A Clinical and Forensic Guide to Cults and Persuasive Leadership

A Clinical and Forensic Guide to Cults and Persuasive Leadership

Edited by

Tyler Durns
University of Utah

Charles Scott
University of California, Davis

Paul Whitehead
University of Utah

Barbara McDermott
University of California, Davis

CAMBRIDGE
UNIVERSITY PRESS

CAMBRIDGE
UNIVERSITY PRESS

Shaftesbury Road, Cambridge CB2 8EA, United Kingdom

One Liberty Plaza, 20th Floor, New York, NY 10006, USA

477 Williamstown Road, Port Melbourne, VIC 3207, Australia

314–321, 3rd Floor, Plot 3, Splendor Forum, Jasola District Centre, New Delhi – 110025, India

103 Penang Road, #05–06/07, Visioncrest Commercial, Singapore 238467

Cambridge University Press is part of Cambridge University Press & Assessment, a department of the University of Cambridge.

We share the University's mission to contribute to society through the pursuit of education, learning and research at the highest international levels of excellence.

www.cambridge.org
Information on this title: www.cambridge.org/9781009643030

DOI: 10.1017/9781009280099

When citing this work, please include a reference to the DOI 10.1017/9781009280099

First published 2025

A catalogue record for this publication is available from the British Library

A Cataloging-in-Publication data record for this book is available from the Library of Congress

ISBN 978-1-009-643030 Paperback

Every effort has been made in preparing this book to provide accurate and up-to-date information that is in accord with accepted standards and practice at the time of publication. Although case histories are drawn from actual cases, every effort has been made to disguise the identities of the individuals involved. Nevertheless, the authors, editors, and publishers can make no warranties that the information contained herein is totally free from error, not least because clinical standards are constantly changing through research and regulation. The authors, editors, and publishers therefore disclaim all liability for direct or consequential damages resulting from the use of material contained in this book. Readers are strongly advised to pay careful attention to information provided by the manufacturer of any drugs or equipment that they plan to use.

To my mother, father, and stepmother,
whose guidance taught me, and
whose love shaped me.

To my brother,
whose compassion protected me, and
whose tenacity inspired me.

And to my wife,
whose spirit lifts me, and
whose love grounds me.

This book is as much yours as it is mine.

– Tyler Durns

Contents

Contributors

Hayat Alvi, PhD, Associate Professor, US Naval War College, RI, USA

Mickey Arieli, RPh, Director of Enforcement, Israeli Ministry of Health (retired); Research Fellow, International Institute for Counter-Terrorism, The Interdisciplinary Center, Israel

Ren Belcher, MD, Clinical Assistant Professor, Department of Psychiatry, Grossman School of Medicine, New York University, NY, USA

Austin Blum, MD, JD, California Department of State Hospitals, CA, USA

Harold J. Bursztajn, MD, Associate Professor of Psychiatry, Co-founder, Program in Psychiatry and the Law at Harvard Medical School, MA, USA; President of the American Unit of the International Chair in Bioethics and American Bioethics & Culture Institute, MA, USA

Eric Y. Drogin, JD, PhD, ABPP, Lecturer in Psychiatry (Part-Time), Harvard Medical School, MA, USA; Affiliated Lead of Psychological Studies, Psychiatry, Law, and Society Program, Brigham and Women's Hospital, MA, USA

Susan Hatters Friedman, MD, The Phillip J. Resnick Professor of Forensic Psychiatry, and Professor of Psychiatry, Pediatrics, Reproductive Biology, and Law, Case Western Reserve University, OH, USA; Director, Division of Forensic Psychiatry, University Hospitals of Cleveland, OH, USA

Reagan Gill, DO, Forensic Psychiatrist and Clinical Assistant Professor, Department of Psychiatry and Behavioral Sciences, Oklahoma State University, OK, USA

Dipak K. Gupta, PhD, Distinguished Professor Emeritus, Department of Political Science, San Diego State University, CA, USA

Thomas G. Gutheil, MD, Professor of Psychiatry, Harvard Medical School, MA, USA; Co-founder, Program in Psychiatry and the Law, Massachusetts Mental Health Center, MA, USA

Ansar Haroun, MD, Professor of Psychiatry, Pediatrics, and Law, UC San Diego School of Medicine, CA, USA

Steven Hassan, PhD, MA, MEd, LMHC, NCC, Founder and Director, Freedom of Mind Resource Center, USA

Trent C. Holmberg, MD, DFAPA, Private Practice of Adult and Forensic Psychiatry, Adjunct Associate Professor of Psychiatry, University of Utah, UT, USA

Carlos A. Larrauri, JD, MPA, MSN, University of Michigan Law School, MI, USA; Harvard Kennedy School, MA, USA

J. Reid Meloy, PhD, ABPP, Faculty, San Diego Psychoanalytic Center, CA, USA; Consultant, FBI Behavioral Analysis Unit, Quantico, VA, USA

Ajay Nair, MD, New York University, Bellevue Hospital, NY, USA

Joseph M. Pierre, MD, Clinical Professor, Department of Psychiatry and Behavioral Sciences, Weill Institute for Neurosciences, University of California, San Francisco, CA, USA

Natalie Pyszora, MBChB, PhD, FRANZCP, MRCPsych, PgLS, Medical Advisor, Countering Violent Extremism, Western Australia Department of Health; Adjunct Professor, Institute for Sustainable Industries and Liveable Cities, Victoria University, Melbourne; Clinical Senior Lecturer, School of Psychiatry and Clinical Neurosciences, University of Western Australia, Australia

Tahir Rahman, MD, Associate Professor, Department of Psychiatry, Washington University in St. Louis, MO, USA

Jason G. Roof, MD, Professor, Division of Clinical Psychiatry; Associate Training Director, Division of Psychiatry and the Law, University of California, Davis, CA, USA

Amanie Salem, DO, MPH, Independent Practice, FPA Med

Zachary Schwartz, MD, MA, University of Utah, Salt Lake City, UT, USA

Debra Smith, PhD, Professorial Research Fellow, Institute for Sustainable Industries and Liveable Cities, Victoria University, Melbourne, Australia

Michael Ashley Stein, JD, PhD, Executive Director, Harvard Law School Project on Disability, Cambridge, MA, USA

Chris Sterwald, MD, Affiliated Assistant Professor, Department of Psychiatry and Behavioral Sciences, University of Miami Miller School of Medicine, FL, USA; Clinical Assistant Professor, Department of Psychiatry and Behavioral Health, Herbert Wertheim College of Medicine, Florida International University, FL, USA

Kelsey N. Tuttle, MD, house staff, Department of Psychiatry, University of Utah, UT, USA

Ashley H. VanDercar, MD, JD, Assistant Professor of Psychiatry, Associate Program Director, Forensic Psychiatry Fellowship, University Hospitals Cleveland Medical Center and Case Western Reserve University School of Medicine, OH, USA; Senior Lecturer, University of Akron School of Law, OH, USA; Staff Psychiatrist, Northcoast Behavioral Healthcare, OH, USA

Diana E. Vukel, BA Candidate, Harvard College, MA, USA

Joslyn K. Wallenborn, MA, Criminal Justice Division, Washington State Attorney General's Office, Seattle, WA, USA

Aviv Weinstein, PhD, Professor, Department of Psychology, The Isadore and Ruth Kastin Chair for Brain Research, University of Ariel, Israel

Chris Winter, BA, Doctoral Research Candidate, Institute for Sustainable Industries and Liveable Cities, Victoria University, Melbourne, Australia

Preface

Tyler Durns and Paul Whitehead

The following chapters endeavor to review and analyze systems of veneration and devotion, otherwise known as cults, in a clinical context. Cults and other forms of persuasive leadership remain a mainstay of modern society worldwide. These include not only classically recognized cult systems but also other forms of persuasive leadership – cults of personality, terrorist factions, and coalitions that may share similar psychopathology. Given notable gaps in the literature, little has been established on how to understand and systematically approach these entities psychiatrically and legally; this book bridges that gap in its focus on cult typologies, origins, pathologies and comorbidities, and treatment – of both cult members and founders – and provides case vignettes when appropriate. Additionally, forensic issues such as approach to mitigation, determination of decisional capacity, existing precedents, and typical outcomes are included to assist experts in the field of mental health and the law.

A Clinical and Forensic Guide to Cults and Persuasive Leadership is tailored to a multidisciplinary audience of psychiatrists, psychologists, social workers, mental health clinicians, or other individuals who work with or interface with individuals who have been members or leaders of cults or similar groups.

The authors included within the text were selected due to their expertise including research, clinical, and other relevant areas relating to their chapters. Many authors have previously contributed to foundational work in the field and continue to build upon such in areas of scientific research. Provided their previous works, many authors herein cite themselves and other chapter authors. References to and citations of such were however subject to peer review by academic journals and publishers prior to their inclusion in order to fulfill standards of academic integrity. Supportive and opposing data for the authors' previous works are presented and discussed throughout when relevant. A full list of references is provided at the conclusion of each chapter for the reader's review. Chapter authors were instructed to specify when conceptualizations and approaches in the absence of peer review are stated.

The editors and authors note several limitations to the content of the book. First, there is no one universally accepted definition of what constitutes a "cult" or "persuasive leadership." Theologians, sociologists, anthropologists, legal professionals, and mental health practitioners have modeled cults based on overlapping but distinct frameworks. Definitional and descriptive opinions may also vary among professionals within the same field. Generally, this textbook characterizes a cult as follows:

> A social group that is defined by its philosophical beliefs and related behaviors, or its common interest in a particular individual, object, or goal outside of the generally accepted beliefs of their culture. These idiosyncratic beliefs may be firmly maintained despite contradictory information but are not necessarily attributable to a major mental disorder and are shared with other affiliated individuals.

Given the anticipated variability of professional opinions, chapter authors have included their qualified designations and descriptions discussed therein with no one interpretation being more authoritative than another.

Second, the term "cult" has also been further diluted in popular culture and applied to a number of mainstream movements in media, and outside of academic context. Indeed, controversies about psychiatric syndromes recognized in the *Diagnostic and Statistical Manual of Mental Disorders, 5th Edition, Text Revision* (DSM-5TR), such as dissociative identity disorder, as well as other psychiatric and psychological constructs such as psychopathy, extreme overvalued beliefs, and pseudologia fantastica also continue within the academic community. This text may offer some insight, debate, and points of contention to such. However, we caution against abstracting interpretations and avoiding social, political, and other biases outside of or otherwise stated within the included peer-reviewed studies. While psychological conceptualizations and descriptive phenomenology may differ between individuals in professional fields and the public at large, readers should appreciate the reviewed literature within the specific methodological confines of each described study and be cautious about extrapolating other ideas, theories, and opinions beyond established facts.

Finally, the evidence-based understanding of cultist phenomena is limited by the dearth of systematic, peer-reviewed research studies on the subject. While the intent of this text is to consolidate such data to be applicable to educational, research, clinical, and forensic contexts, such limitations are also implicit among the reviewed data. Specifically, the majority of extant literature is based on anecdotal accounts and retrospective analysis, often by former followers who may present biased perspectives. The authors have attempted to highlight such when relevant. Cults are comparatively rare, which similarly limits the available data and study. Relatedly, review and discussion of phenomena may not be generalizable to other described groups. The editors have attempted to mitigate this through pairing groups with similar properties in each chapter but have done so in the absence of any generally accepted categorization among the academic community. The partitioning of such was done on a conceptual basis with similarities and differences described within. As such, there exists significant overlap between categories. While the editors and authors recognize this conflicts with traditional nosological approaches often proffered in clinical and forensic psychodiagnostics, we believe this approach is indicative of and true to the psychological and sociocultural complexities of the topics.

The American Psychiatric Association *Principles of Medical Ethics with Annotations Specific to Psychiatry* includes an ethical guideline (The Goldwater Rule) concerning psychiatric comment on public figures who have not been interviewed and who have not given consent. Section 7.3 of the parameter notes:

> On occasion psychiatrists are asked for an opinion about an individual who is in the light of public attention or who has disclosed information about himself/herself through public media. In such circumstances, a psychiatrist may share with the public his or her expertise about psychiatric issues in general. However, it is unethical for a psychiatrist to offer a professional opinion unless he or she has conducted an examination and has been granted proper authorization for such a statement.

While no companion guideline exists for the field of psychology, the American Psychological Association advises psychologists take precautions that any statements they make to the media are in fact based on their professional knowledge, training, or experience in accord with appropriate psychological literature and practice. The majority of the individuals discussed in this text were not directly evaluated by the authors but are instead described through review of scientific literature and available public documents. With these cautions noted, the editors and authors emphasize that the intention of this text is to review the existing body of literature pertaining to cultist phenomena and persuasive leadership. Discussions of the included case examples do not constitute professional opinions about diagnoses, behavior, speech, and risk of any specific individual.

Section 1 Typology

Chapter 1

Eastern Religious Cults

Ansar Haroun, Hayat Alvi, and Dipak K. Gupta

"Nothing is true, everything is permitted."
– *Hassan-I Sabbah, Grandmaster of the Assassins*

Introduction

In our daily discourse, the word "cult" is often used, seldom defined, and never fully comprehended. Understandably, there is no universally accepted objective definition of the term "cult." It is no wonder that researcher James T. Richardson, after critically examining various definitions, concluded that scholars should avoid the term because of its confused and negatively connoted meaning [1]. Yet given the frequency with which the word "cult" shows up in public forums, from acts of terrorism to mass suicide, the term deserves a closer scrutiny. However, unlike in physical sciences, social manifestations are better understood by describing their essential components than by aiming for any one impervious definition.

Joseph Campbell [2], the noted scholar of comparative religion, famously quipped, "mythology is what we call other people's religion" [3]. Like mythology, "cult" is a pejorative term. We do not use it to describe the world's major religious faiths, nor do the members of a movement identify their group as a cult. Hence, the term is loaded with subjective biases. These biases, however, are not unique to the subject matter of this study; they embed most epithets – such as terrorism, fundamentalism, hypernationalism, far-right or far-left movements, and so on. – that freely enter public conversations. Therefore, while we may not be able to define a cult, we can tease out the core elements of what the term implies. These are as follows:

- A cult refers to a physical group, not a single individual actor. Thus, the assassination of President Abraham Lincoln by John Wilkes Booth or the bombing attacks by the solitary Ted Kaczynski, the so-called Unabomber, are not classified as products of a cult, even though these perpetrators might have shared a widespread ideology. This distinction is vital since cult behavior straddles the liminal space between social psychology and psychiatry.
- The second attribute of a cult is the relative size of its membership. Usually, we think of a cult as a small group. Yet, this attribute can be extremely fluid. If we measure size by the number of victims of their violent paths, we can see that the number of victims of mass murder-suicide of Jim Jones' devotees in 1978 was approximately 1,000 [4] while the 1987 Tokyo subway attack by Aum Shinrikyo was 27 [5]. Alternately, measuring by the number of adherents, the group International Krishna

Consciousness (commonly known as Hare Krishna) which currently claims over a million followers worldwide, may qualify [6].

- Although the extent may vary, cults control every aspect of their members' lives and demand submission to their dogma with unwavering fealty [7]. As a result, the members often isolate themselves from the outside world and even sever relationships with their immediate families and friends.
- A cult's religious or political beliefs must be seen as outside the pale of the society at large. For instance, due to Mormonism's adherence to polygamy and other heterodox practices, in its early days, many branded it as a cult despite its widespread following [8].
- Cults, even the atheistic ones, such Heaven's Gate, often derive their belief system by drawing from some established religious faith. The religious foundation provides the leaders and their teachings an aura of divine ordination and incommutability. Therefore, most of those groups that we readily recognize as cult draw from religious imageries to forge group cohesion [9].
- While most cults define their identity through a stark distinction between "us" and "them," some embrace violence while others do not. Depending on the group's ideology, violence may be directed at the "outsiders" and/or its own members, who might be wavering or trying to defect. As all groups impose strict rules for their members, they impose costs for defection, which may vary from excommunication to physical punishment and even death.
- Finally, and perhaps, most importantly, cult groups are created and led by charismatic leaders, who exert total control on their followers. Drawing from Max Weber's classic study of charismatic leadership [10], a burgeoning literature has focused on the role of leaders and followers [11]. Weber argued that leadership rises out of three sources: traditional, legal, and charismatic personalities of the leaders. The traditional leadership is based on long traditions, which varies from the papal tradition in Catholicism, the Mullah tradition of the Shi'as, to the Lamas in Tibetan Buddhism. The law-based leadership is what we see in modern democratic nations, where leaders are elected or nominated according to well-established and recognized process. The third type, charismatic leadership, is typical of cults and other small subnational groups. Based on the extensive literature on social psychology, we can begin to understand the role group formation plays in human society and the impact it has on individual behavior [12].

Group Dynamics in Cults

Unlike the animal world, where group formation is based on genetic proximity, human groups are imaginary [13]. All groups based on nationalism, religious affiliation, ethnicity, linguistics, etc., are founded on mental constructs and exert powerful forces in directing individual actions.

New technologies in brain imaging have allowed neuroscientists to assess the tendency toward and reinforcement of social group formation and identification. The resulting research demonstrates that when we form a group, an essential aspect of our evolutionary path [14], our brains reward us by the secretion of pleasure hormones, such as oxytocin [15]. These findings help social scientists in understanding human proclivities for group formation in pursuit of some utopian vision. Their insight can be profitably used to understand dysfunctional behaviors from cult violence to genocide and terrorism [9, 16, 17].

The manifestation of our need to form groups is seen in the creation of leaders and followers. However, at a micro level, we need to understand the motivations and characteristics of the leaders and followers.

Charismatic Leadership

The question of charismatic leadership begs the question whether these leaders possess certain unique characteristics. There is no record of any (reliable and valid) psychiatric interview using currently acceptable diagnostic measures (International Classification of Diseases [ICD] or Diagnostic and Statistical Manual of Mental Disorders [DSM]) on any Eastern religious cult leader. We do have actual evidence from some notorious cult leaders, such as Charles Manson [18]. Beside those, despite the American Psychiatric Association's Goldwater Rule that prohibits drawing conclusions about states of mind of subjects without proper authorization, there are plenty of analyses based on secondhand information about leaders such as Hitler and other dictators and autocrats [11].

Case Vignettes: The Assassins, Thugs, Aum Shinrikyo, and Rajneesh Movement

Four case studies follow; they are from the family of "Eastern religious cults" to represent separate geographic areas:

- from West Asia: the Assassins
- from South Asia: the Thugs
- from South Asia: the Rajneesh movement
- from East Asia: Aum Shinrikyo

For the Assassins, Aum Shinrikyo, and the Rajneesh movement, we will study the group and offer a macroanalytic perspective. For the Thugs, we can offer both a macro perspective and a more detailed individual-based analysis, from a personal micro perspective (one of us was the court-appointed forensic psychiatrist ordered to evaluate a "Thug," who admitted criminal behavior (murder) but asserted a Thug-like defense ("God told me to kill!"). Moreover, the modern English language has two words – assassin and thug – whose origins derive from these Eastern religious cults.

The Assassins

The original meaning of the word "assassin" is somewhat innocent: the Arabic word *hashashin* refers to a consumer of hash (opium), but in the modern Western imagination, an assassin is not an innocent hedonist using narcotics, but a reviled political murderer [19].

The Assassins cult was born in the Middle East in the twelfth century, a time of great political turmoil. Christians were fighting Muslims in the Crusades, and Muslim sects were fighting each other (i.e., Sunnis vs. Shi'as), and the Shi'as further divided into competing sects, one of which became the Nizaris. The founder of the Assassins was a Nizari named Hasan Sabah who was born in Iran and whose childhood friends included the poet Omar Khayyam and the politician Nizam ul-Mulk, who he later had assassinated [19]. When Sabah died, his cult of the Assassins had 70,000 followers willing to die for their cause [19]. It is remarkable that he created such a powerful cult, but it is unclear how he did it.

The cult left few written records, so scholars are dependent on the writings of a later (fifteenth-century) Egyptian historian, Makkisi, who, being a rival Sunni, may have presented the Nizari Assassins in an unsympathetic light [19].

The Assassins recruited members and offered an alternative view of religious truth. Whereas Judaism and Islam emphasized orthopraxy (correct behavior) and Christianity emphasized orthodoxy (correct faith) as a pathway to paradise, the Assassins taught that correct knowledge was the path to salvation [19].

Traditional Islam believed in the absolute truth of the Quran (scripture) and of the ethics derived therefrom. In contrast, the Assassins taught there was no absolute truth, and that all ethics was situational, so all rules could be rejected or reinterpreted, obviously to coincide with the ulterior motives of the Assassin leadership, which were usually political [19]. Therefore, cult members routinely carried out political assassinations, which led them to be a significant source of fear throughout the Middle East.

The adherents exhibited extraordinary levels of courage, willingly, brazenly, and unflinchingly seeking "martyrdom," because they believed that death would give them a greater reward in the paradise they had briefly tasted through the tricks of the Assassins' leadership. The cult began to decline with the death of its founder Hasan Sabah in 1124 and died out when the Mongols attacked and destroyed Baghdad in 1258 [19].

The Thugs

"A Thug rides his horse! Wears his dagger! And shows a front. Thieving? Never! Never! If a banker's treasures were before me and entrusted to my care, though in hunger and dying, I would scorn to steal. But let a banker go on a journey, and I would certainly murder him. Dacoits and robbers are contemptible. I despise a dacoit. Let him come before me!"

– An eminent Thug leader, narrated by a contemporary author, Thomas Perry [20, p. 35]

The English word, "thug," meaning a violent, aggressive criminal person, has its origin in an Eastern religious cult. "Thugee" is a Sanskrit word for "deceptive concealment," and the Thugs were a religious movement who worshipped the Hindu goddess Kali, the goddess of death. The Thugs killed victims by strangulation and then robbed them. Although cult members worshipped a Hindu goddess, the cult included both Hindu and Muslim members, suggesting the cult had powers of social cohesion [20].

Historically, the first recorded mention of the cult is in 1356 in an account by historian Ziya ud Din Barani, and the cult died out by the nineteenth century. The *Guinness Book of World Records* reports that the Thugs were responsible for about two million deaths [21], so the quantum of harm was enormous.

The success of the cult required deception, social cooperation (cult members worked not as individuals but in teams), and specialization (each cult member was trained in a specific task). While senior or strong cult members committed the murders, a variety of tasks were assigned to junior or weaker cult members; for example, the elderly or infirm, who may have appeared as less threatening, worked as guides or spies [20]. They had an honor code mandating that they were not to kill Brahmins because they were considered too pure; not to kill women because they were incarnations of Kali; and not to kill the sick because they would be an unworthy sacrifice [20].

Theological explanations for killing approved targets included the motivation to appease God with human sacrifice. Some Western readers may express shock at this barbaric practice, but in the Abrahamic religions God also demands the Prophet Abraham to carry out a human sacrifice of his own son, though he changes his mind later. In Christianity, a human sacrifice achieves salvation for all of humanity through divine intervention. The Thug theology is not that dissimilar.

Unlike many cults that have a rigid structure, the Thugs appear to have had no formal membership, no leader, no written records, and no recruitment drives. The Thugs members were recruited through family initiation, that is, fathers recruited sons, ensuring secrecy and loyalty [20]. There was no rigid orthodoxy requiring a correct belief, but there was a devotion to one particular god (or Goddess Kali), and a moral decision to engage in a certain lifestyle characterized by murder and robbery. Although their acts violated the Law of the Land, the Thugs saw their actions as honorable and religiously motivated, appeasing a god for the greater good.

One of the authors of this chapter (Ansar Haroun, MD) served as the court-appointed forensic psychiatrist to examine the mental state of a man who, though not formally professing membership in an Eastern cult by name, believed in such an Eastern cult's ideology.

In 1998, Matthew Cecchi, an innocent nine-year-old boy, was found murdered in San Diego, California. The police suspected, but ruled out, the obvious motives (sexual molestation by a pedophile, robbery, murderous rage). Soon, the police caught the killer, 20-year-old Brandon Wilson, who said that "God told me to kill" [22].

The evidence against him was overwhelming, and he could not deny the behavioral guilt. However, he denied moral guilt, informing the police that he had indeed committed the killing, but only because God ordered him to do so. This assertion was met with disbelief, scorn, astonishment, and obviously invited a psychiatric evaluation. The defendant was evaluated by several psychiatrists, both for the defense and for the prosecution, and also for the (neutral) court. All the mental health experts noted his defense, which consisted of "God told me to kill" [22].

Some opined that this represented a genuine psychotic disorder characterized by a religious delusion, while others speculated that the defendant was malingering and pretending to have such a delusion in order to succeed in a mental health defense. No one considered the possibility that the defendant was a pious Thug, who had actually received, as he claimed, an order from God to kill. Although the court accepted that the defendant suffered from a psychosis at the time of the act, the psychosis was not a "settled" one, so any insanity defense had to be rejected, and the only question was one of behavioral guilt as opposed to moral guilt. The defendant admitted to his behavioral guilt and received the death sentence. While on death row, in 2011 he committed suicide by hanging himself, which is symbolically similar to the strangulation method of the Thugs. The November 17 date of his suicide is psychologically significant, as November 14 signifies the murder anniversary.

The evaluation of the killer's mental state raises many questions pertaining to issues of competency, sanity, *mens rea*, dangerousness, and possibility of rehabilitation, as well as other questions from philosophy and theology. Because the case was so high profile, it was discussed and rediscussed at many clinical, forensic, and scholarly meetings. The majority opinion was that the defendant indeed suffered from a mental disorder of a psychotic type, based on his religious delusion, namely the false belief that God had told him to kill.

Forensic psychiatrist Haroun proposed a minority/dissenting opinion, namely the possibility that there was no mental disorder and that his claim (i.e., God told him to kill) was not a false belief qualifying for a religious delusion; rather, it was a genuine belief.

Many Americans who subscribe to Jewish, Christian, or Muslim beliefs believe that God does order some to kill, as in Genesis 22 where God orders Abraham to kill his son. Also, many in South Asia believe that God does mandate orders to kill as in the example of the Goddess Kali giving such orders to her Thugs. Few would suggest that such pious Jews, Christians, Muslims, and Hindus are mentally ill.

This case fascinates legal and psychiatric scholars for many reasons, including the awareness of bias in psychiatric evaluations. All the psychiatric experts testified that the defendant's belief that God told him to kill was false and not based on any verification from God. On the contrary, the psychiatric experts based their assessments on their Eurocentric biases that convey the belief that God is a benevolent kind-hearted being who could not possibly mandate such a crime, despite the evidence that Kali does give such instructions – both to her Western followers of Abraham, and to her Eastern followers of Kali.

As the American population becomes more diverse, American psychiatry will have to accommodate more diverse images of God to replace the current warm kind-hearted being that is popular among American religious liberals, perhaps with deities from cults.

Aum Shinrikyo

Japan's Aum Shinrikyo cult (often called "Aum") has operated with two principal elements: a) it promotes the concept of establishing a "utopia" and b) it is extremely dangerous, violent, and destructive.

Aum Shinrikyo is a cult that promotes violence for the purpose of creating a utopia, that is, a perfect society based on its ideology, beliefs, and social system. Most cults are not outwardly violent, but Aum Shinrikyo, which combines the Sanskrit word "Aum" with the Japanese for "Supreme Truth," is homicidal and extremely destructive. On March 20, 1995, Aum Shinrikyo operatives carried out a deadly Sarin gas attack on the Tokyo subway. The attack killed 13 and injured nearly 6,000, a number of whom were paralyzed or blinded [23]. Sarin is a highly toxic and lethal military-grade nerve agent that the Nazis invented [23]. Aum Shinrikyo members also attempted to carry out cyanide attacks afterward but were unsuccessful, and after these attacks the group fled and went into hiding. The group's charismatic leader, Chizuo Matsumoto – also known as Shoko Asahara – who claimed to be an incarnation of both Buddha and Jesus Christ, also went into hiding until police found and arrested him [23].

Aum Shinrikyo has achieved global attraction and loyalty with tens of thousands of followers worldwide [23]. Aum's leader, Shoko Asahara, created the Aum ideology based on an amalgam of Hindu, Buddhist, and Taoist principles. Later, he also injected aspects of Christian dogma, particularly messianic and apocalyptic beliefs that integrated well with Asahara's expertise in pharmacology. Asahara claimed to be the creator of yoga and described himself as "God-like" [24]. He loved science fiction and comic books. Asahara had the penchant to use toxic agents to facilitate and accelerate the coming apocalypse that he prophesized based on his obsession with Nostradamus, who predicted that the world would end in 1999 and a "savior" would come from the East [25]. Aum's schemes for mass killings would fulfill the ideology's concept of a postapocalyptic utopia based on Asahara's vision and teachings [25].

Initially, Aum Shinrikyo presented itself as harmless, using animation to depict Asahara and his followers posing in highly spiritual movements and yoga positions [25]. Asahara gained global fame as a religious figure, even posing for a picture with the Dalai Lama. Aum's main message condemned the world's obsession with materialism and lack of spirituality. The group's message went as far as to convey that one must focus on the spiritual or go to hell.

As in all cults, Aum devotees had to sever all ties and give up everything. They had to transfer all worldly belongings and assets to the organization and undergo rigorous initiations that tested their loyalty. Devotees also had to prove their spiritual bonds with Asahara through unbearable physical "training," such as hanging upside down, submerging in very hot water, or staying in an underground box for six days [25]. When some of them died from such physically taxing "training," the group's henchmen secretly cremated the bodies and discarded the ashes [24]. Often, the devotees wore electrically wired headgear that claimed to share brainwaves with Asahara. The Aum leader was worshipped as a divinity, who many believed could levitate, and no one was allowed to question him or the group's beliefs and practices. The consequences would be severe.

The Aum Shinrikyo ideology began to form in the 1980s, but it solidified in 1990 when the group decided to present candidates for election into the Japanese parliament, called the Diet. Upon all Aum representatives getting rejected and ridiculed, the group turned to violence and focused singularly on the apocalyptic aspect of the ideology. Hence, Aum Shinrikyo came to be known as a doomsday cult, mixing its theology with violent acts of revenge and destruction.

Shoko Asahara prophesized that the world will precipitate into the next world war, after which only Aum members will emerge as the survivors [24]. Asahara promoted the idea of a "pure" utopia in the future with life having more meaning as everyone will be Aum followers after World War III, and the Aum ideology will provide the best model for this postwar utopia. Oddly, for the utopia to be realized, everyone outside the cult must be killed in order to be reborn. According to Asahara, "[t]he world and everyone in it could be saved if only they were first destroyed" [24].

Based on this ideology and the insult of rejection from the parliamentary election, Aum Shinrikyo began to stockpile toxins like sarin, firearms, and even biological weapons. The group embraced a strategy of violence and destruction, which encompassed murder, kidnapping, and the use of chemical and biological agents as weapons against civilians. The March 20, 1995 Sarin gas attack on the Tokyo subway became Aum Shinrikyo's most notorious act of mass violence.

In the lead-up to the subway attack, Aum Shinrikyo murdered and attacked numerous targets both within its organization, such as whistleblowers, as well as in society and public figures like judges and journalists [26]. In 1989, Asahara dispatched operatives to drug and murder an anti-Aum lawyer, Tsutsumi Sakamoto, along with his wife and infant son. Sakamoto was helping Aum members who wished to leave the cult. According to *The New York Times* (September 7, 1995), "acting on Mr. Asahara's orders, [the men] broke into the Sakamotos' apartment in Yokohama at about 3 a.m. on November 1989, and killed the family by injecting them with a drug, hitting them with a hammer and strangling them" [26]. The operatives then discarded the victims' body parts in various forested and mountainous areas of the city, not to be discovered until September 1995 [27].

In addition, according to the Organisation for the Prohibition of Chemical Weapons (June 1, 2001):

> While expanding its influence in Japan, Aum also set up branch offices overseas in the United States, Germany and Sri Lanka. In Russia, it is said that over 30,000 people joined the cult. Aum secretly plotted to buy arms and drugs and sent its members for training in shooting. Aum also opened affiliated business firms in Sri Lanka and Taiwan. In Australia, the cult purchased a farm, manufactured chemicals, and tested the chemicals on sheep [27].

Moreover, "[i]n a trial run, the cult successfully sprayed Sarin gas in Matsumoto, and so a chemical plant for Sarin production was started in the autumn of 1994. The cult also succeeded in synthesizing a VX-agent" [27]. The gas attack in Matsumoto resulted in nearly 300 people checking into the hospital's emergency room with similar symptoms after exposure to the nerve toxins, and the following day numerous animal carcasses were found in the attack area.

Separately, a land purchase legal dispute led to another sarin attack that killed seven people and injured three of the judges involved in the case [24]. Aum also targeted journalist Shoko Egawa with toxic gas because she reported on the cult's crimes, but she survived. The legal cases and journalists' negative reports against Aum provide fodder for Asahara to claim that there is a conspiracy against the group. This further fuels the cult's paranoia.

Despite these violent crimes, Japanese police were reluctant to scrutinize and investigate Aum Shinrikyo due to the sensitivities relating to the post–World War II constitution that granted religious freedoms and rights, which were denied prior to the world war eras. The postwar Japanese constitution's legal framework for religious freedoms was deemed untouchable. Undoubtedly, the 1995 sarin gas attack on the Tokyo subway was the last straw. Public anger pressed on the police to act against the violent cult.

In March 1995, five Aum operatives boarded five different Tokyo subway trains. Each man carried umbrellas and plastic bags containing sarin. The men pierced the plastic bags with the sharpened tips of their umbrellas releasing the sarin gaseous vapors and fled. Thirteen passengers died and thousands were injured. A number of victims became blind and paralyzed. Most victims choked and suffocated from the toxic fumes, which linger as long-term effects in survivors. Fortunately, the particular chemical synthesis of the toxin that the Aum operatives used in the Tokyo attack was not conducive to the most lethal sarin components. The chemistry of the sarin was far from perfect, but it still resulted in numerous deaths. Had the toxin's chemistry been perfected, the death count would have been catastrophic.

Aum's goals for this attack included overthrowing the Japanese government and triggering World War III. The sarin gas attacks were also a form of revenge for the rejection and ridicule of the cult from the public during the parliamentary elections. Asahara decried that "[t]he world has rejected the truth!" [24]. These attacks shook Japan to the core, unleashing a national security crisis that the country had not experienced since World War II. Aum Shinrikyo's murderous campaign was actually the nail in the cult's own coffin.

Following the subway attacks, the cult went underground. The authorities finally arrested Asahara on May 16, 1995, and his court trials lasted years due to questions about his sanity and mental stability, which, according to many observers, the blind cult leader deliberately acted out. Ultimately, in July 2018 Asahara and six of his henchmen were executed by hanging in Japan.

The remnants of Aum Shinrikyo have constituted the lower-level adherents who were seemingly nonviolent and claimed they had no knowledge of the violent crimes that the higher echelons of the cult committed at Asahara's command. In 2007, Fumihiro Joyu claimed to be Asahara's successor, and he formed a new organization called Hikari no Wa, which means "Circle of Rainbow Light" [23]. Although the new religious organization is now considered legal in Japan, it continues to be viewed as potentially dangerous and is constantly under surveillance [28].

These Eastern religious cults (Assassins, Thugs, and Aum Shinrikyo) were born and bred in the East and are obviously "Eastern." The psychological profiles of their cult leaders and their followers require a degree of knowledge and sensitivity to Eastern psychologies. But what about a cult that has an Eastern leader with a Western following? Is the applicable psychology Eastern or Western? That cult is Rajneesh.

Rajneesh

The Rajneesh cult, later known as Osho, is named after the founder of the Rajneesh movement, Bhagwan Shree Rajneesh, who first started the movement in his country of origin, India. Eventually, the Rajneesh movement gained a popular following in the West, since Rajneesh set up his New Age Utopia settlement in Oregon.

The Rajneesh cult broke ground in acquiring Western devotees and also operating in the West, though it originated in the East. This begs additional questions about the Eastern–Western dynamics pertaining to cults and their leaders. Some scholars suggest that Western followers may view Eastern leaders in an unrealistic light. Edward Said, who coined the term "Orientalism," argues that the Orient (i.e., the East) is viewed in the Western imagination not as it actually is, but rather as false stereotypes emphasizing grotesque aspects of life, which are not necessarily Eastern [29]. Examples include lewd sex, white slavery, imperial decadence, exotic harems, and hashish. Such themes are indeed apparent in the New Age Utopia in Oregon, where there were suspicions of such practices.

Amartya Sen, the Eastern-born, Western-educated Nobel Prize of Economics laureate also notes the Western caricatures of the East, namely that while the East may have produced gurus, mystics, saddhus, fakirs, and polytheists in abundance, there is a lack of cold, rational, logical nontheists. Sen points out that the reality is that some of the oldest nontheist schools of religious thought have originated in the East, for example the Carvaka, who actually made fun of and mocked the gurus, mystics, saddhus, and the like [30].

The Characteristics of Cult Leaders

This part of the chapter addresses psychiatric analyses pertaining to the characteristics of cult leaders. In doing so, the following key questions need to be addressed:

- Do cult leaders suffer from any DSM psychiatric disorders?
- If not, do they have a psychiatric profile – no disorder, but traits?
- If not, do they have a developmental history with risk factors which may increase risk?

There is no record of any reliable and valid psychiatric interview using currently acceptable diagnostic measures (ICD or DSM) on any Eastern religious cult leader. The majority of such cult leaders lived before modern times. Therefore, modern diagnostic measures were not available. Even if such a cult leader lived today, the American Psychiatric Association's Goldwater Rule prohibits its members from offering psychological opinions about individuals like cult leaders who the psychiatrist has not personally examined. As a result, we have no opinion about the presence or absence of a DSM psychiatric disorder in such cult leaders.

However, there is rich literature on the psychological profiles of leaders, which may or may not be applicable to our subgroup of leaders (i.e., leaders of Eastern religious cults). While leadership in the West may be analyzed from many perspectives, both good (e.g., courage) and bad (e.g., ruthlessness), and neutral (e.g., the propensity for risk-taking), leaders of religious cults are commonly viewed rightly or wrongly as having extreme characteristics around:

- content of belief – the cult belief is surely "false"
- degree of belief – cult followers believe "fanatically"
- deviance of belief – cult followers are certainly weird and most likely dangerous

Leaders of religious cults are thus not viewed favorably, but if the cult is an Eastern religious cult, it carries the added burden of being strange, alien, and foreboding. For most Eastern religious cults, the paucity of information about them precludes scholars from intelligently commenting on the cult leaders. However, in the case of the Assassins, there is some information, albeit biased, but nevertheless available.

The Assassins' leader was born in a time and place of great turmoil, probably raised in an environment of great anxiety wherein survival required keen skills. The fact that he not only survived but flourished suggests he had (either by nature or by nurture) those survival skills, which probably included cunning, the capacity for deceit, good social skills, and the ability to negotiate with different classes, religions, and ideologies. The fact that his childhood friends included a world-famous poet, Omar Khayyam, and a successful politician, Nizam ul-Mulk, suggests that he had an elite education in the company of other elites with plenty of brain stimulation.

Also, the fact that he was born in one culture that is Farsi-speaking Iran but trained in another culture that is Arabic-speaking Cairo suggests that his developing brain had access to two of the then world's most sophisticated civilizations. Thus, he was cosmopolitan, broadly educated, a man of the world, and well equipped to negotiate different ideologies and viewpoints all to his advantage.

The fact that he had his childhood friend (Nizam ul-Mulk) killed over a grudge suggests a cold-heartedness, a lack of empathy, or a lack of virtue (mercy). If it is the former (lack of empathy), then he may have had a psychopathic personality, which is a no-fault condition. The condition is regrettable but not blameworthy. If it is the latter (lack of mercy), then he may have lacked virtue, which is a fault condition and worthy of blame.

The Assassins' leader's ploy of tricking recruits into thinking they were in paradise by surrounding them with the sensuous pleasures of drugs and sex requires a creative imagination and extraordinary planning, which suggests that he had both creative skills and executive functioning skills. The fact that membership in his Assassins cult required not only obedience, but blind, unquestioning obedience, suggests that this gradient of power expressed through behavioral submission is central to the cult follower–leader relationship and further connotes a psychopathic leadership style where the social bond between leader and follower is based not on love, respect, admiration, or need but rather on cold fear.

If we compare and contrast the broad group (i.e., all leaders) with a narrow group of leaders of Eastern religious cults, then the question begging is: What are the similarities and differences? Are the similarities/differences:

- an accident of nature (vs. nurture), suggesting randomness
- a feature of nurture (Eastern parenting styles?)
- a feature of society (does the East encourage cults?)

Although these are worthy questions, so far, there have been few answers from social science research. There may be answers from folk psychology or folk wisdom.

In the last generation, the West has witnessed a demographic revolution. In previous generations, Western parenting was practiced in the geographical West, while Eastern parenting was practiced mostly in the geographical East. In the last generation, migration patterns have changed, and there is now a large population of "Eastern" parents living in the West, allowing the comparison of Eastern parenting styles, in the same space (the West), with the same stresses (those common to the West).

The conventional approach of Western parenting supports an "authoritative" parenting style. However, recent research suggests that Eastern diaspora populations (i.e., Indians from South Asia and others from East Asia) are demonstrating great academic success but with a style of parenting that is not authoritative but rather authoritarian [31]. Thus, apparently the despised authoritarian parenting style is associated with academic success but not necessarily with good emotional health in the context of Eastern populations in Western demographics. If this is true, it may be that "Eastern" leaders, including politicians and cult leaders, are more likely to be the products of one parenting style (authoritarian) rather than the expected – at least in Eurocentric eyes – authoritative. The current political leadership in India is certainly influenced by the Rashtriya Swayamsevak Sangh, which, to its enemies, is considered a political cult which demonstrates an authoritarian style of leadership. Would such findings apply to Eastern religious cult leadership? That question needs to be addressed.

Leaders of Eastern religious cults differ from their Western counterparts in the quality of their followers' religious traditions. All religions differ in detail, but there are some broad differences between the Eastern and Western religions, which may require difference in leadership style. The Western mind, which is influenced by Abrahamic thinking, views the leader (i.e., the Abrahamic God) as having both power and agency to give. As a giver, He may (or may not) give the supplicant things such as rewards, money, gifts, victory in war, forgiveness of sins, salvation, and paradise.

In contrast, the Eastern mind, which is influenced by dharmic thinking, views the leader or guru not as a giver but as a guide. Salvation requires not the supplication of a savior-god but the understanding of karma. If you acquire bad karma, begging or praying for forgiveness will not help, but revised actions may result in a revised karma and a better outcome. Therefore, there is a greater willingness in the Eastern mind to accept guidance from a leader who is a guru, or a guide, and there is no requirement for He/She to demonstrate supernatural qualities (e.g., perform miracles) [32]. Since the guru (Eastern religious leader) is a guide, like a psychotherapist, the bar remains low, and there are numerous gurus, the majority of who do not claim supernatural powers.

In contrast, Western religious leaders claim to talk to supernatural powers. In fact, even secular Western leaders supposedly interact with Western gods who apparently command them to invade preferably non-Western lands, as in the case of US President George W. Bush's claim that his god told him to invade Iraq, not for the oil, but to end the tyranny.

It is rare for an American psychiatrist to have access to the mental state of a practicing member of an Eastern religious cult. However, there is a recent report of the last psychological evaluation of cult leader Charles Manson [33]. Manson was the leader of a Western religious cult but was available for psychiatric evaluation since he was incarcerated in a California prison where he was serving a life sentence after his death penalty was invalidated in 1972. Manson had his psychiatric evaluation in 1997 when he was first admitted to Pelican Bay State Prison in California, but the results were not made public until his death in 2017.

The recently published findings suggest that Manson's symptoms were consistent with a bipolar illness in contrast to earlier findings that emphasized his psychopathy. This is psychiatrically significant because bipolar disorder is very treatable while psychopathy is not.

While there is a report of a psychiatric evaluation of a Western cult leader (the report on Manson, as discussed), there are no comparable rigorous reports on the psychology of any Eastern cult leader. However, the case of Aum Shinrikyo illustrates the fundamental criteria and characteristics of an Eastern cult and leader, along with a few distinctions, including the following:

- Aum was a violent and destructive cult
- Like all cults, Aum engaged in mind control and violence
- Shoko Asahara was characterized by aggressive narcissism and psychopathy
- Asahara proclaimed himself as divine
- Asahara strategically combined other religious beliefs to create his cult
- Aum stockpiled weapons
- Aum was an apocalyptic and utopic cult, which is a common trend among cults
- Asahara combined religion and science (pharmacology)
- A notable difference is Asahara's demise: He was not suicidal; he was arrested, tried, and executed

According to Peter Olsson's book, *Malignant Pied Pipers* (2017), the conventional characteristics and techniques of a cult and its leader include the following [34], which clearly align with Aum Shinrikyo and Shoko Asahara:

- use of intense fear
- charisma
- intimidation
- power and malevolence
- extreme idealism
- erasing one's autonomy
- weakness in character is sought in followers – "less individuated people"
- father/parental figure
- narcissism
- symbiotic relationship between the cult leader and their followers

- control through thought reform
- radical personality changes
- embrace black-and-white thinking without question

In addition, Olsson posits that those seeking to join a cult are searching for "easy answers to the meaning of life – an addictive affiliation with stimulation, excitement, and grandiose action" [34, p. 5]. Moreover, quoting Otto Kernberg, he describes the four elements of malignant narcissism [34], which is wholly consistent with Asahara's personality with the exception of suicidal behavior:

- paranoid regressive tendencies with "paranoid micro-psychotic episodes" (i.e., narcissistic rage)
- chronic self-destructiveness and/or suicidal behavior
- major and minor dishonesty (i.e., psychopathy)
- malignant grandiosity "with overt sadistic efforts to triumph over all authority"

Specifically pertaining to Asahara, Olsson explains that, like many cult leaders, he exercised mind control over his devotees; he presented himself as "divine" but, in reality, he was a charlatan promoting a "pseudo-theology"; he exhibited traits of a criminal psychopath; he preached apocalyptic scenarios; he conveyed a "sinister charisma"; and he employed "treacherous techniques of power and control" [34, p. 78].

Overall, Asahara miscalculated that the Tokyo subway gas attacks would translate to the public that the United States and the West were invading Japan [34], hence triggering World War III and the apocalypse. In the end, Japan learned an important lesson about considering attacking a "new religion" as taboo, when, in fact, it turned out to be an extremely dangerous, violent, destructive, and homicidal cult.

The most suitable summary of this case is embodied in the words of Max Cutler in the introduction of his book entitled *Cults* (2022): Cults and their leaders manifest

> the strange and often deadly symbiosis of belief and charisma and perversity. [These cult figures] may have left trails of bodies in their wakes, but that could never happen without the misguided devotion of their acolytes – their eagerness to step beyond the rules of ordinary life and even the boundaries of common sense. The larger-than-life dominators who seized control of their small but highly profitable bands of believers were gifted at gaining confidence and misdirecting it, but their devotees were willful and energetic in the execution of their faith. It was the cult leaders who lit the fire, and the people trapped within their grip who tragically acted as the fuel [28, p. 5].

The Characteristics of Cult Followers

To examine the cult followers we employ psychiatric analyses with specific criteria and questions. For example:

- Do cult followers suffer from any DSM psychiatric disorders?
- If not, do they have a psychiatric profile (no disorder, but traits)?
- If not, do they have a developmental history with factors that may increase risks, such as:
  1. Being prey-like: attractive to predators, weak, vulnerable, fragile, isolated, few supports.
  2. Being dissatisfied with the reality of their lives (not flourishing), so easily attracted to novel realities, which offer a better life, a more idealistic or idyllic life involving

love, social justice, hope, comradeship, and the like. The old life is portrayed as bad (unjust, dirty, lacking meaning), and the good new life in the new promised land requires rejection of the old, hence the need to avoid contact with old friends, family members, and news sources.

3. Being cognitively confused about the complexities of the world, so they are encouraged to rely on slogans and simple and dogmatic answers from an infallible source, that is, the leader, who removes all confusion. Two common methods to reduce confusion are:

   - replacement of dimensional with categorical thinking
   - replacement of Western logic with Eastern logic

The human mind thinks of constructs either in terms of dimensions (i.e., constructs that are easily quantified, like height, weight, intelligence) or in terms of categories (gender was until recently binary, male/female). For convenience, according to the DSM, some constructs that are actually measures on a dimensional continuum are forced into artificial categories (intelligence). Statisticians use different methods to analyze data from dimensional to categorical.

Often, reducing complex data from dimensional to categorical makes it easier to manipulate or understand. Therefore, some leaders are tempted to reduce complex situations (the world is complicated and wise decision-making requires appreciation of nuance) into apparently simple ones and to offer decision-makers simpler binary choices (e.g., Bush's analysis of the world was simple – the world was either good or bad, and he offered world leaders simple choices – you are either with us or against us) [35].

As in the world of politics, the moral world is in reality complex, and many moral judgments require an appreciation of nuance and greyness. But some Eastern religious leaders are tempted to reduce the world's moral complexities into a simpler frame. The cult recruit is educated in a manner in which their current world, which may be unsatisfying, is portrayed as simply bad, in contrast to the cult world, which promises much satisfaction, as being simply good. Such a binary choice is indeed simple, and many choose that which is good, clean, and noble over that which is not. In making decisions, the cult member may be informed that the cult ideology is based on true facts (not false fictions), and the cult leader has, of course, access to these true facts. But manipulation of the facts requires use of logic, and there is a difference between Western logic (taught in all Western universities) and Eastern logic that is mostly neglected in the Orientalist West.

Western logic, derived from the Greek masters, assumes that a proposition must be either true or false. The statement "2 + 3 = 5" is true, while the statement "2 + 3 = 23" is false. Those are the only two choices, true versus false. In contrast, Eastern (Indic) philosophy is more subtle. It agrees that a statement may be true, or it may be false, but in addition, it offers the rich insights that a statement may be true *and* false, and also *neither* true *nor* false. For example, the statement "lying is good" may be true, and it may be false. The statement "the wind is green" is neither true nor false. Such sophisticated Eastern logic (in contrast to the simpler Western logic) allows for more logical options, and allows for controversial ethical methodologies like casuistry, which is much maligned in the West [29].

4. Being socially confused: Most humans have multiple identities (i.e., race, gender, religion, tribe, moral community) but not all such identities are a source of comfort. By creating an external enemy, the cult creates internal cohesion with a more intense sense of group identity, which is socially comforting. By introducing a moral component, such as the external world is morally corrupt, the cult members are deemed morally pure, and cult membership also becomes morally comforting.
5. Being socially isolated: The cult offers a social group where no member has to be alone. In fact, being alone is discouraged, and there is peer pressure to join in and hence to conform.
6. Being decisionally uncritical/gullible: All humans make decisions, wise or foolish, with various degrees of critical thinking. Some institutions, like academic departments of philosophy, encourage critical thinking. Cults encourage *uncritical* thinking; the decision-making passes from the leader to the devotees, so there is substituted judgment.
7. Search for order, regimentation, discipline, structure, uniformity, and even uniforms, as in militaries, prisons, monastic orders and so on.

Summary

This chapter has reviewed some conceptual topics such as problems in defining the concept of "cult," and it has given a description of some Eastern religious cults, an analytical comparison of cults from different Eastern geographical locations (i.e., East Asia, South Asia, the Middle East) as well as Eastern cults in the Western diaspora.

This analysis has also presented the problems that may confront American psychiatry if an Eastern religious cult ideology is asserted as a mental defense in a Western court of justice. In addition, the authors have attempted to highlight the characteristics of cult leaders and followers that are unique to Eastern religious cults. While there is a rich literature about the social and psychological characteristics of leaders in general, and even of cult leaders, such literature about leaders and followers of Eastern religious cults is sparse.

Nonetheless, scholars may extrapolate findings from the broad category of leaders/followers to the narrower group of cult leaders/followers, to the yet narrower category of "Eastern" cult leaders/followers. Further insights may be gained not from studying actual leaders/followers of Eastern religious cults, which may be difficult, but from studying the dynamics of leadership, and comparing Eastern and Western leadership styles, parenting styles, and examining the differences between Eastern and Western philosophies contextually.

Key Points

- The title of the chapter, "Eastern Religious Cults," implies that the two adjectives – Eastern and religious – when applied to cults give relevant information about the subject of cults.
- While both adjectives are descriptors, they are imprecise. The boundaries between a religious and secular cult (e.g., a political cult) are poorly defined.
- The boundaries between Eastern and other are similarly poorly defined, as Eastern may refer to a geographical space roughly corresponding to Asia, or to the source of

an ideology, perhaps dharmic, as opposed to Abrahamic, or even to a biased interpretation of anything that is alien, or the "other."

- Starting with the biased Orientalist tradition, but continuing to modern (non-Orientalist) scholarship, there is a desire to understand and learn more about the East and Eastern religious cults and how they may differ from their non-Eastern counterparts.
- While there are few findings from hard research, there are more findings from soft research and many opinions from folk psychology, which suggest that Eastern religious cult leaders are narcissistic, scheming, full of oriental cunning, devious, and successful at duping not only followers in the East, but even gullible simpletons in the West.
- Such an analysis may or may not have elements of truth in it, but it may be the result of a tautological fallacy.
- The East and West are full of many social groups with a variety of belief systems.
- Some meet with the approval of the majority – most in the West approve of Jesus and his teachings, and most in the East approve of Buddha and his teachings. These groups are therefore deemed "religions."
- In contrast, some groups do not meet with the approval of the majority.
- In the West, the majority disapproved of Osho, and in the East, the majority disapproved of the Assassins and the Thugs, partly because their leaders were viewed as narcissistic, scheming, and cunningly devious. Based on these characteristics, these leaders are considered cult leaders.
- As a result, it would be a tautology and silly to conclude that Eastern cult leaders are narcissistic or cunning or devious, as our findings presented in this chapter articulate.

References

1. JT Richardson. *Definitions of cult: from sociological-technical to popular-negative.* Routledge; 1998.
2. J Campbell. *Hero with a thousand faces.* 3rd ed. New World Library; 2008.
3. www.goodreads.com/quotes/112690-myth-is-what-we-call-other-people-s-religion
4. J Scheeres. *A thousand lives: the untold story of Jonestown.* Free Press; 2012.
5. RJ Lifton. *Destroying the world to save it: Aum Shinrikyo, apocalyptic violence, and the new global terrorism.* Picador; 2000. p. 7.
6. K Kotela. The Hare Krishna and the counterculture in the light of the theory of the divergent modes of religiosity. *Method & Theory in the Study of Religion.* 2004;16(3):301–20.
7. W Davis. Heaven's Gate: a study of religious obedience. *Nova Religio: The Journal of Alternative and Emergent Religions.* 2000;3(2):241–67.
8. JC Duffy. Is it good to be a good religion? Mormonism and the status politics of novelty. *CrossCurrents.* 2014;64(2):180–201.
9. DK Gupta. *Path to collective madness: a study in social order and political pathology.* Greenwood; 2001.
10. M Weber. *Theory of social and economic organizations.* Free Press; 1947.
11. J Post. *Leaders and their followers in a dangerous world: the psychology of political behavior.* Cornell University Press; 2004.
12. D Kahneman, A Tversky. Choice, values, and frames. *American Psychologist.* 1984;39:341–50.

13. B Anderson. *Imagined communities: reflections on the origin and spread of nationalism*. Verso; 2008.
14. S Atran. *In gods we trust: the evolutionary landscape of religion*. Oxford University Press; 2002.
15. R Sapolsky. *Behave: the biology of humans at our best and worst*. Penguin Books; 2002.
16. DK Gupta. *Understanding terrorism and political violence: the life cycle of birth, growth, transformation, and demise*. 2nd ed. Routledge; 2020.
17. R Sapolsky. This is your brain on nationalism: the biology of "us" and "them," *Foreign Affairs*. 2019 Mar/Apr.
18. https://psycnet.apa.org/record/2023-30761-001
19. B Lewis. *The assassins: a radical sect in Islam*. Basic Books; 1967.
20. M Dash. *Thug: the true story of India's murderous cult*. Granta Books; 2005.
21. The complete story behind India's most interesting thugs. *Homegrown*. 2021 Jun 8. https://homegrown.co.in/homegrown-explore/the-complete-story-behind-india-s-most-interesting-cults#:~:text=According%20to%20the%20Guinness%20Book,there%20are%20no%20reliable%20sources
22. G Morris, A Haroun. "God told me to kill": religion or delusion? *San Diego Law Review*. 2001;4:973–1050.
23. BBC News. Aum Shinrikyo: the Japanese cult behind the Tokyo sarin attack. 2018 Jul 6. www.bbc.com/news/world-asia-35975069
24. E O'Connor. One day that changed Asia: Tokyo's sarin scars: How a false messiah changed Japan forever (ENDEVR Documentary) 2022 Oct 26. https://youtu.be/ig4yr1YqA9U
25. Journeyman Pictures. Japan's strange and deadly insurrectionist cult (1995). 2018 Aug 20. https://youtu.be/xR_FrDbud1E
26. A Pollack. Japanese police find body of a lawyer believed killed by cult. *The New York Times*. 1995 Sep 7. www.nytimes.com/1995/09/07/world/japanese-police-find-body-of-a-lawyer-believed-killed-by-cult.html
27. Japan Today. Thirtieth anniversary of murder of lawyer, family, by Aum observed. 2019 Nov 5. https://japantoday.com/category/crime/30th-anniversary-of-murder-of-lawyer-family-by-aum-members-observed
28. M Cutler. *Cults: inside the world's most notorious groups and understanding the people who joined them*. Gallery Books; 2022.
29. E Said. *Orientalism*. 1st ed. Vintage Books; 1979.
30. D Herbjørnsrud. The untold story of India's vital atheist philosophy. Blog of the APA. 2020 Jun 16. https://blog.apaonline.org/2020/06/16/the-untold-history-of-indias-vital-atheist-philosophy/
31. GHC Huang, M Gove. Asian parenting styles and academic achievement: views from Eastern and Western perspectives. *Education*. 2015;135(3):389–97.
32. R Malhotra. *Being different: an Indian challenge to Western universalism*. Harper Collins; 2015.
33. TA Roy, JL Mihura, AF Friedman, DS Nichols, JR Meloy. The last psychological evaluation of Charles Manson: implications for personality, psychopathology, and ideology. *Journal of Threat Assessment and Management*. 2022;10(3):127–50.
34. PA Olsson. *Malignant pied pipers*. Strategic Book Publishing; 2017.
35. G Priest. Beyond true and false: Buddhist philosophy is full of contradictions. Now modern logic is learning why that might be a good thing. *Aeon*. 2014 May 5. https://aeon.co/essays/the-logic-of-buddhist-philosophy-goes-beyond-simple-truth

Chapter 2 Western Religious Cults

Trent C. Holmberg and Kelsey N. Tuttle

"If the Bible is true, then I'm Christ."
- David Koresh, Branch Davidian leader

Introduction

Identifying groups for discussion in this chapter presented as a challenge, given the limitations of the authors to determine what is "counterculture" in cultures outside of our own. Religious groups fall on a spectrum, along which the transition from organized religion to cult (or vice versa) is not clearly defined. In addition to this, the term "cult" often has a negative connotation associated with it, as historically it has been used to condemn "deviant" and counterculture groups whose effects on individuals and society range from positive to detrimental.

Membership and participation in a new religious movement (NRM), which may also be described as a cult, typically does not cause obvious injury to its followers. In fact, it is generally perceived by the follower as spiritually and/or socially beneficial. In most cases, members stay in the "cult" for a short period of time and then voluntarily leave the movement. In these cases, an individual's progression within the "cult," from investigating the movement, to religious conversion to the organization's doctrines/practices, and then to subsequent religious practice within the group, mirrors the process of individuals who investigate and join larger, more established, and more traditional religions. Similarly, the followers of the NRM tend to be people who lack overt psychopathology and who simply exercise their free will to join and (subsequently in many cases) to leave the "cult." However, in this textbook and particularly in this chapter, we focus on specific groups, frequently referred to as cults, but that also might be termed "destructive" NRMs.

It is probably inevitable that this distinction involves value judgments and could be considered somewhat arbitrary. However, in this chapter, we chose to focus on NRMs that appear to have some destructive elements. These include deceptive recruiting techniques, attempts to exert significant control over the minds and behavior of followers, abuse of followers, criminal activity, and groups associated with violence or harm (including suicide) toward followers or others.

Geographic Tendencies of the Western Hemisphere

In reviewing NRMs/cults in the Western hemisphere (referred to as Western religious cults [WRCs] in this chapter), you will notice that the vast majority of the groups we identify were founded and operated in the United States of America. There are approximately 2,500 different religious groups in the United States, and roughly half of those are considered "nonconventional" [1]. Moreover, NRMs are also growing at the clip of 20 per year. Cowan and Bromley have written that "this makes the United States one of the most religiously diverse countries both in the world and throughout history" [1, p. 6].

The reason for this is likely multifactorial, but a widely accepted theory relates to the laws protecting religious freedoms in the United States of America. One key law is the First Amendment to the Bill of Rights of the United States Constitution, which states: "Congress shall make no law respecting an establishment of religion, or prohibiting the free exercise there of; or abridging the freedom of speech or of the press or the right of the people peaceably to assemble, and to petition the Government for a redress of grievances" [2]. The Free Exercise Clause of the First Amendment was added in 1791 and is utilized by both mainstream and counterculture groups [3–6]. Its interpretation first came into question in the late 1800s when the practice of polygamy was brought to court in the case *Reynolds* v. *United States* [7]. Ultimately, Congress dissolved the religious organization until they agreed to exclude polygamy from their religious practices. In this case, the distinction between belief and action and what is protected under the First Amendment was debated. Some individuals argued for full religious freedom to include both belief and action. Other individuals argued that the law should be interpreted to protect beliefs only, not actions, with the concern that it undermines the value of government if members of specific religious organizations are allowed to disobey laws that apply to all other individuals outside of that religion. The courts have interpreted the First Amendment to mean the latter.

As time went on, in the United States, it continued to be the prominent opinion that religious expression should be allowed to flourish and that government should not interfere with this at the national or state level. To ensure this, the Fourteenth Amendment to the United States Constitution was ratified in 1868 and prohibited state-level interference with religious freedoms as well as addressing multiple other freedoms. The Fourteenth Amendment reads: "No state shall make or enforce any law which shall abridge the privileges or immunities of citizens of the United States; nor shall any state deprive any person of life, liberty, or property, without due process of law; nor deny to any person within its jurisdiction the equal protection of the laws" [8]. With this amendment, states could not enforce laws that contradict national laws, including the First Amendment.

More recently, a key law in the United States of America was the Religious Land Use and Institutionalized Persons Act of 2000 [9]. This Act allows religious institutions to operate outside of state property zoning restrictions that might prohibit their use of certain land/buildings. This Act

> [p]rohibits any government from imposing or implementing a land use regulation in a manner that imposes a substantial burden on the religious exercise of a person, including a religious assembly or institution, unless the government demonstrates that imposition of the burden on that person, assembly, or institution: 1) is in furtherance of a compelling governmental interest; and 2) is the least restrictive means of furthering that compelling governmental interest. [9]

This Act has allowed religious groups to build churches, compounds, and other facilities in locations that otherwise would be restricted.

In addition to laws protecting religious freedoms, there are some traditional Western philosophies that may promote the conception of NRMs as well as membership to these groups. Historians refer to multiple "Great Awakenings" that have cyclically occurred over the lifespan of the USA. Each awakening indicates a time of ideological transformation in which people find it necessary to change their mindset, behavior, and institutions (including religions) to reflect the larger group's new view (s) that result from having a more relevant understanding and ability to cope with changes in the world [10]. Though there is debate about the number and dates of each awakening, it seems that social change and religious change often happen alongside each other. During each awakening there have been various sects that separated themselves from the accepted religions of the time as well as the formation of brand-new organizations. These smaller groups would not be limited by existing institutional restrictions, rituals, interpretations, and doctrine. The Fourth Great Awakening started in the 1960s and a number of movements and value systems around weapons, Earth health, animal safety, and oppression of women and people of color came to the forefront, some in the form of religions [11]. Conditions thought to play a role in a person converting to a new religion are largely debated, overgeneralized, and research of hypothesized models has not been consistent in results. However, aspects of the Lofland–Stark model [11] are supported by Western philosophies. This includes being exposed to intensive interaction with other converts – as we have outlined, some laws facilitate communal living. Western philosophy may also more easily allow for isolation from noncult members as independent living is more common than the multigenerational homes seen in other cultures. Cultural preferences in the West favor individualism over collectivism and this mindset of autonomy and protecting individual rights provides the space for people to consider religions other than the one(s) they were raised in and to question tradition.

Case Vignette

"Are you gonna come in and kill me?," a Branch Davidian child can be heard cautiously asking during a recording of negotiations between the Branch Davidians, the FBI, and the Bureau of Alcohol, Tobacco, Firearms and Explosives (ATF) [12] on April 19, 1993 in Mount Carmel Center outside of Waco, Texas.

The Branch Davidians were a splinter group that broke away from the Seventh-day Adventist Church. In the 1930s, an active but controversial member of the church, Victor Houteff, was expelled from the Seventh-day Adventist Church due to disagreements about his teachings. Houteff established a church and went on to publish two books, *The Shepherd's Rod Vol. 1* and *Vol. 2* (Figure 2.1 and Figure 2.2) [13, 14]. Out of this, he gained followers whom he initially called the Shepherd's Rod Seventh-day Adventists. One such follower was the mother of a child named Harriet (Harriett was the individual who later introduced Vernon Howell to the Branch Davidians). Houteff believed he was a living prophet and moved his followers from California to the outskirts of Waco, Texas on a property called Mt. Carmel.

The new sect's beliefs were centered around the Book of Revelation and the seven seals that are discussed within it. The seals were believed to provide information around the sequence of events that will lead to judgment day, or Advent (the second coming of Christ). It was their belief (and the belief of many Christians) that the true meaning of

Figure 2.1 "The Harvest Period and the Close of Probation," one of 21 teaching charts by Victor Houteff
Source: Baylor University Library, Special Collections, The Texas Collection, 1931
Credit: The Texas Collection, Baylor University, Baylor, Texas

these seals would be explained or revealed by the Messiah, who would come during the last days before judgment day.

Houteff and his followers lived for years outside of Waco studying the Bible and were described as pleasant and kind people by local law enforcement [12]. Eventually, Houteff changed the movement's name to Davidian Seventh-day Adventists. Houteff died in 1954 and his followers continued to wait for the Advent that his wife, Florence, predicted would be on April 22, 1959 [15].

A Davidian Seventh-day Adventist follower by the name of Benjamin Roden disagreed with Florence Houteff's prophecy, and believed the second coming would occur in 1960. Roden also campaigned that he should be Houteff's successor. When the prophesied date arrived and the Advent did not occur, the group began questioning Florence Houteff's leadership and divided into multiple smaller groups, one being dubbed the "Branch Davidians" and led by Roden [12]. Roden changed his prediction about the Advent. He also obtained the Mt. Carmel property for himself and his group of followers. Less than a decade later (in the late 1970s) Roden died and his wife, Lois, assumed leadership of the Branch Davidians [15].

Shortly after Florence Houteff's prophecy did not come true, a child by the name of Vernon Wayne Howell was born. He was born on August 17, 1959, to Bobby Howell and

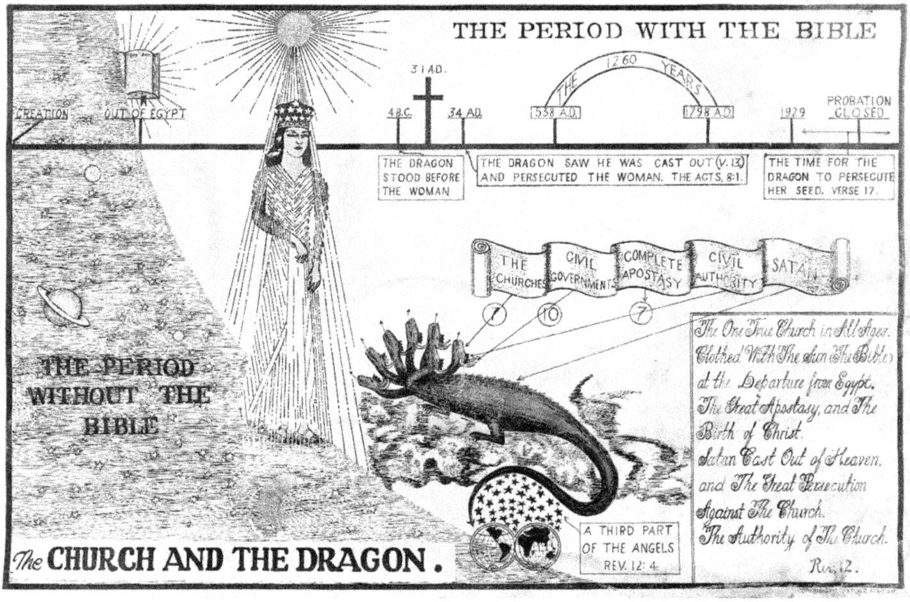

Figure 2.2 "The Church and the Dragon," one of 21 teaching charts by Victor Houteff
Source: Baylor University Library, Special Collections, The Texas Collection, 1932
Credit: The Texas Collection, Baylor University, Baylor, Texas

14-year-old Bonnie Clark [16]. Vernon would later change his name to David Koresh. Vernon's father was not involved in his life; instead he was predominantly raised by his mother, maternal grandmother, and other family members. Early in his life, Vernon was described by his mother as cute, sweet, always talking, curious, and always telling stories. He enjoyed attending church and Sabbath school. From age two to four, Vernon lived with his maternal grandmother who introduced him to her church, the Seventh-day Adventists. During this time, Bonnie married a man named Joe shortly after he was released from jail and divorced him when he returned to jail.

At age 18, Bonnie met a man by the name of Roy Haldeman who was 16 years her senior. They began a romantic relationship. Bonnie became pregnant with Haldeman's child. They married when Bonnie was six months pregnant. Vernon lived with his mother and new stepfather. He struggled in school and his mother described him as having a learning disability. She said: "It was not dyslexia. It was called a language disability. Kids who have this disability have high IQs, but they just can't get certain things" [16, p. 15]. Despite this, his mother described him as making friends easily and engaging in outdoor activities including riding bikes and going to the lake; church was not initially a regular part of Vernon's life when he moved in with his mother. However, church attendance became a large part of his life when Vernon was age nine, as his mother and grandmother increased their involvement in church. By age 13, Vernon asked to go to a religious school, so Bonnie sent both of her sons to a church-sponsored school in a neighboring town. She cleaned houses to help pay their tuition. Vernon, his half-brother, and Bonnie were very active in the church during this time and Vernon had his first girlfriend [16].

For high school, Vernon returned to public school, joined the track team, learned to play guitar, listened to rock music, and began listening to radio preachers. He argued with his parents about common topics of the time, including wanting to have long hair, of which they disapproved – later in life he never made any of his children get haircuts. Bonnie recalled Vernon punching his stepfather when his stepfather was drunk and physically disciplining Vernon's little brother. Bonnie also recounted an instance in which Vernon intentionally set fire to his own vehicle. Vernon dropped out of 11th grade and went to work with his stepfather as a carpenter [16].

At age 20, Vernon was living in his car and had impregnated his high school girlfriend. He was forbidden by the girl's father to ever see her or their child, Shae. Emotional distress and many questions came to weigh heavily on Vernon, and he would bring his questions and occasional "visions" to his Seventh-day Adventist Church congregation. His frequent questioning and claims of the Holy Spirit being feminine (per a vision he had) were not received well by the church. Vernon began asking why there were no present-day prophets. Harriet (referenced at the beginning of this section), a member of the congregation, became close with Vernon and informed him that those in the Branch Davidian sect at Mt. Carmel (led by Lois Roden at the time) believed in present-day prophets [16].

Vernon joined the group at Mt. Carmel and immersed himself in the religion, memorizing multiple sections of the Bible including the passages pertaining to the seven seals. In 1983, he had a revelation that he was to have a live-in relationship with Lois Roden, who was in her sixties at the time [1, 17]. Shortly thereafter, Lois passed away. Vernon believed he should become the leader of the group, while Lois' son, George, felt he should be her successor. As this disagreement continued, Vernon, age 24, wed a lifelong member of the group, Rachel Jones, age 14. Her parents were also followers and gave their consent. Nevertheless, this union resulted in Vernon and Rachel being forced out of the Mt. Carmel compound by George Roden. They consequently moved to Palestine, Texas and lived primitively in tents [12, 1].

In 1985 and 1986, members of the now George Roden-led Branch Davidians began to leave the group at Mt. Carmel to follow Vernon. He was able to eventually attract a wide range of individuals to follow his teachings, including international individuals and Harvard Law School graduates [12]. While in Israel furthering his religious understanding, Vernon had a revelation that he was called to follow in the path of King Cyrus of Persia and defeat modern Babylon, identified as the government [15]. Over the next year, Vernon took three more wives, all under the age of 18 at the time of the union. Vernon and multiple followers became involved in acts of armed violence with the Branch Davidians that remained at Mt. Carmel, namely George Roden and his followers. Vernon and some of his followers were charged with attempted murder, but they were found not guilty (Figure 2.3) [12, 15] .

In 1988, Vernon and his followers moved back to Mt. Carmel. Over a year later, in late 1989, Vernon began preaching to the Branch Davidians about the "new light" doctrine, which made him the rightful husband of all women in the religion, even if they were currently married to someone else [12, 1]. Per the New Testament, "at the time of the end, those who have wives, should live as if they have none" and according to the seven seals, as the time of the Advent approached it was the group's obligation to be celibate. However, it was the final figure's obligation to have 24 children, who would eventually become the elders that would rule the earth. The Branch Davidians believed

Figure 2.3 Mug shot of David Koresh, November 3, 1987
Source: www.atf.gov/sites/default/files/media/2018/02/korseh-2.jpg
Author: McLennan County Sheriff's Office

these children would be pure, as they were raised in the Branch Davidian sect. They were therefore exposed to the Bible and did not watch television or eat processed foods [12, 1].

In early 1990, Vernon changed his name to David Koresh. He chose David because he related to King David in the Bible, from whom Jesus Christ was thought to descend. Koresh was a Persian king who is known in the Bible for freeing Jewish people during Babylonian captivity. In accordance with his preaching, Koresh and his followers believed he was the seventh and final messenger referenced in the Book of Revelation leading up to the Advent [1, 12, 17, 18].

Since 1934, long before Koresh was born, there was a prophecy that the Branch Davidians would have a confrontation with an armed power, Babylon, later interpreted to be the United States government. To prepare, Koresh and the Branch Davidians began acquiring firearms and would also buy and sell firearms for a profit. This activity was legal, but there were reports made to the ATF that firearms were being converted to automatic firing, which is illegal [18, 15]. As a result, plans were made to serve a search warrant at Mt. Carmel to investigate the illegal weapon modification charges, as well as to investigate allegations of child abuse and statutory rape [12, 15, 19].

Over the years, state Division of Family Services representatives had been sent to Mt. Carmel to investigate Koresh and his followers on multiple occasions, but no cases were brought against Koresh or other members of the group [19]. It was noted that parental consent prevented local authorities from building cases related to certain potential violations [12]. It was reported by Koresh's arms dealer that Koresh offered for the ATF to inspect his firearms when he found out he was being investigated, but the ATF did not take him up on this offer. During congressional hearings after the Waco standoff, the possibility that the ATF intentionally pursued a raid when a less invasive option may have existed was discussed. Potential motives for this decision were thought to include producing positive press, creating fear about fringe groups, and simultaneously helping build a case for increased funding for the Bureau, given that the department's hearing for appropriations was scheduled for one week after the raid [12].

Figure 2.4 ATF agents attempting to enter the Branch Davidian compound on February 28, 1993
Source: Retrieved from the Texas Ranger Evidence Locker at Austin, Texas, by Mike McNulty, and published to the blog https://copsproductions.wordpress.com/ in 2012.
Author: United States Government

Figure 2.5 ATF agents arrive at the Branch Davidian compound in cattle trucks
Source: Wikimedia, public domain
Credits/Author: Mike McNulty

On the morning of February 28, 1993 local media were made aware of the ATF's plan for a raid. Numerous media outlets descended on the Mt. Carmel compound to document the raid. On their way to the compound, representatives of one media outlet stopped a mailman to ask for directions to the compound. Unknown to them, that mailman was a Branch Davidian member. The member dutifully alerted Koresh to the raid. The ATF had an undercover agent who had infiltrated the Branch Davidians, so the ATF also quickly became aware that Koresh had been alerted to the coming raid. Despite this, the ATF moved forward with the raid and plans to serve the search warrant (Figure 2.4 and Figure 2.5) [12, 20].

Dispatch recordings include that of a Branch Davidian by the name of Wayne Martin who called 911 once the raid was underway, stating that there were women and children in the home and asking for the raid to be called off. He also stated he had a right to defend himself and that the government agents had fired first. The dispatcher is heard trying to radio to the ATF and reports no response back. At the completion of the raid, four ATF agents had died, and tens of others were injured [20]. There were also multiple Branch Davidians who were killed or injured prior to the ceasefire being called (Figure 2.6). Koresh was injured, sustaining gunshot wounds to his side and hand. His followers viewed this to be not unlike the wounds of Christ on his final day [12].

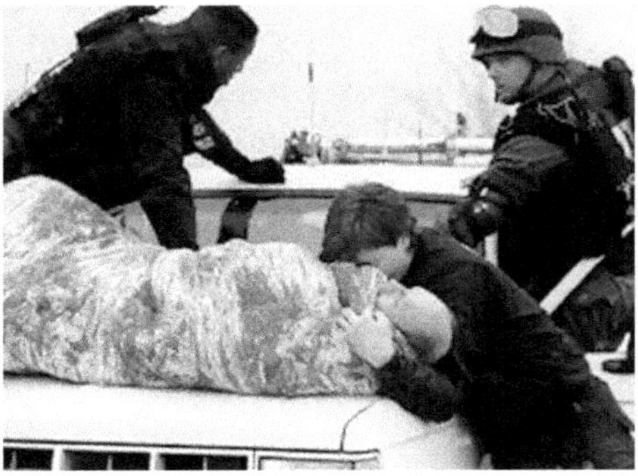

Figure 2.6 Wounded ATF special agent being transported
Source: www.atf.gov/our-history/photo-gallery/photo-gallery-waco

After the ceasefire, the Branch Davidians largely remained in their compound and the FBI gave a video camera to them. Some of the comments made on camera included: "I've always wanted to understand the Bible, and I wanted to know about the seven seals. Now I've found what I've been looking for"; "Is he the son of God? I hope he is"; and "I want to know what the truth is, if he happens to be the vehicle that shows me, I thank God for him" [12].

On March 1, 1993, the ATF transitioned control of the situation to the FBI who continued negotiations but also brought in a hostage recovery team, though it is argued there was no clear evidence that a hostage situation existed [1]. Negotiations were initially positive, with Koresh releasing children two by two every time a sermon of his was played on the local radio station. Some adults also left the compound, reportedly at Koresh's direction. The adults were arrested and later tried for the murder of the ATF agents who were killed in the initial raid. None were found guilty. As surviving children and adults recount it, leaving was not viewed as having saved their lives. Rather, they blamed themselves for having given up on their beliefs. They described this as extremely hard for them, but they were willing to move forward with something Koresh had instructed them to do [12, 21].

This point was further illustrated by a Branch Davidian who was severely injured in the raid. Rather than leave the compound, surrender to federal agents, and seek medical help, he begged for other Branch Davidians to kill him, which they did. Koresh then promised that if a videotaped sermon of his were to be broadcast nationally, he and the remaining children, women, and men inside Mt. Carmel would exit peacefully. However, after the broadcast occurred, Koresh claimed that he was told by God to "wait." As a result, no additional Branch Davidian members exited the compound [12].

At this time, the FBI began to realize that it was unlikely that Koresh or his followers were going to exit the compound voluntarily. The FBI had multiple snipers surrounding the compound and began resorting to other tactics outside of hostage negotiation, including playing loud songs and animal noises throughout the night and directing bright lights at the compound throughout the night [12, 21]. With both parties disgruntled, the situation continued to unravel. The FBI's negotiation tapes document a Branch Davidian member, Steve Schneider, confronting the negotiator about agents that were "flipping off" the Branch Davidians and "mooning" them when the Branch Davidians would look out the windows. This confrontation was acknowledged by the negotiator.

David Koresh's grandmother offered to talk to Koresh in an effort to have him surrender his firearms and leave the compound, but this offer was not accepted. Koresh told negotiators he was instructed by God to write his interpretation of the seven seals, and that he and the rest of the Branch Davidians would come out of Mt. Carmel once this task was completed. The FBI viewed this as a delay tactic. They were concerned no writing was being done, and that the Branch Davidians would not exit. The FBI seemed to be at a loss, as they struggled to grasp and negotiate around Koresh's beliefs. Their tactics to get followers of Koresh to leave the compound were largely unsuccessful as the Branch Davidians proved to be highly committed to their beliefs and extremely loyal to their leader. Koresh's interpretation of the biblical description of the seven seals included a prophecy of a fiery death during battle that would result in the chosen people returning as God's army, ultimately returning them to a paradisiacal Garden of Eden–like state. This was the sequence of events for which the Branch Davidians were prepared [12].

Dr. Park Dietz, a forensic psychiatrist, was contracted by the FBI to assess and give recommendations regarding their strategy during the standoff. Dr. Dietz's interpretation included the opinion that Koresh was unlikely to voluntarily leave the compound, that he may be suicidal, and that he had a manipulative personality. Dr. Dietz recommended that the FBI express sympathy with Koresh's anti-ATF views. He also advised that Koresh would likely choose death over losing power, so he recommended that negotiation strategies not highlight the potential for prison but rather should insinuate that Koresh may emerge to find an influx of followers if he were to exit and end the conflict [21].

On April 19, 1993 (day 51) the FBI felt they could wait no longer and began using their tanks to punch holes in the walls of the compound, injecting tear gas in the process [18, 21]. Over loudspeakers they announced: "We are in the process of placing tear gas in the buildings. This is not an assault" [12, 21]. Tear gas is flammable, and when burned produces hydrogen cyanide. Hydrogen cyanide is also flammable, and both hydrogen cyanide and tear gas are known to produce fireballs. The FBI asserted that they did not fire at the Davidians; however, forward looking infrared (FLIR) imaging, verified by two independent FLIR analyses, showed infrared patterns consistent with the firing of automatic weapons from the tanks circling and punching holes in the walls of the buildings. There were also 50 boxes of Ferrets (barricade-penetrating cartridges) found on the grounds of the compound – consistent with the Department of Justice's written report that tear gas was inserted using command engineering vehicles and Ferret rounds [21].

During the insertion of tear gas, multiple storage vessels were crushed by armored vehicles and the fuels they contained were released in addition to the flammable tear gas that had settled out into dust. Shortly after the insertion of tear gas, multiple fires started throughout the compound (Figure 2.7 and Figure 2.8). How these flames were originally ignited is unknown. However, the ultimate conclusion of the courts was that the Branch Davidians set fire to themselves as a mass suicide. The Department of Justice evaluation of the standoff documents that a woman who emerged from the compound during the April 19 series of events ran away from an agent and threw herself into the burning building, though ultimately was pulled out and survived [21]. Koresh along with a majority of his followers died in the fire, although Koresh's body was found with a bullet hole through the forehead, likely indicating his death prior to being engulfed by flames [12].

Those Branch Davidian members who survived the fires professed no knowledge of how the fires were started. When the survivors exited, they did bring with them a typed copy of Koresh's interpretation and teachings of the seven seals, which he finished in the early hours of April 19. His writings contained multiple statements in line with his

Figure 2.7 Aerial view of the Branch Davidian compound near Waco, Texas in flames on April 19, 1993, following a 51-day siege by the FBI and law enforcement
Source: https://multimedia.fbi.gov/item?type=image id=901
Author: FBI

Figure 2.8 Aerial view of the Branch Davidian compound with ongoing fire
Source: www.atf.gov/our-history/photo-gallery/photo-gallery-waco
Credits/Author: United States Government

pledge to exit Mt. Carmel once he finished the manuscript [22]. Of course, it remains unknown if he would have followed through with this promise.

Characteristics of Leaders

Demographics

Gender

The majority of the WRCs identified were led by men, which is in line with the study of millennial groups, a subset of WRCs [23]. One of the only groups led by women was Fiat Lux. The Children of God were initially led by a man but after his passing they were led by a woman, Karen Zerby. There were a few groups that were coled by a woman and a man including the Children of God [23] and Heaven's Gate [24]. Other groups were temporarily led by women after the man leading the cult died, such as with the Branch Davidians prior to Koresh taking leadership [12, 16, 15]. After review of the groups in this chapter, there were no overt differences in groups led by women versus men.

According to a study conducted by the Information Network Focus on Religious Movements (an educational charity that provides information about minority religions and spiritualities) about 12% of millennial groups (they identified 213) had some element of a significant female leadership. Therefore, it can be deduced that generally, most NRMs, at least of the millennial type, were and are led by men [25].

Age

The age at which WRC leaders were starting their organizations varies widely. Of the groups considered in this chapter, the age at which the leader came into power ranges from 23 to 60 years old (Table 2.1). This is partially affected by the status of the leader, specifically whether they incepted the group or if they achieved leadership through succession. Jim Jones was the youngest leader at age 23 when he began attracting followers [26]. The eldest was Joseph di Mambro of the Order of the Solar Temple at age 60 when the group was gaining traction [27].

Table 2.1 Approximate age of each leader at the time they began leading their respective group

Leader	Born	Year began leading	Approximate age when leading began
Jim Jones	1931	1954	23
Aldolfo Constanzo	1962	1986	24
Vernon Howell (David Koresh)	1959	1985	26
Paul Kingston	1959	1987	28
Claude Vorilhon	1946	1974	28
Roch Thériault	1947	1977	30
Warren Jeffs	1955	1986	31
Geody Harman	1973	2004	31
Charles Manson	1934	1967	33
Terrill Dalton	1967	2004	37
Luc Jourre	1947	1984	37
Paul Schäfer	1921	1961	40
Karen Zerby	1946	1988	42
Uffe Eidorff Hove	1956	1998	42
Marshall Applewhite	1931	1975	44
Charles Dederich Sr	1913	1958	45
Bonnie Nettles	1927	1975	48
James Baker (Father Yod)	1922	1971	49
David Berg	1919	1968	49
Charles Kingston	1884	1935	51
Erika Hedwig Bertschinger-Eicke	1929	1980	51
Joseph di Mambro	1924	1984	60

Childhood Upbringing

Among WRC leaders, Jim Jones, Warren Jeffs, Geody Harman, Terrill Dalton, Paul Kingson, Roch Thériault, Marshall Applewhite, and David Koresh all had religious upbringings. Jones was exposed to and active in many Christian religions including Methodism, Pentecostalism, and the Independent Assemblies of God – all of which he drew from in his own preaching [28]. Warren Jeffs (Figure 2.9) was born and raised in the Fundamentalist Church of Jesus Christ of Latter-Day Saints (FLDS) group he later came to lead [29].

Thériault was raised Catholic (though this was noted to be a fringe Catholic group called the "white berets") and later was a member of the Seventh-day Adventist Church. Applewhite was raised in a Presbyterian church [24]. Koresh was first exposed to the Seventh-day Adventist Church from an early age and then transitioned to being a member of the Branch Davidians, an offshoot of the Seventh-day Adventist Church, before becoming their leader [16].

Aside from religion, some of these cult leaders often had highly supportive parents. This includes Jim Jones, who was told frequently by his mother that he was destined to do something great [28], and Warren Jeffs whose father favored him and viewed him as special [29]. However, this is not the case for many other cult leaders who experienced absent parents, unstable childhoods, or parents/stepparents who used substances in excess. One such cult leader was David Koresh who did not know his father until age 19, had a stepfather who used alcohol in excess, a mother who dropped out of school at age 14, and who was raised by his grandmother for a significant period of time [16]. Charles Manson's mother was 16 years old when she had him and was later known for heavy alcohol use often resulting in leaving Manson alone or with sitters. Manson's mother also received a 10-year prison sentence for robbery and he was raised by his aunt and uncle during this time [30].

Figure 2.9 Photo distributed by the government in the hopes of catching Warren Jeffs
Source: www.fbi.gov/wanted/topten/topten-history/hires_images/FBI-482-WarrenSteedJeffs.jpg/view

Education

The level of education obtained by each WRC leader varies from professional degrees to dropping out of junior high school. Jim Jones had a bachelor's degree from Butler University [31]. Marshall Applewhite graduated from Austin College [32, 24]. Bonnie Nettles graduated with a nursing degree from Herman Hospital School of Professional Nursing [30, 33]. Paul Kingston was initially an accountant and an attorney indicating graduate-level education – at the time of this writing he was a member of the Utah State Bar [34]. Warren Jeffs completed high school at Jordan High School [35]. Roch Thériault was said to have dropped out of school in the seventh grade [36]. Charles Manson attended multiple reform schools, but it is unclear if he completed a high school education. However, Manson's IQ was tested at the National Training School for Boys in 1951 and again at Terminal Island in 1956 and was documented as 109 and 121 respectively [37]. Perhaps more consistent with his frequent moves from reform school to reform school and institutionalization from a young age, his Wide Range Achievement Test Reading (WRAT-R) subscale, administered in 1997, was a third grade equivalent [37].

Psychological Traits

Thirst for Power and Absolute Authority Resulting in Harm to Others

Having a thirst for power and absolute authority is a common trait of WRC leaders. This need for power and authority was often asserted through harm to others with a clear willingness to use physical violence and other forms of coercion and abuse to establish and maintain their position of power. Paul Schafer of Colonia Dignidad tortured "political" detainees for political intelligence [38, 39]. Jim Jones of Peoples Temple locked people in "the box" (a coffin-sized dark box) and induced fear in followers (e.g., forcing members to have snakes slither all over their bodies) [40]. Despite being in prison, Warren Jeffs described his leadership style over the FLDS community as "a benevolent dictatorship" [29]. Even after being arrested and incarcerated, he continued to attempt to lead the FLDS from prison rather than cede leadership to someone else.

Multiple WRC leaders evidenced a willingness to perpetrate or order violent acts, sometimes on a shocking scale. Other practices were more primitive, including stonings, amputations, intentionally breaking bones, and performing surgery without training or anesthesia, all of which were done by Roch Thériault on the members of the Ant Hill Kids and resulted in the death of a member [41]. At least 24 human sacrifices were completed by Adolfo Constanzo and his followers [42]. David Koresh and some of his followers also instigated an armed shootout with a prior member in order to take over the compound from which they had previously been expelled [12]. There is also the question of whether Koresh committed arson during the 1993 conflagration that ultimately killed his followers who remained in Mt. Carmel. This remains unclear, though, as investigations never definitively identified who or what started the conflagration [12, 21].

Bonnie Nettles and Marshall Applewhite instructed their Heaven's Gate followers to be celibate, that "sensuality" was a major offense, and that they should prepare for the lack of gender distinction in the "Next Level" [1]. Consequently, some of their male followers had themselves surgically castrated [1].

Charles Manson had 31 mug shots. After his death, some of his psychological testing while imprisoned became available to the public. In 1997, he was administered the Psychopathy Checklist-Revised (PCL-R) and scored 36/40, indicating severe psychopathic personality traits at a 95% confidence interval (the construct of psychopathy as it relates to WRC leaders is discussed in detail in Chapter 11 in this volume). Manson was also administered the Rorschach test to rule in/out mental illness (not to analyze personality organization or motivation) and he was positive on the Schizophrenia Index, the Hypervigilance Index, and was elevated on the cognitive Special Scores [37].

Elevated Self-Esteem/Grandiosity/Narcissistic Traits

Inflated self-esteem, grandiosity, and narcissistic traits were commonly demonstrated by the leaders of the more destructive WRCs (see Chapter 11 in this volume). As outlined in the "Childhood Upbringing" section, some leaders were known to have caregivers that praised their specialness/individuality without appreciation for "common" things they did or limitations that may exist. According to psychiatrist and author Jerrold Post, "[t]he more unrealistic the expectations, the more likely we will find a narcissistic individual driven by dreams of glory" [43, p. 51].

Referring to themselves as prophets, messiahs, God, and/or reincarnations of Jesus Christ are easily identifiable grandiose acts of multiple group leaders. Warren Jeffs, Geody Harman, Terrill Dalton, Paul Kingston, Uriella, Bonnie Nettles, Marshall Applewhite, and David Koresh all used such high terms to refer to themselves and their followers used these terms to refer to them. It is not uncommon for the leader of a group to be unemployed, as their main work is leading, while members of the group are employed and helping to support the group financially. Across much of the literature, WRC leaders are described as being narcissistic or having narcissistic personality disorder, though formal evaluation is often not outlined or cited. Again, this topic is discussed in detail in Chapter 11.

Among other examples, Father Yod of the Source Family crashed and died while hang gliding without lessons and without ever having done it before. As we have mentioned, Warren Jeffs continues to lead the FLDS from prison and requires members of the group to visit regularly to transcribe his oral preaching [29]. Charles Manson believed that after the race war (that he was going to start) ended, the United States of America would look to him and the Manson Family to lead the country. Of note, some claim this belief attributed to Manson was actually invented by the prosecution and that the more likely motive for the Helter Skelter murders was revenge on Terry Melcher, a music producer who did not move forward with recording and sharing Manson's music [44].

Spells, human sacrifice, and animal sacrifice were all used by Adolfo Constanzo. He believed he was able to channel the powers of Satan and was able to therefore protect himself and others [42]. It was claimed by Claude Vorilhon that the International Raëlian Movement had cloned a human, but despite repeated requests, he never produced evidence of the clone [45]. Frequently and without known hesitation, Roch Thériault performed multiple unanesthetized surgeries on members of the Ant Hill Kids [41]. Many WRC leaders greatly embellished the numbers of followers they had.

WRC leaders' inflated self-esteem appears to have facilitated their speaking and acting with confidence, which likely helped them attract and retain followers.

Hyperreligiosity, Religious Grandiosity, and Radical/Fundamentalist/Apocalyptic Doctrine

Being leaders of religious organizations, it does not come as a surprise that multiple leaders professed that they were God or that God was speaking through them. This included (among others) Jim Jones, Warren Jeffs, Terrill Dalton, and David Koresh. Jim Jones claimed to have come from another planet and to, therefore, be a man far ahead of his time here on earth [46]. Adolfo Costanzo felt as though he could channel the powers of Satan for protection. Per their preaching, Terrill Dalton was perceived by himself and his followers to be the Holy Spirit and Geody Harman was perceived to be "God in the flesh" [47]. These grandiose claims may represent anything along the spectrum from psychotic delusions to extreme overvalued ideas, to overvalued ideas, to "normal" religious beliefs, to fabricated claims intended to manipulate followers.

When attempting to determine if a WRC leader's religious beliefs represent "mental illness," wide deference must be given to accommodate the broad spectrum of religious beliefs that exist, particularly when there are no other signs of mental illness (other than religious beliefs that appear to be extreme, grandiose, or fundamentalist in nature). True delusions are fixed, false (or highly improbable), generally unshareable (i.e., idiosyncratic) and are associated with a disintegration of personality, while overvalued ideas are shareable and occur in an intact personality without such disintegration [48]. Navigating this middle ground between "normal" religious belief and delusion has been a challenge for the mental health field.

The concept of "extreme overvalued belief" is gaining traction as a recently validated concept providing helpful terminology as the mental health field struggles to conceptualize the diagnostic assessment of individuals with extreme religious ideas who carry out what appear to an outside observer to be horrific and inexplicable acts of violence [48]. These individuals hold odd and bizarre beliefs, but the beliefs are shared by others in their culture or subculture and therefore are probably not delusions. Tahir et al. defined "extreme overvalued belief" as follows:

> An extreme overvalued belief is one that is shared by others in a person's cultural, religious, or subcultural group. The belief is often relished, amplified, and defended by the possessor of the belief and should be differentiated from an obsession or a delusion. The belief grows more dominant over time, more refined, and more resistant to challenge. The individual has an intense emotional commitment to the belief and may carry out violent behavior in its service. [48, p. 181]

Many WRC leaders changed their names or added one or more titles in an effort to forge a new and higher identity, at least in the minds of their followers. Warren Jeffs uses the terminology that he is God's mouthpiece and is a divinely appointed prophet. David Koresh was originally named Vernon Howell but changed his name to emulate King David and Koresh, the Hebrew name for Cyrus, the King of Persia. He also referred to himself as the Messiah for conquering Babylon [12]. Marshall Applewhite and Bonnie Nettles called themselves (at various times) "Guinea and Pig," "Tiddly and Wink," "the Two," "Bo and Peep," and finally "Ti and Do" [1].

When "Ti" (Nettles) died from liver cancer, "Do" (Applewhite) taught their followers that a suicidal "exit" from their "vehicles" (bodies), and from Earth, would reunite the members with Ti, who they believed was piloting a flying saucer behind the Hale-Bopp comet that was approaching Earth at the time (March 1997) [46]. Accordingly, 39 members of Heaven's Gate (dressed in black with patches on their shirts that read "Heaven's Gate Away Team") consumed pudding or applesauce mixed with phenobarbital, drank vodka, and, with assistance, pulled plastic bags over their heads [48].

Uffe Eidorff Hove, Claude Vorilhon, Ervil LeBaron and David Koresh [22] all wrote their own gospel or religious text. Ervil LeBaron wrote the 400-page *The Book of the New Covenants* while he was in prison. The book included not only theological content but commandments to kill specific people [49].

In serving God, many leaders at least appear to have been willing and ready to die for their beliefs and to show their commitment to God and/or their religious tenets. This included Marshall Applewhite, Jim Jones, and David Koresh. It should be noted, however, that the manner of death (suicide vs. homicide) of both Jones and Koresh remains in question as both were found with gunshot wounds to the forehead [48].

Criminal Behavior

Violating the law was a common occurrence among WRC leaders. Warren Jeffs, Charles Manson, Terrill Dalton, Uffe Eidorff Hove, Roch Thériault, Marshall Applewhite, and Paul Schafer were all arrested and incarcerated, some with life sentences and parole denied [50, 51, 52]. Geody Harman and Charles Dederich were both on probation for their charges. Charles Dederich had multiple followers who were found guilty and given lengthy prison sentences for attempted murder, while he only received probation. Before the Waco standoff and fire, David Koresh was charged with (but not convicted for) attempted murder related to a shootout he and his followers had with George Roden and his followers [12, 15]. A search warrant for illegal firearms, child abuse, and statutory rape was attempted to be served to David Koresh, and had the standoff not ended with his death, he would have likely been incarcerated as there were illegal firearms being used by the Branch Davidians during the raid [12, 21].

Substance Use

Accounts from the destructive WRC leaders themselves or from their close followers indicated regular use of substances in many cases. There were also accounts of various substances being found on the property of the groups when they were raided/disbanded; one such instance was at Jonestown, where the *New York Times* reported that findings included quaaludes, Demerol, Valium, morphine, and Thorazine [53]. Methamphetamine was presumed to be the substance of choice for Jim Jones; however, his autopsy was positive for high levels of pentobarbital [54]. If he were using a stimulant, it likely contributed to his energy and enthusiasm while traveling the country performing staged miracles. It also probably allowed him to minimize time lost to sleep in Guyana, allowing him to oversee construction and preach into the night. It is thought that his signature look – wearing dark tinted glasses – was how he hid bloodshot eyes from minimal sleep [28].

Warren Jeffs was in possession of cocaine when he was arrested [29]. Charles Dederich was reported to have consumed alcohol in excess by a prior Synanon member, Laura Johnston Kohl [55]. This led Dederich to create what was initially a residential treatment program for substance use disorder and over time transitioned to what became known as the Church of Synanon. Adolfo Constanzo had access to marijuana. The *New York Times* reported that his drug operation was smuggling approximately one ton of marijuana into the United States weekly [56]. Charles Manson was known to use marijuana and presumed to use LSD – this is supported by the diagnostic impression by psychologist, Dr. Tod Roy, in 1997 – when Manson was incarcerated and was diagnosed with cannabis abuse (confirmed) and hallucinogen abuse (suspected) [37]. In an interview, Isis Aquarian (previously named Charlene Peters), a member of the Source Family and one of the wives to leader James Baker ("Father Yod"), reported that Yod regularly used marijuana and intermittently used cocaine and mushrooms [57]. The quantity and frequency of substance use for most leaders is not clear, but accounts regarding Jim Jones suggest he was using amphetamines regularly [28].

Hypersexuality

Although most professed that the practice was in line with their religious beliefs, polygamy could be interpreted as hypersexual behavior on the part of WRC leaders. Polygamy was, and continues to be, a common practice for leaders and their followers. James Baker had 14 wives within the Source Family and fathered multiple children [58]. Many women in the Ant Hill Kids were married to and impregnated by Roch Thériault, resulting in over 20 children [41]. In Emenkaya-Ordenen, Uffe Eidorff Hove took multiple wives with which he practiced sadomasochism and child pornography [59]. Hove was convicted of having intercourse with a minor, Krista, who married Hove on her 18th birthday [59, 60].

David Koresh also had multiple concurrent marriages, some to girls as young as 14 years old [21], and possibly as young as 10 years old [46]. He began taking "spiritual wives" as early as 1987 in an effort to father a new lineage of God's children, that is, a new "House of David" [1]. At the age of 33, Koresh had already fathered 12 children, all eight years of age or younger [46]. In 1989, he also revealed to his believers the "New Light" doctrine – that he was the messianic husband to all female members of the community and that all male members of the community (except himself) were to be celibate [46].

In regard to number of wives, Warren Jeffs is the leader who has the most known wives with some documentation indicating that at the time of his arrest he had 78 wives, 24 of which were under the age of 17 (Texas' legal age of consent). Estimates are that Jeffs fathered approximately 60 children [61]. Audiotape evidence revealed that he participated in the rape of multiple young girls while some of his other wives were present [29].

Charisma

Unusually strong psychological and emotional investments on the part of WRC members in charismatic leadership has been consistently linked to violence. Charismatic leaders are able to "mysteriously" galvanize the "commitment" of followers in ways unparalleled by other forms of authority. Leaders of NRMs, particularly destructive WRCs, have been known for their charm and talent that allowed them to form deeply personal relationships with their followers and to inspire a profound devotion in them [11].

Jim Jones and his followers would eavesdrop on potential followers at his healing ceremonies and then would incorporate this information into his preaching to these recruits, making him appear to be divinely inspired [62]. Jones was also known to preach for hours on end into the early hours of the morning (apparently often fueled by methamphetamine) and it appeared that his excitement to preach could not be contained [28]. Father Yod was the lead singer of the Source Family's psychedelic rock band, Ya Ho Wha 13 [58], bringing captivating energy to life in the form of music [63]. Charles Dederich inspired his followers to come to a life of sobriety and inspired the government to research and endorse the Syanon method, as seen in a Congressional Record report section titled "Study in Heroism – Synanon Foundation. A New Method for Treating Narcotics Addicts" by Senator Thomas Dodd Sr. [64].

Techniques Employed to Gain Followers and Maintain Control

Isolation

Limiting contact of members with nonmembers was a common tactic used by most leaders to varying degrees. Some allowed their followers to work in the community or for ministration of their messages, while others required complete isolation from nonmembers, television, and specific reading material. One of the more severe instances of isolation for maintaining membership was when Jim Jones moved members of his group to Guyana, taking possession of their passports and therefore precluding them from leaving the country [28]. Jones also directed his members what to write in their letters home. He screened the letters prior to allowing them to be sent [65].

Another radical example is the FLDS members under Warren Jeffs who lived in self-contained colonies including the Yearning for Zion Ranch, almost completely isolated from "Gentile" outsiders. They were not allowed to speak with members that left the church, and there was a complete absence of outside television and news programs. All books required approval and/or editing [29].

Bonnie Nettles and Marshall Applewhite isolated their followers from family and friends by living in a nomadic fashion, moving all over the country and camping in rural areas. Members were not to interact with people outside of the group unless it was to ask for help or to hold a public recruitment meeting – the latter being limited to only discussing "the message" and providing stereotyped answers. Isolation was taken even a step further, as members of this WRC were isolated from their own members. Each person was assigned a partner by Nettles and Applewhite. The pair was to stay together 24 hours a day, but friendships and sexual relations between the pair were strongly discouraged. Each pair was also to travel in a vehicle, separate from other couples, and was to camp away from other members [24].

Many other groups lived communally at the direction of the leader, including Heaven's Gate, the Source Family, Church of the First Born, Church of Syanon, the Children of God, the Kingston Clan, Colonia Dignidad, Emenkaya-Ordenen, and the Branch Davidians. The Colonia Dignidad compound still exists but people are able to leave freely.

Websites

While most leaders used basic recruiting tactics such as evangelization and word of mouth, some groups that were still operating in the 1990s utilized the internet to get their message out and attract new followers. This exclusive group included Heaven's Gate and the Source Family. The Heaven's Gate website provides contact information to request informational kits and, though maintained by past members, they have preserved its content and appearance to largely reflect its original inception [66]. The Source Family has stickers and Ya Ho Wah 13 music available for purchase [63].

Direct Evangelization

Direct evangelization is common practice for most WRC groups. The expectations around evangelization and the form in which it manifested were different across groups.

The Children of God used "flirty fishing," a form of evangelization in which members were encouraged to use their sexuality to entice new members [11, 25].

The Peoples Temple participated in direct evangelization by traveling the country and performing healing rituals in which Jim Jones would remove false cancers and other ailments from planted members in the audience. Jones and his followers also traveled across the country from California to Pennsylvania to evangelize and attempt to overtake Father Divine's congregation after his death. The Peoples Temple also participated in more sophisticated evangelization including starting soup kitchens and nursing homes, which allowed them to interact with vulnerable individuals. Jones was a strong "advocate" for these individuals and was known to contact utility companies and government officials to demand current and potential members get their electricity or other utilities turned back on. His work caring for the elderly and economically burdened was viewed with favor and incentivized people to be committed to the group, with the promise that they would receive similar treatment should they need it [40].

During the 51-day standoff, David Koresh (with the help of some of his followers) made voice and video recordings of his sermons that Koresh demanded be played on local and national stations as part of the attempted negotiation. Koresh quickly called for the media and wanted his message to be heard worldwide [12, 1].

Financial Control and Exploitation

As we have discussed, the Peoples Temple nursing homes were viewed with favor but along with the care members received came complete control of their finances and seizure of their assets. Jim Jones had nursing home members sign all of their assets over to the church, allowing him to use or sell assets as needed [28]. It is common practice in many religious organizations for members to give donations or tithings, but FLDS members are required to provide a specific amount of their income to the church. Some prior FLDS members report this required amount could be as high as 90% of their income [29]. The leaders of the FLDS as well as the Kingston Clan also engaged in financial control in a less direct but illegal way, through welfare fraud in order to obtain more money for the collective group [67, 68].

Creating Dependence and Stifling Independence

Intragroup dependence not only on the leader but on other members of the group creates a social system that is highly distressing to leave because it affects one's religious, social, occupational, and familial circles. Jim Jones would provide care to aging individuals and would feed financially burdened individuals, creating a dependent relationship with them. Jones also held all of his followers' passports when they lived in Guyana so that he had control over their ability to leave or cross country borders [28]. Warren Jeffs specifically targeted creating dependency among the women in the FLDS group. Jeffs promoted the role of homemaker as well as impregnation of girls and young women in order to create a system of financial and emotional dependence on the FLDS community. His directives to "keep sweet" and "pray and obey" had the effect of suppressing independent thought. Young men in the FLDS were often forced to be independent when they were involuntarily removed from the group in order to maintain a ratio of men to women that supported the polygamous lifestyle [29].

Psychological Tactics

Tactics akin to aversive exposure, gaslighting, mantras, and celebrity influence were used to attract and retain followers. Jim Jones enacted many "practice" Flavor-Aid sessions in which he told members they were drinking poison in a mass suicide when in fact the drinks were not poisoned. Jones did this repeatedly as a way for him to "test" the commitment and loyalty of his followers [26]. Incidentally, the Jonestown tragedy served as the origin of the expression "drinking the Kool-Aid" [69].

Warren Jeffs classically dictated all marriages within the FLDS community based on revelations he had. However, Jeffs would allow "chosen" marriages in the group in order to retain individuals he was highly concerned were going to leave the movement or to bring back individuals that left. Jeffs also kept control of the culture and expectations of the FLDS women by denying allegations of rape brought forward by them. Jeffs and his predecessors propagated the mantras "keep sweet," and "pray and obey" among the group. This mantra appeared written on their buildings and other FLDS objects [29].

In an attempt to use well-known marketing strategies, Father Yod marketed the Source Restaurant and, in turn, the group, to celebrities in Los Angeles by placing it on the Sunset Strip and promoting a professed culture of health and well-being. The allure of encountering celebrities at the restaurant was an appealing feature of being a follower.

Reproduction

A simple yet effective tactic to increase the number of followers a group had was to endorse large family sizes, often supported by the practice of polygamy. Groups including the FLDS, Church of the First Born, the Source Family (James Baker [Father Yod]), the Ant Hill Kids, the Kingston Clan, Emenkaya-Ordern, and the Branch Davidians all practiced polygamy – see the section on "Hypersexuality."

Perception by Followers

Whether a result of their preaching or the collective interpretation of their followers, leaders of WRCs were viewed positively by their followers. The authority of the WRC leader typically depends upon the leader fostering the attachment of the follower to the leader by forging a deep and very personal relationship, leading the follower to develop progressively stronger feelings of faith and trust in their leader [11]. The predictable result is dependency on the leader, and a comforting belief that the leader will either "save" them or teach them how to save themselves.

Warren Jeffs and David Koresh were viewed as prophets with direct lines to God [12, 29]. Terrill Dalton and Geody Harman preached that they were the Holy Spirit and "God in the flesh" respectively, and they were viewed by followers to be just that. The Peoples Temple members viewed Jim Jones to be a socialist and man of the people [28]. An advocate for general wellness of body and mind was a common perception of Father Yod.

One example of the way followers viewed WRC leaders is the statement of former Davidian Alisa Shaw. Discussing David Koresh's taking of multiple wives in sacred marriages, Ms. Shaw explained that marriage to "The Lamb" was "the way to salvation." Davidian women believed that there were few women that would be deemed "worthy to be sown with the seed of God and produce children." The Davidian women considered it "an honor to have a baby for Christ." The prevailing belief was that Koresh was given "inspiration," and that was how he knew who was worthy of his "loins." Parents of the girls or women who Koresh took as spiritual wives, at least the ones who were part of the Mt. Carmel community, consented to these polygamous marriages to Koresh because they believed that their daughters were "going to have children for the Lord" [46, p. 83].

Characteristics of Followers

Contrary to prevailing assumptions, WRC followers are generally not recruited through public interactions such as street contacting or other public displays. Most recruits join these cults through preexisting social networks and interpersonal bonds. In other words, they know someone within the cult and accept their invitation to investigate the movement. In fact, single contacts in public places with cult recruiters unknown to the target are quite unlikely to result in the target joining the movement [11].

There are limited data in this area, but a study was conducted in Great Britain evaluating the way in which individuals joined a group known as Nichiren Shōshū. This study showed that introductions to the group occurred 42% by friends, 23% by partners or family, 14% by casual acquaintances, and 6% through media (exhibitions, concerts, media accounts, etc.) [11].

For example, David Koresh was initially introduced to the Branch Davidians through Harriet, a member of the Seventh-day Adventist Church to which they both belonged. Harriet's mother had been a member of the Branch Davidians and, according to Koresh's mother, Harriet and Koresh had become close, so when Koresh began struggling with the congregation and was looking for present-day prophets, Harriet informed him of the Branch Davidians [16]. Harriet's mother, Bonnie, later became a member of the Branch Davidians for a period of time when she left her marriage [16].

Jim Jones also obtained his first followers after he left his role as a pastor at the Laurel Street Tabernacle. The board of directors did not take well to Jones' inclusion of people of color and as a result he left this role, taking with him about half of their congregation [28]. Geody Harman and Terrill Dalton both knew each other prior to forming the Church of the First Born and the General Assembly of Heaven, because they were both excommunicated members of the FLDS. Members of the Children of God engaged in "flirty fishing" to deepen affective bonds with prospective new members [11, 25]. Groups like The Order and the FLDS both broke away from the Church of Jesus Christ of Latter-day Saints and took members of this original group with them when they left.

An exception to groups being formed through affective bonds and pre-existing social networks is Heaven's Gate. Firsthand accounts from Robert Balch and David Taylor, who joined the cult in the 1970s as "hidden observers," detail the importance of isolation during induction and continued membership in the group. They recount that contact with outsiders was limited to asking for help and holding recruitment meetings. When individuals were interested in joining the group, they would be invited to a follow-up meeting after the initial meeting. After the follow-up meeting, if people chose to join, they would be given the location of a "buffer camp" to report to – the buffer camps were for new recruits only, and no old members were present. Balch and Taylor recount that new recruits got very little social support from the current members. For example, buffer camps were a day's or more drive away from the original meeting place, as a test of the new member's commitment. Once at the buffer camp, new members were assigned partners – the expectation being that partners spend 24 hours a day together but sexual relationships and friendships within the partnership were discouraged. Partnerships were for developing "friction" and awareness of the human qualities each person had to overcome in order to complete Human Individual Metamorphosis (overcoming human emotion and worldly attachments in order to be taken to heaven in UFOs). Partnerships were the main social structure of the group. The expectation when traveling was one partnership per vehicle and each partnership was to camp away from other members of the group to avoid unnecessary social interaction (as this would prevent "friction" and subsequently metamorphosis) [24].

Demographics

Education

Contrary to popular belief, followers of WRCs are generally not uneducated or cognitively impaired individuals on the fringes of society. Followers tend to be highly educated, markedly better educated than the general public [11]. Western religious cult leaders have typically expected followers to study and understand writings they view as sacred. They require recruits to be able to grasp new religious ideas or idiosyncratic extensions of more mainstream religious concepts. In order to become dedicated believers and followers, recruits must be comfortable thinking deeply about abstract religious concepts and topics. Therefore, in many cases, being a literate individual with an inquisitive mind, and having average to above-average intellect is almost a prerequisite to membership in a new religious movement [11].

Some of the more destructive WRCs, including the FLDS and the Peoples Temple, have chosen to educate children within their community, which also provided additional opportunities for indoctrination and controlling the flow of information within the community.

Among the Branch Davidians there were Harvard Law School graduates [12]. The Peoples Temple had scholarships at one point for members to use toward college expenses [28]. According to "hidden observers" who joined Heaven's Gate, "a large majority" of Heaven's Gate followers had attended college, but "their median occupational status was rather low, reflecting the cult's overall youthfulness and the fact that most members had changed jobs frequently, preferring not to be tied down to a routine that would limit their personal freedom" [24, p. 39].

Gender

The followers of WRCs have predominantly been coed, with a few exceptions. There is no consistent trend to allow for a generalization that males or females are more prone to join cults [11]. However, there has been a study that suggested that women are more religiously devout, which may play a role in people attracted to WRCs. In the study, data were collected from 84 countries from 2008 to 2015. Results included that women were more committed in areas of religious affiliation, in religion playing an important role in their life, and in the frequency of their service attendance, along with other measures [25]. This same study estimated that 83.4% and 79.9% of women and men respectively identify with a faith group. Of note, this gender gap was more or less pronounced depending on the religion studied.

In polygamous WRCs (e.g., the Ant Hill Kids, FLDS, Branch Davidians, the Kingston), the marriage of one man to multiple women tends to move the cult toward a predominantly female population. For example, Warren Jeffs alone had 78 wives at the time of his arrest [29]. Balch and Taylor comment that when they joined Heaven's Gate in the 1970s there were roughly equal numbers of males and females but for the weeks they observed the group they reported a greater number of men were recruited during that time, for reasons that were unclear [24]. Uffe Eidorff Hove's followers were largely female as he focused his recruiting efforts on women to be his partners and to engage in sadomasochism [60].

Age

With a few exceptions, WRC followers have generally been young (teens and young adults) people who have more free time to devote to religious pursuits/study [11, 70]. It is common that people in their late teens and early twenties do not have children or aging parents to care for yet. As a result they have few responsibilities and obstacles inhibiting them from joining a group, going missionizing, or moving to a new location. It could also be hypothesized that individuals often join cults in their teens and twenties because it aligns with the fourth requirement in the Lofland–Stark model of conversion – "encounter the cult to which they convert at a turning point in their lives" [11]. Certainly, this timeframe is known to be the transition to adulthood, adult identify formation, and early career/legacy creation.

In the 1970s and 1980s, more than half of the members of Krishna Consciousness joined before their 21st birthday [11]. Most early members of Heaven's Gate were in their early twenties, with an age range from 14 to 58 reported by two "hidden observers" who joined the group in 1975 for a number of weeks [24]. The Children of God had an average age of around 23 in the 1970s. When this was reassessed in the 1990s the average age was unchanged [70]. An explanation for this comes from the movement's "Law of Love," and discouragement of the use of contraceptives, which resulted in many children being born into the group, thereby keeping the average age low, despite almost no new converts joining. The WRCs that are communal and have had some staying power have generally seen high dropout rates as followers reach middle age [11].

Marital/Family Status

Followers of WRCs are more commonly single than married or involved in committed relationships. Most do not have children. As we have mentioned, older, married people with children generally have less free time to devote to an NRM and might have more fixed value systems. Many WRCs demanded prioritizing communal pursuits and individual spiritual pursuits above anything else. Dawson wrote, "the demands and desires that accompany family life and the raising of children often conflict with the obligations of membership" in such a movement [11, p. 83; 71].

Social Status

Followers of WRCs tend to enjoy a relatively high socioeconomic status. Believers are disproportionately from middle- to upper-middle-class households [11, 71]. Having a relatively higher socioeconomic status theoretically gives followers the freedom to pursue religious or spiritual enlightenment and to have time to pursue endeavors. In terms of social connectedness, WRC involvement is "strongly correlated with having fewer and weaker extra-cult social ties" [11, p. 78]. This may explain the popular perception that cults recruit on college campuses, as college students are away from home and away from any social connections they had at home. College students presumably also have the freedom to investigate the cult further.

Although members may have started out with some social ties external to the WRC, those ties seem to diminish or completely dissolve over time. For example, members of Heaven's Gate were traveling almost constantly, making it difficult for friends and family outside of the group to stay in contact with them [24]. This was also seen in the Children of God/The Family International, as members had to be willing to move all over the country and the world in response to the call of leadership by their leader, David Berg [1].

Religious Background

While one might assume that individuals who join WRCs come from religious backgrounds, the opposite is true [11]. Potential recruits are more likely to join cults if they are "unchurched" or were raised in a more secularized denomination. Lavine also said after his many interviews of prior members that "[y]oungsters from very intense religious backgrounds, in fact, seem exempt from radical departures." As Lavine mentions, a pattern has been observed that if individuals are from religious backgrounds, they often are not from intense religious organizations. Catholic and Jewish individuals were recognized as more likely to join WRCs, but specifically Reform and Conservative Jews, not Orthodox [71, p. 76]. Dawson also noted that Jews are extraordinarily overrepresented in many WRCs (though did not specify Orthodox, Reform, Conservative, etc.), probably due to a combination of secularization of the American Jewish community, along with the higher educational attainment and socioeconomic status of Jewish people. It would appear that the prototypical WRC member would characterize him or herself as spiritual (see "Seekers" section) but not religious [11].

Psychological Traits

Next we list several prevailing hypotheses about psychological traits that might make people more likely to join and/or maintain loyalty to a WRC. Most of these areas require further study before firm conclusions can be reached.

As we have discussed, WRCs that successfully recruit new members generally find the most success among young, single, educated, somewhat prosperous people who have a somewhat weak religious background, have limited social and economic commitments, and, therefore, also have the ability to commit a substantial amount of time and (often) money to the cause.

Idealists

A psychologist who worked exclusively and extensively with ex-cult members and cult survivors, Dr. Keith Harary, wrote, "Those who join cults don't do so with the intention of demeaning themselves or torturing children. They join in the hope of creating a better world, and because they believe in a lie, or a series of lies" [72].

An individual who left Jonestown before the deaths occurred there, Deborah Layton, explained her motives for joining: "I was 18 years old when I joined the Peoples Temple. I had grown up in affluent circumstances in the permissive atmosphere of Berkeley,

California. By joining the Peoples Temple, I hoped to help others and in the process to bring structure and self-discipline to my own life" [73].

Edith Roller, living in San Francisco in the 1960s, was disturbed by the injustices of the Vietnam War and the "racist policies" of the US government. She had watched her father, a miner, die from black lung disease and had developed a commitment to helping the weak stand up against the powerful. After she quit her job in protest, she was invited (at Jim Jones' direction) to attend a church service at the Peoples Temple. There, "Roller was pleased to find a community where she could work for the ideals she cared about so deeply." One author wrote that Jonestown members should be remembered as "noble idealists" [74].

Seekers

From a psychological standpoint, WRCs have tended to be most attractive to "seekers." These are individuals who are looking for a sense of direction (usually spiritual but not always) and who are dissatisfied with current/mainstream religious practices. Almost half of all converts to WRCs had either previously been members of a different NRM or were actively practicing a religion other than the religion in which they were raised [11]. In other words, they already have a history of religious conversion when they are introduced to the WRC.

The impression we get from the literature on the topic is that individuals who remain in WRCs are typically not just seekers but are principled and disciplined seekers who crave an opportunity to demonstrate their devotion/faith to an ideal, once they have found a religious ideology that they can fully support. Dr. Harary opined that the "only real difference" between WRC members and those of us who do not join WRCs is "the extent to which they are led to carry those same sorts of feelings [the hope of creating a better world described above] to extremes" [72].

Conformists

Among FLDS leader Warren Jeffs' favorite mantras was "keep sweet" (also the title of a recent documentary on Jeffs' FLDS community). At first glance, this appears to be a harmless and simple edict to be kind to others. However, this statement, delivered by a prophet, God's mouthpiece upon the earth, is also a clear message to followers that the expected relationship of followers to their prophet was one of unquestioning submission to his (which was also God's) will. The women in the cult were expected to wear long, pastel-colored dresses, long underwear, no makeup, and to each wear the same distinctive hairstyle.

After the Heaven's Gate mass suicide, the bodies were discovered all clothed in black shirts, sweatpants, the same Nike shoes, and purple shrouds. They each had $5 and a few quarters in their front shirt pocket, along with identification, a bag neatly packed with clothes, a spiral notebook, and lip balm [46]. Before the mass suicide, members of the cult were expected to abandon gender roles by dressing in the same shapeless clothing, not wearing makeup, and having similar hairstyles. Celibacy was required and some, including Applewhite, underwent surgical castration [24].

Fiat Lux followers live together, follow the same prayer schedule, are all vegetarians, and all wear ceremonial robes [75]. All members of the Church of Synanon were required to shave their heads. These examples illustrate how WRC leaders typically create an expectation of conformity in their cults.

Strong Need to Belong and to Find a Higher Purpose

The need to belong to something larger and more meaningful than our own individual existence is a basic human need. Deborah Layton, a Jonestown survivor, explained, "[w]hen I joined Peoples Temple, I was 17 and it was like joining the Peace Corps," she said. "I felt we were doing something that had meaning. I wanted to be part of something that was doing things for other people, and besides, Peoples Temple offered a community of friends" [76].

One Jonestown survivor wrote about "the personal, social and psychological rewards of the communal, politically engaged life." It was these rewards, claimed another follower, that "at least while Peoples Temple was still stateside, made so few of us members seriously entertain the idea of leaving" [74].

Dr. Harary was able to identify a prototypical cult member during his therapy sessions with former cult members. He wrote, "[t]hose who became involved in cults had a frightening underlying commonality. They described their experiences as finding an unexpected sense of purpose, as though they were becoming part of something extraordinarily significant that seemed to carry them beyond their feelings of isolation and toward an expanded sense of reality and the meaning of life." Dr. Harary further concluded, "[p]eople end up joining cults when events lead them to search for a deeper sense of belonging and for something more meaningful in their lives" [72].

Need for Structure and Routine

A corollary to the need to belong to something and find meaning in life is the reassuring nature of structure and routine, even if daily tasks are mundane or even aversive. In Deborah Layton's 1978 affidavit (discussed in the "Idealists" section), she emphasized that she was raised in a permissive environment and desired to add structure and self-discipline to her life. The Peoples Temple seemed to offer that to her.

In Heaven's Gate, initially there was minimal structure with one meeting in the morning and one in the evening, otherwise members were to be "communing" (forming a mental connection with a member of the next level) or developing "friction" (identifying and rejecting their human traits) between themselves and their partner. With such minimal structure, members began challenging Nettles and Applewhite's authority, starting to make their own claims and interpretations that were often against the leaders' teachings. Nettles and Applewhite responded to this crisis by substantially increasing regimentation and implementing strict rules, predominantly around communication, but other aspects of commune life as well. With time, they restructured their communication with the Next Level such that all information from the Next Level first came to Peep (Nettles) who communicated it to Bo (Applewhite), who communicated it to the members. As a result, defections dropped and commitment increased – they had learned how to keep members occupied and obedient. The group also created structure by having members shave their heads and wear uniforms [24].

In Guyana, Peoples Temple members were known to work long days (often 12 hours and at times approaching 20 hours) at the instruction of Jim Jones. They would build their town nearly continuously, often with Jones preaching over the loudspeaker. This left little to no time for other things, including sleeping and eating [26].

Fiat Lux had daily prayer schedules that members adhered to. Structure in diet and appearance was present through necessitating a vegetarian diet and wearing ceremonial robes [75].

Submissiveness

The second of Warren Jeffs' favorite mantras – "pray and obey" – was important enough to him that he had the phrase engraved in huge block letters on the chimney of his home. At Jeffs' direction, children were removed from their homes in Utah/Arizona and taken to his Yearning for Zion ranch in Texas. Followers were expected to accept these orders without questioning.

Deborah Layton explained why she initially flourished in Jim Jones' cult: "The reason I did well," Layton said, "is that I'm a little soldier and I follow orders so well" [76].

Large numbers of adult women and underage girls submitted themselves sexually to WRC leaders, although almost certainly not all of it was voluntary. Roch Thériault married and impregnated all the women in his cult. Uffe Eidorff Hove had multiple wives who joined him in sadomasochism and the use of child pornography. Warren Jeffs had 78 wives, 24 of whom were under the age of 17. David Koresh slept with and/or married most (and possibly all) of the adult women living at Mt. Carmel and many of the postpubescent adolescent females. Jim Jones was noted by Jonestown survivors to have "sick" sexual fantasies and to engage in a variety of "sexual perversions" [72].

It should be noted that submissiveness does not suggest that WRC members are brainwashed automatons who have become unable to think for themselves. The known high turnover rate in WRCs provides compelling evidence that WRC members are thinking for themselves and are capable of changing their minds and deciding to leave the group [46]. However, the trait of submissiveness does seem to correlate with ongoing participation in these organizations.

Those Seduced by Power

Warren Jeffs admitted that his role within the FLDS community was a dictatorship, but attempted to soften it by saying that it was "a benevolent dictatorship." There were positions of power awaiting David Koresh's children. When Koresh began preaching the New Light revelation, that his mission was to be the messianic husband of all female members of the community and father offspring through them, he preached that at the end of time his children would become rulers of the universe, both heaven and Earth [1]. Dr. Harary, after working with ex-cult members, concluded, "[u]ltimate power is seductive not only to those who achieve it themselves but also to those who give up their own power in order to help others achieve it" [72]. While the idea that cult leaders are omnipotent within their organizations is more of a myth than reality, it is also true that the outsized influence that many WRC leaders obtained over their followers could not have been achieved without the agency and complicity of their followers [46].

Suggestible

A member of Heaven's Gate who did not participate in the 1997 mass suicide, Rio DiAngelo, later stated to CNN, "I can say with absolute, undeniable certainty that Do [Applewhite] was a second coming of Jesus" [77].

Jim Jones orchestrated fake "healing" ceremonies to trick people into believing he was able to cure cancer, read minds, etc. David Koresh made increasingly grandiose claims to the Branch Davidians, including that he was descended from King David (hence his name change from Vernon to David), that he was able to unlock the seven seals mentioned in the Book of Revelation in the Bible because he was the seventh angel mentioned in Revelation 10:7, that he was a messiah, and that he was "the Lamb" descended from the "root of David," not the historical Jesus Christ [1]. His followers accepted these claims. It was only when Koresh extended the "Lamb" concept into the New Light doctrine in which he was to take the members' wives as spiritual wives, that significant defections occurred within the ranks at Mr. Carmel [1].

Although it remains unproven whether WRC followers are more suggestible than the general population, we mention it here because suggestibility may underlie the ability of cult leaders to radicalize some of their followers. This is an area that merits further study.

Groupthink

The term "groupthink" was first coined by Irving Janis in 1972 [11]. In *Foundations of Modern Sociology*, Metta Spencer describes the phenomenon as follows: "Each member wants the approval of all the others, and this produces a strong tendency toward uniformity. No one wants to raise controversial issues, question weak arguments, or puncture unrealistic hopes . . . Each person censors his or her doubts instead of voicing them" [78, pp. 171–72]. Although this phenomenon was first described in an effort to explain political fiascos, it is easy to see how this phenomenon would occur even more strongly in a WRC.

There is no more powerful manifestation of the power of groupthink than in the mass suicides associated with WRCs. Over 900 died in Jonestown, Guyana, at least some of which were voluntary suicides. Thirty-nine died in the Heaven's Gate mass suicide, all wearing shirts with patches that read "Heaven's Gate Away Team" [46]. Fifty-three members of the Order of the Solar Temple also died, although it is unclear how many were killed and how many completed suicide.

Swiss investigators concluded that 15 of the 53 Solar Temple deaths in Quebec and Switzerland in 1994 were suicides. The individuals who died by suicide regarded themselves as "The Awakened." Some of the 16 Solar Temple deaths in France in 1995 had left behind notes about going to "see another world." A third group suicide involving five adults occurred in 1997 in Quebec. The Solar Temple suicide deaths represented believers deciding together to make a transit to a higher world where salvation, a glorious solar body, and a higher realm of consciousness awaited them [46].

Cognitive Distortions: Black and White Thinking

People are attracted by the answers provided by the cult leader to age-old mysteries such as the existence of a higher power and the meaning of life. The security of having a belief system that appears to solve some of life's most vexing problems can be extremely appealing. Followers likely respond strongly to the comfort of believing that a positive spiritual outcome is guaranteed by simply doing what the leader asks them to do. A common belief within cults is that cult members are enlightened and on a higher spiritual plane, while the "outside world" is ignorant, fallen, lost, or evil. This kind of thinking may lay the groundwork for dehumanizing and (in some cases) perpetrating violence against others outside of the cult.

Defense Mechanisms: Denial and Repression

To put it simply, denial is a primitive (as opposed to higher-level defenses) defense mechanism first described in Freudian times that involves refusal to accept an external reality. The external reality is essentially forced from conscious awareness into the subconscious. Repression is a different primitive defense mechanism and involves taking an internal emotion, drive, idea, or other reality, and actively (but unconsciously) preventing it from coming into one's conscious awareness. The primary differences between the two defenses, then, is that one involves external material being forced from conscious awareness and the other involves preventing internal material from entering conscious awareness. These defenses are often utilized to reduce dissonance and the anxiety it generates and underlie the sometimes astonishing human capacity for self-deception.

In our opinion, these dissonance-reducing defense mechanisms are likely to underlie the well-known phenomenon of the survival of the failure of apocalyptic prophecies. This refers to the fact that many groups not only survive the failure of their apocalyptic prophecy, but actually grow and thrive [11]. When a prophesied date arrives and the prophesied event does not come to pass, certain adaptational strategies – proselytization, rationalization, and reaffirmation – are employed by religious leaders and their followers [11]. Proselytization involves recruiting others to join the cause as a way of resolving the conflict generated by being confronted by the failure of the prophecy, and as a preferred alternative to abandoning their faith. Rationalization involves leaders quickly providing believers with a plausible reinterpretation of events after the prophesied date passes. Typically this involves spiritualization (claiming a physical and verifiable event was actually an unverifiable and spiritual event), reframing the event as a test of faith, and/or attributing the failure of the prophecy to human error or otherwise blaming others for the failure of the prophecy. Reaffirmation involves immediately praising believers for being faithful and changing the focus to building group cohesion [11].

When Florence Houteff assumed leadership after her husband Victor died, she told the Mt. Carmel Davidians that she had solved the biblical puzzle of the seven seals and prophesied that God's earthly reign would be established on April 22, 1959 [1].

Bonnie Nettles claimed to have received a message from the "Next Level" and prophesied that a flying saucer would land that same evening [46]. When Nettles died of cancer in 1985, it ostensibly disconfirmed Ti and Do's teachings that their bodies were being transformed into Next Level extraterrestrial bodies and that the transition to the Next Level was a physical one. Applewhite quickly reinterpreted Nettles' death, stating that her cancer was merely the physical manifestation of the stress that existed because Nettles' mind had evolved so far that her body could no longer function adequately as a container for it. Applewhite also began claiming that he could communicate telepathically with Nettles (the "Older Member"), and she had assured him that she had successfully transitioned to the Next Level [1].

Writers have made claims that Rulon Jeffs (the FLDS prophet who preceded his son Warren) told members that he would live to be 350 years old (he died in 2002 at age 92) and that an apocalyptic event would occur on June 12, 1999. One writer claimed that before that day (when 2,500 church members were told to meet in one place where they would be taken to heaven) ended, the prophet informed the FLDS members that the people lacked the faith for this event to take place, an example of rationalization. They were told that God had given them more time to repent [79].

Summary

A finding consistently replicated in various studies is that most of the people who join NRMs leave voluntarily within a few years [11]. This undercuts the contention that cult

Figure 2.10 US Congressman (California) Leo Ryan, pictured in 1977, who was murdered with his staff while investigating reports of abuse at Jim Jones' Peoples Temple in the jungle near Jonestown, Guyana on November 18, 1978
Source: https://multimedia.fbi.gov
Author: FBI

followers are "brainwashed" and lack the ability for independent thought. However, if cult members are more intelligent and free thinking than most assume, the actions that some cult leaders have been able to convince followers to take become that much more difficult to understand. Cult leaders have repeatedly demonstrated the ability to convert well-meaning recruits into enforcers willing to perpetrate crimes, sometimes involving horrific violence, in the service of the "cause."

Sexual crimes against adults and children are noted to have occurred in many WRCs. Jim Jones convinced his followers to murder perhaps several hundred of their peers, in addition to a US congressman, Leo Ryan (Figure 2.10), and his associates.

Charles Manson persuaded his followers to carry out the Helter Skelter murders. Followers of David Koresh engaged in a gunfight with federal agents, killing four agents from the ATF. Cult leaders may also have been responsible for starting the fire inside the Waco compound that incinerated 74 cult members, including David Koresh. Church of Synanon members attempted to kill an attorney via a rattlesnake bite, willingly left their spouses to take new partners within the cult, and willingly submitted to vasectomies and abortions. Marshall Applewhite (who led by example) was able to convince several of his followers to voluntary undergo surgical castration.

Labels such as "brainwashing," "mind control," and "thought reform" are reductionistic and often inaccurate ways to describe the dynamics that have produced the negative outcomes in these totalistic groups headed by seemingly unstable but charismatic leaders. However, more broadly accepted and applicable sociological and psychological concepts such as coercion/coercive persuasion, influence, conditioning, groupthink and other group dynamics, social isolation, and physical stress (exhaustion, malnourishment, etc.) probably do play a role. Although it is a less dramatic conclusion than "brainwashing," it appears that the tragic outcomes associated with certain WRCs may come down to mostly "normal" people exhibiting extreme behavior due to very abnormal social circumstances. Nevertheless, it is a worthwhile pursuit to continue to also try to identify individual factors that could predispose certain individuals to engage in extreme and harmful behaviors driven by radical religious beliefs.

Dr. Keith Harary, the psychiatrist who worked extensively with former cult members wrote, "[m]ost of us don't think of ourselves as the kind of person who could ever possibly become embroiled in a cult like the Peoples Temple. We are not at all correct in that assumption" [72].

Key Points

- The vast majority of NRMs are not destructive – they involve new members entering voluntarily, often followed by a relatively rapid and equally voluntary exit. Participation in the movement is generally perceived by both the leader(s) and the follower as spiritually and/or socially beneficial.
- Destructive NRMs (referred to as WRCs in this chapter) involve some combination of deceptive recruiting techniques, attempts to exert significant control over the minds and behavior of followers, abuse of followers, criminal activity, and violence or harm (including suicide) toward followers or others.
- Followers of both nondestructive and destructive cults are by and large free of overt psychopathology and are more intelligent and free thinking than most assume.
- The siege and subsequent fire at the Waco, Texas Branch Davidian compound is one example of a destructive WRC.
- There are some characteristics that destructive WRC leaders have in common.
- Tactics employed by destructive WRC leaders follow a somewhat identifiable pattern regardless of the religious/doctrinal basis for the movement.
- There are identifiable demographic and psychological traits that religious cult followers tend to share.
- Labels such as "brainwashing," "mind control," and "thought reform" as applied to WRC cult dynamics are reductionistic and often inaccurate.
- A more productive framework for understanding the sometimes horrific outcomes associated with destructive WRC involves sociological and psychological concepts such as coercion/coercive persuasion, influence, conditioning, groupthink and other group dynamics, social isolation, and physical stress (exhaustion, malnourishment, etc.).

References

1. DE Cowan, DG Bromley. *Cults and new religions: a brief history.* Wiley Blackwell; 2015.
2. United States of America Congress. U.S. Constitution – First Amendment. Library of Congress. https://constitution.congress.gov/constitution/amendment-1/
3. Oyez. *Wisconsin* v. *Yoder*. www.oyez.org/cases/1971/70-110
4. Oyez. *Thomas* v. *Review Board of the Indiana Employment Security Division.* www.oyez.org/cases/1980/79-952
5. Oyez. *Sherbert* v. *Verner*. www.oyez.org/cases/1962/526
6. Oyez. *Heffron* v. *International Soc. for Krishna Consciousness, Inc.* www.oyez.org/cases/1980/80-795
7. Oyez. *Reynolds* v. *United States*. www.oyez.org/cases/1850-1900/98us145
8. Constitution Annotated. U.S. Constitution – Fourteenth Amendment. Constitution Annotated Analysis and Interpretation of the US Constitution. https://constitution.congress.gov/constitution/amendment-14/

9. Civil Rights Division US Department of Justice. Religious Land Use and Institutionalized Persons Act. 2023. www.justice.gov/crt/religious-land-use-and-institutionalized-persons-act

10. WG McLoughlin. *Revivals, awakenings, and reform: an essay on religion and social change in America.* University of Chicago Press; 1978.

11. LL Dawson. *Comprehending cults: the sociology of new religious movements.* 2nd ed. Oxford University Press; 2006.

12. W Gazecki. *Waco: the rules of engagement* [Motion picture]. Journeyman Pictures; 1997.

13. V Houteff. *The shepherd's rod.* Vol. 1. The Davidian Seventh-day Adventists Association; 1930. https://gadsda.com/shepherds-rod-volume-one/

14. V Houteff . *The shepherd's rod.* Vol. 2. The Davidian Seventh-day Adventists Association; 1932. https://gadsda.com/shepherds-rod-volume-two/

15. S Harvey. David Koresh and the Branch Davidians. *Critical Dictionary of Apocalyptic and Millenarian Movements.* 2021 Jan 15. www.cdamm.org/articles/koresh-davidians

16. B Haldeman, C Wessinger. *Memories of the Branch Davidians: the autobiography of David Koresh's mother.* Baylor University Press; 2011.

17. H Steinberg. On Victor Houteff: the way to Waco. *Cabinet.* 2001 iss 5. www.cabinetmagazine.org/issues/5/steinberg.php

18. Gale. David Koresh. In: *Encyclopedia of world biography online.* Gale, part of Cengage Group; 2019. https://go-gale-com.ezproxy.lib.utah.edu/ps/i.do?p=BIC&u=marriottlibrary&id=GALE|K1631010898&v=2.1&it=r

19. United States FBI. David Koresh Part 1 of 2. FBI Records: The Vault. n.d. p. 6. https://vault.fbi.gov/David%20Koresh/David%20Koresh%20Part%201%20of%202/view

20. Bureau of Alcohol, Tobacco, Firearms and Explosives. Remembering Waco: timeline of events. n.d. www.atf.gov/our-history/timeline-events

21. E Dennis. Evaluation of the handling of the Branch Davidian stand-off in Waco, Texas February 28 to April 19, 1993. www.justice.gov/archives/publications/waco/evaluation-handling-branch-davidian-stand-waco-texas-february-28-april-19-1993#A1

22. D Koresh. *The decoded message of the seven seals.* J Tabor, J Arnold, editors. Reunion Institute; 1994. https://dc.library.txstate.edu/node/6879

23. E Barker, S Harvey. Children of God/The Family International. *Critical Dictionary of Apocalyptic and Millenarian Movements.* 2021. www.cdamm.org/articles/children-of-god

24. GD Chryssides. *Heaven's Gate.* Routledge; 2016.

25. S Harvey, S Newcombe. Gender and contemporary millennial movements. *Critical Dictionary of Apocalyptic and Millenarian Movements.* 2021. www.cdamm.org/articles/gender-and-contemporary

26. S Harvey. Jim Jones, Jonestown, and the Peoples Temple of the Disciples of Christ. *Critical Dictionary of Apocalyptic and Millenarian Movements.* 2021. www.cdamm.org/articles/peoples-temple

27. M Introvigne. The Order of the Solar Temple. 3. Joseph Di Mambro and Luc Jouret. *Bitter Winter.* 2021 Dec 27. https://bitterwinter.org/solar-temple-3-joseph-di-mambro-and-luc-jouret/

28. San Diego State University. Alternative considerations of Jonestown & Peoples Temple. F McGehee III, editor. 2013. https://jonestown.sdsu.edu/

29. *Keep sweet pray and obey.* Netflix; 2022.

30. Charles Manson and the infamous Tex Watson murders. n.d. www.charlesmanson.com/childhood/

31. The Editors of Encyclopedia Britannica. Jim Jones. *Encyclopedia Britannica.* 2023. www.britannica.com/biography/Jim-Jones

32. J Steinberg. From religious family to reins of deadly cult. *The New York Times.* 1997

Mar 29. https://archive.nytimes.com/www.nytimes.com/library/national/0329mass-suicide-leader.html

33. Encyclopedia of Occultism and Parapsychology. Bonnie Lu Truesdale Nettles. Gale; 2001. https://go-gale-com.ezproxy.lib.utah.edu/ps/i.do?p=BIC&u=marriottlibrary&id=GALE|K1656001842&v=2.1&it=r
34. Utah State Bar. Paul Kingston. n.d. https://services.utahbar.org/Member-Directory/Profile?customercd=5738
35. Jordan High School. Jordan High (JHS) class of 1972 alumni list. High School Network Jordan High School. n.d. http://jordanhighschool.org/sandy-ut/class-of-1972.html
36. M Cutler, K Conley. *Cults: inside the world's most notorious groups and understanding the people who joined them.* Gallery Books; 2022.
37. T Roy, J Mihura, A Friedman, D Nichols, J Meloy. The last psychological evaluation of Charles Manson: implications for personality, psychopathology, and ideology. *Journal of Threat Assessment and Management.* 2023;10(3), 127–50.
38. J Hammer. Lost colony. *New Republic.* 1997;217(12).
39. B Falconer. The torture colony. *The American Scholar.* 2008 Sep 1;77. https://theamericanscholar.org/the-torture-colony/
40. FBI. Jonestown. n.d. https://vault.fbi.gov/jonestown/
41. C Babstock. Life sentence for murder of cult leader Roch Theriault. *The Gazette.* 2012 Mar 5. https://web.archive.org/web/20120308223121/http://www.montrealgazette.com/news/Life+sentence+murder+cult+leader+Roch+Theriault/6254854/story.html
42. E Humes. Buried secrets: a true story of serial murder, black magic, and drug-running on the US Border. US Department of Justice Office of Justice Programs; 1991. www.ojp.gov/ncjrs/virtual-library/abstracts/buried-secrets-true-story-serial-murder-black-magic-and-drug
43. J Post. Dreams of glory and the life cycle: reflections on the life course of narcissistic leaders. *Journal of Political and Military Sociology.* 1984;12(1):49–60.
44. J Lewis. Helter Skelter: an American myth. *Journal of American History.* 2021;108(1):222–24.
45. R Flaherty. International Raëlian Movement. *Critical Dictionary of Apocalyptic and Millenarian Movements.* 2021. www.cdamm.org/articles/international-raelian-movement
46. C Wessinger. *How the millennium comes violently: from Jonestown to Heaven's Gate.* Seven Bridges Press, LLC; 2000.
47. E Morgan. Man sentenced to probation for sex with teen in religious sect case. KSL. 2012 Jul 10. www.ksl.com/article/21195816/man-sentenced-to-probation-for-sex-with-teen-in-religious-sect-case
48. T Rahman, R Meloy, R Bauer. Extreme overvalued belief and the legacy of Carl Wernicke. *Journal of the American Academy of Psychiatry and the Law.* 2019 May 13; 180–87. https://jaapl.org/content/jaapl/47/2/180.full.pdf
49. Associated Press. Book by Ervil LeBaron calls for Yocom's death. *Deseret News.* 1992 Sep 17. www.deseret.com/1992/9/17/19005191/book-by-ervil-lebaron-calls-for-yocom-s-death
50. J Jones. *Jeffs* v. *State.* Casetext. 2012 Mar 29. https://casetext.com/case/jeffs-v-state-2
51. *People* v. *Manson.* 1976 Aug 13. https://law.justia.com/cases/california/court-of-appeal/3d/61/102.html
52. *State* v. *Dalton*, No. 20120477-CA. 2014 Mar 27. https://case-law.vlex.com/vid/state-v-dalton-no-888696685
53. *The New York Times.* Jones commune found stocked with drugs to control the mind. 1978 Dec 29. www.nytimes.com/1978/12/29/archives/jones-commune-found-stocked-with-drugs-to-control-the-mind-perhaps.html
54. K Mueller. Clinical record autopsy protocol. 1978 Dec 15. https://jonestown.sdsu.edu/wp-content/uploads/2013/10/JimJones.pdf.

55. L Kohl. I am a cultist, two times over. 2016 Oct 10. https://jonestown.sdsu.edu/?page_id=67567
56. P Applebome. 13th victim is found on ranch where drugs and occult mixed. *The New York Times.* 1989 Apr 14. www.nytimes.com/1989/04/14/us/13th-victim-is-found-on-ranch-where-drugs-and-occult-mixed.html
57. F Emilie. Our father: line in the Source Family. The Fader. 2013 May 1. www.thefader.com/2013/05/01/our-father-life-in-the-source-family
58. I Aquarian, E Aquarian. *The Source: the untold story of Father Yod, Ya Ho Wa 13 and the Source Family.* Process; 2007.
59. I Nielsen. Documentary on deadly violence: Sadomasochistic cult leader resurrects. Randers. 2021 Jan 19. https://amtsavisen.dk/randers/dokumentar-om-doedsvold-sadomasochistisk-sektleder-genopstaar
60. R Bureau. Cult leader found guilty of capital violence. Inland. 2002 Jun 27. https://jv.dk/indland/sektleder-kendt-skyldig-i-doedsvold
61. T Escobedo. Warren Jeffs' son, daughter allege sexual abuse. CNN. 2015 Sep 29. www.cnn.com/2015/09/29/us/warren-jeffs-children-allegations/index.html
62. D Carpenter. Countdown to Armageddon: the Reverend Jim Jones and Indiana. Indiana Historical Society. 2018. https://indianahistory.org/stories/countdown-to-armageddon-the-reverend-jim-jones-and-indiana
63. Drag City. YaHoWha 13. n.d. www.dragcity.com/search?query=yahowha
64. Congressional Record – Senate. 1962 Sep. p. 18750–751. www.congress.gov/bound-congressional-record/1962/09/06/senate-section
65. M Armstrong. It's time to stop saying "drink the Kool-Aid": interview with Jonestown author Julia Scheeres. Longreads. 2014 Nov 18. https://longreads.com/2014/11/18/its-time-to-stop-saying-drink-the-kool-aid-interview-with-jonestown-author-julia-scheeres-2/
66. Heaven's Gate – how and when it may be entered. n.d. www.heavensgate.com/
67. District of South Dakota | arrests made, indictment unsealed in Federal case charging FLDS church leaders and others with conspiracy to divert SNAP benefits, money laundering | United States Department of Justice. United States Attorney's Office District of South Dakota. 2016. www.justice.gov/usao-sd/pr/arrests-made-indictment-unsealed-federal-case-charging-flds-church-leaders-and-others
68. S Lemons. Blood cult. Intelligence Report. 2017 Aug 8. www.splcenter.org/fighting-hate/intelligence-report/2017/blood-cult
69. A Cirjak. What does it mean to drink the Kool-Aid? WorldAtlas. 2020. www.worldatlas.com/articles/what-does-it-mean-to-drink-the-kool-aid.html
70. E Barker. The not-so-new religious movements: changes in "the cult scene" over the past forty years. *The Finnish Society for the Study of Religion.* 2014;50(2):235–56.
71. SV Levine. *Radical departure: desperate detours to growing up.* Harcourt Brace Jafanovich; 1984.
72. K Harary. The truth about Jonestown. *Psychology Today.* 1992 Mar 1. www.psychologytoday.com/us/articles/199203/the-truth-about-jonestown
73. San Diego State University. Affidavit of Deborah Layton Blakey. Alternative Considerations of Jonestown & Peoples Temple. 2021 Oct 20. https://jonestown.sdsu.edu/?page_id=18599
74. V Weaver-Zercher. The lure of Jonestown. The Christian Century. 2012 May 30. www.christiancentury.org/reviews/2012-05/lure-jonestown
75. Fiat Lux. 2001. wwwuser.gwdg.de/~agruens/UFO/fiatlux.html
76. M Taylor. 20 years later, Jonestown survivor confronts horrors. *San Francisco Chronicle.* 1996 Nov 2.
77. CNN. Heaven's Gate suicides remembered. 2011. www.youtube.com/watch?v=IzWpfq103q4
78. M Spencer. *Foundations of modern sociology.* 4th ed. Prentice-Hall; 1985.
79. JR Llewellyn. *Polygamy under attack.* Agreka Books; 2004.

Chapter 3

Cults of Personality

Joseph M. Pierre

"It is recognition on the part of those subject to authority which is decisive for the validity of charisma."
– *Max Weber, sociologist*

Introduction

To date, an evidence-based understanding of cults has been limited by a lack of systematic, peer-reviewed research studies on the subject along with an extant literature dominated by anecdotal accounts published in books by self-styled experts. Many of these accounts have been written from a clinical perspective based on the select experiences of ex-followers of specific groups, limiting their generalizability to the broader cult spectrum and its membership. To make matters worse, there is no universally accepted definition of the term "cult" that adequately balances its intended meaning with the diversity of the phenomenon. As such, just what a cult is remains open to debate.

Historically, the term "cult" was most often applied to religious groups where differentiation from a "sect" depended on whether a deviant religious organization was based on traditional or novel beliefs and practices. In other words, unlike religious sects that are schismatic offshoots of established religious groups, cults have been defined as lacking ties to existing groups with a firm foothold in mainstream society [1]. The phenomenon of cults has since been scrutinized across a variety of academic disciplines. Consequently, theologians, sociologists, anthropologists, and psychiatrists have each modeled cults according to distinct frameworks (e.g., sociologists emphasize a group's relationship to society whereas psychiatrists focus on the psychological make-up of its individual members) [2]. Cults also have been widely covered in the media, resulting in the use of the term to encompass all manner of social organizations centered around ideological beliefs including political, entrepreneurial, psychotherapeutic, self-help, and pseudoscientific movements.

The term "cult" been diluted through the years such that it has been used indiscriminately to describe mainstream political movements (e.g., "the cult of Donald Trump") or loose affiliation with ideologies that have spread around the world without any central organizational structure or leadership (e.g., QAnon). Moreover, it also has become almost uniformly pejorative. This negative valence began in the 1970s as part of a moral panic in response to the perceived risk of young people being lured away from their families and lost to the likes of the Hare Krishnas and the Unification Church along with the extremist violence of the Manson Family and Jim Jones' Peoples Temple. This in turn gave birth to the "anticult" movement that popularized cults as a threat to society due to their alleged ability to use "mind control" to "brainwash" members into subservience. The anticult movement, spearheaded by ex-cult members and mental health professionals with newfound careers trying to help them, popularized the practice of involuntary extraction from cult affiliation and forced "deprogramming" as the best hope for a cult member's salvation [3]. By the time of the Branch Davidians' incendiary standoff in Waco, Texas and the mass suicide of Heaven's Gate in the 1990s, this mainstream view of cults as dangerous if not outright evil and cult members as victims robbed of free will and in need of rescue and rehabilitation became firmly entrenched so that it remains a prominent trope within public consciousness today.

The demonization of cults in the public eye has occurred despite significant push-back by some academic scholars who have noted that the methods of "coercive persuasion" often used to identify cults can often be found in the recruitment tactics of mainstream religious groups, the military, or corporate entities like Amway [4, 5]. This counterargument was strongly supported by a 1992 study that presented participants with a vignette describing a young male college student who left school to join a group that subjected him to "isolation of the individual, total control of the individual's environment, control of all channels of information and communication, and manipulation of guilt" [5, p. 532]. When the study participants were told that the group was the Moonies (i.e., the Unification Church), they were significantly more likely to prefer the term "brainwashing" to describe the indoctrination process and more likely to rate the group as "negative," "unfair," and "coercive" than when the groups was identified as the Marines or a Catholic seminary. Similarly, respondents were also significantly more likely to rate the young man as unhappy, less intelligent, less responsible, and lacking in power to resist when the group was identified as the Moonies compared to the Marines or the Catholic Church. Notably, the vast majority of the sample described "television, newspapers, magazines, or radio" as their primary source of information about cults.

Given this negative bias against cults and the parallels between modern anticult attitudes and historical prejudices against Masons, Mormons, and Catholics before they became part of mainstream religion in the US, it has been recommended that the term "cult" be replaced by value-neutral terms like "new religious movement" or "emergent religion." However, there remains no nonpejorative alternative to describe nonreligious ideological groups.

That the term "cult" is often used as a pejorative should not be taken to mean that there is no such thing as a cult or that the concept lacks validity. Rather, it could be argued that the term's utility lies in calling attention to the fact that cults are by definition "highly manipulative groups that exploit and otherwise abuse their members" [6]. Indeed, some authors have attempted to resolve the indiscriminately pejorative use of the term "cult" by specifying that it should be reserved for groups guilty of abusive practices and a significant potential for membership to cause personal harm. For example, Chambers and colleagues defined cults as "groups that often exploit members psychologically and/or financially, typically by making members comply with leadership's demands through certain types of psychological manipulation ... through the inculcation of deep-seated anxious dependency on the group and its leaders" [7, n.p.]. This definition was based on factor analysis of results from administering the Group Psychological Abuse Scale to 308 former cult followers from 101 different groups. In a similar vein, West and Martin specified that a "totalist cult" ought to be defined as

> a group or movement exhibiting a great or excessive devotion or dedication to some person, idea, or thing, and employing unethical, manipulative or coercive techniques of

persuasion and control (e.g., isolation from former friends and family, debilitation, use of special methods to heighten suggestibility and subservience, powerful group pressure, information management, promotion of total dependency on the group and fear of leaving it, suspension of individuality and critical judgment, and so on, designed to advance the goals of the group's leaders, to the possible or actual detriment of members, their families, or the community). [8, n.p.]

Cults of Personality

The term "personality cult" (or "cult of personality") has been around since at least the late 1800s when it was used to describe the public's widespread devotion to certain political leaders. It was given new life when Nikita Khrushchev, while addressing the Communist Party of the Soviet Union in 1956, denounced the "personality cult" of Joseph Stalin in the name of heralding a return to the principles of Marxism-Leninism [9]. Much like the evolution of the word "cult" itself, the terms "cult of personality" and "modern personality cult" [10] have since been applied in casual discourse to political regimes with leaders like Stalin, Vladimir Lenin, Benito Mussolini, Adolf Hitler, Mao Zedong, Kim Jong-Il, and Donald Trump. Moreover, it is also applied to a wider range of religious and secular cults with prominent leaders such as Reverend Sun Myung Moon, Charles Manson, Jim Jones, and David Koresh. Indeed, owing to the fact that having a central cult leader has become a stereotypical cult feature, "cults" and "cults of personality" have become almost synonymous. For example, Levine defined a cult as a "group of people which follows a dominant leader [who] makes absolute claims about his being . . . that he is divine . . . omniscient and infallible" and whose "membership is contingent on complete and literal acceptance of his doctrines and dogma" with "unquestioning loyalty . . . and total willingness to obey the cult leader's commands without question" [11, p. 593]. Adopting this broader meaning of the term without limiting it to the political sphere, this chapter defines "cult of personality" as any cult whose members are held in thrall by an identifiable leader.

Characteristics of Leaders

Central to the concept of a cult of personality is a relational dynamic that involves the reverence if not outright worship of its leader by its followers. Along with the extremes to which cult followers are often willing to go at the behest of their leader, this dynamic naturally begs the question of what characteristics the leader of a "personality cult" might possess that would command such authority, obedience, and devotion.

Charisma

In order to account for "cults of personality" in the political realm, the sociologist Max Weber developed a theory of "charismatic leadership" to describe the ability of some leaders to attract substantial followings by virtue of their extraordinary personal characteristics rather than through an appeal to tradition or rationality. Weber described charisma as a "certain quality of an individual personality, by virtue of which he is set apart from ordinary men and treated as endowed with supernatural, superhuman, or at least specifically exceptional powers or qualities" [12, p. 538]. However, he did not delineate what those qualities were and instead characterized charisma in value-neutral and utilitarian terms without distinguishing between the charisma of Jesus Christ or

Napoleon Bonaparte [13]. To Weber, who wrote "it is recognition on the part of those subject to authority which is decisive for the validity of charisma," the defining feature of charismatic leadership isn't *how* a charismatic leader attracts a following – whether through one's personality, persuasiveness, or espoused ideology – but *that* the leader is able to do so [12, p. 539].

Looking beyond mass political movements to the broader spectrum of cults that includes leaders with more modest numbers of followers, it becomes apparent that charisma, like beauty or sex appeal, lies in the eye of the beholder. Indeed, such subjectivity is central to the cult concept inasmuch as the labeling of leaders and followers as part of a cult requires that the rest of society looks upon them with incredulity. In other words, were everyone wholly impressed by the charisma of a cult leader, no one would be claiming that they were a leader of a cult – "cult" labels are typically assigned by those unimpressed if not repulsed by cults and their leaders.

Characterizations of political "cults of personality" have long recognized that charisma may be as much an inherent inspirational quality of a leader as it is manufactured through propaganda and misinformation, media depiction, and statecraft, as well as by instituting a culture of fear in the populace. For example, the "cult of Stalin" has been attributed to his iron-fisted rule including publicly witnessed "purges and mass killings" of political opponents [10]. This is also true of smaller religious and secular cults where "boundary controls" [14] – including all of the geographical, digital, or ideological factors that restrict interaction between cult members and the outside world – together with ritual practice create a closed social order where followers are exposed to a simulated, ideal representation of a leader.

Personality

If "cults of personality" are defined by the presence of a charismatic leader, it follows that charisma ought to be definable in terms of personality traits. At the same time, since the term "cult" is typically used as a pejorative, it should come as no surprise that cult leaders have almost invariably been characterized in "negative" terms of personality disorder rather than in "positive" terms of personality traits that might account for their charisma.

Notably, such characterizations have not typically involved any systematic psychological or psychiatric assessment of cult leaders, but rather suppositions about individual cases based on news reports, the testimony of ex-cult "survivors," and overarching generalizations based on backward reasoning that presumes that a cult leader must be "bad" in some way. For example, in their provocatively titled 1994 book *Captive Hearts, Captive Minds*, Tobias and Lalich claimed that "researchers and clinicians who have observed these individuals describe [cult leaders] variously as neurotic, psychotic, on a spectrum exhibiting neurotic, sociopathic, and psychotic characteristics, or suffering from personality disorder ... we can surmise that there is a significant psychological dysfunctioning in some cult leaders and that their behavior demonstrates features rather consistent with the disorder known as psychopathy" [15, pp. 68–69]. They enumerate 15 traits of psychopathy including pathological lying, lack of remorse, incapacity for love, callousness, promiscuous sexual behavior, and criminal or entrepreneurial versatility as a "tool to help ... label and demystify traits" of cult leaders [15, p. 72]. In a similar vein, Burke cited "a number of peer-reviewed studies ... based on clinical interviews with ex-cult members, which report various antisocial acts and behaviors ... [that] detail examples of mistreatment, psychological intimidation, and physical and sexual abuse of cult members by cult leaders" to conclude that the behavior of cult leaders can be explained by antisocial personality disorder or possibly narcissistic personality disorder [16, n.p.].

Turning to individual case studies, Akimoto proposed that Shoko Asahara – the leader of the Aum Shinrikyo cult responsible for the 1995 sarin gas attacks in Tokyo – suffered from "pseudologica phantastica" and "severe incarceration psychosis" [17]. This assessment seems to have been based on news accounts of Asahara including his reported behavior in court rather than any independent medical examination. Goldberg similarly described psychodynamic therapy with an "ex-cultist prosecuted for criminal behavior" and, based solely on her patient's claims, attributed her "antisocial behavior" to the influence of "her idealized cult leader's version of morality" [18, p. 15].

Owing to a lack of rigorous study of cult leaders and a biased sampling of the accounts of ex-cult members, it would be prudent to view existing generalizations about the personality of cult leaders with a skeptical eye. This statement does not deny that some cult leaders who are guilty of abusive criminal behavior might have personality traits such as narcissism, sociopathy, or psychopathy, but at the same time cautions against claims that this is necessarily true of any leader of a group labeled as a "cult." Acknowledging that "the study of the cult leader has been rather neglected" [2, p. 18], the Group for Advancement of Psychiatry provided a less pathological typology of cult leaders including the "charismatic figure," the "hero," the "outsider," the "narcissist," and the "entrepreneur" that highlights that there is no one-size-fits-all profile of a cult leader.

It should be noted that, as with cult followers, it remains possible that the behavior and personality traits of cult leaders are characteristics that emerged as a consequence of involvement within the interpersonal dynamics of cult groups. Psychological studies of role identity such as the well-known Stanford prison experiment [19] provide support for the dictum that "power corrupts and absolute power corrupts absolutely," suggesting that the apparent personality stylings of cult leaders may be more of a "state" than a "trait" phenomenon. In the absence of prospective personality assessments of cult leaders prior to and throughout their cult affiliation, however, this possibility remains untested.

Brainwashing, Mind Control, and Coercive Persuasion

Cult leaders are often portrayed as Svengalis, capable of manipulating and exploiting hapless victims through a psychological process of indoctrination that has been variably referred to as "brainwashing," "thought reform," "mind control," or "coercive persuasion." After all, casual observers might ask, how else could followers come to fall under the apparent spell of charismatic leaders?

Unfortunately, efforts to detail this process have been thwarted by failures to validate a scientifically plausible explanatory mechanism or to convincingly demonstrate that it compromises free will. For example, some authors have theorized that the process involves hypnotic suggestion and have invoked the "Stockholm syndrome" to account for cult followers' identification with an oppressive cult leader [8, 20]. Others have referred to the induction of dissociative states [21] and the practice of "love bombing" [22] and "grooming" [23] to seduce converts. Still others have emphasized how overarching efforts to control behavior, information, thinking, and emotions within a cult's closed system can result in conformity and a new "pseudo-identity" or "dual" identity of cult followers [8, 23].

In contrast to such proposals, the notion that the free will of cult followers is truly compromised has been challenged with the contention that "the concept of coercive persuasion as a means of thought control fails to pass scientific muster" [4]. Calling attention to the biased subjectivity of the term, Robbins quoted Thomas Szasz who wrote, "[w]e do not call all types of personal or psychological influences 'brainwashing.' We reserve this term for influences of which we disapprove" [22, p. 241]. Indeed, as noted earlier, it has also been argued that much like the term "cult" itself, the term "coercive persuasion" has been overgeneralized across a spectrum of indoctrination practices. It has been further noted that, upon closer scrutiny, the process of deprogramming promoted by anticultists could be considered to be just as coercive as cult indoctrination so that it amounts to "counterbrainwashing" [24].

Characteristics of Followers

Just as cult leaders have often been portrayed as all-powerful Svengalis, so too have cult followers been portrayed as mindless automatons. While the concept of "coercive persuasion" suggests that this is a universal liability such that anyone could fall victim to "mind control," it has also been proposed that cult followers may represent a particularly vulnerable population.

Personality and Psychopathology

Given the diversity of cults, we might expect that accounts of the psychopathology of cult followers might be inconsistent. Indeed, some reports have noted that the majority of cult members are "basically normal" and "stable individuals" prior to joining cults [2]. Ungerleider and Wellisch likewise performed psychiatric interviews and psychometric testing of 50 unspecified cult members and found no evidence of "insanity of mental illness in the legal sense," but did report evidence of "strong ideological hunger" among followers [25, pp. 279, 282].

Most other accounts have claimed some degree of psychopathology among cult members. For example, several authors have made claims about overrepresented personality traits and disorders among those affiliated with cults including features of dependent, obsessive-compulsive, and antisocial personality disorders though such case analyses have included only a few individuals [16, 18, 26]. Turning to larger datasets, Clark conducted interviews with over 60 religious cult followers in Germany and reported that 60% were "substantially and chronically disturbed and unhappy for many years" while the remaining 40% were "essentially normal, maturing persons" [21, p. 279]. Summarizing the results of several anecdotal reports, Galanter similarly observed that "psychological distress is a frequent antecedent to joining a [charismatic religious] sect" and that members often have limited social ties before joining [14, p. 1539]. He further noted that "certain sects attract members with considerable psychopathology," citing previous studies finding that "virtually all" members of one sect reported "histories of chronic unhappiness and unsatisfactory parental relations" while the followers of other sects reported 30–38% rates of seeking "professional help" prior to group affiliation [14, p. 1540]. Based on a study of 200 interviews with followers across some 25 different cults,

Levine concluded that there was "little doubt that [members] joined the cult because of personal dissatisfaction with their lot" with a sense of alienation, demoralization, and a poor sense of self prominent among the young adult sample [11, p. 594].

A critical and more thorough review of this literature was published in 2000 by Aronoff and colleagues, who noted considerable variation in rates of psychological and psychiatric morbidity across studies and detailed a number of methodological issues that have thwarted firm conclusions [27]. For example, most studies have lacked control groups to determine whether reports of generalized experiences such as unhappiness, alienation, or ideological hunger among a predominantly young sample of cult followers represent anything out of the ordinary. In addition, due to the significant potential for biased retrospective reporting, it is unclear whether such reports reflect antecedents or subsequent effects of cult membership [20]. Studies involving ex-cult members also represent a biased sample wherein the disgruntled "witness of apostates" may be exaggerated or at the very least not necessarily generalizable to those that remain within cults [28]. While Galanter and others have argued that cults have the potential to offer group cohesion and relief of distress [14, 29, 30], the professed happiness of those actively affiliated with cults has often been questioned. Recent studies of terrorist group members provide evidence of the potential for psychological distress and mental disorder to worsen with group affiliation [31].

In what might be considered the most methodologically sound study of psychiatric aspects of cult membership to date, Rousselet and colleagues conducted semistructured interviews with 31 ex-cult followers in France and found evidence of anxiety disorder among 51% of the sample, mood disorders among 45%, and either substance use or eating disorders among 13% during the year preceding cult affiliation [32]. Rates of anxiety disorder increased throughout affiliation and peaked at 61% during the year following departure while rates of mood disorder decreased to 35% during membership and then increased to 55% after departure. These data suggest variable degrees of premorbid psychopathology among cult members and inconsistent effects of cult membership and departure on mental health. Given that the study's assessments were made retrospectively during a single interview session, however, definitive statements about the effects of joining and leaving cults on symptoms of psychopathology remain unproven in the absence of prospective, longitudinal data.

The review by Aronoff and colleagues drew three conclusions from existing studies exploring the association between cult membership and psychological or psychiatric morbidity [27]. First, it is not always the case that those joining cults suffer from psychopathology in any way. Second, while many active cult members can appear psychologically well, it is possible that evidence to the contrary is either underreported or otherwise masked. And finally, a significant proportion of those who leave or are otherwise "rescued" from cults struggle with adjustment or psychological difficulties after doing so. Taken in aggregate, the heterogeneity of findings about the psychopathology of cult members at different stages of cult affiliation suggest that the individual assessment is likely to be more reliable than attempting broad generalizations about cult followers as a group or about the psychological impact of joining or leaving a cult.

Group Dynamics

Recalling the political origins of the term "cult of personality," it is both tempting and almost tautological to speculate that cult followers' seemingly blind obeisance to a

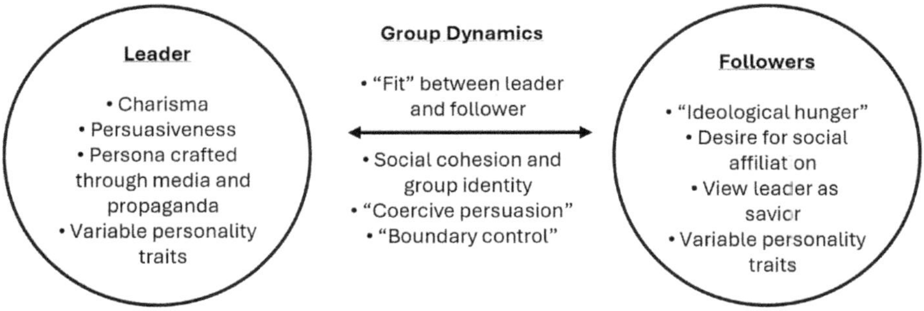

Figure 3.1 Characteristics of cults of personality

charismatic leader could be explained by the concept of the "authoritarian personality." Developed by Theodor Adorno to account for public support of fascist and antisemitic ideological movements such as that of Nazi Germany, the concept drew heavily on psychoanalytic theory to theorize that repressed and displaced hostility toward one's parents resulted in a need among certain individuals to submit to authority and, in doing so, to tolerate prejudice and out-group aggression [33]. Following critiques of the theory, more recent revisions have cast aside its explanatory psychoanalytic mechanisms to describe a willingness to submit to authority figures, a tendency to adhere to in-group conventions, and aggression against those who challenge authoritarian establishment [34]. Given that "cults of personality" are defined by the power dynamic between cult leader and cult follower, these features have face validity in reference to both the specific political and broader meanings of the term "cult." To date, however, there have been no attempts to research an explicit connection between authoritarianism and the phenomenon of cults.

Offering further critique of the concept, Duckitt noted the failure to validate the authoritarian personality as an individual trait or dimension and instead proposed that authoritarianism be conceptualized as a social phenomenon in terms of group dynamics [33]. This perspective has particular relevance to cults. For example, as previously mentioned, charisma is a subjective quality that lies in the eye of the beholder such that the apparent power and influence a cult leader has over followers is less an issue of their respective individual characteristics than it is an issue of "match" or "fit" (see Figure 3.1). Accounting for cults therefore need not rely on stereotypes involving an all-powerful Svengali followed by brainwashed automatons. Instead, the specific relationship between cult leader and followers within a group could vary substantially from cult to cult as well as from one follower to another within the same group. A better accounting of such relational dynamics is vital to understanding specific cult groups and their individual members.

As we have already noted, Galanter and others have theorized that followers typically join cults because of psychological distress and a lack of social connection, which are relieved by a sense of social cohesion and a newfound identity attained from group affiliation and a shared belief system [14, 29, 30]. The notion that cult membership can create a kind of soothing "social cocoon" for followers provides a useful and more normalizing counter-explanation of cults that stands in contrast to claims of "mind control" [29]. As with intimate relationships, this perspective does not refute that members can be victims of abuse within cults, but rather provides an alternative account of why some individuals cede authority and control to cult leaders and remain in groups despite such victimization.

Returning to cults of personality in the political realm and Weber's theory of charismatic leadership, it has been similarly noted that distress on the part of a populace paves the way to following leaders who can convincingly portray themselves as saviors. Tucker argues that charismatic leadership is inherently "salvationist or messianic in nature" with leaders who reject old rules and demand change and followers who are "charisma-hungry" and looking for someone to "lead them out of [a] predicament" [13, pp. 742, 743, 745]. This characterization can apply just as well to cults in the broader sense of the term and reinforces the notion that the key to understanding cult dynamics lies in the match between the psychological needs of followers and the advertised benefits of cult membership, whether related to the attributes of a cult's leader, ideology, or social system.

Social Conditions

While much of the literature on cult followers has focused on distress or lack of identity attributed to an individual's personality style or psychopathology, the phenomenon of political personality cults highlights that such characteristics can also apply to large swaths of a population or society due to specific social conditions that render a populace desperate for salvation. As suggested earlier in reference to cult leaders, this means that cult followers might also be better understood in terms of "state" rather than "trait." For example, the emergence of "cults of personality" in communist history has been attributed to public demand for societal change and "revolutionary necessity" satisfied through a renewed sense of nationalism [9]. The rise of Naziism has likewise been attributed to a need for a new national identity in the wake of "the fragmentation of Germany's collective self following the narcissistic injury of defeat in World War I" [30, p. 242]. Just so, the emergence and proliferation of religious cults in the US during the 1970s has been theorized to have stemmed from "rebellion against conventional society" in the midst of the Vietnam War and political unrest that led many down a countercultural path in search of "alternative source[s] of structure, purpose, and support" [2, p. 26].

Within the broad spectrum of cults, it should be recognized that the social conditions that give rise to them can emerge – as well as be manufactured – on both microscopic and macroscopic scales. Just as political "cults of personality" have been described as typically arising within closed societies [10], so too has the phenomenon of religious cults been attributed to enforced "boundary controls" in the form of social and ideological as opposed to physical confines [14]. Indeed, it has been argued that "totalist" cults create the conditions that result in coercive persuasion and undue influence by demanding control of all aspects of a follower's behavior to include how they dress, when and how they eat or sleep, their sexual activity, what information they consume, and even what they think and feel [23].

Just as Weber noted that charisma is unstable and often proves transitory, so too does the dynamic between cult leaders and followers shift over time. Modeling the factors that influence cult affiliation as "state" rather than merely "trait" conditions aids an appreciation of why some people join cults and leave them while others do not. For example, the study by Rousselet and colleagues found that cult members typically leave due to loss of faith in the cult's ideology, perceptions of a cult leader's imperfection or contradiction, conflicts within the hierarchy of a group, and experience of psychological abuse [32]. These are best understood as changes in the social conditions and interpersonal dynamics of a cult rather than changes within individuals per se.

The depth and fluidity of cult involvement can also be meaningfully conceptualized along a stage-wise model of ideological commitment that includes "nonbelievers," "fence-sitters," "true believers," "activists," and "apostates" [36]. Such a model recognizes the potential for the fusion of identity and ideology among "true believers" as well as the potential for violence when ideological threats are perceived as existential threats. When cults come into conflict with the society that surrounds them, "activists" feel the need to "do something" and often take it upon themselves to defend against such perceived threats. Modeling cult affiliation in this way – that is, as a social interaction both within cult groups as well as between cults and society at large – can facilitate a better understanding of the violent potential of cults and cult members beyond the mere pejorative labeling of a group as a cult or an individual as a cult follower.

Case Example: Sherry Shriner and the "Alien Reptile Cult"

Few verified facts are known about Sherry Shriner's life. By her own account detailed in the book *Bible Codes Revealed: The Coming UFO Invasion*, she was born in Cleveland, Ohio in 1965, was "reborn" in Jesus Christ at age 5, and attended a private Christian school and church every Sunday while growing up [37]. She "read the Bible from front to back" at age 12 and was "partial to the Book of Revelation" [37, p. 2]. She then attended college at Liberty Baptist University where she worked as a campus news reporter and radio director and later transferred to Kent State University, graduating in 1991 with degrees in criminal justice, journalism, and political science. By that time, she was married, had her first child, and was aspiring to land a position at the Washington bureau of CNN.

Shriner's life instead took a different turn as she

> embarked on an intense research over the next 5 years into spiritual warfare, hell, demons, Satan, and continued into [her] favorite areas of end time events and last days prophecies . . . [studying] deception in the churches, UFOs, government black operations, the New World Order, and much, much more . . . [culminating in] an enormous journey of unraveling conspiracies and lies in our government and churches. [37, p. 4]

In 1994, she began having "visions from God" and developed an "intimate relationship with Yahweh Himself" and by 2001, she had taught herself how to "decode" the Bible and began to claim that God had called her to be "messenger, an emissary and mouthpiece" as well as "a Watchman, a Prophet, and a warrior for Him" [37, pp. 5–6]. Soon thereafter, she also claimed that God had "led me into what I have termed the Alien Agenda" including "the coming UFO and Alien invasion to America and our Earth" and revealed to her that she was the granddaughter of King David [37, pp. 6, 7]. By 2004, Shriner was running an internet talk radio show where she monologued about "the Luciferian New World Order, UFOs, Aliens, the Alien agenda, the coming UFO invasion, Planet X, NESARA, the deceptions in the churches, and the coming of the Antichrist in power" [37, p. 7].

In 2008, Shriner launched an eponymous YouTube channel where, over the next decade, she posted some 240 videos. These videos provided a sprawling account of apocalyptic biblical prophesies and conspiracy theories related to alien reptilian shape-shifters and vampires occupying the bodies of celebrities and infiltrating the highest levels of government. All of this was accompanied by an increasingly right-wing political rhetoric that claimed that mass shootings and hurricanes were "false flag operations" orchestrated by the likes of "NATO, the Illuminati, or the Democratic Party" [38]. She made a living running numerous websites that she used to proselytize, promote the three e-books she had written (including *Aliens on the Internet*, *Interview with the Devil: My Conversation with Lucifer*, and the aforementioned *Bible Codes Revealed*), and sell "orgone" – an alleged source of energy contained in crystals that she claimed could repel evil – and "Orgone Blasters" that were marketed to keep aliens, zombies, and demons at bay. In 2014, Shriner managed to raise over $150,000 through a GoFundMe crowdfunding page and by the time of her death by natural causes in 2019, she had attracted over 20,000 YouTube subscribers with over 3 million views of her videos and had come to refer to her following that "congregated" and interacted with her on her Facebook page as her "ministry" [38].

While still relatively unknown with an undetermined number of online devotees, Shriner's "fringe religion" attracted local public attention in Detroit following the 2012 suicide of Kelly Pingilley [39], a 22-year-old follower who worked as a transcriber for Shriner's radio show, accompanied her on "missions" to battle the New World Order, and was wearing an orgone pendant at the time of her death by overdose [40]. Shriner went on to claim that Pingilley had been killed by a "NATO hit squad" [39].

Shriner finally garnered national attention as the leader of an "alien reptile cult" in 2019 after Steven Mineo, another one of her former followers since the early 2000s, was fatally shot in the head at point-blank range by his girlfriend Barbara Rogers, another one-time Shriner acolyte. Although Rogers was convicted of third-degree murder and sentenced to 15–40 years in prison, the circumstances of Mineo's death remain something of a mystery. As the lone surviving witness, Rogers claimed that Mineo had urged her to end his life with his hands held together with hers on the gun due to stress related to "issues" as members of Shriner's "religious cult" [41]. In the months prior to his death, Rogers and Mineo had both been harassed and attacked online by Shriner and her followers after a falling-out that involved Shriner declaring that Rogers was a reptilian and a witch and Mineo responding by posting a series of videos denouncing Shriner as a fraud [41].

On her website following Mineo's death, Shriner denied that she was in any way responsible, noting: "They're trying to spin it that I'm responsible for Steve's death? No, Barb is . . . They want to call me a cult leader? I'm just a humble servant and Messenger of the Most High. I've spent my life serving HIM and for that, I get beat up by Cain's kids, libtards, witches, Satanists, and haters everywhere" [41]. In subsequent media interviews and on her radio show, she went on to declare, "I'm not a cult and I'm not a cult leader" [41] and "I don't run a cult. You can turn on my video or turn it off. You can turn on my podcast or turn it off. I don't have a list or a membership rule" [42].

Forensic Implications

This chapter offers a cautiously skeptical take on "cults" in recognition of the pejorative use of the term offered through the "armchair diagnosis" of those biased against their deviance, the considerable diversity of ideological groups that are labeled as such, and the lack of systematic research on cults, cult leaders, and cult followers to inform a better understanding of such a maligned entity (see also Table 3.1). While this chapter loosely applies the term "cult of personality" to account for a wide variety of political, religious, and other types of ideological cults on both large and small scales that are identifiable by a charismatic leader and devoted followers, it concludes that more specific characterizations of cults based on coercive and abusive practices might help to avoid getting mired in debates about what constitutes a cult while potentially justifying the use of the term as a pejorative when appropriate.

Although mental health professionals may be called to serve as expert witnesses in forensic cases involving cult affiliation, it should be acknowledged that the word "cult" is not a term of clinical psychology or psychiatry and, as previously suggested, the group dynamics governing cult interactions might be understood just as well if not better within theological, sociological, and anthropological frameworks. Accordingly, the psychiatric "medicalization" of cult phenomena risks a biased and prejudicial amplification of the potential mental health issues of cult leaders and followers alike with significant implications regarding the potential liability of cult members charged with committing crimes [24]. Some have argued that the term "cult" should be prohibited in legal proceedings since allowing the label in court would amount to a "social weapon" that would be prejudicial in the extreme [43].

Rather than lumping all "cults" into a wastebasket category of derision and following backward reasoning that necessarily views cult leaders and followers through a lens of pathology, forensic discussions should instead acknowledge a spectrum of "cultic" or "cult-like" groups that can be differentiated by the degree to which they employ specific practices that might be more universally regarded as exploitative, abusive, or harmful. In doing so, they must remain vigilant for biased judgments, especially in cases falling within the "gray area" of the cultic spectrum.

Psychiatric Diagnosis

For alleged cult leaders, the potential disconnect between the perception of their constructed public image and the reality of their true personality highlights an important distinction that challenges attempts at forensic psychiatric assessment based on post-hoc review of media portrayals. For example, what we know of Sherry Shriner is largely limited to her own writing and radio show monologues where her previous experience in journalism and radio production is noteworthy. Similar to the Goldwater Rule that offers an ethical prohibition against armchair diagnosis for public figures, forensic experts should exercise considerable caution about offering opinions about purported cult leaders in the absence of a face-to-face examination.

For cult followers, unsubstantiated claims about their mental health often emerge in the wake of unfortunate outcomes that make newspaper headlines or result in criminal charges. Kelly Pingilley's family speculated that she had schizophrenia after she died by suicide [40] while Barbara Rogers claimed to be off her medications for bipolar disorder when she was arrested by police [38]. While such claims could be valid, they should in general be regarded skeptically due to their vulnerability to both the confirmation bias of hindsight and the motives of defense strategies within forensic proceedings. In the absence of objective data to refute them, however, such claims often have an intuitive appeal to those who read media reports about cults as well as those who find themselves sitting on trial juries. As with cult leaders, face-to-face assessment of cult members along with a thorough review of available medical records is essential for objective diagnosis.

Forensic experts should resist the temptation to limit the framing of cult involvement, whether as a leader or follower, to the level of the individual psychopathology. Instead, the "triangulation of [the] psychological, social, and relational aspects" [44, p. 9] of cults should be the guiding principle in order to gain a more nuanced and thorough understanding of this enduring and vexing phenomenon. With regard to the specific diagnostic significance of ideological beliefs shared within cults, forensic assessors must likewise take care to avoid pathologizing group beliefs and citing them as evidence of mental illness without appropriate justification. In doing so, assessors should bear in mind that religious and other subculturally sanctioned beliefs are excluded from the definition of delusion [45] as well as the fact that courts of law have not typically allowed defendants to evade culpability for criminal behavior through claims of incompetency or insanity pleas based on the delusion-like beliefs found within cult ideologies [46, 47]. While novel terminology like "extreme overvalued belief" has been recently proposed to fill the void of an appropriate psychiatric vocabulary to account for the belief systems of cults and terrorist groups while differentiating them from delusions [48, 49], the use of such medicalized terminology lacks validity and likewise presents significant potential for prosecutorial bias [45, 50]. Nonpsychiatric accounts of group beliefs and the relevant group dynamics that give rise to them, drawing from research on both peaceful new religious movements and violent terrorist groups alike, can offer a more evidence-based explanation for beliefs that are odds with mainstream society [50]. As noted previously, staging ideological commitment may offer a more useful model to understand the potential for beliefs to result in violent or other criminal behavior [51].

Coercive Persuasion

Forensic experts should be wary of claims regarding "coercive persuasion" on the basis of allegedly cult involvement without clear evidence of coercion. In order to more clearly separate them, some have drawn a brighter line between the involuntary tactics of "brainwashing" and torture in the historical context of prisoners of war that are clearly coercive and the voluntary process of cult participation that involves mere deception or the "manipulation of social variables" [52]. This distinction is more consistent with how the courts have not traditionally allowed the conflation of cult membership with claims of mental incompetency or not guilty by reason of insanity pleas when evidence of physical coercion has not been demonstrated [4, 46, 47, 52]. In the same vein, courts have also not looked favorably upon cult members' claims about loss of free will through "mind control" or "coercive persuasion" in cases involving the prosecution of cult leaders [4, 46].

Another option to resolve conflicts over coercive persuasion lies in acknowledging that terms like "coercion" can be conceptualized on a continuum "ranging from extreme physical coercion to totally autonomous decision making" [4, p. 96]. In doing so, assessments of coercion and competency within cultic environments can be decoupled and should be considered separately on a case-by-case basis [46]. The same could be said of "cults" more generally. Although the legal system typically prefers "crisp lines" when it comes to categorical definitions, in reality the borders that define "cults" and "coercion"

Table 3.1 Cautions for forensic evaluations involving cults of personality

Identifying "cults"	• Identification is subject to bias • Use of the term "cult" in legal proceedings is often pejorative and prejudicial
Describing coercive persuasion	• Coercive persuasion should be specified within a spectrum of coercive practices • Claims of "brainwashing," "mind control," or loss of free will lack validity, often fail to outline a cognitive mechanism, and must be distinguished from culpability
Characterizing psychiatric morbidity among leaders and followers	• Reliability depends on face-to-face evaluation and review of medical records rather than third-party accounts and media portrayals • Psychiatric morbidity before, during, and after cult affiliation should be differentiated • Psychopathology as the basis for cult affiliation should not be assumed at the expense of considering social dynamics and staging ideological commitment

alike are often blurry, just as they are with psychiatric diagnosis [45]. Additionally, while the definitions of "cult" and "coercion" are rooted in folk intuitions about free will, a neuroscientifically informed perspective highlights that the assumption of contracausal free will in forensic proceedings may be more illusion than reality [53]. This sobering conclusion has crucial implications for any attempts to define coercion based on distinctions between voluntary and involuntary action.

References

1. R Stark, WS Bainbridge. Of churches, sects, and cults: preliminary concepts for a theory of religious movement. *Journal for the Scientific Study of Religion*. 1979;18:117–31.
2. Group for the Advancement of Psychiatry. *Leaders and followers: a psychiatric perspective on religious cults*. American Psychiatric Press, Inc.; 1992.
3. AD Shupe, R Spielmann, S Stigall. Deprogramming: the new exorcism. *American Behavioral Scientist*. 1977;20:941–56.
4. JL Young, EEH Griffith. A critical evaluation of coercive persuasion as used in the assessment of cults. *Behavioral Sciences & the Law*. 1992;10:89–101.
5. JE Pfeifer. The psychological framing of cults: schematic representations and cult evaluations. *Journal of Applied Social Psychology*. 1992;22:531–44.
6. MD Langone. Clinical update on cults. *Psychiatric Times*. 1996 Jul 1.
7. WV Chambers, MD Langone, AA Dole, JW Grice. The Group Psychological Abuse Scale: a measure of the varieties of cultic abuse. *Cultic Studies Journal*. 1994;11:88–117.
8. LJ West, PR Martin. Pseudo-identity and the treatment of personality change in victims of captivity and cults. *Cultic Studies Journal*. 1996;13:125–52.
9. JP Pittman. Thoughts on the "cult of personality" in Communist history. *Science Society*. 2017;81:533–48.

10. D Leese. The cult of personality and symbolic politics. In: SA Smith, editor. *The Oxford handbook of the history of communism*. Oxford University Press; 2014. p. 339–54.
11. SV Levine. Role of psychiatry in the phenomenon of cults. *Canadian Journal of Psychiatry*. 1979;24:593–602.
12. M Weber. *Theory of social and economic organization*. The Free Press; 1947.
13. RC Tucker. The theory of charismatic leadership. *Daedalus*. 1968;97:731–56.
14. M Galanter. Charismatic religious sects and psychiatry: an overview. *American Journal of Psychiatry*. 1982;139:1539–48.
15. ML Tobias, J Lalich. *Captive hearts, captive minds*. Hunter House Publishers; 1994.
16. J Burke. Antisocial personality disorder in cult leaders and induction of dependent personality disorder in cult members. *Cultic Studies Review*. 2006;5:390–410.
17. H Akimoto. The Aum cult leader Asahara's mental deviation and its social relations. *Psychiatry and Clinical Neurosciences*. 2006;60:3–8.
18. L Goldberg. Influence of a charismatic antisocial cult leader: psychotherapy with an ex-cultist prosecuted for criminal behavior. *International Journal of Cultic Studies*. 2012;3:15–24.
19. C Haney, WC Banks, PG Zimbardo. Interpersonal dynamics in a simulated prison. *International Journal of Criminology and Penology*. 1973;1:69–97.
20. LJ West. A psychiatric overview of cult-related phenomena. *Journal of the American Academy of Psychoanalysis*. 1993;21:1–19.
21. JG Clark. Cults. *JAMA*. 1979;242:279–81.
22. T Robbins. Constructing cultist "mind control." *Sociological Analysis*. 1984;45:241–56.
23. SA Hassan, MJ Shah. The anatomy of undue influence used by terrorist cults and traffickers to induce helplessness and trauma, so creating false identities. *Ethics, Medicine and Public Health*. 2019;8:97–107.
24. T Robbins, D Anthony. Deprogramming, brainwashing, and the medicalization of deviant religious groups. *Social Problems*. 1982;29:283–97.
25. JT Ungerleider, DK Wellisch. Coercive persuasion (brainwashing), religious cults, and deprogramming. *American Journal of Psychiatry*. 1979;136:279–82.
26. F Rahmani, A Hemmati, SJ Cohen, JR Meloy. The interplay between antisocial and obsessive-compulsive personality characteristics in cult-like religious groups: a psychodynamic decoding of DSM-5. *International Journal of Applied Psychoanalytic Studies*. 2019;16:258–73.
27. J Aronoff, SJ Lynn, P Malinoski. Are cultic environments psychologically harmful? *Clinical Psychology Review*. 2000;20:91–111.
28. T Robbins, D Anthony. Cults, brainwashing, and counter-subversion. *Annals of the American Academy of Political and Social Science*. 1979;446:78–90.
29. M Galanter. Cults and zealous self-help movements: a psychiatric perspective. *American Journal of Psychiatry*. 1990;147:543–51.
30. TB Feldmann, PW Johnson. Cult membership as a source of self-cohesion. *Bulletin of the American Academy of Psychiatry and Law*. 1995;23:239–48.
31. E Corner, P Gill. Psychological distress, terrorist involvement and disengagement from terrorism: a sequence analysis approach. *Journal of Quantitative Criminology*. 2020;36:499–526.
32. M Rousselet, O Duretete, JB Hardoiuin, M Grall-Bronnec. Cult membership: what factors contribute to joining or leaving? *Psychiatry Research*. 2017;257:27–23.
33. J Duckitt. Authoritarian personality. In: JD Wright, editor. *International encyclopedia of the social & behavioral sciences*. 2nd ed. Elsevier; 2015. p. 255–61.
34. M Kemmelmeier. Authoritarianism. In: JD Wright, editor. *International encyclopedia of the social & behavioral sciences*. 2nd ed. Elsevier; 2015. p. 262–68.

35. J Duckitt. Authoritarianism and group identification: a new view of an old construct. *political psychology.* 1989;10:63–84.

36. JM Pierre. *False: How mistrust, disinformation, and motivated reasoning make us believe things that aren't true.* Oxford University Press; 2025.

37. S Shriner. *Bible codes revealed: The coming UFO invasion.* iUniverse; 2005.

38. J Flanagin. How YouTube became a breeding ground for a diabolical lizard cult. *The New Republic.* 2019 Jun 3. https://newrepublic.com/article/154012/youtube-became-breeding-ground-diabolical-lizard-cult

39. FX Donnelly. Metro Detroit family blames fringe religion for Redford woman's suicide. *Detroit News.* 2013 Mar 10.

40. K Weill. Reptile cult leader says her follower was killed by NATO. *The Daily Beast.* 2017 Jul 31. www.thedailybeast.com/reptile-cult-leader-says-her-follower-was-killed-by-nato

41. K Weill. Reptile cult feud ends in death. *The Daily Beast.* 2017 Jul 27. www.thedailybeast.com/reptile-cult-feud-over-raw-meat-ends-in-death

42. K Swenson. It looked like a simple domestic murder. Then police learned about the alien reptile cult. *The Washington Post.* 2019 Jun 11. www.washingtonpost.com/nation/2019/06/11/alien-reptile-murder-cult-barbara-rogers-sherry-shriner

43. JT Richardson. Definitions of cult: from socio-technical to popular-negative. *Review of Religious Research.* 1993;34:348–56.

44. JL Epley. Weber's theory of charismatic leadership: the case of Muslim leaders in contemporary Indonesian politics. *International Journal of Humanities and Social Science.* 2015;5:7–17.

45. JM Pierre. Forensic psychiatry versus the varieties of delusion-like belief. *Journal of the American Academy of Psychiatry and the Law.* 2019;48:327–34.

46. JL Young, EEH Griffith. Expert testimony in cult-related litigation. *Bulletin of the American Academy of Psychiatry and the Law.* 1989;17:257–67.

47. B Holoyda, W Newman. Between belief and delusion: cult members and the insanity plea. *Journal of the American Academy of Psychiatry and the Law.* 2016;44:53–62.

48. T Rahman. Extreme overvalued beliefs: how violent extremist beliefs become "normalized." *Behavioral Sciences.* 2018;8:1–11.

49. T Rahman, JR Meloy, R Bauer. Extreme overvalued belief and the legacy of Carl Wernicke. *Journal of the American Academy of Psychiatry and the Law.* 2019;47:180–87.

50. JM Pierre. Integrating non-psychiatric models of delusion-like beliefs into forensic psychiatric assessment. *Journal of the American Academy of Psychiatry and the Law.* 2019;47:171–79.

51. JM Pierre. Conspiracies gone wild: a psychiatric perspective on conspiracy theory belief, mental illness, and the potential for lone actor ideological violence. *Terrorism and Political Violence.* 2024. https://doi.org/10.1080/09546553.2024.2329079

52. DT Lunde, HA Sigal. Psychiatric testimony in "cult" litigation. *Bulletin of the American Academy of Psychiatry and the Law.* 1987;15:205–10.

53. JM Pierre. The neuroscience of free will: implications for psychiatry. *Psychological Medicine.* 2013;44:2465–74.

Section 1 **Typology**

Chapter 4

Cults and Terrorism

Natalie Pyszora, Debra Smith, and Chris Winter

"Terrorism is the tactic of demanding the impossible, and demanding it at gunpoint."
– *Christopher Hitchens*

Introduction

In 1995, when five members of the Aum Shinrikyo doomsday cult each pierced vials of poisonous sarin gas on peak-hour trains across Tokyo's sprawling subway system, they not only unleashed horrific death and injury on innocent commuters going about their daily business, they also triggered a spirited debate around the changing nature of terrorism. Central to this debate was the question of whether terrorism had entered a "new" era characterized by increasingly religious and apocalyptic movements.

Within the social sciences, the definition of terrorism remains contested. For many scholars, any attempt to apply a single definition to encompass a tactic employed by a diverse range of actors for differing social and political reasons would perhaps be futile [1]. Furthermore, the terms "terrorism" or "terrorist" have become so value-laden that they have become political tools in themselves, applied to particular groups or individuals as an effective way to invalidate the basis of their particular political grievances. Indeed, it is the political nature of terrorism that is fundamental to any definition, with this captured in most legal and scholarly classifications of the concept. At its simplest, terrorism is the use of violence to achieve strategic or symbolic political impact. It involves the threat or use of unlawful violence against noncombatants, with the aim of inspiring fear in the wider population for the purposes of bringing about or communicating some kind of political goal [2]. In this sense, terrorism is a tactic that can be used by state or nonstate actors, by religious or nonreligious groups, or by individuals, organized cells, or social movements. The political goal can be clear and immediate or it can be distant and vague. However, because of the political character of terrorism, terrorist groups are often recognized and categorized by governments and international bodies as security threats, with specific counterterrorism strategies aimed at dismantling them. This differs from cults in that, while sometimes recognized as dangerous, they are generally not subject to the kinds of government mechanisms designed to tackle terrorism.

The Tokyo subway attack is generally considered an act of terrorism because political goals were strongly intertwined with Aum Shinrikyo's religious philosophies. Aum's leader, Shoko Asahara, prophesized an impending apocalypse but sought to position the group strategically to emerge as a dominant force in a postapocalyptic world. He aimed to acquire military and chemical weapons and to establish an autonomous, theocratic state with a society governed by Aum's ideology [3]. However, Aum Shinrikyo was not the first cult to use tactics that could meet the definition of terrorism. In 1984, for example, the Rajneeshee cult manufactured salmonella and used it to contaminate 10 salad bars in The Dalles, Oregon. The Rajneeshee cult was aiming to influence a local election and, to this day, it remains the largest bioterrorist attack in US history, hospitalizing over 750 people [4]. Similarly, the Tate–LaBianca murders committed by the Manson Family in 1969 were an outcome of both the cult's apocalyptic beliefs and Manson's desire to instigate a race war he dubbed "Helter Skelter" [5]. At the culmination of the race war, Manson, a white supremacist, saw himself as ruling over African Americans who he considered incapable of governing themselves. While the connection between inspiring members of The Family to brutally murder people so as to usher in societal revolution is fantastical, the idea that the downfall of the existing social and political structures can be hastened through acts of horrendous violence threads through contemporary terrorist groups, primarily (although not exclusively) associated with white supremacist and neo-Nazi movements [5].

While The Family and the Rajneeshees used terrorism as a tactic, it was the potential scale and horror of the Tokyo subway attack that amplified already simmering debates around the changing nature of terrorism. While "old" terrorism was generally considered to be rooted in secular political struggles, with the subsequent violence manifesting in calibrated forms designed to bring attention to the particular cause, "new" terrorism was characterized by religious zealotry that unleashed apocalyptic and indiscriminate violence.

Prior to the mid-1990s, terrorism was primarily driven by specific political objectives, such as national liberation, revolutionary change, or ideological dominance. The groups were organized and incorporated command structures, were often hierarchical, and used conventional weaponry [6]. Attacks were usually targeted at emblematic symbols of the state and often sought to minimize civilian casualties to avoid alienating public support [6, 7]. For example, Sànchez-Cuenca's study [7] of the dynamics of national terrorism using the cases of the Irish Republican Army (IRA) and Euskadi Ta Askatasuna (ETA) found that both groups moderated the lethality of their attacks in order to engage in a war of attrition against the state, while maintaining broader support from their respective communities. These groups were rarely referred to as cults or even cultish. Rather, people who joined terrorist groups perceived themselves to be soldiers sacrificing themselves on behalf of their communities, drawing more parallels with joining a military service than a cult.

In contrast, the new terrorists were seen as unconstrained religious fanatics, driven by rage and hate rather than instrumental goals. Collectively, these religiously driven individuals were viewed as forming a new "wave" of terrorism with little regard for wider strategic or moral considerations [6]. While the specifics of the wave theory of terrorism are contested, the overall recognition that terrorism has evolved to be somehow different is largely uncontroversial [8, 9]. Lacking regard for human life, a desire for destruction had become an end in itself. Levy's study into the lethality of terrorist groups found that it was the apocalyptic ideology of jihadist groups that correlated with higher lethality rates [10]. Rather than calculating the impact of violence in terms of alienating potential supporters, the "new" apocalyptic terrorists were supposedly committed to causing the largest possible number of indiscriminate deaths. The goals of the "new" terrorism were understood in terms of reaching paradise or the millennium rather than political change in the current moment. These characteristics of "new" terrorism began to attract comparisons to new religious movements or cults, with scholars such as Dawson pointing to the parallels between terrorist groups that draw on apocalyptic beliefs and charismatic forms of authority, and violent cults [11]. Both, he argues, claim that the world is fundamentally corrupt and claim the right to cleanse it via destruction. Where they differ, suggests Lawson, is when the violence is condoned, with apocalyptic terrorist groups utilizing violence from the beginning, and the violence of cults tending to manifest toward the end of their operations.

This debate only intensified in the face of the September 11, 2001 attacks in the United States by al-Qaeda [12]. The rise of the Islamic State of Iraq and Syria (ISIS) in 2014 provided further evidence of a terrorist group that, on the surface, seemed to present some strong commonalities with other so-called destructive cults such as Aum Shinrikyo, the Peoples Temple, the Branch Davidians, and the Solar Temple [12].

Both al-Qaeda and ISIS became the subject of debate around whether the groups constituted "cults," "terrorist groups," or sometimes even "cult terrorist groups." Particularly after September 11, al-Qaeda's actions were explained as being that of a "terror cult" led by Osama bin Laden, an "apocalyptic cult leader" much like David Koresh or Jim Jones [13]. Bin Laden and other terror cult leaders were described as "[m]alignant Pied Pipers," preying on vulnerable communities and indoctrinating them into their sacred war against the Great Enemy [12]. It was perhaps this latter element – the sanctity and "holiness" of their mission – that prompted the comparison with cults. Here, the doctrinal fundamentalism and the moral and spiritual authority of the cult were recognized in the writings of bin Laden and the mission of al-Qaeda [14]. However, other scholars during this period noted that there were fundamental differences between al-Qaeda and what was traditionally defined as a cult. For example, al-Qaeda represented an exaggerated and distorted version of a mainstream religion with a nondivine leader [15].

The cult comparison once again arose with the emergence of ISIS, with the group's brutality and penchant for public executions and graphic violence prompting many commentators to brand the group a "death cult" [16, 17]. This term was also adopted by numerous world leaders opposed to the group, including President Barack Obama, British Prime Minister David Cameron, and Australian Prime Minister Tony Abbott. The latter, in particular, heavily employed the term, drawing upon deeply rooted social norms against cults to delegitimize and demonize the group rather than any particular desire for categorical and theoretical accuracy [18]. However, like al-Qaeda before it, ISIS also attracted scholarly attention, with various authors making arguments that ISIS did indeed strongly resemble a cult. The following vignette explores the cultic elements of ISIS, exploring the various ideological and methodological features of the group that closely resemble similar structures in totalist cultic groups. However, it is important to note that despite these similarities, ISIS remains, conceptually, a terrorist group.

Case Vignette: ISIS

The Islamic State of Iraq and Syria shocked the world when, in 2014, the group successfully overran significant portions of Iraq and Syria in defiance of significant material support provided to the Iraqi government forces by the United States and other

Table 4.1 Mapping Lifton's eight criteria for thought reform onto ISIS

Lifton's Criteria for a Cult	Description	Present in ISIS
Milieu control	Manipulating information to sustain influence over group members.	Yes
Mystical manipulation	Claiming that the group ideology is supported by a higher, often divine, purpose.	Yes
The demand for purity	Setting a harsh standard for purity and morality, dividing the world into "good" versus "evil."	Yes
Sacred science	Presenting the group's beliefs as the absolute truth.	Yes
Loading the language	Using specialized jargon, making it harder for outsiders to understand or critique the ideology.	Yes
Doctrine over person	Degrading the individual's experience, perspective, or reality in favor of the group ideology.	Yes
The dispensing of existence	The group claims the right to decide who is worthy of existence.	Yes
The cult of confession	Group members are encouraged to confess their sins or faults publicly.	No

allies. However, the group was not a new one, with elements of modern ISIS originating with Abu Musab al-Zarqawi's Jamaat al-Tawhid wa-I-Jihad, created in 1999. By 2004, this group was active in the ongoing insurgency in Iraq, becoming famous for performing numerous suicide bombings and beheadings of various targets. After a period as an al-Qaeda affiliate and several name changes, the group became the Islamic State of Iraq in 2006. This rebranding positioned the group as being more than another insurgent group – it now represented a proto-state. In 2010, a man named Abu Bakr al-Baghdadi became the leader of the group. It would be under this man's leadership that ISIS would see its greatest territorial gains. In 2013, the group made its territorial aspirations clear when it again rebranded, this time adding "Syria" to the group's name. With the declaration of the Caliphate in 2014, the group again changed names, this time referring to itself as simply " the Islamic State," portraying itself as a legitimate manifestation of the politico-religious successor of the Prophet Muhammad. With this history in mind, it is worth examining why so many have attached the "cult" descriptor to ISIS.

In his seminal 1969 work *Thought Reform and the Psychology of Totalism*, Lifton argued that when immoderate individuals combine with immoderate ideologies, a state of *ideological totalism* emerges. Where this totalism exists, any group or entity becomes a cult [19]. He notes eight criteria for a group to satisfy the definition declaring a group as totalist in nature. These are milieu control, mystical manipulation, the demand for purity, the "sacred science," loading the language, doctrine over person, the dispensing of existence, and the cult of confession. It is clear that ISIS demonstrates seven of these criteria, as explored throughout this vignette. Other studies have supported the use of these criteria as being useful in assessing ISIS to be a cult (Table 4.1), with the exception that ISIS lacks a cult of confession [20].

The Exceptionality of ISIS

For many, the figure of Abu Bakr al-Baghdadi is one of the most enduring memories of the Islamic State. Even before his ascension to head of ISI in 2010, al-Baghdadi had been noted as a particularly brutal figure; from his emergence with the ISIS predecessor, Islamic State of Iraq, to his death during a raid by US special forces in 2019, al-Baghdadi was ISIS's most prominent figure, both internally and externally. Indeed, so great was his presence that al-Baghdadi's role in ISIS strongly resembles that of a cult leader more so than other similar terrorist group leaders.

Al-Baghdadi's public persona of a divinely appointed leader was an intentionally developed one. Five days after the declaration that ISIS was now the Caliphate, al-Baghdadi made his first-ever public appearance. He declared that,

> I have been appointed to rule over you, though I am not the best among you . . . If you see that I do right, help me, and if you see that I do wrong, set me right. And obey me so long as I obey God touching you. If I disobey Him, no obedience is owed me from you. [21, p. 31]

In saying this, al-Baghdadi was quoting the first caliph of Sunni Islam, Abu Bakr al-Siddiq, and therefore positioning himself as the rightful ruler of all Sunni Muslims. Indeed, al-Baghdadi's pseudonymous name (Abu Bakr al-Baghdadi) referred to al-Siddiq, again reasserting al-Baghdadi's claim as a legitimate caliph. Additionally, al-Baghdadi became an apocalyptic figure, claiming the name "al-Qurayshi," or the Prophet Muhammad's tribe. This positioned al-Baghdadi with the fulfilment of a prophecy that a descendant of the Prophet would rule shortly before the apocalypse [22].

It is perhaps in this approach to the Caliphate that ISIS diverges heavily from other seemingly similar jihadist groups and perhaps where ISIS most strongly resembles a cult. A comparison with al-Qaeda and Osama bin Laden is useful here. Though hugely influential in the development of international jihadist thought, bin Laden was not regarded as having special powers of divine revelation. Rather, from the perspective of the followers of his ideology, he was a well-educated and pious Muslim, able to draw upon Koranic inspiration in articulating his message [15]. This differs from al-Baghdadi, who, despite his claims to modesty, directly linked himself with the Prophet. Additionally, this self-characterization gave al-Baghdadi a messianic quality – a sense that he was more than simply the leader of another jihadist group. Rather, he was a figure of supreme historical importance, possibly at the end of days. Moreover, by designating himself as caliph, he asserted his right to rule not just over his followers but all Muslims.

This last point is a crucial one. The declaration by ISIS of the Caliphate represented a significant rupture with the rest of the Islamic world. This is not to say that ISIS previously represented Muslims generally. Rather, the declaration *forced* all Muslims to either accept allegiance to the group or be declared to be infidels or heretics through the process of *takfir*. In the speech declaring the Caliphate, Abu Mohammad al-Adnani, the primary spokesperson for ISIS, said, "[w]e inform Muslims that, with the announcement of the caliphate, it has become obligatory for all Muslims to give *bay'a* [an oath of allegiance] and support to Caliph Ibrahim [al-Baghdadi]" [21, p. 41]. This declaration was also a clear example of ISIS's self-proclaimed role as Lifton's dispensator of existence; that is, they clearly could define the world into "believers" and "nonbelievers," the latter of which were not worthy of human consideration.

This polarized view of the world is also reflected in the group's language, which is notably totalistic. Lifton's conceptual loaded language is on display here, where certain terms act as highly categorical shorthand for the hated Other. Anyone outside the ISIS umbrella represented either a *kuffir* (nonbeliever), a non-Muslim who was contributing to the persecution of true believers, or an apostate, an individual who had denounced the "true Islam" of ISIS and was deserving of death.

Little regard is required for the view of the other because of this. The material of ISIS is full of terms like "unbeliever," "disbeliever," "infidel," "kufr," "crusader," and so on. Again, it is not unusual for religious terrorist groups to establish a strong in-group/out-group divide. However, it is the totality and starkness of ISIS's approach to other Muslims and non-Muslims that makes it exceptional among other Salafi jihadist groups. Many Islamist extremist groups have engaged in *takfir* against their enemies as justification for their violence; however, in comparison to ISIS, their targets were more limited. For example, al-Qaeda did not declare the general Muslim population to be nonbelievers, reserving the designation for specific groups and individuals [23]. Indeed, it is crucial to note that the majority of ISIS's victims are themselves Muslim. More than simply serving to dehumanize the other, however, it is the act of murder and destruction itself that serves as a psychological bond to the group, with the advocation of sacred murder and the act itself tying leaders and supporters together in a "codependent cult group" [13].

Eschatology: ISIS versus the World

"The spark has been lit here in Iraq, and its heat will continue to intensify – by Allah's permission – until it burns the Crusader armies in Dabiq."

This quote from al-Zarqawi appeared on the front-page matter of each issue of one of ISIS's publications, *Dabiq*. This quote references a statement from the Prophet in which he predicts the end of days occurring when the "Romans" come to al-A'maq [in Turkey] or Dabiq [in Syria] [23]. These predictions seemingly became true when an international coalition decided to intervene in the quagmire of the Syrian Civil War, largely to stymie the growing power of the ISIS proto-state. Suddenly, aircraft from Western nations were flying overhead, and Turkish forces threatened Dabiq itself. The end of days was at hand.

This kind of apocalyptic thinking was pervasive in ISIS propaganda. The group's primary English-language publication was called *Dabiq*, referencing the city and prophecy. Indeed, the invocation of the apocalypse through these references was a key aspect of ISIS's recruitment strategy, particularly aimed at would-be supporters outside the immediate conflict zone. As McCants notes, this messaging was not particularly novel, with al-Qaeda similarly adopting apocalyptic messaging at times [24]. However, ISIS was able to combine this message with physical, tangible success, as well as spectacular and gruesome propaganda. The fact that, seemingly, the entire world had aligned itself against ISIS reaffirmed this messaging, creating a self-motivating cycle of prophecy, violent action, and violent reaction. This was a similar dynamic to cult groups, which have seen themselves as victims of government or societal repression.

It is important to note that the brutal and excessive violence carried out by ISIS was not just reactionary or born out of the circumstances of a brutal sectarian war. Cruel violence was a core element of this apocalyptical worldview. ISIS's violence was part of an intentional brutalization strategy to create "regions of savagery" in which ISIS could insert its governance [25]. This was a mission of decivilization, the subversion and destruction of the existing order. Thus, the genocide of the Yazidi people and other ethnic groups, the ritualistic mass executions of anyone deemed to be an enemy, and the spectacular and brutal terrorist attacks carried out globally were key aspects of ISIS's mission of destabilizing global society. ISIS's mission of destruction also extended to historical objects, with supporters targeting various antiquity-era ruins throughout Syria and Iraq.

The Rule of Heaven: The Utopian State and Control

Another cult-like element of ISIS is the level of control the group exercised over those who found themselves (willingly or unwillingly) in the ISIS proto-state. The result of this control was a "strange dichotomy of ultra-violence and civil order" [26]. On one hand, ISIS propaganda depicted life in the Caliphate as one of pure sharia law, untainted by the worldly vices associated with such decadent institutions such as democracy or secularism. Indeed, ISIS propaganda presents the Caliphate as a utopian society, "free of corruption and sin, where one can go to worship freely and properly" [27, p. 117]. The Caliphate was further presented as a complete society with everything that entailed, from hospitals, education, sanitation, media (including official, ISIS-produced video games), justice, and banking. Naturally, all of these institutions were sharia-compliant (according to ISIS's version of sharia). The Caliphate was even portrayed as the ideal place to raise a family, with *Dabiq* promoting a child-focused online learning series, complete with images of cartoon weaponry [27]. Promoting the Caliphate in that way was particularly appealing to prospective supporters from the West, who would expect this level of service from the state. However, it also allowed ISIS to impose a level of milieu control over its supporters, controlling what its supporters saw and read in an anti-Western "cocoon of fog" [28].

It is not surprising then that underneath this "utopian paradise" was a totalitarian, all-controlling theocratic body. Government bodies like the ISIS Research and Fatwa Department existed purely to incorporate sharia law into day-to-day life in the context of the Caliphate. Dissent was forbidden. Anyone who managed to travel to Syria or was in an area that fell under ISIS control suddenly found themselves subject to strict laws, the breach of which resulted in extreme punishments, ranging from public lashings to dismemberment and execution. These punishments were carried out by religious police who had little accountability. Groups like the all-woman Al-Khansaa Brigade served to enforce strict gender norms. One such example of justice meted out by these units of religious police was a group of women who were found to be wearing "overly form-fitting" abayas. When their face covers were removed, the women were found to be wearing makeup. Finally, the police determined that the women had too much attitude and were not meek enough in the face of Al-Khansaa's authority. For these offences, the women were lashed 25 times [29]. This demand for religious purity clearly meets Lifton's demand for purity, further establishing ISIS as being cult-like.

However, those outside ISIS's narrowly defined in-group found themselves brutalized and placed into a state of slavery, often including sexual slavery. Indeed, ISIS formally incorporated sexual slavery into its judicial system, with the Research and Fatwa Department releasing manuals for would-be slavers [30]. This was Lifton's "sacred science" in action, where ISIS were the undisputed arbiter of the truth and law.

Finally, it is worth considering the sheer brutality of ISIS. When combined with the apocalyptic narrative that ISIS relied on, the brutal push and pull of the Syrian and Iraqi civil wars and the intense group control exerted by the group meant that ISIS followers effectively existed in a period of "moral holiday." This refers to a period where the usual morality and ethical structures of an individual are suspended in favor of excessive violence and other deviant behavior, like sexual abuse of others. As previously mentioned, this kind of moral holiday was an inherent feature of ISIS's program of decivilization. However, it also speaks to Lifton's doctrine over the person, where individual experience and views are subordinated to the demands of doctrine. This is not to remove one's agency; rather, the totalist environment provides a seductive psychological appeal in which the individual chooses to subordinate their agency to the ideology of the group. In the totalism of the group, there is also a sense of the communitarianism of the various cults associated with the human potential movement, though perhaps in a perverse, inverted sense of human potential.

It must be pointed out that, as of writing, the physical Caliphate no longer exists beyond its influence in numerous refugee camps across Syria. This does not mean ISIS is not a threat – the group still maintains a large network of affiliate organizations across the globe and is no doubt attempting to plan and carry out attacks internationally. Moreover, one of the most challenging aspects of ISIS was the group's ability to inspire otherwise unaffiliated individuals to commit terroristic violence. To these people, ISIS offers a message of redemption and purpose – commit an attack in the name of the Islamic State, and you will achieve a level of immorality in martyrdom, no matter the individual's past. This remains one of the greatest challenges of ISIS's message, a message that is no less totalistic and cult-like in its appeal. However, without the organizing structure of the Caliphate to compound this message, those responding to the challenges of radicalized individuals have numerous opportunities to respond to them.

Mental Disorder and Terrorism

Although there has been a significant amount of research conducted over the past two decades examining any correlation or causation of mental disorders in terrorist offenders, it has rarely been based on data gathered through structured clinical assessment by a suitably trained mental health professional. Many of the most widely cited studies are based on open-source information of terrorist offenders that typically relies on media coverage and court documents and from which mental health disorders are inferred.

Analyses of datasets have generally not separated terrorist group leaders from group members when examining the prevalence of mental disorders. Some individual case reports have looked in detail at a terrorist's psychopathology, including cult leaders who were terrorists. For example, the in-depth clinical examination of Charles Manson provides fascinating detail on his psychopathology, including an extremely high psychopathy rating [5]. Such examination of terrorist group leaders is rare, as many are killed and therefore never undergo thorough clinical examination. The diagnoses that do exist are largely distal in nature. Indeed, the post-9/11 period saw the release of dozens of examinations of bin Laden's psychological profile [31]. However, these studies were based on what the authors could observe from bin Laden's writings, developmental history, and role in al-Qaeda. These studies, though often useful, also reflected a tendency to pathologize terrorists during this period, seeking answers for their behavior in their mental configuration. This contrasts with earlier profiles of effective terrorist leaders that depict them as being "rigid, dedicated, over suspicious ... highly motivated ... convicted of [their] righteousness ... dedicated, but not delusional ... She or he is not mentally ill. The leader can read people well and appeal to their needs" [32, p. 89].

Research carried out on various terrorist organizations and groups across Europe, South America, and the Middle East provided evidence that group-based terrorists are psychologically quite normal [33, 34, 35]. Group leaders seek to recruit those most capable of undertaking assigned tasks. Most tasks require an element of secrecy, calibrated violence, and/or technological skill. Therefore, terrorist organizations prefer recruits who can be trusted, are reliable, and can take direction. It has been argued that those who seek to join but display signs of mental illness may be weeded out in the selection process [36]. Clinical examination of lone actor terrorists is more common, often as part of the court process where they survive their attack and are prosecuted for their terrorist acts [37].

In the past decade, there has been a paradigm shift in much terrorist offending, at least in the Western World, with a move to lone actor attacks involving low levels of capability and planning. This has been particularly prevalent with the rise of ISIS, which calls on supporters to commit low-capacity attacks whenever and wherever possible [38]. Correspondingly, there has been a focus on examining the prevalence of mental disorders in this cohort compared with group actor terrorists. Although the prevalence rates of mental disorders vary considerably across studies, with estimates ranging from 6% to 41% among radicalized individuals to 3–49% among those who commit acts of terrorism [39], the prevalence of mental illness seems to be significantly higher among those who commit lone acts of terrorism than group acts, at 31.9% and 3.4% respectively [40]. Put another way, the odds of a lone actor terrorist having a mental illness is 13.49 times higher than the odds of a group actor having a mental illness. Several individual disorders have been found to be more prevalent in lone actors than in the general population, including autism spectrum disorder (ASD; 3.3%), schizophrenia (8.5%), and delusional disorder (2%) [40]. Again, the tendency for groups to filter out individuals perceived to be unreliable and self-select for operational security may be a reason why an individual becomes a lone actor rather than operating in a group. Indeed, it is the decision to operate independently that is the key conceptual distinction between a group-based and lone actor, with even the latter involved in social processes in coming to embrace the use of violence in furthering an ideology. Mental health, in this instance, merely influences how the individual is able to relate to those around them rather than being a precipitator for violent action.

A recent systematic review that focused on mental health and its association with terrorist involvement examined 56 papers reporting on 73 terrorist samples [41]. It estimated that the lifetime prevalence rate of diagnosed mental disorder in the general population is 29%. The lifetime prevalence rate of diagnosed mental disorder in terrorist samples was 17.4%. This increased to 23.2% for the studies reporting lifetime prevalence rates of suspected disorder, and 28.5% for studies reporting any psychological problems. At any one time, 14.4% of those involved in terrorism had a disorder or suspected disorder (as opposed to a psychological problem). They found some evidence that lone actor terrorists have higher rates of difficulties than other terrorist populations. The authors conclude that at most mental health difficulties present a background nondeterminative predisposing factor nested among other factors and that may present a vulnerability to terrorism through the depletion of resilience, impairment of judgement, restriction of opportunity, and an almost unlimited range of other life experiences and situational factors.

Neurodevelopmental disorders, predominantly ASD, have increasingly been highlighted in those individuals convicted of terrorism in Western cultures. There is no causal link between ASD and violent extremism [42]. Yet, for those with ASD who are drawn to violent extremism, facets of ASD can contribute to push and pull factors that shape an individual's pathway to engagement [43, 44].

Recent research has examined how neurodivergent traits and symptoms (with a focus on ASD and attention deficit hyperactivity disorder) may contextualize vulnerability to extremism engagement, as well as resilience and disengagement [45]. Analysis of closed source data on 18 cases suggested that neurodivergent features alone do not directly cause vulnerability or risk to extremism [46]; rather, they can combine with or exacerbate other vulnerabilities, such as those associated with social isolation and rejection; comorbidities and complex needs; difficulties in transitional periods; a lack of support from support systems; and socioenvironmental factors such as the impact of the COVID-19 pandemic and the time spent online.

A systematic review in 2021 examined the functional role of an individual's personality in radicalization and terrorism with some evidence that sensation-seeking, poor self-control, low empathy, and impulsivity are common among this population rather than a specific personality type [47]. Some reports have identified the role of paranoid, antisocial, and sadomasochistic personality traits [48]. Examination of Palestinian terrorists identified more Cluster B traits in the control and organizer groups, and more Cluster C avoidant and dependent personality traits among the suicide bombers. These traits made them more amenable to group, leader, and public influence [49]. A review of articles examining group actor terrorism in the Middle East suggested that pathological personality traits were highly prevalent including psychopathic, paranoid, depressive, and hypomanic traits compared with nonterrorist controls [39].

Threat Assessment and Risk Assessment in Terrorism

Just as a terrorist group can resemble a cult, cults can resemble terrorist groups. In some cults, de-facto acts of terrorism have clearly been committed, such as Aum Shinrikyo's attack on the Tokyo subway, while in other cults links to a terrorist motivation for violence have been more ambiguous; for example, Charles Manson has been described by some authors as a terrorist who commanded an autonomous cell to further his accelerationist ideology [5]. For practitioners conducting assessments on a member of a cult promoting violent extremist narratives, it will be important to evaluate any immediate threat of violent or otherwise illegal action based on ideology as well as an assessment of the medium- to longer-term risk of radicalization to violent extremism/terrorism. Ultimately, the aim of risk assessment is not to predict outcomes but to identify strategies for risk mitigation as well as interventions to support the individual's disengagement from harmful ideologies and groups.

The task of threat assessment and risk assessment in these scenarios involves several complexities, including an understanding of why the individual was drawn to that particular group membership, as well as a need to assess the individual within the context of their current environment and influences, especially if they remain in the cult or extremist group. Sociopolitical and geopolitical contexts at the time of assessment will also affect the level of concern that the individual may progress to violent action in ways that are not typical in the assessment of nonideologically motivated violence or other types of offending. The ideology itself may also influence the likelihood of suicidal or homicidal acts, for instance, where promises of redemption through death/martyrdom are made (e.g., in the case of ISIS) and/or the shared narrative is one of apocalyptic violence. There is increasing recognition of the contributory role of real or perceived grievances in many of those who progress to acts of targeted extremist violence [50], and where a personal grievance is combined with moral outrage concerning historical or contemporaneous religious or political events, an ideology can provide the justification for an act of violence that has its roots in more personal motivations [51]. In some cases, specific triggering events associated with these grievances may accelerate the movement toward violent extremist action.

Threat assessment tends to be a dynamic task, often based on limited information, and focuses on the motivation, intent, and capability of the individual or group. The presence of each of these factors (motivation, intent, and capability) will be present to differing degrees, and the ability to assess their presence or absence will depend on access to information on the person, much of which may only be accessed by other agencies such as law enforcement or security services. Motivation and intent may be revealed through direct clinical interviews or through other sources of information such as online posting. Although many have questioned the validity of information that would be provided during an interview with a terrorist offender [52], this concern is not unique to terrorist offenders, and forensic practitioners working with nonterrorist offenders are skilled in incorporating information from clinical interviews (including the nature and quality of the interaction with the practitioner) into an overall assessment of clinical issues and risk. Capability may be determined through various sources of information including any records of strategic weapons training and/or financial resources to fund weapons. Aum Shinrikyo, for instance, developed significant capability in weapons, including the production of sarin used in the Tokyo subway attack. With Charles Manson and the Tate–LaBianca killings, the homicidal intent of the perpetrators was expressed clearly at trial, and the motivation was hypothesized through collateral information of witnesses and established at trial, namely that "Helter Skelter" would precipitate a race war, but cult members would survive [53]. Capability in the homicides was less sophisticated, with the use of easily accessible weapons (knives) as well as a gun.

The basic principles of risk assessment in violent extremism/terrorism remain the same as assessment of risk in any type of offending and ideally involves direct clinical interview of the individual, collateral sources of information such as information from family and/or agencies already involved with the individual, and review of records. However, when compared to risk assessment for general, violent, and sexual offending behaviors, the process of risk assessment of violent extremism is comparatively new [54]. Several violent extremism risk assessment tools have been developed in the past few years, but each have their own limitations [54]. None have predictive validity, and it is arguable whether this can ever be developed in view of the low base rates in terrorist offending and reoffending, as well as the heterogeneous risk factors present in perpetrators of the wide range of acts defined as terrorist offences [55]. Terrorist offences may include foreign incursion and recruitment offences, terrorist act and preparatory offences, membership of proscribed terrorist organizations, collecting or making documents likely to facilitate terrorist acts, and financing terrorism. Therefore, many of the offences do not directly involve an act of violence but are indirectly involved because of the terrorist organization's support of violence to achieve its ideological goal, whether domestically or overseas.

Violence risk assessment tools generally assume a cumulative risk model that purports that the more risk factors that are present, the higher the chance of engaging in violence. This assumption is not supported within the violent extremist literature, whereby it is not the number of risk factors that is important but the nuance within each risk factor [56]. Individual risk factors may impact an individual's commitment and motivation to engage in an act of violent extremism. Although there is overlap with many of the risk indicators for criminal violence, additional factors such as having extremist associates, extremist beliefs, and/or skills and resources for committing violence are relevant to terrorism or violent extremist offending [50]. In addition, acts of terrorism are often influenced by, or take place in, the context of groups both online and offline, which differs from risk factors in most other types of offending [57].

Risk assessments for violent extremist offenders aim to identify how motivations, criminogenic needs, responsivities, vulnerabilities, and protective factors interact at a given point in time and within a given context. The aim is to provide a narrative to understand each individual's drivers, motivations, and level of conviction for committing a terrorist act in order to inform decisions about how risk can be mitigated, and interventions can be provided to support the individual to disengage from violent extremism and reengage with pro-social supports and lifestyle.

Violent extremism risk assessment tools use a structured professional judgment (SPJ) approach, which is an amalgamation of empirical knowledge and practitioner experience. The SPJ tools most commonly used in terrorism and violent extremism assessment include the Terrorist Radicalization Assessment Protocol-18 (TRAP-18), the Violent Extremist Risk Assessment – version 2 Revised (VERA-2R), and the Extremism Risk Guidance 22+ (ERG 22+). All three are SPJ tools and all three are described as ideologically neutral. Additional tools exist for specific extremist cohorts [58].

The TRAP-18 was developed as an investigative template to assess the risk of targeted terrorist violence across all ideological spectrums [51]. The TRAP-18 has eight proximal warning behaviors that are derived from the pre-attack signals identified in the targeted violence literature on lone perpetrators of mass killings, assassinations, spousal homicide, and terrorist attacks. There are 10 distal background factors that align with the theorized features of the mindset of a lone actor "violent true believer" that create their vulnerability to targeted violence [59]. The assessor develops a narrative for understanding the case given the presence or absence of indicators and other idiosyncratic circumstances that might apply in the individual case. A growing number of postdictive studies are building evidence for the validity and reliability of the TRAP-18 [58].

The VERA-2R includes a set of dynamic risk indicators identified as relevant for violent extremism [56]. It provides a structure for the analysis of an individual's risk of violent extremism, based on the person's beliefs, attitudes and ideology; social context and intention; history, action, and capacity; commitment and motivation; protective and risk-mitigating indicators; relevant criminal and personal history; and potential mental disorders. The purpose of the assessment is to establish a clear case formulation that, in turn, informs risk identification, treatment needs, and the nature of the intervention required.

The ERG 22+ was developed by the UK Prison and Probation Service. Assessors consider the 22+ factors significant to an individual's pathway into extremism (i.e., engagement), how they overcame inhibitions against offending and/or harming others (i.e., intent), and their ability to contribute to or commit a further extremist offence (i.e., capability). The ERG 22+ was designed to be used as part of a multidisciplinary decision-making process to inform proportionate risk management, to increase understanding and confidence in frontline staff and in decision-makers working with extremist offenders, and to facilitate effective and targeted intervention [60]. Although the ERG 22+ focuses on the individual, it also identifies the role of factors and circumstances external to the individual that may have influenced their engagement and/or involvement in extremism, including the group, cause, or ideology that is being supported, the individual motivations and protective and contextual factors, as well as their role within the extremist activity.

The factors within the engagement dimension of the ERG 22+ include need to redress injustice, need for identity, meaning, and belonging, need for status, susceptibility to indoctrination, need to dominate others, political/moral motivation, transitional periods, the influence of family and/or friends, opportunistic involvement, and mental health. The term "intent" refers to the mindset associated with a readiness to act illegally and/or violently on behalf of a group, cause, and/or ideology. The intent dimension is best described as the endpoint of an engagement process if uninterrupted and includes, for example, overidentification (as an end state of engagement and identification), us and them thinking, dehumanization (as an end state of us and them thinking), and harmful objectives; all of which represent a state of mind where inhibitions against offending and causing harm have been overcome or where the individual sees no other course of action in pursuit of their goals.

Most individuals who commit terrorism are not mentally ill [40]. When mental illness is present, it tends to be more prevalent in specific subgroups (e.g., lone actors compared to members of organized terrorist groups) and may or may not be relevant to risk [61]. Where it has some relevance, it may not be causal, and if it is partly causal, it is likely to interact with a range of political, social, environmental, situational, and biological factors at any given time. A forensic mental health case formulation process is important to provide an understanding of the nature of the individual's mental health needs and the ways some, if any, relate to vulnerability/risk. When formulating an individual's pathway into terrorism, this is structured in terms of "push" factors – aspects of an individual's mindset or life that push them toward terrorism – and "pull" factors, or aspects of the terrorist cause, ideology, group, or modus operandi that appeal to an individual and pull them in [54]. The shifting balance of push and pull factors, influenced by a range of personality, social, political, and operational factors, influence the pathway to radicalization and engagement in terrorist offending. Individuals are motivated to commit acts of terrorism for a range of ideological, psychological, and social motives. In most cases, an individual's needs are met by terrorism/extremism, with each push and pull factor possibly varying in its influence at different points in that pathway. Certain extremist narratives that offer escapism, hope, redemption, and meaning may be particularly compelling to individuals suffering with a range of mental health issues and psychological vulnerabilities [62]. Self-destructive and suicidal ideation may provide generic "push" factors for harmful acts of self-destruction, while anger and vengefulness may act as further push factors for violence, especially where grievances are prominent. In particular, ISIS was adept at capitalizing on individual vulnerabilities, with much ISIS media presenting a narrative of empowerment and redemption, where past transgressions and personal failings are wiped away by the commission of violence [63, 64].

It is important when assessing an individual that this is done within a multidisciplinary and multiagency framework including subject matter experts where required. Understanding an ideology or a terrorist group will provide insight into the push and pull factors of why that particular ideology or group were attractive, and what influenced the radicalization toward violent action. It is important where possible that the operational and clinical experts inform each other's insights. Each country, state, organization, and professional group will have its own protocols on multidisciplinary working and information-sharing.

Psychological and behavioral pathways into violent extremism may be similar to those factors that make an individual vulnerable to engagement in a cult, and in some cases the violent extremist group itself may have cult-like qualities, as described earlier in the case of ISIS. Both violent extremist groups and cults may be harmful to an individual's mental health, and mental health practitioners may therefore form a key part of a multiagency approach to providing interventions to support disengagement.

Disengagement from violent extremism or terrorism reflects a behavioral change whereby the individual no longer acts violently in support of their beliefs. Deradicalization refers to psychological and ideological change whereby the individual may distance themselves from their previously held beliefs [65]. A comprehensive review of the literature around successful approaches to disengagement from violent extremism is beyond the scope of this chapter, but key elements to the approach have been outlined in Barrelle's pro-integration model [66]. This model describes five domains of need that influence an individual's engagement in violent extremism, namely coping and well-being, social relations, sense of self and identity, behavioral orientation, and attitudes and beliefs (otherwise described as ideology). These domains provide the platform for interventions that aim to support disengagement and ongoing desistence from violent extremism achieved through the individual becoming engaged in an alternative and healthier environment.

Once push and pull factors that shaped the pathway to extremism and the protective factors that can divert from it are identified, support and therapeutic strategies can be put in place. Support and interventions may vary and should build on evidence-based practice and well-researched intervention approaches for mental disorder (where this is present) while also taking into consideration nonpsychiatric approaches that enhance resilience for that individual. In some cases, family is also key to intervention approaches, and their ability to identify and respond to the individual's risk/needs assists greatly in safe and sustainable community reintegration. Regardless of the intervention and support approach taken, the common principle needs to be to help the vulnerable/at risk individual to recognize the functions and needs that extremism met for them and to either alleviate the factors that exacerbate that need or else to meet those needs in healthy alternative ways [62].

Conclusion

This chapter has explored the conceptual overlap between terrorist groups and cults, using the example of ISIS to explore how some terrorist groups can be highly cultic in nature. Conversely, several examples of cults engaging in terrorist violence have been identified. In the end, this chapter does little to resolve the "terrorism or cult" debate. Instead, it has taken the position that this debate represents a false dichotomy, with each group capable of sharing attributes of the other. However, these comparisons are largely limited to religious terrorist groups. This is not to say nonreligious terrorist groups cannot be cultic – they most certainly can. Most terrorist groups will present a Mancichean dichotomy between its members and the targeted out-group. Most will also enforce this worldview through a period of indoctrination and radicalization. However, it is the fundamental nature of extremist religious ideology that lends itself to similarities with cultic movements, whose messages and ideologies often converge around divine and transhumanistic conceptions of the universe and the place of the chosen people within it. In this way, religiously motivated terrorists and violently minded cult members are highly similar. However, categorizing a cult as a terrorist group will shape the context in which responses are framed, with those that are members of a terrorist group subject to specific military and legal measures. Members of a terrorist group are unlikely to be viewed as victims of manipulation or cultish practices, but rather as security threats to the state and therefore subject to more punitive responses. Nevertheless, it is the similarities that enable existing risk management tools and frameworks to function with both types of individuals effectively. This is because, fundamentally, these are people with human needs. Identifying and responding to these needs in prosocial ways remains the goal, regardless of whether they are a terrorist or a cultist.

Key Points

- Unlike cults, terrorist groups are defined by their *political* nature and threat to state security.
- Being designated a terrorist group brings additional state and international responses, including military and legal responses not utilized against cults.
- Cults can use terrorist tactics, and terrorist groups can utilize cultish tactics.
- Threat assessment and risk assessment in terrorism requires multiple sources of information and an understanding of the specific ideology.
- Understanding an individual's push and pull factors for radicalization toward a violent extremist ideology or terrorist group provides a basis for supporting their disengagement and reintegration into a prosocial and healthy lifestyle.

References

1. M Sedgwick. The concept of radicalization as a source of confusion. *Terrorism and Political Violence.* 2010;22(4):479–94.
2. P Jenkins. *Images of terror: what we can and can't know about terrorism.* Aldine de Gruyter; 2003.
3. M Juergensmeyer. *Terror in the mind of God: the global rise of religious violence.* University of California Press; 2001.
4. M Wheelis, M Sugishima. Terrorist use of biological weapons. In: M Wheelis, L Rózsa, M Dando, editors. *Deadly cultures: biological weapons since 1945.* Harvard University Press; 2009.
5. TA Roy, JL Mihura, AF Friedman, DS Nichols, JR Meloy. The last psychological evaluation of Charles Manson: implications for personality, psychopathology, and ideology. *Journal of Threat Assessment and Management.* 2023;10(3):127–50.

6. DC Rapoport. The fourth wave: September 11 in the history of terrorism. *Current History.* 2001;100(650):419–24.
7. I Sànchez-Cuenca. The dynamics of nationalist terrorism: ETA and the IRA. *Terrorism and Political Violence.* 2007;19(3):289–306.
8. M Gallagher. The 2016 'lone wolf' tsunami: is Rapoport's 'religious wave' ending? *Journal of Strategic Security.* 2017;10(2):60–76.
9. T Parker, N Sitter. The four horsemen of terrorism: it's not waves, it's strains. *Terrorism and Political Violence.* 2016;28(2):197–216.
10. I Levy. Lethal beliefs: ideology and the lethality of terrorist organizations. *Terrorism and Political Violence.* 2023;35(4):811–27.
11. LL Dawson. The study of new religious movements and the radicalization of home-grown terrorists: opening a dialogue. *Terrorism and Political Violence.* 2009;22(1):1–21.
12. PA Olsson. The mind of Osama Bin Laden: the ultimate malignant pied piper. In: J Piven, editor. *Jihad and sacred vengeance.* Bloomusalem Press; 2002. p. 99–115.
13. PA Olsson. Group death myths and terror cult groups. *Journal of Psychohistory.* 2007;3(34):241–54.
14. Á Rodríguez-Carballeira, J Martín-Peña, C Almendros, J Escartín, C Porrúa, M Bertacco. A psychosocial analysis of the terrorist group as a cult. *International Journal of Cultic Studies.* 2010;1:49–60.
15. CM Centner. Cults and terrorism: similarities and differences. *Cultic Studies Review.* 2003;2(2).
16. S Malik. The Isis papers: behind "death cult" image lies a methodical bureaucracy. *The Guardian.* 2015 Dec 7. www.theguardian.com/world/2015/dec/07/isis-papers-guardian-syria-iraq-bureaucracy
17. I Tharoor. How the Islamic State is like a Christian death cult. *The Washington Post.* 2015 Mar 23. www.washingtonpost.com/news/worldviews/wp/2015/03/23/how-the-islamic-state-is-like-a-christian-death-cult/
18. P Lentini. Demonizing ISIL and defending Muslims: Australian Muslim citizenship and Tony Abbott's "death cult" rhetoric. *Islam Christ-Muslim Relations.* 2015;26(2):237–52.
19. RJ Lifton. *Thought reform and the psychology of totalism: a study of 'brainwashing' in China.* University of North Carolina Press; 1989.
20. B Barron, DL Maye. Does ISIS satisfy the criteria of an apocalyptic Islamic cult? An evidence-based historical qualitative meta-analysis. *Journal of Terrorism Research.* 2017;8(1):18–33.
21. C Bunzel. *From paper state to caliphate: the ideology of the Islamic State.* Center for Middle East Policy (The Brookings Project on US Relations with the Islamic World).
22. F. Gaub. The cult of ISIS. *Survival.* 2016;58(1):113–30.
23. E Poljarevic. Theology of violence-oriented takfirism as a political theory: the case of Islamic State in Iraq and Syria (ISIS). In: MA Upal, CM Cusack, editors. *Handbook of Islamic sects and movements.* Brill; 2021. p. 485–512.
24. WF McCants. *The ISIS apocalypse: the history, strategy, and doomsday vision of the Islamic State.* 1st ed. St. Martin's Press; 2015.
25. J Fromson, S Simon. ISIS: the dubious paradise of apocalypse now. *Survival.* 2015;57(3):7–56.
26. J Stern, JM Berger. *ISIS: the state of terror.* William Collins; 2015.
27. SJ Baele, KA Boyd TG Coan. The matrix of Islamic State's propaganda: magazines. In: *ISIS propaganda: a full spectrum extremist message.* 1st ed. Oxford University Press; 2020. p. 84–126.
28. A Baczko, G Dorronsoro, A Quesnay, M Youssef. The rationality of an eschatological movement: the Islamist State in Iraq and Syria. *SSRN Electronic Journal.* 2016. www.ssrn.com/abstract=3732243

29. A Moaveni. ISIS women and enforcers in Syria recount collaboration, anguish and escape. *The New York Times*. 2015 Nov 21. www.nytimes.com/2015/11/22/world/middleeast/isis-wives-and-enforcers-in-syria-recount-collaboration-anguish-and-escape.html

30. S El-Masri. Prosecuting ISIS for the sexual slavery of the Yazidi women and girls. *International Journal of Human Rights*. 2018;22(8):1047–66.

31. A Locicero, SJ Sinclair. Terrorism and terrorist leaders: insights from developmental and ecological psychology. *Studies in Conflict and Terrorism*. 2008;31(3):227–50.

32. T Strentz. The terrorist organizational profile: a psychological role model. In: Y Alexander, JM Gleason, editors. *Behavioral and quantitative perspectives on terrorism*. Pergamon Press; 1981. p. 86–104.

33. M Crenshaw. The causes of terrorism. *Comparative Politics*. 1981;13(4):379–99.

34. M. Sageman. *Understanding terror networks*. University of Pennsylvania Press; 2011.

35. J Post, E Sprinzak, L Denny. The terrorists in their own words: interviews with 35 incarcerated Middle Eastern terrorists. *Terrorism and Political Violence*. 2003;15(1):171–84.

36. L Lindekilde, F O'Connor, B Schuurman. Radicalization patterns and modes of attack planning and preparation among lone-actor terrorists: an exploratory analysis. *Behavioral Sciences of Terrorism and Political Aggression*. 2019;11(2):113–33.

37. I Melle. The Breivik case and what psychiatrists can learn from it. *World Psychiatry*. 2013;12(1):16–21.

38. C Winter, R Spaaij. Lone actor terrorism in 2019 and 2020: trends and implications. In: L Close, D Impiombato, editors. *Counterterrorism yearbook 2021*. Australian Strategic Policy Institute; 2021. p. 19–22.

39. M Trimbur, A Amad, M Horn, P Thomas, T Fovet. Are radicalization and terrorism associated with psychiatric disorders? A systematic review. *Journal of Psychiatric Research*. 2021;141(July):214–22.

40. E Corner, P Gill, O Mason. Mental health disorders and the terrorist: a research note probing selection effects and disorder prevalence. *Studies in Conflict and Terrorism*. 2016;39(6):560–8.

41. KM Sarma, SL Carthy, KM Cox. Mental disorder, psychological problems and terrorist behaviour: a systematic review and meta-analysis. *Campbell Systematic Reviews*. 2022;18(3):e1268.

42. F Druitt, D Smith, R Spaaij, D Kernot, A Laver. Do autism spectrum disorders (ASD) increase the risk of terrorism engagement? A literature review of the research evidence, theory and interpretation, and a discussion reframing the research-practice debate. *Journal of Policing, Intelligence and Counter Terrorism*. 2023;18(3):307–32.

43. Z Al-Attar. Autism spectrum disorders and terrorism: how different features of autism can contextualise vulnerability and resilience. *Journal of Forensic Psychiatry & Psychology*. 2020;31(6):926–49.

44. Z Al-Attar. Framework for the Assessment of Risk & Protection in Offenders on the Autistic Spectrum. www.nota.co.uk/wp-content/uploads/2021/09/FARAS-Guidelines-Final-1.pdf

45. N Salman, Z Al-Attar, G McKenzie. Practitioner perspectives on counterterrorism and neurodiversity. Centre for Research and Evidence on Security Threats. https://crestresearch.ac.uk/resources/practitioner-perspectives-on-counterterrorism-and-neurodiversity/

46. N Salman, Z Al-Attar, N Pyszora, D Smith, M Iqbal. Neurodivergence and violent extremism: 18 international case studies. Centre for Research and Evidence on Security Threats. https://crestresearch.ac.uk/site/assets/files/4838/23-059-01_neurodivergence_and_ve_case_studies_overview.pdf

47. E Corner, H Taylor, I van der Vegt, N Salman, B Rottweiler, F Hetzel, et al. Reviewing the links between violent

extremism and personality, personality disorders, and psychopathy. *Journal of Forensic Psychiatry & Psychology.* 2021;32(3):378–407.

48. D Weatherston, J Moran. Terrorism and mental illness: is there a relationship? *International Journal of Offender Therapy and Comparative Criminology.* 2003;47(6):698–713.
49. A Merari, I Diamant, A Bibi, Y Broshi, G Zakin. Personality characteristics of "self martyrs"/"suicide bombers" and organizers of suicide attacks. *Terrorism and Political Violence.* 2009;22(1):87–101.
50. AG Smith. *Risk factors and indicators associated with radicalization to terrorism in the United States: what research sponsored by the National Institute of Justice tells us.* National Institute of Justice; 2018.
51. JR Meloy. *TRAP-18 user's manual version 1.0.* Multi-Health Systems Inc. Risk Management Authority; 2021.
52. LL Dawson. Taking terrorist accounts of their motivations seriously: an exploration of the hermeneutics of suspicion. *Perspectives on Terrorism.* 2019;13(5):74–89.
53. V Bugliosi, C Gentry. *Helter Skelter: the true story of the Manson murders.* Arrow; 2018.
54. S Copeland, S Marsden. Extremist risk assessment. Centre for Research and Evidence on Security Threats; 2020 Nov 4. (Knowledge Management Across the Four Counter-Terrorism 'Ps.').
55. C Smith, M Nolan. Post-sentence continued detention of high-risk terrorist offenders in Australia. *Criminal Law Journal.* 2016;40(3):163–79.
56. E Pressman, N Duits, T Rinne, J Flockton. VERA-2R violent extremism risk assessment version 2 revised: A structured professional judgement approach. *Netherlands Institute of Forensic Psychiatry and Psychology.* 2016.
57. M Dernevik, A Beck, M Grann, T Hogue, J McGuire. The use of psychiatric and psychological evidence in the assessment of terrorist offenders. *Journal of Forensic Psychiatry & Psychology.* 2009;20(4):508–15.
58. M Lloyd. Extremism risk assessment: a directory. Centre for Research and Evidence on Security Threats; 2019 Mar.
59. JR Meloy, P Gill. The lone-actor terrorist and the TRAP-18. *Journal of Threat Assessment and Management.* 2016;3(1):37–52.
60. M Lloyd, C Dean. The development of structured guidelines for assessing risk in extremist offenders. *Journal of Threat Assessment and Management.* 2015;2(1):40–52.
61. E Corner, P Gill. A false dichotomy? Mental illness and lone-actor terrorism. *Law and Human Behavior.* 2015;39(1):23–34.
62. Z Al-Attar. *Extremism, radicalisation & mental health: handbook for practitioners.* RAN; 2019.
63. G Barton. Understanding key themes in the ISIS narrative: an examination of *Dabiq* magazine. In: F Mansouri, Z Keskin, editors. *Contesting the theological foundations of Islamism and violent extremism.* Springer International Publishing; 2019. p. 139–61.
64. AN Awan. The impact of evolving jihadist narratives on radicalisation in the West. In: S Staffell, A Awan, editors. *Jihadism transformed.* Oxford University Press; 2017.
65. JF Morrison, A Silke, H Maiberg, C Slay, R Stewart. A systematic review of post-2017 research on disengagement and deradicalisation. Centre for Research and Evidence on Security Threats; 2021 Aug. https://dspace.lib.cranfield.ac.uk/handle/1826/17508
66. K Barrelle. Pro-integration: disengagement from and life after extremism. *Behavioral Sciences of Terrorism and Political Aggression.* 2015;7(2):129–42.

Chapter 5

Groups of Prejudice and Intolerance

Carlos A. Larrauri, Diana E. Vukel, Harold J. Bursztajn, Michael Ashley Stein, Mickey Arieli, and Aviv Weinstein

"Ignorance leads to fear, fear leads to hatred, and hatred leads to violence. This is the equation."
— *Ibn Rushd,* Averroes: Antología

Introduction

This chapter examines hate groups by analyzing attributes common to both their leaders and followers. To do so, we first delineate a historical case study, that of Father Charles Coughlin and the National Union for Social Justice. Next, we extrapolate from the Father Coughlin context and adjacent historical examples such as Henry Ford and Charles Lindbergh to identify and analyze the psychological and social characteristics predisposing leaders and followers to participate in these groups. Finally, we conclude with some thoughts on the contemporary relevance of learning lessons from the past.

Father Coughlin possessed many characteristics that aided his antisemitic movement. The presence of these features among other demagogues and their impact on followers suggests that there are characteristics common among leaders of hate groups. For instance, Charles Coughlin and Henry Ford demonstrated the critical role of mass media in successfully distributing hateful agendas. Father Coughlin and Charles Lindbergh further showed how a charismatic personality is often a component of these leaders, enabling them to blind the public and employ deception.

Our research also indicated that some element of messianism (e.g., the belief in a messiah who is seen as the savior of humanity, ensuring eternal life) is often present within hate groups. This belief system is associated with notions of achieving purity, perfection, and spiritual as well as material resurrection, and, in the hate group context, the idea of eliminating marginalized and dehumanized individuals, often foreigners, to attain this desired state. Leaders often intentionally cultivate a malignant messianic image, enabling them to exert substantial influence over their followers. When confronted with their vulnerability to mortality, isolation, and powerlessness, these followers seek solace in the assurance of belonging to a group led by a messiah figure. This sense of belonging is fostered through the promise of eternity, a shared identity founded on mutual hatred, and the allure of empowering violence.

These qualities worked in tandem with one another to grant Coughlin, along with other antisemites like Ford and Lindbergh, the power and motivation necessary to fuel hateful movements against the Jewish population. The Jewish community served as a tangible reminder of historical events and uncomfortable truths, specifically, the absence of a messiah and human beings' existential vulnerability and mortality.

Analyzing the common characteristics among followers of these leaders helped us understand what made them so receptive to the agendas of these demagogues. What we found is that many followers tended to experience some traumatic event that left them in a state of vulnerability. In the case of Coughlin's followers, that event was World War I, which was coupled with the Spanish flu and followed by the Great Depression – a trio of society-wide events that caused and compounded trauma and grief.

World War I occurred between 1914 and 1918, but the United States did not enter the war until April 1917. When the US relinquished neutrality, it joined the war on the side of the Allied Powers led by Britain, France, and Russia [1]. Woodrow Wilson, who served as president during this era, determined that a declaration of war was necessary following a series of events, including a violation of the Sussex Pledge and the discovery of the Zimmerman Telegram.

The Sussex Pledge was an agreement between the US and Germany in which the German government agreed to cease attacks on passenger ships. The need for this pledge followed an incident in which German forces sank an unarmed French vessel, the *Sussex*. Unless Germany complied with this agreement, President Wilson represented that the US would sever diplomatic ties with Germany. However, Germany violated this agreement in 1917. Germany justified its action with the argument that the US abandoned neutrality by supplying Allied forces with resources. During February and March of 1917, Germany resumed its practice of unrestricted submarine warfare, attacking several civilian and commercial US ships. Wilson provided US ships with naval personnel and resources through an executive order. This support was met with backlash from many antiwar politicians and individuals who opposed the US's involvement in the war. One of those individuals was Charles Lindbergh, who held isolationist views.

The Zimmerman Telegram was another source of contention. British intelligence intercepted a telegram in which German officials promised the return of territory lost during the Mexican–American War to Mexico in exchange for Mexican support. Ultimately, both events contributed to Wilson's decision to declare war on Germany in 1917.

As World War I neared its end, the world was confronted by another catastrophe: the Spanish flu (Figure 5.1). When this virus emerged, the war encouraged its spread through conditions like overcrowding [2]. This pandemic consisted of three waves, each killing large numbers of people. The extensive reach of the Spanish flu can be attributed to the fact that a vaccine for influenza had not been developed yet, nor were there any antibiotics to treat infections associated with it. Consequently, people had to rely on methods like isolation or quarantine and resources like disinfecting agents. The Spanish flu infected approximately 500 million people, with about 50 million succumbing to the virus.

Immediately following World War I, the United States experienced a postwar depression [3]. But economic conditions changed around 1923 when an upward trend started to develop. That trend lasted for most of the 1920s but suffered a dramatic turnaround when the stock market crashed in 1929. Among other factors, such as the collapse of world trade, the market crash jump-started one of the worst economic periods in US history, the Great Depression (Figure 5.2). The impact of the Great Depression was far-reaching and affected all aspects of life. Unsurprisingly, some of

HEALTH ORDER DOOMS LODGE HALL COBWEBS

Grip Ban on All Meetings Until Places Are Renovated; 21 Theaters Reopen.

GRIP VIGILANCE STILL NEEDED

Dr. Robertson Warns Against Relaxing Precaution, Despite Wane of Epid-mic

'OPEN-FACE' SNEEZERS TO BE ARRESTED

Orders to arrest any [illegible] seen indulging in the "open face" sneeze or cough in

POLICE RAID SALOONS IN WAR ON INFLUENZA; KEEP CHURCH WINDOWS OPEN

Stringent New Orders Are Issued for Preventing Spread of Epidemic; Police Ambulances Are Drafted; 100,000 Doses of Vaccine on Way.

1,613 NEW CASES SHOW DECREASE IN CITY; DOWNSTATE HIT WORST

FLU CURFEW TO SOUND FOR CITY SATURDAY NIGHT

Persons Not on Business Expected to Quit the Streets at 9 o'Clock.

The curfew will ring or, rather, blow in Chicago tomorrow night.
Promptly at 9 o'clock the whistles of

DRAFT MEN TO BE FIRST INOCULATED FOR "FLU"

'NONESSENTIAL' CROWDS BARRED IN EPIDEMIC WAR

Churches and Saloons Exempt; Conventions, Athletics, Parties Hit.

FREE DOCTOR

Influenza victims unable to pay for a doctor can obtain one by calling Main 447, Local 108, day or night.

CHURCH WINDOWS MUST STAY OPEN, SAYS ROBERTSON

Health Department Gives Out New Rules in Fight on Influenza.

CHICAGO DEP'T. OF HEALTH - CUT

Figure 5.1 Chicago newspaper headlines, 1918
Source: Public domain

the most prominent facets were social and financial; unemployment, food insecurity, loss of community, and material and emotional deprivation skyrocketed while industrial production fell dramatically. These consequences, in turn, affected families and led to a decrease in marriage rates. Families experienced the Great Depression's compounding impacts while still recovering from World War I and the Spanish flu aftermath.

As we will see, this trio of events combined to devastate US society, exposing appreciable vulnerabilities. Such exposure generated a deep desire for a group identity that would alleviate individual followers' insecurities. This resulting group affiliation allowed for cognitive and affective identification with Coughlin's movement by creating an argument based on fallacies: Coughlin's listeners were the victims and Jewish people were the perpetrators. Unfortunately, the media and methods by which information spread only strengthened these misguided views, leaving those exposed unguarded against demagogues.

Case Vignette and Historical Context

Father Coughlin was one of the US's early radio stars and remains among its most infamous antisemites (Figure 5.3). He leveraged the first mass media medium, the ubiquitous radio, to command a regular weekly audience of 15–20 million listeners throughout most of the 1930s, leaving an undeniable influence on US culture and politics for years to come. In addition to his weekly radio program, Father Coughlin published a weekly periodical and founded and directed the National Union for Social Justice, providing a platform for

Figure 5.2 Unemployed men gather during the Great Depression
Source: US National Archives and Records Administration, public domain

Figure 5.3 Charles Coughlin
Source: Photo by Craine, Detroit, via Library of Congress website, public domain

increasingly extreme hatred and calls for violence. He used his bully pulpit to mesh political populism, celebrity culture, and bigotry to a toxic degree, cheering on demagogues and rising to prominence as one of the US's most influential people [4].

Father Coughlin's rise coincided with the Great Depression, which left millions unemployed and homeless. By voicing the disarray and deprivation felt by his listeners, Coughlin provided what many thought a reassuring presence during a period of unprecedented economic uncertainty. Many blamed the Depression on President Herbert Hoover and the Republican Party; however, Coughlin blamed Jewish people, bankers, politicians, and communists, and he spread the theory that the US was under attack by the Russians. Father Coughlin began espousing the Judeo-Bolshevism conspiracy – alleging that Jewish people were the originators of the Russian Revolution and that they held primary power among the Bolsheviks who led the revolution – to feed into fears of Jewish people coming into power. He described American society as controlled by powerful "banksters," "plutocrats," "atheistic Marxists," and "international [commonly understood to mean Jewish] financiers," whom Coughlin blamed for the misfortune of everyday American citizens [5, p. 3068].

Coughlin offered simple solutions by blaming these groups and reinforcing nativist ideologies, calling for a crusade "against the anti-Christian forces of the red revolution" [6, p. 120]. A longstanding history of antisemitism and the exceptional achievement of American Jews in attaining mainstream success in the 1930s (e.g., Albert Einstein, Jack Benny, Hank Greenberg) provided Coughlin with ample fodder for scapegoating and reactionary rhetoric. Additionally, as his interests and ambition grew on America's largest and most powerful stage – national politics – he used his platform as a weapon to attack political opponents such as President Franklin D. Roosevelt. His sophisticated political attack campaign successfully sowed fear, uncertainty, and doubt in the minds of his listeners with ominous and fearful proclamations.

Father Coughlin recognized that religion could be as dynamic and popular as variety-hour entertainment, so he tailored his message and delivery accordingly. He spoke in what listeners considered a pleasant, familiar, and grandfatherly fashion, writing simply and directly and toning down his language and metaphors to be unassuming and human. Coughlin overemphasized certain vowels and purposely mispronounced words, giving his speeches dramatic flair. He mastered communication techniques such as quotable, memorable language, alliteration, and language that ignited visual imagery and imagination [4].

Early in life, Coughlin earned a reputation at the University of Toronto for his lengthy speeches and oratory abilities; his charisma was due, in part, to his appealing voice. Writer Wallace Stegner credited Father Coughlin's listenability to his dynamic baritone, which could range from a soothing soft tempo to soaring, passionate intensity. Stegner described Coughlin's voice as being of such "mellow richness, such manly, heartwarming, confidential intimacy, such emotional and ingratiating charm that anyone turning past it almost automatically returned to hear it again" [7, p. 90]. Arguably, Father Coughlin is considered to have possessed one of the greatest speaking voices of the twentieth century.

Among Father Coughlin's most devoted listeners were right-wing, working-class Catholic immigrants in New York and Boston. Catholics had been the subject of discrimination by Protestants in the US but were beginning to gain a foothold. Coughlin served as a spokesperson for a swelling populism drawn to his message of

Figure 5.4 Coughlin's *Social Justice* magazine
Source: Library of Congress, public domain

social and economic justice that he expertly exploited. However, as his message became more political and strayed into antisemitic conspiracy theories, his audience grew to include more white supremacist groups and other extremist organizations. He considerably influenced members of the Christian Front who were closely associated with pro-Nazi groups. Some of them believed the threat of Communism was so severe and imminent that any violent actions would be in self-defense and thus permissible under Christian teachings. Father Coughlin leaped to their defense despite the Front's violent plans to mount an antigovernment uprising and destroy Jewish-owned newspapers and stores. He supported them, claiming the arrest of Christian Front members by the FBI was a political plot. Instead of denouncing their violence and ideologies, he continued to incite them [4].

When CBS radio decided that Father Coughlin was crossing too many lines, he argued that nameless enemies were perpetrating an attack to thwart free speech. Although CBS dropped him from its broadcasting schedule, by 1932, he assembled his own network of 27 stations, financially supported by regular donations from his listeners [4]. Nevertheless, by the end of his radio career, his rhetoric had become so brazen and explicit that he was finally denounced as a fascist sympathizer and indisputable antisemite. Father Coughlin's *Social Justice* magazine (Figure 5.4) became almost indistinguishable from Nazi propaganda as it propagated the ideology propounded by the German propaganda minister Joseph Goebbels.

The National Association of Broadcasters (NAB) decided to pull the plug on Father Coughlin, banning radio broadcasters from continuing to sell airtime for his divisive religious or political commentary. After the NAB edict, Father Coughlin's syndicated network fell apart. The Roman Catholic Church hierarchy ordered him to return to his ministry in Royal Oak, Michigan, where he often spoke hatefully within the confines of his clerical pulpit [4]. Still, for decades, Coughlin's speeches and *Social Justice* articles would be circulated as neo-Nazi recruitment tools.

Henry Ford (Figure 5.5) influenced American politics similarly and was one of Coughlin's good friends and inspirations. Ford was best known for his revolutionary

Figure 5.5 Henry Ford
Source: United States Library of Congress Prints and Photographs division, under the digital ID cph.3b34530, public domain

Figure 5.6 Model T, 1908
Source: Ford Motor Company, public domain

work within the automobile industry, specifically with the assembly line [8]. An improved assembly line enabled Ford to make automobiles (the "Model T") affordable for citizens who otherwise could not afford them (Figure 5.6). This beneficial innovation was accompanied by a growing concern for the well-being of his employees. In response, Ford set a new wage for his workers: he increased their pay from $2.34 to $5.00 per day and reduced their workday by one hour [9]. While he informed his fellow industrialists that this act was strictly business, Ford's decision remarkably impacted his status in US society. Ford took advantage of his elevated social position to cultivate a new image of himself. He spoke about his journey to success as one of exceptional perseverance, as he overcame poverty and other obstacles. The accuracy of these claims is unreliable in light of Ford's sister's allegation that they were untruthful [9].

Despite this, Ford continued to amass a large following and acquire significant wealth. His popularity reached extraordinary levels, which, as with Coughlin, was

Figure 5.7 Charles Lindbergh
Source: Gale Family Library, Minnesota Historical Society, public domain

dangerous once he started to espouse antisemitic views. Coughlin and Ford relied on many of the same maneuvers to disseminate their views; for example, both utilized mass media to manipulate the public into perceiving Jewish people as threats.

When Henry Ford purchased *The Dearborn Independent*, he transformed it into a national platform through which his antisemitic ideas could be transmitted [10]. *The Dearborn Independent* was used to circulate a document known as The Protocols of the Elders of Zion, which contained false claims about Jewish people, whom it portrayed as craving control of the entire world. Once it became clear that *The Dearborn Independent* was merely a distribution center for antisemitism, Ford and his newspaper organization faced backlash. Following a libel suit against Ford, *The Dearborn Independent* shut down. Ford issued an apology in which he stated that it was never his intention to cause any harm to anybody or to appear prejudiced [9]. The apology was insufficient for some and came across as a poor attempt to salvage a threatened reputation.

Regardless of the motives behind Ford's actions, there is no doubt regarding their consequences. He served to influence individuals far beyond Charles Coughlin, including the genocidal demagogue Adolf Hitler [9]. Additionally, Ford was a good friend of Charles Lindbergh, who, as we will see, embarked on a path nearly identical to that of Coughlin and Ford.

Charles Lindbergh (Figure 5.7) served as a pioneer in the field of aviation. On May 21, 1927, he completed the first solo transatlantic flight from New York to France in 33.5 hours [11]. The moment forever changed both the possibilities for aviation and the trajectory of Lindbergh's life [12]. He was hailed as a hero for his courage and commitment (Figure 5.8). His rise to national prominence was reminiscent

Figure 5.8 Medals given to Lindbergh following his transatlantic flight
Source: *Chicago Tribune*, public domain

of Ford's, but with one significant difference: Lindbergh had risked his life, making his accomplishment, in the public's eye, all that more impressive.

Lindbergh's accomplishment awarded him a type of credibility that gave him tremendous power. For example, he and his wife, Anne, whom he married in 1929, visited Germany in 1936 to observe the German Air Force. They did so against the advice of Roger Strauss, chairman of the National Conference of Christians and Jews in the US [9]. Strauss warned Lindbergh that a visit of this nature could be interpreted as support for Hitler and his antisemitic regime. But Lindbergh did not seem concerned about the optics and went through with the trip. He even commented favorably afterward, seemingly praising Hitler and how Germany was being governed. His comments raised some concern in the US, but his role as an influential figure persisted.

The charismatic aviator also used his newfound celebrity status and power to advocate his isolationist views. Lindbergh believed the US shouldn't enter World War II since the country wasn't affected by it. He began to deliver speeches at the America First Committee (AFC) rallies in which he became increasingly vocal about his opposition to the war. The AFC was established to oppose US entry, and Lindbergh officially joined the organization in 1941 [13]. His speeches on behalf of the AFC, fueled by prejudice and antisemitism, contributed to his decline in popularity. Lindbergh's prime argument for opposing the war relied on the notion that it would destroy the white race, which needed protection [9]. He blamed Jewish people for instigating the war and attempting to drag the US into their conflict.

Despite Lindbergh's declining popularity, his words had severe repercussions. They contributed to an already rampant environment of antisemitism. The effects were devastating; when individuals of Coughlin, Ford, and Lindbergh's stature uttered hate-fueled rhetoric, many were inclined to believe them, regardless of how harmful or preposterous what was said may have been.

Characteristics of Leaders

Hate group leaders have several common characteristics: as demagogues, they elevate themselves through mass media; possess charisma and portray themselves as heroic; and may possess malignant narcissistic and messianic traits.

The Ford–Coughlin Connection: Mass Media–Elevating Demagogues

Henry Ford inspired Father Coughlin as the latter ascended to the role of a powerful demagogue. Coughlin's admiration stemmed in part from the knowledge that Ford, too, arose from humble origins, as Ford claimed to have grown up poor on a farm with four younger siblings. Coughlin believed that Ford epitomized the power a person could manifest through hard work, creativity, and access to avenues of amplification, such as mass media [4].

Ford acquired power that he would later employ to spew hateful, antisemitic propaganda, much as Coughlin did with the power and influence he amassed. Coughlin's views eventually became so hatefully direct and violent that his popularity dwindled. And while there are many plausible reasons for why Coughlin devolved into bigotry, some "prefer a psychological explanation, seeing him [Coughlin] as fitting the classical pattern of [an] antisemite, and pinpoint the influence of Henry Ford, a folk hero of the time and publisher of the American edition of 'The Protocols of the Elders of Zion,' a notorious forgery purporting to link Jews to a conspiracy for world domination" [14, p. 236]. Ford's influence on Coughlin was so strong that some associate this influence with Coughlin's ultimate career demise.

Both Ford and Coughlin had an avenue through which they could amplify their voices and diffuse hateful propaganda unrestrictedly. Initially a fan of the media, Ford was quick to denounce them once his public image took a turn for the worse following a failed peace mission to Europe in 1915, losing a race for a US Senate seat, and his involvement in two court cases.

He took an accusatory tone and declared that the press targeted him directly, twisting his words to spread lies about him [15]. Ford wanted a purely self-driven route to deliver his views: "What he sought, in effect, was a paper and print version of a megaphone: an instrument that would amplify – but not alter – what he wanted to say" [15, p. 19].

Consequently, Ford took matters into his own hands by purchasing *The Dearborn Independent*, a small newspaper, in the early 1920s. Ford was committed to constructing a national platform through this newspaper to reach thousands of ordinary people directly. He grew the publication and transformed it into one of the most accessed newspapers in the US. By giving antisemitism a platform of this magnitude, Ford contributed to an already antisemitic atmosphere that aimed to vilify Jews and cast them out of society [15].

Coughlin followed a modus operandi like that of his muse. For Coughlin, however, the radio was his megaphone. Coughlin's timing was impeccable – his tactic coupled economic uncertainty with the emergence of radio broadcasting in the early 1920s, marking the first time that messages could be transmitted to a large audience across vast distances [7]. Taking advantage of this new form of mass media worked in Coughlin's favor: In the 1930s, he boasted the title of the most listened-to radio speaker.

Further, Coughlin's use of the radio broadcast as a mass communication medium was instrumental in affecting and altering the views of many. A 2021 study found that counties with more exposure to Father Coughlin's broadcasting station gave less support to Franklin D. Roosevelt in the 1936 presidential election. The researchers conducted a falsification test to boost confidence in this study and isolate the findings to Coughlin's radio broadcasting. This test allowed them to conclude that their findings resulted specifically from exposure to Coughlin's radio station, as opposed to other influences [7, p. 3066].

Coughlin's attributes and the radio broadcasting station worked concurrently to help him amass a following and expand the significant influence he had. The Ford–Coughlin connection thus highlights the instrumental role that mass media play in the rise of demagogues and the creation of groups driven by hate.

The Lindbergh–Coughlin Connection: Exploiting Charisma and Heroism

Father Coughlin's acquisition of power wasn't solely a product of mass media communication. His success was the culmination of factors both tangible and intangible. Personal qualities, for instance, were paramount to his success and the success of many other individuals who contributed to the growing antisemitism in the United States, especially Henry Ford and Charles Lindbergh. Among the most notable similarities between these men were their charismatic personalities. Charisma, which was instrumental in powering their rise to fame, continues to be an asset for like-minded individuals, one powerful enough to elicit concern regarding individuals who can skillfully wield it in tandem with media savviness to manipulate public opinion for political gain [7]. Father Coughlin, Henry Ford, and Charles Lindbergh are prime examples of how charismatic personalities can galvanize movements characterized by hate, brutality, and prejudice.

With the whole world watching, Lindbergh completed a solo transatlantic flight from New York to France [8]. The success of his flight had an impact more significant than anyone could have ever imagined, Lindbergh included. In an instant, "Lindbergh achieved what no person, living or dead, has ever accomplished ... He has occupied the front page of every cosmopolitan newspaper in Europe and America ... he has made himself the hero of every son, the sweetheart of every daughter," stated one US senator [8, p. 74]. It was reverence for an individual to a degree never seen before, for a man who, through his humble persona, captivated the hearts of people everywhere [8].

America transformed Lindbergh into a hero who epitomized the country's perception of its perfect youth [8]. By this time, mass media were booming, making it easy to broadcast his charisma worldwide. New technology paved the way for important events to be recorded using methods and tools that could capture the dramatization and detail of such moments and be played for people throughout the globe [16]. The impact was powerful: "[F]or the first time all of civilization could share as one the sights and sounds of an event – almost instantaneously and simultaneously. And in this unusually good-looking, young aviator – of apparently impeccable character – the new technology found its first superstar" [16, p. 6].

This revered stature necessitated caution, as it came with tremendous power. Lindbergh's charisma and popularity allowed him to disseminate his agenda and narrative to the public. Lindbergh's followers readily accepted his words and beliefs, and his rhetoric contributed to a hostile atmosphere toward Jews. He found himself capable of exerting significant influence on the political climate of this time, despite his only credentials seeming to appear from the completed transatlantic flight [9].

Nevertheless, regardless of how Lindbergh acquired his "credentials," they were effective, and his use of them was destructive. In his public standing, he saw an opportunity to advance his isolationist policies to prevent American entry into World War II at the expense of the Jewish population in the US and worldwide. As the face of the AFC, Lindbergh delivered several speeches that emphasized the importance of defending the white race, which Hitler did not threaten: "[I]f the white race is ever seriously threatened, it may then be time for us to take our part in its protection, to fight side by side with the English, French, and Germans, but not with one against the other for our mutual destruction" [9, p. 209]. His overtly racist words were even more dangerous given his global reach. Lindbergh's speeches were regularly reproduced and disseminated in the US, Germany, Italy, and South America.

In one particularly harmful speech by Lindbergh at an AFC rally in Iowa, Lindbergh declared three groups responsible for potential American entry into the war: the Roosevelt administration, the Jewish population, and the British [8]. Among these groups, the Jewish population was the most criticized as Lindbergh accused them of ignorantly instigating a war that would harm them [16].

By blaming Jewish people for the situation that was unraveling, Lindbergh supplied antisemites and demagogues with ammunition. Arnold Foster, chief attorney of the Anti-Defamation League (ADL), which fought antisemitism, stated, "[w]e had come so far, yet with this one statement he did a tremendous amount of damage. Here was this so-called hero saying these things and it was like an invitation for antisemites to blame us" [9, pp. 290–91]. Foster understood the dangers of such a statement, specifically when delivered by a man of Lindbergh's notoriety.

In his Iowa speech, Lindbergh continued, "[t]their greatest danger to this country lies in their large ownership and influence in our motion pictures, our press, our radio and our government" [9, p. 290]. Yet, it was Lindbergh and other antisemites whose influence within the media and among the public posed a danger. And Lindbergh was undoubtedly aware that individuals held in high regard by the public had an exceptional capacity to charm, impress, and influence people. This self-awareness is evident when, upon convincing Henry Ford to grant his support to the AFC, he thanked him in a letter in which he acknowledged the personal power possessed by Ford: "[Y]our stand against entry into the war has already had great influence, and if we are able to keep out of it, I believe it will be largely due to the courage and support you have given us" [9, pp. 250–51].

Although there came a time when the media no longer defended Lindbergh, and many viewed him with disapproval, he still had a significant following and managed to do a great deal of damage before being questioned and distrusted. It was as if his charismatic personality and hero status granted him immunity against society's judgment. At one point, Lindbergh enchanted the entire world with his courage and modesty – he was a man who could do no wrong. Therefore, the threshold for what Lindbergh could do "wrong" was raised. His charisma and status undoubtedly helped him maintain such a large following, even once he began to share his racist sentiments. And it likely aided in his redemption.

But Lindbergh was not the first, or the last, example of how charismatic individuals use and abuse the devotional nature of the public to propagate ignorant views. One of Lindbergh's biggest fans, Father Charles Coughlin, wielded the same power. His charisma and oratory ability helped him become known as the Radio Messiah [5, p. 3065]. He, too, understood how to weaponize his charisma and elevated social status. Hence, he would reiterate Lindbergh's messages and employ Lindbergh's likeness to bolster the appeal and reach of his own antisemitic communication [16].

Father Coughlin also used his association with Henry Ford to disseminate his hateful rhetoric. The public regarded Ford as a hero after instituting a five-dollar workday. In addition, Ford had his own charm and charismatic style by "blend[ing] folksy wisdom with a homespun philosophy on life" on whatever subject he spoke about [9, p. 10]. However, when the topic turned antisemitic, the only thing that mattered was the person behind the spoken or written words; for the public, the name Henry Ford was its own form of authority and credibility. To fully grasp Ford's influence, it is necessary to recognize his relationships among the most famous antisemites: He was a good friend of Charles Lindbergh and a source of inspiration for Father Charles Coughlin and Adolf Hitler.

The Father Coughlin, Charles Lindbergh, and Henry Ford nexus demonstrates how influential people can use their charisma and elevated status to disseminate hate. History has shown us its damaging and destructive effects.

Malignant Narcissism and Malignant Messianism: Perceptions of Self and Salvation among Leaders

Malignant Narcissism

When evaluating the potential harm done by an individual aspiring to fame, it is worth considering whether they exhibit characteristics and traits associated with malignant narcissism. This syndrome, expounded upon by psychoanalyst Otto Kernberg, can be viewed as one of the "most vicious and dangerous form[s] of human orientation" [17, p. 23]. It entails an extreme self-perception of superiority, difficulty or inability to empathize with others, paranoid and antisocial conduct, and egosyntonic aggression [18]. The severe and intense consequences of malignant narcissism prevent the affected individual from existing peacefully among normal populations as they struggle to distinguish between reality and fantasy [19]. For this reason, a leader of this kind is most infectious among vulnerable people – those who have suffered economic, political, or social turmoil [20].

Aspiring leaders with malignant narcissistic traits may use their grandiosity and perceived superiority to grant followers a false sense of security by cultivating a new, dangerous group identity [20]. Sigmund Freud highlighted the perilous nature of this tendency by describing the typical behavior of a "masse," which is to allocate moral responsibility to the group's leader, allowing followers to live and act without moral constraint [20]. A leader who displays traits consistent with malignant narcissism will use this power irresponsibly – rationalizing violence against an out-group while dehumanizing them. In this way, followers (who have relieved themselves of moral responsibility) readily accept the leader's false self-depiction as morally virtuous.

French historian Jacques Semelin studied the genocides in Rwanda, Bosnia, and Germany [20]. Social turmoil exacerbated the tensions between social groups in all three instances. Aggressive, paranoid, and grandiose personality types came to power during these periods, personalities compatible with malignant narcissism. The dangers accompanying the ascension of leaders with these traits are profound, and we have seen its destructive effects throughout history [20]. In retrospect, many characteristics consistent with malignant narcissism are readily visible in demagogues like Adolf Hitler and

Charles Coughlin. One of the syndrome's defining characteristics, antisocial behavior, was exhibited by Hitler on multiple occasions.

We find examples of these traits in Hitler's public deceit concerning his plans for the Jewish population. Despite having delivered directions to exterminate Jewish people under his power, Hitler failed to address this subject with the public [20]. Likewise, Father Coughlin's actions and words displayed patterns consistent with traits characteristic of malignant narcissism via innuendo, or "dog whistles."

Charles Coughlin supported policies in Hitler's Nazi Germany and Mussolini's "Blackshirt" Italy [21]. Consequently, his broadcasts, often centered on politics and the economy as opposed to religion, were dubbed an adaptation of these policies for the American people [21]. In 1938, his *Social Justice* magazine reprinted weekly installments of the antisemitic text "The Protocols of the Elders of Zion." Although he denied being antisemitic, he received indirect funding from Nazi Germany during this period. He was described as "the German hero in America for the moment" with sympathetic statements toward Nazism, defending it as "a defensive front against Bolshevism" [22, p. 79]. Coughlin attempted to refute claims of his being an antisemite and a Nazi sympathizer: "I was accused of being un-American, a defender of Nazism, a sadist, and an anti-Semite" [4].

Confusion may arise from Coughlin's unwillingness to be associated with a title or organization that fervently favored his espoused views. But an understanding of malignant narcissism can help resolve this confusion. According to Kernberg, a unique challenge that comes with selecting good political leadership is that individuals with narcissistic and paranoid traits are often aware of the need to hide their true intentions and beliefs to "present themselves as open and friendly, attentive to others' wishes and needs, and disguise their resentful selfishness and self-absorption, and their true thinking, if the moment 'is not right'" [20, p. 22]. Coughlin likely recognized many Americans' distaste for the Nazi movement and knew he would not garner widespread favor by publicly supporting Hitler and the Nazis (Figure 5.9). At that moment, he realized that aligning himself with the Nazi cause would harm his movement rather than help it. So, whether Coughlin truly supported or agreed with Hitler's views and mission did not matter because he recognized that moment called for the concealment of such beliefs – the moment was "not right."

Malignant Messianism

Similarly, malignant messianism functions as an extension of malignant narcissism. Demagogues with malignant narcissistic traits often create a malignant messianic image, offering followers comfort as they confront vulnerabilities such as mortality. Messianism, which scholars usually understand in a religious context, especially among the Abrahamic faiths, creates a unique relationship between an individual and their followers that can quickly turn dangerous if abused. When a group designates an individual as their "messiah," it is in the belief that this person will bring about salvation in some form. The specific type of salvation can be subject to the group's needs and desires during a particular period. For instance, salvation may be perceived as economic relief during financial hardships. For Christians, Jesus as messiah will grant them redemption from sin. In Judaism, the belief in a messiah exists as well. However, the Jewish faith maintains the messiah has not yet arrived to bring eternal peace and accomplish his final task of assisting Jewish people (23). It is thus vital to note that the

Figure 5.9 Adolf Hitler
Source: Public domain

specific function of the messiah can vary between religious sects and certainly among different religions.

The longing for a messiah is strengthened in times of difficulty, which can expose significant vulnerabilities that leave people hungry for stability. Throughout history, when there has been a threat of political, social, or religious oppression, the desire for salvation and, consequently, the hope for a messiah becomes paramount [23]. Individuals have sometimes manipulated messianism to the degree that it became malignant to cater to agendas driven by hate, brutality, and injustice, as was the case for the most notorious antisemites and their followers during the twentieth century. Individuals like Father Charles Coughlin, Charles Lindbergh, Henry Ford, and, significantly, Adolf Hitler recognized the instability that consumed society because of the Great Depression, which brought fear, want, and insecurity. This vulnerability allowed these demagogues to promise salvation and immortality to a crowd that would receive the promises as music to their ears. Ultimately, it led to a perception of these individuals as potential messiahs. But in contrast to traditional religious messianism, in the context of hate groups, malignant messianism requires an out-group to direct hatred against and ultimately harm, even to the point of extermination.

The malignant messianic perception of Coughlin is evident from how his followers treated him. Coughlin's followers believed that their purpose was to spread the word of Father Coughlin by distributing his works, like his *Social Justice* periodical. Edwin Westphal, an especially devout follower, declared that the Father would oversee the reinstatement of America to the militant national Christian. Coughlin did not dispute depictions of him as a messiah; instead, he allowed the continuous portrayal of this image because he felt entitled to it. This attitude explains why Coughlin refused to concede to the demands of Archbishop Ed Mooney, which entailed reviewing Coughlin's works before publication. Coughlin was resolute in not allowing anyone to hinder or obstruct his path toward the recognition and acclaim he felt rightfully entitled to. Another of Coughlin's admirers, Roberto Farinacci, referred to him as an "apostle of Christianity," further perpetuating the image of Coughlin as a sacred being [4].

The malignant messianic perception among followers was a common trend among antisemites spewing hate. Henry Ford, for example, was deemed the "new Messiah" by a newspaper upon becoming an American hero – a hero who would later advocate for the destruction of Jewish people by asserting that they were a threat [8]. Lindbergh, too, claimed to hold the key to salvation, arguing that "we, the heirs of European culture, are on the verge of a disastrous war, a war within our own family of nations," that could be avoided by constructing a "Western wall of race and arms" [24, p. 173]. The tragic death of Lindbergh's baby also led several followers to parallel it with the death of Jesus and insinuate that it had been "for their sins" [16, p. 277]. Similarly, Hitler promised to save the German people from their vulnerabilities and mortality. He painted Jewish people as an obstruction to that goal to justify his extermination of them [11]. Leaders could sell these hollow promises by exploiting the public's perception of them in a malignant messianic light.

The mechanisms through which this malignant messianic perception comes to be, and followers readily come to accept it, are complex. But self-hatred and insecurity serve in some capacity as driving forces in the evolution of this relationship. Consider German doctors who joined the Nazi Party, an organization antithetical to the core value of healing among physicians. The doctors were not inclined to question the immorality of the Nazis' practices and beliefs because they "presented to the German people a solution to the doubt-ridden, tireless, Dostoevskian wrestling of the mind" by promising to alleviate insecurity and susceptibility to mortality [24, p. 3]. It was clear that mortality presented a grave threat to the Germans, and the fear and anxiety that surrounded it thus culminated in an obsession with immortality. They wanted salvation from this inevitable fate, and Hitler's promises provided a source of hope for this deliverance. Perhaps this fear of mortality made the German population so willing to accept the Jewish population as a threat. The Germans craved immortality to relieve the trepidation of being a "mortal being" [24]. In contrast, a standard component of Judaism is the denial of immortality and a concession that death is inevitable and must be accepted [25].

Germans also tended to use the Jewish population as an excuse for their shortcomings. By allocating blame elsewhere, they did not have to deal with the reality of their faults. For a familiar recent example of this dynamic, consider Eric Harris and Dylan Klebold. In April 1999, these individuals opened fire at Columbine High School in Littleton, Colorado, killing 12 students and a teacher. An analysis of the Littleton killers found connections to Nazism and emphasized the role of self-hatred in dictating the level of aggression the killers directed at their victims [26]. The killers' superficial mask of superiority could not conceal their true self-perception "as 'losers' being put down by their targets, conventionally regarded as 'winners'" [26].

Likewise, German doctors felt compelled to expel Jewish physicians from academia and professional leadership [25]. German doctors were suffering economically and, rather than addressing their fallibility, they found an alternative by blaming Jewish physicians. When insecure members of a group encounter a leader promising to free them from their insecurity, they discover a way to make sense of and justify anger and violence directed at those toward whom they express jealousy. This insecurity is transformed into a destructive "murderous group identity" [26].

Indeed, followers were compelled to view the leaders as malignant messiahs because it would make them valued contributors to what they perceived as a meaningful and admirable cause. It helped alleviate some of their insecurities to the point where their self-hatred became unwarranted self-worship, and they could delude themselves into feeling superior to their victims through a newly acquired group identity [26].

Self-hatred and insecurity are not confined to group followers but also apply to the leaders. In the end, Hitler himself could not bear defeat. In an odd twist of fate, when he could not cope with his failure to deliver promises of immortality to the German people, his mortality gave him an escape.

Characteristics of Followers

Victimization toward Self and Others: Impairing Moral Judgment and Rationalizing Acts of Violence

Victimization, as defined by the American Psychological Association, is "the act or process of singling someone out for cruel or unfair treatment, typically through physical or emotional abuse" [27]. Leaders and followers of antisemitic groups and initiatives in the twentieth century provide an extraordinary example of how victimization is used to create false pretenses that unite a community of people to partake in a common goal. Followers disposed toward self-victimization are susceptible to joining cults and hate groups. This tendency to victimize oneself, particularly as it relates to cults, is analogous to the kind observed in patients with factitious disorder, who feign or self-induce illness to elicit sympathy or fulfill a psychological craving to be perceived as sick or injured [28]. The willingness of Germany's citizens to aid in the formation of a Nazi Germany and to worship Hitler presents a notorious example of this tendency.

The Nazi Party strategically manipulated the public into believing that Jewish people posed a risk to German citizens' physical health. Propaganda to perpetuate this idea included distributing posters whereby Jews were seen holding animals commonly associated with disease and filth, including rats and snakes [25]. Thus, the Nazis spread the belief that the Jewish population had to be exterminated to ensure protection and self-preservation against feared illnesses.

Further, the looming prospect of war, followed by its grim reality, presented challenges for the Nazis that they addressed by conducting horrific experiments on Jewish people [25]. One of these challenges was "hostile thermal environments" [25, p. 477]. To tackle this issue, the Nazi Party subjected Jewish people to experimentation that often resulted in the drowning or freezing to death of both Jewish and Russian captives [25]. These experiments aimed to discover ways to prevent hypothermia and better handle bitter weather. It was an unheard-of form of cruelty, rationalized as necessary to address the ordeals faced by Nazi soldiers, despite such threats being the product of a war instigated by the Nazis' leader, Adolf Hitler. Instances like these, of which there were many, illuminate how Hitler and his followers led much of the German public to perceive themselves as the victims and the Jewish population as the antagonists.

But the tendency toward self-victimization alone does not account for what compelled so many humans to partake in genocide. An additional explanation can be found in the emotions that could be quieted through perceived victimization – emotions like guilt, which had to be suppressed to accept Hitler's nefarious practices and beliefs [29]. Many Germans saw Hitler as an omnipotent figure through whom they could idealize and stabilize their fragile self-esteem [30]. He enabled troubled German citizens to disperse blame and find a solution for the misfortunes of their lives. From their perspective, the perceived threats against the "pure" German population posed by Jewish people constituted a justification for Hitler's brutal and finally murderous conduct toward them.

Alleviating Germans' feelings of guilt removed the necessity for accountability and the capacity to recognize injustice and rectify wrongs [29]. Alexander Mitscherlich, a German psychoanalyst who wrote *The Inability to Mourn*, touched upon how the "pathology of repression, denial, and projection [allowed] the Germans as a people [to dissociate] themselves from crisis of conscience or threats to self-esteem" [31, p. 328]. Repressing certain emotions results in passivity, and the adoption of an apathetic stance enabled the practices by which Hitler first assumed control [31].

Under these circumstances, perceived victimization, however unwarranted, predisposes people to become involved with groups of hate by laying to rest any internal moral conflict. The leader resolves followers' conflictual beliefs, and their attendant anxieties, by mirroring and thereby highlighting and magnifying hateful views. As the followers, in turn, mirror the leader, their tentative or questionable beliefs become unquestionable convictions and then delusions.

This use of victimization is observed in many demagogues, including Charles Coughlin. Coughlin lauded "The Protocols of the Elders of Zion," which framed Jewish people as planning to take over the world [32]. He defended the persecution of Jews by asserting that Christians were the initial victims of persecution [32]. It did not matter that Coughlin denied being an antisemite or created distance from Nazi organizations such as the German American Bund. Convincing his followers that Jewish people were threatening them gave rise to a victimhood mentality. As Hitler and the Nazis amply demonstrated, this mentality obscured the moral repercussions of the acts committed against Jewish people.

How Resilience and Group-Identity Formation Become Toxic during Catastrophic Times

The Great Depression plagued society with fear and insecurity, revealing vulnerabilities among residents and systemic structures. Life became volatile as this event uncovered the insecurity that often resides within economic systems and organizations [33]. The impact was so profound that many likely endured poverty-related psychological trauma [34]. This economic uncertainty and insecurity predisposed some of those individuals to accept the fallacious and violent rhetoric of Father Charles Coughlin.

One potential explanation for this predisposition is the realistic group conflict theory, which touches upon the relationship between economic difficulty and increased discrimination and prejudice [35]. Individuals and groups of people become more willing to act unfairly to help alleviate the burdens they face themselves. For this reason, when confronted by conflict over material goods, individuals in a group tend to blame members of a different group. Competition heightens the desire to identify an obstacle in order to construct a solution for its perceived consequences. In a study conducted by Muzafer Sherif in 1954, researchers found that when two groups of fifth-grade boys were pitted against each other in a series of competitions for a reward, such as a tug-of-war, they became increasingly aggressive and began to perceive the other team as an obstruction to their reward, and thus as an enemy [35]. This study exemplifies how times of stress, loss, and competition increase the ease with which humans turn on others.

To strengthen confidence in this theory and recognize its application to followers of Coughlin and other antisemites and racists, consider America during the post-Civil War era. During the Reconstruction Era, the government attempted to put the country back together by readmitting the Southern States and integrating African Americans into the legal framework of society [36]. However, in a country devastated by the Civil War, the main concern became reestablishing equilibrium between Northern and Southern states for political and economic stability. Consequently, many Northerners adopted a new viewpoint, portraying black suffrage as problematic for the South. Northerners permitted more racial antagonism and oppression than they would have without socioeconomic instability [37]. This example further illustrates how vulnerability can make certain groups more willing to engage in or tolerate biased and discriminatory perceptions and practices.

Followers of Coughlin were especially vulnerable, as the Great Depression was preceded by two other catastrophic events: World War I and the Spanish flu. These three misfortunes compounded to form an existential threat people had to face. They confronted severe and diverse concerns: loss of life, economic hardship, political instability, and unpredictability. Consequently, individuals and families experienced helplessness, fear, and despair, allowing many vulnerabilities to surface.

In only a few weeks, New York City and Philadelphia mourned the loss, respectively, of 33,000 and 13,000 lives due to the Spanish flu [38]. In as little as four months, the pandemic had killed at least 21 million people worldwide. The world had suffered a death toll greater than both world wars combined. The situation was so dire that some families starved because their primary provider was ill or deceased. At this point, many could no longer deny the gravity of the situation. They recognized that despite an initial attempt to keep the war at the forefront of consciousness, another problem of equal magnitude had arisen [39]. These two overlapping events devastated the country and the world.

Eventually, the Allies were victorious, and the Spanish flu ran its course. However, while both catastrophic events appeared to resolve, their impact was long-lasting [40]. Calamities like these rob survivors of a healthy sense of security and personal agency, making them more susceptible to humiliation and avoiding professional help [41]. Moreover, people faced another catastrophe only a decade later: the Great Depression.

Survivors of this kind of trauma must proceed through a grieving process. Unfortunately, this grieving process can sometimes devolve from healthy grieving into complex grieving [42]. Under these circumstances, the grief pathway can become pathological and amplify symptoms like poor self-esteem, insecurity, guilt, and a fixed conviction of defeat [42]. It often brings about feelings of guilt on behalf of a loved one who has passed or for circumstances of a tragedy or hardship that are out of the individual's control [42]. Unfortunately, this toxic mentality has predisposed many individuals to the rhetoric of demagogues like Father Charles Coughlin.

Father Coughlin was an influential religious figure who viewed the collective vulnerability of Americans as an opportunity to impose his views. He preyed on their emotional, mental, and physical instability and, in the eyes of his followers, served "as a champion of the poor, a foe of big business, and a critic of federal indifference in the face of widespread economic distress," appealing to both the worries and desires of struggling Americans [43].

He provided his audience with a scapegoat, the Jewish population, and he crafted a false and hate-filled narrative for the scapegoat to account for the difficulties specific to this period, including economic anguish. His periodical *Social Justice* became filled with baseless allegations that Jewish people were in control of the financial institutions in America [43]. The vulnerable condition of Coughlin's followers enabled them to conform more easily to the narrative he spread about the Jewish population. Such conformity offered simplicity under complex conditions characterized by chaos, uncertainty, and variability – "stereotypes provide us with those simpler models that allow us to deal with the 'great blooming, buzzing confusion of reality'" [35, p. 767]. It formatted the world in a way that avoided ambiguity, offering stable permanence in place of unstable transience. The picture he painted was simple in that society was composed of "good" and "bad" individuals; in doing so, he cultivated an "us" versus "them" mentality.

By imposing this mentality, Father Coughlin nurtured a sense of community and group identity among his followers. Unsurprisingly, this feeling of community and group identity was in high demand as many individuals grappled with their sense of self. The threefold catastrophe of the Spanish flu, World War I, and the Great Depression transformed the lives of individuals into one entirely foreign to them; for instance, men who were previously accustomed to providing for their families could no longer do so because of the unemployment that resulted from the Great Depression [34].

Experiences like these lead to feelings of shame, embarrassment, and guilt, thus heightening the desire to belong to a community and identify with a group. This desire occurs because forming a group identity can help regulate self-esteem. Social identity theory explains how self-esteem derives from the standing and achievements of the various groups we affiliate with, instead of only personal accomplishment [35]. For this reason, members of a particular group, the "in-group," are more likely to degrade an "out-group." For Coughlin and his followers, White Catholics were the "in-group" and Jewish people constituted the "out-group."

Once individuals join a group or cult, it becomes challenging to leave. This difficulty can be partly attributed to followers' dependence on the group or its leader, compelling them to stay despite any threats [44]. Coughlin exploited the vulnerabilities of his followers to manipulate them into remaining loyal and dedicated to his cause. And it worked – belonging to Coughlin's group of followers became an identity for many of them.

Social identity theory also maintains that "group memberships are part of every individual's identity. If so, then people will often be motivated to denigrate outgroup members not just when they personally are under threat, but when their groups are" [35, p. 765]. This dynamic increases the likelihood of an individual experiencing deindividuation – whereby they partake in collectively violent activities they would not perpetrate on their own. The consequences of their actions appear to be reduced when it is not just they, but their entire group that engages in those actions [35].

In sum, social identity theory provides a framework for understanding how the vulnerable state of Coughlin's followers made them more susceptible to his rhetoric and manipulation. He provided them with a solution to cope with financial and other tangible uncertainties, such as unemployment, while also tackling mental, emotional, and intangible insecurities, such as self-esteem and postcatastrophe mental health struggles. Affiliation with Coughlin became a quick fix for aloneness, helplessness, deprivation, grief, fear, and uncertainty. It established a group identity that provided community, strength, and an intoxicating sense of supremacy, entitlement, and security. Yet, the cost was high, including a dangerous dependence on demagogues and their shallow models for making violent sense of an inherently uncertain world.

The Spread of Information among Followers Reinforced Their Views

The evolution of mass media confers enormous societal benefits. But accompanying it is the threat of immoral and harmful view solidification and rationalization of vicious aggression. The destabilization compounded by the motto of "bad news sells" became evident as early as the Great Depression, when it was through the use of mass media that Coughlin acquired so much power. Thus, as it assumed ubiquity in the 1930s, people experienced the dual nature of mass media, which could result in either liberation or in entrapment via fear-mongering and scapegoating vulnerable minority groups, with calamitous consequences [45].

Radio's power, therefore, lay in its ability to serve not only as a megaphone for Coughlin and other demagogues but also as a demonstration of future harms: "[T]he modern culture that radio represented threatened to overpower individuals, leaving them with little control either in their own lives or in the wider world" [45, p. 3]. While some individuals can resist this effect, many do not. Instead, they become dominated by the desire to reinforce views that are favorable to oneself or to find information that validates rather than threatens existing beliefs [46].

This self-serving psychological bias can help explain why Coughlin's followers were so receptive to him as a news source. Given conditions that induced low self-esteem and insecurity, many understandably tuned into Coughlin's rather than an opposing figure's radio broadcasts. To cope with their threatened self-image, many of Coughlin's followers enchanted themselves into believing they were not at fault. Coughlin was a friendly voice over the radio who would validate this tale and construct a favorable, self-exculpating narrative (i.e., the Jewish population serving as antagonists and instigators of society's ailments).

Another famous example of delusion based on mass media's fear-mongering (intentional or otherwise) is Orson Welles' "War of the Worlds" radio broadcast in 1938, a fictional account of Martians attempting to destroy humanity. This radio program became a major historical event because of the panic it caused. Listeners devolved into chaos, with some even contemplating suicide rather than being murdered by Martians [45].

Within moments, a voice on the radio convinced a population that imminent death awaited them. In his effort to make an outlandish fantasy sound dramatically convincing, as now seems clear, Welles unintentionally triggered a public hysteria with nothing more than his imagination and the media at his disposal. American journalist Dorothy Thompson explained that this event revealed "the appalling dangers and enormous effectiveness of popular and theatrical demagoguery" [47]. Rather than demonizing Welles for his charade, Thompson expressed gratitude to him "for having made the most amazing and important contribution to the social sciences. For Mr. Orson Welles and his theater have made a greater contribution to an understanding of Hitlerism, Mussolinism, Stalinism, anti-Semitism" [47].

What Are Hate Groups?

The critical commonality among the followers and leaders discussed in this chapter is that they can be generally categorized as belonging to a hate group. To clarify the definition of a hate group and how it relates to our definition of a cult is a complex task, since there are many organizations with their own definition of a "hate group," creating a broad range of meanings with overlapping interpretations.

The Office of Justice, for example, defines a hate group as a collection of individuals who share a commonality concerning their prejudices or fears [48]. They seek a quick fix for issues they encounter, which often entails finding an easy target in populations with differing demographics from the hate group, such as a contrasting religion or race. Similarly, the FBI defines a hate crime as a criminal offense committed toward someone or against property, with an incentive that stems, whether partly or entirely, from "an offender's bias(es) against a: race, religion, disability, sexual orientation, ethnicity, gender [or] gender identity" [49]. The Southern Poverty Law Center (SPLC), an organization dedicated to combating white supremacy and advancing human rights, provides another variation on the definition [50]. According to the SPLC, a hate group is an organization inhabited by beliefs or operations that target entire populations of people "through its official statements or principles, the states of its leaders, or its activities" and generally "for their immutable traits" [50].

Within all these definitions, an element of direct discrimination can be found – that is, hatred directed against an individual or group, rooted in some sort of bigotry against a particular feature or demographic. This understanding aligns well with our definition of a cult, a social group that is characterized by its philosophical views and shared behaviors or that has in common an interest in a specific individual, object, or goal that differs from its own – for instance, a group that is interested in denigrating a particular demographic. Cults encourage the survival of idiosyncratic beliefs among their members regardless of disproof. In this way, some cults may be perceived as cults of hatred. They direct their anger and violence toward a particular demographic or value that deviates from theirs. For Coughlin and his followers, that demographic was the Jewish population. Despite a lack of evidence to support the harmful claims circulated about Jewish people at the time, those beliefs persisted. Such enduring beliefs can be attributed to the strong unity these groups achieve by fostering shared values and objectives. This feature is essential to note since the last part of our definition of "cult" holds that these beliefs persist, but not mainly because of a major mental disorder.

From these three organizations alone, we see how, despite similar underlying components, formulating a single definition for hate groups can be challenging. The absence of a consensus definition introduces uncertainty, making it difficult to designate organizations as hate groups and thereby oppose their prejudicial practices. This lack of consensus is especially problematic since organizations rarely self-identify as hate groups, leaving that designation to be made by external sources. Moreover, this label may arouse hostility in some groups, creating another source of contention that can lead to legal issues. The SPLC's entanglement with the Coral Ridge Ministry offers an excellent example of this dilemma.

The Coral Ridge Ministry, a Christian organization committed to sharing its views with the public, sued SPLC for defamation [51]. Coral Ridge applied for AmazonSmile in 2017, which would have allowed it to receive contributions from Amazon customers as a nonprofit organization. However, the organization learned it could not participate in the program because SLPC had designated it as a "hate group." The SPLC accused Coral Ridge of being anti-LGBT due to its stance on homosexuality. Coral Ridge argued that SPLC knew it was not a hate group but decided to identify it as one anyway. In response, SPLC argued that its designation of Coral Ridge as a hate group was permissible under the First Amendment. The court ultimately ruled in favor of SPLC, arguing that there was not enough evidence that the organization "acted with actual malice," nor was the hate group label "provably false" due to the varied and ambiguous interpretations of "hate group" [51, p. 2454].

Despite the controversy and ambiguity present in hate group designation, it remains a vital instrument for keeping track of groups that potentially pose a threat to the well-being of others. It promotes vigilance to counter the rise of movements like those discussed in this chapter. Organizations such as the SPLC and ADL continually monitor groups and incidents related to hatred and prejudice. The SPLC identified 1,225 hate and antigovernment organizations throughout America in 2022. These organizations range from anti-immigrant to hate music [52].

Moreover, the ADL has a map that enumerates incidents related to hate, extremism, antisemitism, and terrorism [53]. From 2020 to 2023, the ADL tracked approximately 26,193 such incidents in the United States. These numbers speak to the many manifestations of hate groups and the presence and persistence of threats against the objects of their hatred. For instance, the Ku Klux Klan is one of the more well-known race-based hate groups, while QAnon, which believes a "Deep State" controls society, is an example of a more recent, internet-based hate group [54].

While each hate group is unique regarding what motivates it and whom it chooses to attack, John R. Schafer and Joe Navarro have developed a model to better understand their etiology and evolution [55]. In this model, a hate group progresses through seven stages. In the first and second stages, the group gathers and defines itself. In the third, fourth, and fifth stages respectively, the group disparages, taunts, and attacks the target without weapons. In the sixth stage, the group uses weapons to attack. In the final stage, the target is destroyed.

This model accounts for and is consistent with much of the phenomena observed among followers of Coughlin, Ford, Lindbergh, and Hitler. These groups offered individuals an identity wherein they could find solace and comfort. Although the antisemitic movement appeared to begin with a seemingly harmless distribution of ignorant and ridiculous tales about Jewish people, it evolved into something far more dangerous and destructive. Verbal violence evolved into physical attacks. For the Nazis, this evolved into outright genocide. Such historical events reveal the perilous nature of the seven-stage model. However, as its authors point out, early identification of a hate group can help develop programs to intervene and disrupt this process [55].

Leaving a hate group is a challenging endeavor. Many former members of hate groups experience psychological hardships following their departure [56]. Nevertheless, researchers have found that disengagement and deradicalization can contribute to a person's decision to exit such groups. For instance, disengagement occurs when a member renounces the obligations of their role in the group, which the member now views as unacceptable. Deradicalization takes this a step further – rather than merely creating a physical distance between the group and individual, deradicalization alters a person's belief system. With disengagement and deradicalization, the individual creates physical and mental separation from their former group.

Push and pull factors also encourage individuals to renege on their affiliation with hate groups. Disagreeing with the group's violent practices is an example of a push factor, whereas a pull factor could be a desire to interact with members outside of one's group. Other factors that may contribute to a person's decision to exit are "self-reflection that results from contact with law enforcement and the experience of incarceration" [57, p. 14].

However, research in this area is minimal, and more effective methods than incarceration likely exist [57]. What is certain, however, is that exiting hate groups is a complicated and understudied process. It is difficult to say with certainty what compels an individual to escape, but initially promising research has shown that these are likely contributing factors to a person's decision.

Conclusion

In hate groups, the relationship between leader and followers is a process of reciprocal mirroring, a dynamic recognized in neoclassical psychoanalytic explorations that have largely been lost as psychoanalysis became Americanized [58]. Any human being has conflictual feelings and beliefs. We all have the capacity to love and to hate, often both simultaneously. Conflict leads to anxiety and fear, and the conflictual beliefs from which anxiety and fear can arise are the raw material for hate group leaders. Rather than create new views for followers to adopt, the leader takes beliefs that may not yet be fixed in followers' minds and brings them to the forefront, making them more intense and ultimately dominant. The leader turns followers' tentative or questionable beliefs into unquestionable convictions and delusions, as one might persuade someone to make a place they have visited their permanent residence.

As the leader holds up a mirror that highlights and magnifies the hateful side of followers' beliefs, followers start to mirror the leader, to see themselves as the leader sees them. The cult of hate (like a cult of love) becomes a funhouse of mirrors in which only what is reflected in monstrous size and shape is seen. Beliefs that are not reflected and magnified are no longer held, and feelings that are not reflected and magnified are no longer felt.

Now more than ever, we must remain vigilant of our present-day vulnerabilities, as we have seen historically how demagogic leaders can exploit psychosocial vulnerabilities in order to disseminate destructive agendas and amass power. Present-day society remains susceptible to conditions and individuals like those that emerged in the first half of the twentieth century. For instance, the coronavirus pandemic subjected the global population to the brutal consequences of a public health emergency. These conditions are like those that occurred during the Spanish flu in 1918. In both instances, a shortage of healthcare professionals exacerbated the physical and psychological impacts of the pandemic [34].

Additionally, much as Coughlin's followers were desperately searching for a scapegoat to account for the suffering produced by the triple catastrophe, COVID-19 evoked a similar reaction. The pandemic resulted in increased violence and discrimination against the Asian population as Asian communities were accused of creating and spreading the coronavirus and faced consequent bigotry [44]. This turn of events strongly recalls how Jewish people have been falsely libeled for centuries for spreading disease and how notorious antisemites like Coughlin have destructively amplified this false narrative.

Hate-filled rhetoric has not been confined to the pandemic context but instead has spread into all realms of society. A violent display of hatred erupted at the highest levels of politics when, on January 6, 2021, rioters stormed the US Capitol because they were unhappy with the presidential election results, which designated Joe Biden as the president-elect [59]. Some attackers came from organizations such as the Proud Boys, which SLPC identified as a hate group. This attack left five people dead and many more injured. It was the first time a Confederate flag had entered the US Capitol [56]. Many individuals identified as rioters were also present at another violent rally in Charlottesville, Virginia, on August 11, 2017. This rally consisted of white supremacists marching and reciting chants such as "Jews will not replace us" [60]. One neo-Nazi, James Fields, went so far as to drive a car into a crowd of counter-protesters, killing a 32-year-old woman named Heather Heyer.

These instances are only a few of many. Both cases highlight how far individuals are willing to go in their beliefs when the elements of fear and personal threat are employed along with the mobilizing force of mass media. While such phenomena have been observed throughout many historical events, their occurrence has not diminished. The dangers of mass media–mobilized hate remain ever present, with an even more significant number of avenues through which it can manifest. With social media platforms like Facebook, Instagram, and X (Twitter), the dislocations incited or exacerbated by mass media during the Great Depression are now an even more pressing risk. Social media algorithms push content to users that they are more likely to engage with based on their previous behavior. Consequently, individuals inclined toward extremist content are usually served more of the same, further entrenching them in their beliefs and isolating them from diverse and dissenting perspectives.

Researcher C. Thi Nguyen explains the unique dangers presented by modern-day media sources through two concepts known as *epistemic bubbles* and *echo chambers.* Nguyen defines an epistemic bubble as "a social epistemic structure which has inadequate coverage through a process of exclusion by omission" [61, p. 143]. Thus, an epistemic bubble atmosphere operates by prohibiting information that opposes what the environment favors. Such an environment is cultivated by a desire to strengthen already established views. Coughlin's followers became entrapped in an epistemic bubble when they made individuals like Coughlin, Ford, Lindbergh, and other notorious antisemites their only or primary source of information. Another source of epistemic bubbles is algorithmic filtering by modern media sources [61].

Nguyen emphasizes an essential distinction between epistemic bubbles and echo chambers in that echo chambers actively seek to discredit other sources of information rather than just prohibit their entrance. Under these circumstances, members may face exposure to other sources but are hesitant and unwilling to consider what those sources say. This occurs because they have been led to believe that information that comes from those external sources lacks validity.

Father Coughlin created an echo chamber by stripping the opposition of credibility, such as attacking President Franklin D. Roosevelt while he was running for a second term as president of the US. For instance, "[h]e criticized President Roosevelt and attacked the government's fiscal policy in the aftermath of the Depression" [62]. This tactic likely deterred many followers from logical contemplation of alternatives, such as the possibility that Jewish people were not at fault for their problems and that, at their core, the challenges accompanying the Great Depression were systemic.

We must recognize how group identities are cultivated from hatred so that we can mitigate the harmful consequences of their formation. This challenge is even more critical from a contemporary perspective as we attempt to combat the diffusion of toxic rhetoric by influential individuals facilitated by more expansive media. Technology and media are used to a greater degree than ever before and will continue to evolve. As we have seen, these tools can be used to perpetrate real harms and must therefore be protected against weaponization.

The stories of Father Coughlin, Charles Lindbergh, and Henry Ford offer parallels and precedents to the social media and digital-age debates over the limits of free expression [63]. New digital and social media make it easier for charismatic individuals to gain influence. Social media companies have profited by segmenting users into information bubbles fueled by algorithms designed to increase engagement, often driven by outrageous and inflammatory stories. Although the media have changed, the narratives remain painfully familiar.

We hope that through an analysis of historical figures and events, the parallels between past and present dangers are made apparent so that these threats can be confronted. By recognizing the avenues and methods through which these dangers come to manifest, we can be better prepared to address them before they jeopardize the stability of democratic society.

Finally, emerging areas of neuropsychiatric research can shed light on the mechanisms and pathways by which followers bond with leaders who act as malignant compounding mirrors, magnifying and distorting. These areas of study include brain-wave synchronization or "mind meld," whereby a leader fomenting a mob can be understood as a pathological variant of the neural bonding or alignment that occurs in normal interpersonal and social interaction [64]. From a cognitive linguistic perspective, the leader's rhetorical devices (e.g., dehumanizing metaphors) can "switch on" fear-driven biochemical responses in listeners whose neural pathways are already wired to believe rather than critically assess emotionally laden but factually unsupported statements. Absent the development of neural mechanisms for receiving and considering contradictory evidence, these beliefs harden into enduring convictions [65].

Summary

In his emotional rhetoric, blending religion, politics, and entertainment, Father Coughlin, supported by Henry Ford's capital, pioneered a form of intoxicating amusement for his followers – the reactionary, personalistic radio show – later emulated by Rush Limbaugh and Alex Jones [66]. Coughlin used tactics such as self-victimization to pull on the heartstrings of his listeners, for instance, by claiming he was a victim of injustice when the KKK burned a cross outside his chapel. Although he told this story numerous times, and the media reported it, there is no evidence that the publicized cross-burning occurred. Nevertheless, facts would not impede Father Coughlin's provocative rhetoric.

Research has shown that a charismatic individual can manipulate the media to influence political behavior. For instance, Wang found evidence that places more exposed to Father Coughlin's antisemitic and isolationist broadcasts in the late 1930s were more likely to form a local branch of the pro-Nazi German American Bund and sold fewer war bonds during World War II [5]. Similarly, Charles Lindbergh used his brave aviator allure to advocate for isolationism to keep the United States from entering World War II. He did so by delivering harmful speeches that targeted the Jewish population on behalf of the America First Committee [16]. Given the popularity of Coughlin and Lindbergh with the media and their well-liked personas, their words had a devastating impact.

Elements of malignant narcissism typically present themselves among such charismatic demagogues. Coughlin defended the Nazis and their practices by claiming that Hitler's antisocial behavior was required to help defeat Bolshevism; essentially, Coughlin justified it as a necessary evil. But despite all his support, Father Coughlin still tried to distance himself from the Nazi movement. One component of malignant narcissism entails recognizing when the moment is not right to take a particular action, and Coughlin acknowledged that such an association would merely diminish his popularity with the American people.

A malignant messianic perception of demagogues evolved in the twentieth century as an outgrowth of malignant narcissism. Leaders like Coughlin and Ford provided a calming and confident presence in times of difficulty. Insecurity was a persistent struggle among the population. Consequently, the belief that these leaders could deliver salvation provided comfort. For example, German doctors who feared mortality easily fell victim to Hitler's promises of immortality. This kind of idolatry also occurred among Coughlin's, Ford's, and Lindbergh's followers. It contributed to the success of their movements while encouraging the elimination of an out-group.

Followers – that is, individuals who felt compelled to engage with these groups – also shared many characteristics. The idea of victimization, for example, was often used to justify the atrocities committed against the Jewish population. Developing a victimhood mentality enabled followers to believe Jewish people threatened their well-being, making violence directed at Jews morally permissible. Hitler even persuaded the German people that Jewish people posed a direct threat to their physical health.

During this upheaval, many people experienced a crisis of insecurity. Followers of Coughlin struggled with World War I, the Spanish flu, and the Great Depression, which led to economic and psychosocial instability. As the realistic group conflict theory outlines, such an environment increases the risk that hate groups will arise and cause harm. For example, Coughlin provided simplicity during a time of great uncertainty and suffering. By offering his followers a new community they could identify with, Coughlin helped relieve their insecurities. Social identity theory explains how people can alleviate their individual self-esteem issues by celebrating their group's claimed or perceived achievements as their own.

The strategies employed by hate group leaders, coupled with the vulnerabilities of followers, facilitated the formation and propagation of hate groups in the twentieth century. Defining a hate group can be challenging given its subjective nature, but in all its definitions, one common feature remains: Hate groups target a specific demographic different from their own. Apart from this commonality, the concept's ambiguity can present challenges due to a lack of consensus. Nevertheless, the hate group designation is essential for tracking and countering potential harms – for example, by supporting the disengagement and deradicalization that are helpful strategies for exiting a hate group.

Key Points

- Leaders can use mass media and information dissemination in two very different ways: one can polarize and harm society, while the other can work toward its advancement.
- Sometimes, the most potent weapons leaders of hate groups leverage are intangible – a charismatic and courageous persona, for example, can immunize an individual from the consequences of their damaging rhetoric.
- Leaders of hate groups typically are aware of their power and influence, allowing them to strategically plan how to utilize that power in service of their personal goals.
- Insecurity is one of the most significant risk factors for being predisposed to follow demagogues and their agendas.
- Political, social, and economic instability creates environments that are vulnerable to power-hungry individuals, and it is during these times that vigilance is of utmost importance.
- Individuals are sometimes idolized to an unhealthy and destructive degree, evidenced by how leaders like Coughlin, Ford, and Lindbergh were perceived in a messianic light.
- Psychodynamically informed social theories can help better explain why individuals behave the way they do and join hate groups.
- It is possible for an individual's grieving process to undergo complications and result in a strengthened negative self-perception.
- Justifications used by members of hate groups are commonly grounded in a victimhood mentality. This mindset enables the repression of certain emotions, like guilt, which relieves followers of their actions' moral repercussions.
- In hate groups, the relationship between leader and followers can be understood as a process of reciprocal mirroring. The leader reflects and magnifies the hateful, fear-driven side of followers' conflictual beliefs, while followers, mirroring the leader, come to see themselves as the leader sees them. In this house of mirrors, tentative or questionable beliefs become unquestionable convictions and then delusions.
- Hate groups, especially those that adhere to ideologies such as white supremacy, frequently justify their hatred by framing it as an existential battle. They adopt credos like "we shall not be replaced" to express this viewpoint.
- Hate groups remain a fundamental threat to a democratic society and can take many variations based on race, ethnicity, culture, gender, religion, sexual orientation, or gender identity. The SPLC helps keep track of designated hate groups throughout the country.
- Technology can amplify the challenges faced by hate groups through epistemic bubbles and echo chambers, reinforcing and validating hateful mentalities and baseless accusations.
- The dangers posed by demagogues throughout history, such as Adolf Hitler and Charles Coughlin, remain ever present, as manifested by contemporary hate group leaders and influencers.

- There is no academic consensus for what constitutes a hate group, which presents ambiguity around its definition, thereby leaving room for conflict in the designation of hate groups.
- Departing from a hate group can be difficult. Still, research has shown that disengagement and deradicalization are important steps. The former creates a physical distance between the individual and the group, whereas the latter generates an ideological and emotional distance. It is also necessary to address the underlying aloneness, fear, and helplessness that make people vulnerable to the appeal of hate groups.
- The success of movements driven by hate is dependent upon multiple factors. But the strategies and characteristics common among both leaders and followers work in tandem with one another to create the perfect storm.

References

1. Office of the Historian. U.S. Entry into World War I, 1917. U.S. Department of State. n.d. https://history.state.gov/milestones/1914-1920/wwi
2. Centers for Disease Control and Prevention. History of 1918 flu pandemic. 2019. www.cdc.gov/flu/pandemic-resources/1918-commemoration/1918-pandemic-history.htm
3. W Woytinsky. Postwar economic perspectives 1. Experience after world. *Social Security Bulletin*. 1945;8(12). www.ssa.gov/policy/docs/ssb/v8n12/v8n12p18.pdf
4. A Lapin. Radioactive: The Father Coughlin Story. PBS. n.d. www.pbs.org/wnet/exploring-hate/series/radioactive/
5. T Wang. Media, pulpit, and populist persuasion: evidence from Father Coughlin. *American Economic Review*. 2021;111(9):3064–92.
6. L Dinnerstein. *Antisemitism in America*. Oxford University Press; 1995.
7. A Brinkley. *Voices of protest: Huey Long, Father Coughlin, and the Great Depression*. 1st ed. Knopf; 1982.
8. PBS. A Science Odyssey: People and Discoveries: Ford installs first moving assembly line. n.d. www.pbs.org/wgbh/aso/databank/entries/dt13as.html
9. M Wallace. *The American axis: Henry Ford, Charles Lindbergh, and the rise of the Third Reich*. Macmillan; 2004.
10. Z Feldstein. Henry Ford and antisemitism: the notorious "Dearborn Independent." American Jewish Archives. 2021. www.americanjewisharchives.org/snapshots/henry-ford-and-antisemitism-the-notorious-dearborn-independent/
11. Minnesota Historical Society. New York-to-Paris flight. n.d. www.mnhs.org/lindbergh/learn/aviation/famous-flight
12. National Air and Space Museum. The first solo, nonstop transatlantic flight. n.d. https://pioneersofflight.si.edu/node/324
13. Minnesota Historical Society. America First and WWII. n.d. www.mnhs.org/lindbergh/learn/controversies
14. R Modras. Father Coughlin and anti-semitism: fifty years later. *Journal of Church and State*. 1989;31(2):231–47.
15. VS Woeste. *Henry Ford's war on Jews and the legal battle against hate speech*. 1st ed. Stanford University Press; 2012.
16. AS Berg. *Lindbergh*. Berkley Books; 1999.
17. E Fromm. *The heart of man, its genius for good and evil*. Harper & Row; 1964.
18. O Kernberg. Factors in the psychoanalytic treatment of narcissistic personalities. *Journal of the American Psychoanalytic Association*. 1970;18(1):51–85.
19. ME Deveze-Villarreal, CA López-Acevo. Malignant narcissism: a case report and literature review. *Revista Medicina Universitaria*. 2022;24(2):8535.
20. OF Kernberg. Malignant narcissism and large group regression. *The Psychoanalytic Quarterly*. 2020;89(1):1–24.
21. BP Coppola. "Father Coughlin is already explaining it to the American people"

(June 13, 1939). 2019. https://sites.lsa.umich.edu/bcoppola/2019/01/01/father-coughlin-is-already-explaining-it-to-the-american-people-june-13-1939/

22. Three stations refuse Coughlin three talks for allegedly inciting race prejudice. *Broadcast Advertising*. 15(11):17, 79.

23. QS Alma'itah, Z ul Haq. The concept of Messiah in Abrahamic religions: a focused study of the eschatology of Sunni Islam. *Heliyon*. 2022;8(3):e09080.

24. DM Friedman. *The immortalists: Charles Lindbergh, Dr. Alexis Carrel, and their daring quest to live forever*. Ecco; 2007.

25. OS Haque, J De Freitas, I Viani, B Niederschulte, HJ Bursztajn. Why did so many German doctors join the Nazi Party early? *International Journal of Law and Psychiatry*. 2012;35(5–6):473–79.

26. HJ Bursztajn. Preventing neo-Nazi cult violence in our schools. *Forensic Psychiatry & Medicine*. n.d. www.forensic-psych.com/articles/artNeoNazi.html

27. APA Dictionary of Psychology. Victimization. n.d. https://dictionary.apa.org/

28. Cleveland Clinic. Factitious disorder imposed on self (formerly known as Munchausen Syndrome). n.d. https://my.clevelandclinic.org/health/diseases/9833-munchausen-syndrome-factitious-disorder-imposed-on-self

29. A Mitscherlich, M Mitscherlich. *The inability to mourn: principles of collective behavior*. Grove Press; 1975.

30. A Mitscherlich, M Mitscherlich. "The Inability to Mourn" (A. and M. Mitscherlich). Psychic coping with the situation in Germany after 1945. PCCA – Partners in Confronting Collective Atrocities. 2020. https://p-cca.org/a-the-inability-to-mourn-a-and-m-mitscherlich-psychic-coping-with-the-situation-in-germany-after-1945/

31. M Drekmeier. The inability to mourn. Mitscherlich A, Mitscherlich M, editors. *CrossCurrents*. 1976;26(3):328–33.

32. C Haberman. Exploring hate. Today in History: The Father Coughlin story. PBS. 2022. www.pbs.org/wnet/exploring-hate/2022/03/09/today-in-history-the-father-coughlin-story/

33. M De Witte. The Great Depression demonstrated the indispensable role of government. Stanford News. 2020. https://news.stanford.edu/2020/04/29/great-depression-demonstrated-indispensable-role-government/

34. J Gregory. Everyday life during the Depression. Great Depression in Washington State. 2019. https://depts.washington.edu/depress/everyday_life.shtml

35. T Gilovich, D Keltner, S Chen, R Nisbett. *Social psychology*. 5th ed. W.W. Norton & Company; 2018.

36. T Nast, AR Waud, HL Stephens, JE Taylor, J Hoover, GF Crane, et al. The African American odyssey: a quest for full citizenship. Library of Congress. 1998. www.loc.gov/exhibits/african-american-odyssey/reconstruction.html

37. EJ Blum. *Reforging the White republic: race, religion, and American nationalism, 1865–1898*. LSU Press; 2015.

38. S Fujimura. Purple death: the Great Flu of 1918. Pan American Health Organization. n.d. www.paho.org/en/who-we-are/history-paho/purple-death-great-flu-1918

39. AW Crosby. *America's forgotten pandemic: the influenza of 1918*. Cambridge University Press; 2003.

40. KR Robinson. Comparing the Spanish flu and COVID-19 pandemics: lessons to carry forward. *Nursing Forum*. 2021;56(2):350–57.

41. G Tanaka, H Tang, O Haque, HJ Bursztajn. Preserve Enduring Personality Change After Catastrophic Experience (EPCACE) as a diagnostic resource. *The Lancet Psychiatry*. 2018;5(5):e9.

42. Pan American Health Organization. Protecting mental health during epidemics. 2009 May 4. www.paho.org/en/documents/protecting-mental-health-during-epidemics

43. PBS. Reverend Charles E. Coughlin (1891–1979). n.d. www.pbs.org/wgbh/

americanexperience/features/holocaust-coughlin/

44. M Rousselet, O Duretete, JB Hardouin, M Grall-Bronnec. Cult membership: what factors contribute to joining or leaving? *Psychiatry Research.* 2017;257:27–33.
45. B Lenthall. *Radio's America: the Great Depression and the rise of modern mass culture.* University of Chicago Press; 2008.
46. J Matthew. A cognitive scientist explains why humans are so susceptible to fake news and misinformation. Nieman Lab. 2019 Apr 17. www.niemanlab.org/2019/04/a-cognitive-scientist-explains-why-humans-are-so-susceptible-to-fake-news-and-misinformation/
47. D Thompson. Mr. Welles and mass delusion. *New York Herald Tribune.* 1938 Nov 2.
48. S Thompson. Hate groups. Office of Justice Programs. n.d. www.ojp.gov/ncjrs/virtual-library/abstracts/hate-groups
49. FBI. Hate crime statistics. n.d. www.fbi.gov/how-we-can-help-you/more-fbi-services-and-information/ucr/hate-crime
50. Southern Poverty Law Center. Frequently asked questions about hate and antigovernment groups. 2024 Jun 4. www.splcenter.org/20220216/frequently-asked-questions-about-hate-and-antigovernment-groups#hate-group
51. *Coral Ridge Ministries Media, Inc.* v. *S. Poverty Law Ctr.*, 142 S. Ct. 2453 (2022).
52. Southern Poverty Law Center. Hate map. n.d. www.splcenter.org/hate-map
53. ADL. ADL H.E.A.T. map™. n.d. www.adl.org/resources/tools-to-track-hate/heat-map
54. ADL. QAnon. n.d. www.adl.org/resources/backgrounder/qanon
55. J Schafer, J Navarro, Office of Justice Programs. Seven-stage hate model: the psychopathology of hate groups. 2003 Mar. www.ojp.gov/ncjrs/virtual-library/abstracts/seven-stage-hate-model-psychopathology-hate-groups
56. JB Liguori, LB Spanierman. Walking out on hate: a qualitative investigation of how and why White supremacists quit hate groups. *Journal of Counseling Psychology.* 2022;69(4):389–402.
57. BF Bubolz, P Simi. Leaving the world of hate: life-course transitions and self-change. *American Behavioral Scientist.* 2015;59(12):1588–1608.
58. M Klein, J Riviere. *Love, hate and reparation.* Hogarth Press; Institute of Psycho-analysis; 1953.
59. PBS. Frontline: members of several well-known hate groups identified at Capitol Riot. n.d. www.pbs.org/wgbh/frontline/article/several-well-known-hate-groups-identified-at-capitol-riot/
60. D Elliott. The Charlottesville rally 5 years later: "it's what you're still trying to forget." NPR. 2022 Aug 12. www.npr.org/2022/08/12/1116942725/the-charlottesville-rally-5-years-later-its-what-youre-still-trying-to-forget
61. CT Nguyen. Echo chambers and epistemic bubbles. *Episteme.* 2020;17(2):141–61.
62. United States Holocaust Memorial Museum. *Father Charles Coughlin opposes Roosevelt* [film]. n.d. https://encyclopedia.ushmm.org/content/en/film/father-charles-coughlin-opposes-roosevelt
63. T Doherty. The deplatforming of Father Coughlin. Slate. 2021 Jan 21. https://slate.com/technology/2021/01/father-coughlin-deplatforming-radio-social-media.html
64. L Denworth. Brain waves synchronize when people interact. *Scientific American.* 2023 Jul 1. www.scientificamerican.com/article/brain-waves-synchronize-when-people-interact/
65. M Danesi. *Politics, lies and conspiracy theories: a cognitive linguistic perspective.* 1st ed. Routledge; 2023.
66. PK Manning. Review of *Radio Priest: Charles Coughlin. The father of hate radio. Michigan Sociological Review.* 1997;11:114–20.

Chapter 6

Multilevel Marketing Groups

Reagan Gill

"I mean I could blow your, your mind away by telling you that we have over 100 people that make a lot of money, like between 50 thousand to 500 thousand dollars a month, and I'm not lying."
– *DeAnne Stidham, LuLaRoe founder [1, p. 11]*

Introduction

Multilevel marketing groups (MLMs) are businesses that incentivize the member (or "distributor") to sell products or services through person-to-person sales and recruit others to do the same [2]. In context, "multilevel" refers to the process in which distributors graduate in level or status as they acquire increasing numbers of customers or recruits. These groups may also be referred to as using "network marketing" or "direct marketing." Legally sanctioned MLMs do not directly pay a distributor for recruiting new members. They can, however, increase the distributor's commissions, bonuses, and other incentives based on the number of individuals that they recruit [3]. In 2014, MLMs had an estimated $34.47 billion in retail sales and approximately 18.2 million distributors [4].

In some specific instances, and often colloquially and in the media, MLMs may be referred to as "pyramid schemes" (Figure 6.1). However slight, definitional nuances significantly impact the legality of such groups. Those MLMs that are not functioning as pyramid schemes might leave participants with little to no profit or, at worst, financially destitute. They are, however, often legally sanctioned. Pyramid schemes are subsets of multilevel marketing that compensate a distributor based heavily, if not solely, on their recruitment [5]. Pyramid schemes are, in contrast to legitimate businesses and

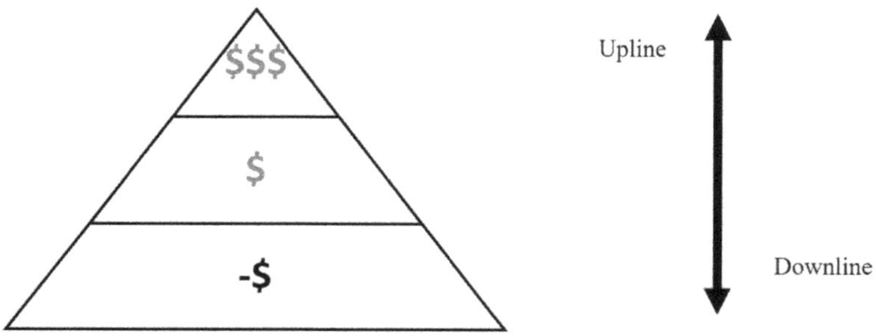

Figure 6.1 Visual depiction of compensation structure of a pyramid scheme

other MLMs, illegal [5]. To become a distributor for an MLM or pyramid scheme, one must first spend money upfront, typically on the products that one is expected to sell [6]. A distributor then receives bonuses for each person that they recruit. Pyramid schemes require members at the lower levels to contribute to those in the higher "levels" or status within the organization, with the assurance that they will similarly be supported by newer, subordinate members. The recruit then provides equity for startup costs, and the cycle continues. This arrangement is, however, inherently limited in the benefits it promises. Eventually, base-level subordinate members are left with little to no support and compensation, despite their initial offerings. Base-level distributors are then left with products purchased as a condition of their acceptance, yet are unable to sell.

Many MLMs use coercive tactics to expand recruitment and increase their profits. These maneuvers might include isolating members from friends and family, encouraging members to pay large sums of money to the larger organization, using evangelist rhetoric to indoctrinate members, and relying on vulnerabilities that will be discussed in this chapter. Some MLMs expand their influence and, in extreme cases, resemble cultist mentalities themselves.

While few definitional distinctions have been formally made by governing bodies, subsequent examples proffered in this chapter are presented in an effort to delineate the spectrum of MLMs in implementation, recruitment, coercion, legality, and potential for harm.

Case Vignettes

Amway

Amway is one of the largest multilevel marketing organizations globally [7]. Amway was founded by long-time friends Jay Van Andel and Richard DeVos in 1959. Andel and DeVos explained that being successful from working hard was the "American way," deriving the company's namesake [8]. Initially, this company sold one cleaning product but quickly grew to generate more than $500,000 in sales during its first full year. Amway now manufactures and distributes nutrition, beauty, personal care, and home products and claims distributors in 100 countries across the world [9].

Amway products can only be purchased from Amway Independent business owners (distributors or sellers). Distributors increase their potential profits when they recruit new distributors to create their own "downline" [6]. A recruit is encouraged to purchase a startup kit, leading to profit for their recruiter, also known as their "upline." Although Amway's website explains that selling actual products is the only way that distributors profit, some former distributors allege that a large majority of Amway's profits derive from distributors' down payment to establish their new business [10, 11].

Before the creation and widespread dissemination of the internet, Amway distributors recruited new members by distributing "ad packs." This included motivational tapes and brochures. Members were encouraged to listen to training tapes repeatedly [10, 12]. For example, one former member described driving to a company seminar and listening to nothing but these tapes for the entire 13-hour journey [10]. It is alleged that Amway produced false and misleading earning claims to encourage members to sell items and recruit new members [8].

Although there have been many lawsuits against Amway, the US Federal Trade Commission ruled in 1979 that Amway was not an illegal pyramid scheme. *In re*

Amway Corp., Inc., the Federal Trade Commission (FTC) ruled that Amway "avoided the abuses of pyramid schemes" because the company required a consultant to sell 70% of their inventory to 10 different customers every month, in order to qualify for a bonus [8, p. 700]. Additionally, the FTC noted that Amway provided distributors a method to sell back any unsold inventory. These safeguards became known as the Amway Safeguards, and precluded its inclusion as a pyramid scheme under US Federal definitions. Specifically, the FTC determined that a company does not qualify as a pyramid scheme if it follows the "10 retail sales rule" (requiring sales to 10 separate people to receive downline commission), the "70% rule" (requiring the sale of 70% of inventory in order for a distributor to reorder), and a "buyback policy" (requiring the company to buy back inventory that the distributor did not sell).

However, many former distributors attested false guarantees and unduly coercive tactics of this organization. Former Amway distributors have described sequestration from their family and friends if they refused to join [13]. Related allegations suggest the monetary and time commitment required by the company left distributors with little free time and minimal social contact outside of the group meetings. A former Amway distributor, Lori Mauldin, stated: "It's not a business, it's a community. They provide you with family, love and friendship. They feed you ideas on religion, politics and relationships. They tell you everything about how to act and how to think" [10, para. 28].

The company hosts group meetings and conferences with motivational, charismatic speakers [14]. These speakers include some of the company's highest-earning members, known as crowns or diamonds. In order to advance in the ranking hierarchy, one must recruit new members. For example, to be a diamond member, one must have six or more groups in one's downline that each makes a required amount of profit [6, 9].

Historically, new members have been recruited with the belief that they can pay to join and eventually yield significant profit [6]. Firsthand accounts allege that at major Amway functions, the company displays videos of top earners "pulling glittery ballgowns out of a closet" and "living in these incredible mansions" while encouraging members, "[t]his all can be yours" [10, para. 31]. However, this is not the case for many members who leave the company with varying levels of debt due to failure to meet the requisite sales goals to profit, or even maintain financial security [10, 12]. Amway's 2021 income disclosure states that the average monthly gross income for distributors at the Founders Platinum level and below was $766 before expenses [15]. Amway explains that expenses can include registration/renewal fees, shipping charges, taxes, travel, and training. The top 1% of distributors reportedly earned an average of $87,901 in 2021.

Today, Amway employs nearly 15,000 people operating company management as well as over 1,000,0000 "business owners [distributors]" [16]. According to the Amway Global Impact Report Summary for 2022, Amway is "the No. 1 direct selling business in the world" [16, p. 5]. This document further states that Amway exists "to [help] people live better, healthier lives" [16, p. 5]. The company reported $8.9 billion in global sales for 2021 with its top market in China followed by the United States [15].

LuLaRoe

LuLaRoe is a clothing company best known for its "buttery soft," brightly patterned leggings. LuLaRoe was founded in 2013 by DeAnne Brady (also known as DeAnne Stidham) and her husband Mark Stidham [17]. At this company, members are recruited to become "fashion consultants," "fashion entrepreneurs," or distributors. They are then expected to sell clothing and recruit new fashion consultants to the company. At its zenith in 2017, LuLaRoe reported sales of over $2 billion with approximately 80,000 distributors throughout the United States [18].

Former LuLaRoe fashion consultant, Katie Willis, told reporters that she paid $10,000 to join the company in 2016 [18]. By 2018, she was approximately $50,000 in credit card debt due to her business. Willis went on to recall spending thousands of dollars to attend LuLaRoe conferences and events. She alleged that constantly working was part of the LuLaRoe culture and that she worked seven days a week in order to keep up with her business, leaving little time for her to spend with her family.

LuLaRoe encouraged its distributors to buy large amounts of products to better meet the future demands of their clients [1]. The strategy for success of "buy more, sell more" left many distributors with more product than they could sell. This process of "inventory loading" led to distributors selling product at cost without turning much, if any, profit [1, p. 15]. Leaders of LuLaRoe encouraged distributors to use whatever profit they made to buy more product. Additionally, distributors could not purchase specific items. Instead, they were required to purchase at least 33 items per shipment that arrived in an array of patterns and sizes, usually including only a few popular items [19]. Training materials for LuLaRoe quoted in the *Complaint of Injunctive and Other Relief for Washington* v. *LLR, Inc.* explain this process as follows:

> Having a wide selection will lead to more customer engagement and bigger sales. It is crucial that you carry a significant number of pieces in every size before moving onto other styles. We have found that our Consultants who carry several hundred items in their inventory have the highest rate of success. Of course there are no set-in-stone rules, and you may proceed at your own pace, but we have learned that abundant inventory often creates abundant sales! [19, p. 15]

In addition to selling products, independent fashion consultants were rewarded for recruiting new members. When independent fashion consultants recruited new distributors, they would then become a "sponsor" [1]. With more recruits, their rank could progress to a "trainer," a "coach," and finally a "mentor" [1]. With each new rank, the distributor earned more profit through bonus incentives. These awards were based on the amount of product purchased from a distributor's recruits, or their downline.

Former members describe attending extravagant leadership conferences hosted by LuLaRoe [18]. These meetings made distributors feel empowered, accepted, and important. Some high earners within the company reached internet stardom and amassed their own following of thousands of fans [18]. The largest LuLaRoe celebrity is the founder herself, DeAnne Brady. DeAnne grew a social media following and frequently posted on social media sites encouraging fashion consultants to continue selling and recruiting [18].

By October 2017, a class action lawsuit was filed in California accusing LuLaRoe of being a pyramid scheme [20]. An additional lawsuit filed by the Washington State Attorney General's Officer in 2019 alleged the same [19]. According to Attorney General Robert Ferguson, "LuLaRoe's marketing and sales activities, misleading income and lifestyle claims, emphasis on recruiting and inventory purchases over emphasis on sales to consumers outside the LuLaRoe organization, and inventory loading practices ensured that the primary business opportunity with LuLaRoe was through recruitment"

[19, p. 17]. This lawsuit was settled in February 2021 causing the company to pay $4.74 million and publish accurate income disclosures [21]. Throughout these lawsuits, LuLaRoe continuously denied any wrongdoing.

Today, LuLaRoe continues to recruit new members to "join the movement" [17]. According to the 2021 LuLaRoe Income Disclosure Statement, the majority of retailers had an annual sales profit between $1 and $5,000 [22].

NXIVM

Keith Raniere began as a founder of an MLM before later being convicted of racketeering, sex trafficking, and forced labor conspiracy [23]. Raniere, also known by his followers as "Vanguard" or "Grandmaster," founded Consumers' Buyline in 1990 [24]. He made the decision to start his own MLM after working for Amway [24]. Consumers' Buyline claimed to be a company that recruited members who could receive discounts on various items such as groceries and other consumer goods. However, the members were reported to have been solely reimbursed based on their recruitment of new members, rather than commissions from sales or set pay schedule [24]. This company closed its doors in 1996 after multiple state investigations into it functioning as a pyramid scheme. One such investigation alleged that affiliates or distributors of Consumers' Buyline earned commissions not on selling actual products but instead on downline memberships and the monthly fees paid by those members [25].

Raniere then founded Executive Success Programs, Inc. (ESP) in 1998 [26]. This was a series of self-help workshops with a goal to "actualize human potential." Raniere founded NXIVM (pronounced "nex-ee-um") in 2003 as an umbrella company to encompass ESP as well as his other affiliated entities [26]. This company described itself as a "business providing education tools, coaching and trainings" to corporations and people from all walks of life through a philosophy that allows "humanity to rise to its noble possibility" [27, para. 10].

The company recruited young professionals who hoped to better themselves and targeted wealthy heiresses and celebrities [28, 29]. To enter the group, one needed to enroll in workshops that cost up to $5000 for a five-day course [26]. Recruits were encouraged to spend thousands of dollars to attend these workshops that would more grant them downstream profits. Members were informed that they could also receive commissions to recruit new members to sign up for workshops. Some members even became employed by NXIVM to ostensibly pay off their debts [26]. Members of NXIVM were encouraged to sign nondisclosure agreements promising that they would not reveal certain aspects of NXIVM's teachings to nonmembers and the general public [26].

Around 2015 a secret society, called "DOS" or "The Vow," was created within NXIVM [26, 30]. "DOS" is an acronym for "Dominus Obsequious Sororium," which is derivative of Latin, roughly translating to "Lord/Master of the Obedient Female Companions." It operated with a pyramid-like structure in which higher-level "masters" recruited lower-level "slaves." Slaves would recruit slaves of their own and then themselves become a master. Slaves owed service to not only their direct master, but also to their master's master, and so on. The individual at the top of the hierarchal structure, the master of all masters and all slaves, was Raniere himself [26]. Notably, Raniere was also the only male in the group, as only women were allowed to be recruited [26].

Slaves of DOS were recruited through the ranks of NXIVM. A master would target women who were experiencing dissatisfaction that they generally attributed to disappointment with their lack of advancement within the ranks of NXIVM. The recruit was told that this secret organization, DOS, was a women's mentorship group that would result in significant personal betterment [26]. The recruit was first required to provide personally damning information as collateral [26, 29, 30]. Examples of accepted collateral included sexually explicit photographs or videos, as well as confessions (either in video or through written documentation) about something detrimental for her or her family/ friends. Additional indemnification was required after the member joined DOS, including the transfer of financial assets [26]. Members were informed that if they left the organization, spoke publicly about the organization, or failed their obligations within the organization, this collateral would be released.

The DOS group sermonized the notion that women are inherently weak [26]. The group would explain to members that women needed to be trained to overcome such weakness. If a recruit showed hesitation about joining, she would be told that her hesitation was a sign of weakness and evidence of why she needed DOS [26].

Slaves were required to perform many acts within the organization, termed "acts of care" [26]. These amounted to becoming personal assistants to their masters and running personal errands [26]. In addition to acts of care, slaves were also required to perform "readiness drills." These drills required slaves to respond to their masters via text message at any given time of the day or night, resulting in severe sleep deprivation [26, 29]. Slaves were also given specific assignments by their masters. Assignments included sexual encounters with Raniere [26]. Another frequent pledge was for slaves to adhere to a low-calorie diet, demanded due to Raniere's sexual preference for thin women [26]. Other examples include taking only ice-cold showers, standing upright for an hour at 4.00 a.m. every morning, and performing strenuous exercise. If the slave did not perform her assignments, she was at risk of having her collateral released publicly [26].

During "branding ceremonies" DOS slaves were branded in their pubic regions with a cauterizing pen (Figure 6.2) [29, 30, 31]. The brand was a symbol that the slaves were

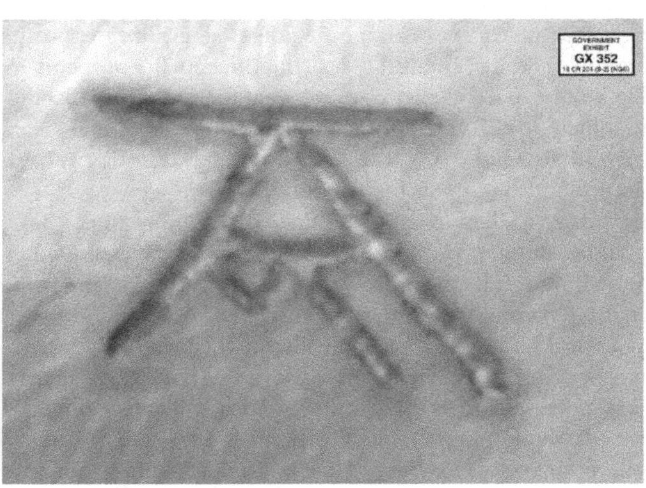

Figure 6.2 Symbol branded on DOS slaves alleged to represent water, air, earth, and fire but which includes Keith Raniere's initials [26]

told represented the four elements – water, air, earth, and fire. However, the brand included the initials "KR" that Raniere later described as a form of tribute to him [26].

Characteristics of Leaders

Leaders and figureheads of MLMs are primarily salespeople whose primary objective is to recruit new members in order to increase profit and personal gain [2]. Similar to groups colloquially termed "cults," multilevel marketing leaders seek to entice potential recruits to join, or buy into, their group with indemnification, explicit, and often implicit collateral. A leader might be selling the promise of a supportive family-like group structure, profitable business venture, or generally successful life.

Personality traits and psychopathology found in many more classically associated cult contexts may be found among high-ranking members of MLMs such as Amway and LuLaRoe and include secrecy, charisma, and narcissism. These companies may recruit members through misleading advertising, portraying their organizations as money-making ventures for any recruit who is willing to front initial funds and pledge time and labor for the group's systematized objective and induction. They are often alleged to employ a level of deception and otherwise covert agendas.

Recruiters in MLMs may share information about the company with recruits through a specific lens based on the recruit's desire to conform to a particular religious or gender identity [2]. Economist and attorney at law, Heidi Liu, describes this type of information sharing as "imperfect disclosure." She defines imperfect disclosure of MLMs by their appeal to the emotional biases of recruits while engaging in base-rate neglect, similar to misleading potential recruits to ignore warning signs found in studies on cult groups [32]. This occurs when MLMs heavily market the successful but rare outcomes for its distributors, in order to persuade potential members. For example, MLMs commonly highlight the small percentage of its members who attend lavish parties, embark on expensive vacations, or earn outrageous bonuses. On July 13, 2015, the founders of LuLaRoe posed for a picture with a distributor after presenting her and her husband with an oversized bonus check at Vision Leadership Conference in the amount of $1,425,701.18 [19]. It is much more difficult to find the fine print that explains exactly how much money an average distributor makes within the company.

Multilevel marketing groups repetitively speak about the potential, albeit rare, profits that could be acquired by potential recruits [2]. Simply hearing the benefits of membership repeatedly, a new member will be more likely to believe what the recruiter is saying. This creates repetition bias, which means the more frequently an individual hears something, the more likely they are to believe it is true [33]. Ultimately, familiarity with information becomes more important than its factual validity [34].

These groups rely on charismatic leaders to motivate their distributors to continue working with their company and earn them profits [35]. Members may be exploited or pressured by their upline to buy more products, pay for more meetings, and spend more money on educational materials. This motivation may be provided in an environment created to feel like a religious revival because these highly charged, emotionally intense situations create a higher likelihood of a recruit investing in an MLM [2]. Similarly, MLMs frequently use other deific dialogue to assert cultural identity outside of financial gain. For example, leaders of MLMs commonly refer to their success and profits as "blessings" [36]. In her deposition for the case *Washington* v. *LuLaRoe*, DeAnne Stidham states: "If they know that they've got an ability to make money sitting in their home, then this could be a blessing into their family's lives" [37, time 18:35]. More overtly, one of the founders of LuLaRoe, Mark Stidham, would frequently read passages from the Book of Mormon (the guiding text for the Church of Latter-Day Saints) at companywide sales events [38].

Leaders may also create an isolated, restricted environment for members. Former distributors speak about feeling alienated from people in their lives who were not involved with their MLM [10]. They describe an "us versus them" mentality in which they were told that anyone who was not in the group was less successful, less hard-working, and less likely to reach their financial goals. Those who do not become successful distributors are described as the "unmotivated majority" [2, p. 130]. Motivation is, however, controlled by the distributor. Therefore, a prospective recruit may join an MLM regardless of the risk because they believe that they have everything (i.e., motivation) necessary to become a high earner if they put in the effort.

Padilla et al. describe characteristics of destructive leadership that they define as leadership that results in negative organizational outcomes [39]. As seen by the inner workings and eventual downfall of NXIVM, Raniere represents one such destructive leader. Beyond his business management style, his leadership exemplifies the characteristics that were required for his reign, effectively, as a cult leader. Raniere was motivated by his own power and success, engaged in exploitative behaviors toward others, and portrayed himself as smart, more enlightened, and overall better than others [26, 31].

Destructive leaders are motivated by enhancing their personal power [39]. As seen by Raniere, his goal for leading NXIVM was primarily for his own personal financial interest and predatory sexual gratification. Destructive leaders focus on self-promoting to build support for themselves. Indeed, Raniere placed himself at the top of the DOS slave/master hierarchy. Although NXIVM and DOS claimed to be organizations made to promote personal growth and development, Raniere's leadership goals were instead to further his own personal interests that were intentionally opaque, if not altogether concealed from NXIVM members.

Destructive leaders may share personality traits consistent with and endemic of classic psychoanalytical frameworks of malignant narcissists. Psychologist Erich Fromm coined the term *malignant narcissism* in 1964, which he equated to "the quintessence of evil" [40, p. 37]. He defined malignant narcissism as having a narcissistic personality with antisocial behavior, aggression with sadism, and paranoia [41]. Someone with a narcissistic personality believes that they are more important than other people, desires unlimited success, power, brilliance, beauty, or ideal love, requires excessive admiration, exploits others, lacks empathy, and acts enviously and arrogantly [42, p. 748]. A malignant narcissist is likely to gain satisfaction from harming others in addition to having traits of typical narcissism including being self-absorbed and seeking attention. Malignant narcissists ignore others' viewpoints and welfare while claiming special knowledge and demanding unquestioning obedience. Additionally, malignant narcissists frequently dehumanize others as they have feelings of rage alongside a mistrust of others [43]. Raniere highlighted these traits in his treatment of what he considered to be his slaves. He demanded their unquestioning obedience to himself as he was the god-like "Vanguard." He displayed antisocial behaviors and showed a lack of empathy to others as he manipulated his power to abuse DOS members psychologically and sexually.

Characteristics of Followers

Most members, consultants, or distributors in MLMs are women who work part-time [2]. Doctor of Philosophy, Tiffany Lamoreaux, says that MLMs "deliberately tap into women's anxieties and desires to blend their perceived gender roles with their need for income" [44, p. 44]. Companies like LuLaRoe specifically recruit women and frequently espouse the potential "freedom" that can be found within the company [17]. LuLaRoe emphasizes its desire to "empower women" through both their clothing as well as their career potential. Marketing material is fraught with feministic dialogue such as "boss babe" and "girl boss" [38]. While potentially sincere, such verbiage appears to draw on the desire for women to help women, allowing women to fulfil their own goals while helping others fulfil their own. However, this goal is often unfulfilled, self-defeating, and creates a framework within MLMs.

Many MLMs emphasize the alleged flexibility of becoming a distributor, in order to attract women with already busy schedules, such as primary caretakers for children and families who do not hold full-time jobs otherwise. In the film *LulaRich*, founder of LuLaRoe, Mark Stidham, plainly told a documentarian: "If you want to create incredible wealth, identify an underutilized resource – And you know what? There is an underutilized resource of stay-at-home moms" [38]. On its website, LuLaRoe specifically targets this demographic with statements including "make your own schedule as a mom" and "mompreneur inspiration" [17]. LuLaRoe's official mission statement includes: "Where through fashion we create freedom, serve others & strengthen families" [19, p. 18].

Members may see the company's values as aligning with their own personal values [2]. Intense labor, high levels of motivation, or empowerment of like-minded distributors may be seen as a cause more important than personal profit. When values intertwine, the boundary between work, home, and values may become blurred and consumed by the MLM itself [35]. Political scientist J. Busher and colleagues summarize, "[this] provides an effective means of exerting control over the eliciting affiliation from distributors" because a member is less likely to quit the company if they see the company as associated with their own values, home, and family [45, p. 12].

For most MLMs, followers tend to be motivated initially by their unmet financial need. Many recruiters evangelize to potential new members about prospective profits and enticing status or other awards [2]. Those who feel as if they are not contributing to their household income in a substantial way will be more ready to join these groups to enhance their self-esteem and their quality of life [2].

Companies like Amway and LuLaRoe emphasize a type of familial connection between members. This, in turn, leads members to feel an emotional association and identity to the company itself. Feeling valued and even loved by high-ranking members within the company reinforces the member's need to belong. Marketing strategies used by MLMs emphasize this idea by stating that they are a supportive community of friends who rally around each other. LuLaRoe's website says: "Join a supportive community of thousands of retailers who build each other up, and who've created lifelong friendships. Your fellow retailers are an amazing group that acts as a support system and can help wherever you are at in your business" [17]. These statements often play on the emotional needs of recruits who may feel isolated, lonely, or in need of a social group. Someone who is seeking inclusion in a community with a desire to feel wanted, needed, or as if they belong is more vulnerable to joining a potentially exploitative group [46].

Members are encouraged to view their own identity as one enmeshed with the company. Not only does the company become their employment but also their support system. In this context, failure within the company becomes more than a failed financial venture – it becomes a personal malfunction and unfulfilled need [2]. Multilevel marketing groups emphasize that distributor success is directly linked to the distributor's effort and work ethic [2]. Therefore, if the venture is not profitable, distributors commonly blame themselves, indoctrinated with the belief that they would have been successful if only they had worked harder or more auspiciously. Because they believe that their success is solely under their own control, they are more likely to continue with the company under a false pretense that they can succeed if only they improve their work ethic. To leave the company would evidence that the distributor was in the "unmotivated majority," potentially damaging their self-confidence and sense of self-worth [2].

Additionally, distributors who have invested into starting their MLM business may fall into the sunk-cost fallacy. This belief occurs when an individual is reluctant to abandon a strategy in which they have heavily invested even though leaving is clearly the sounder financial decision [47]. Self-preservation, along with the sunk-cost fallacy, makes it more difficult for a member to quit the company and ultimately leads to members staying long after they start losing money.

Padilla and colleagues reviewed characteristics of those who help bring destructive leaders to power – susceptible followers [39]. Susceptible followers make up two groups: conformers and colluders. Conformers are followers who comply with destructive leaders due to fear and a means to avoid negative consequences. Colluders, on the other hand, actively participate in the destructive leadership for personal gain.

A conformer is vulnerable to a destructive leader due to unmet basic needs, negative self-evaluation, and psychological immaturity [39]. Basic needs often include shelter, food, and safety. Those without these necessities may conform to destructive leadership as a means for survival [48]. Similarly, an individual who feels alienated from mainstream society may be more likely to follow a destructive leader to gain a sense of community and a group with which to belong.

A negative self-evaluation includes low self-esteem, external locus of control, and limited self-efficacy [49]. Someone with low self-esteem sees their own value as being less than others around them. These individuals often want to be more desirable, aligning them with charismatic leaders [39]. Having an external locus of control causes an individual to believe that their life is determined by outside forces and that they are incapable of controlling or changing this outcome. An individual with this mindset is more likely to be manipulated by a controlling leader who appears willing to care for them [50]. Finally, self-efficacy is defined as one's belief about their capability to perform well [51]. Someone with low self-efficacy assumes that they are incapable of making good decisions. This leads to spending less time and effort on decisions that can lead to following a leader who is willing to make such decisions for the potential follower [39].

In the case of NXIVM members, the conforming followers sought to have their unmet needs of personal and professional growth met by the organization's promise of self-development workshops and trainings. Belonging to DOS provided some of these members with a more exclusive community in which they could belong. Those with lower self-esteem would be more readily willing to join a group that promised personal fulfillment and overall self-improvement [39, 26].

Unlike conformers, colluders are usually ambitious, selfish, and share the destructive leader's worldviews. A highly ambitious individual is more likely to collude with a destructive leader in order to gain success, prestige, or profit [52]. If an ambitious follower is highly self-interested, they are more likely to engage in destructive acts alongside a leader [53]. Additionally, followers are more likely to align with a leader with whom they see similarities [54, 55]. If an individual identifies their own personal values within a destructive leader, this will strengthen their bond and willingness to join the leader's cause [54, 55].

Additionally, psychologically immature recruits are more likely to adopt the views of the group and accept the authority of the destructive leader [39]. Psychological immaturity causes individuals to be more willing to conform to authority and potentially commit destructive acts at the behest of their leader. In a group or community setting, one's own ideas or mindset can be set aside and replaced with that of the group or the group's leader. Psychological immaturity is more common in youth and young adults, especially those who have not yet developed a strong sense of identity [39]. Like many other MLMs and pyramid schemes, NXIVM actively recruited individuals who were actively seeking personal growth and identity development [24, 31].

Some of NXIVM's colluder-type followers were seen in the hierarchy of DOS. The higher-level masters, although still considered slaves of Raniere, mirrored his leadership approach in their systematized control over their own slaves [26]. This allotted high-tiered members to abuse others as a means of meeting their own personal agendas to obtain power and higher esteem in the eyes of Raniere.

Beyond those characteristics of members who keep MLMs functioning, there are specific factors that keep these members from exiting the group. Once a recruit joins an MLM, leaving the group is made to be difficult. Upon becoming a distributor and actively recruiting other members, distributors now have the additive pressure of the guilt and shame for not only upsetting their upline who would likely lose profits if they were to quit, but they also have the guilt of leading astray the new members that they recruited. Leaving an MLM may feel as if a distributor is not only betraying others but that they may be left unhappy or even unsafe. As psychologist Eunice U. Choi encapsulated: "Inclusion in our in-groups makes us feel happier, safer, and more certain of ourselves and our place in the world" [56, p. 483]. Todd Rose related, "[w]hen our reputations are on the line [or] we are emotionally invested in an outcome . . . [w]e do everything we can to avoid acknowledging the truth" [33, p. 20].

Summary

Multilevel marketing groups are organizations that require the participating person (or "distributor") to sell products or services through person-to-person sales and to recruit others to do the same. Distributors of MLMs earn profits based on sales of products to retail customers. A pyramid scheme is a multilevel marketing group that pays its distributor based heavily, if not solely, on their recruitment. Pyramid schemes require members at the lower levels to contribute to those in the higher levels or status within the organization, with the assurance that they will similarly be supported by newer, subordinate members.

Amway and LuLaRoe are MLMs that have been alleged to act as pyramid schemes. However, these companies deny such allegations, have avoided legal sanctions, and continue to run their respective business models recruiting new distributors and selling products in adhering to FTC safeguard practices [9, 17].

NXIVM is one extreme example of a multilevel marketing group that expanded to become a cult by exerting physical and psychological control over its members. Under the leadership of Keith Raniere, NXIVM members branched off into a suborganization called DOS that recruited new members referred to as "slaves." Slaves were required to perform acts of service for their masters, including sexual favors with Raniere [26].

Multilevel marketing groups commonly have charismatic leaders who recruit others to join based on promises of making large amounts of money. Some of these groups use cultist strategies to enhance member commitment such as alienation from those outside the group, maintaining an "us versus them" mentality, and creating feelings of emotional connectedness between members and leadership. Multilevel marketing groups often emphasize a familial alliance between members. This leads members to feel an emotional connection and intertwinement with the company. Feeling valued and even loved by high earners in the company subsequently reinforces the member's need to belong and validates their role. These features of MLMs create and perpetuate a framework, wherein members often find it difficult to leave without financial, emotional, and social damages.

Key Points

- Multilevel marketing groups are businesses that require a consenting person (the "distributor"), often under false pretexts, to sell products or services through person-to-person sales and to recruit others to do the same.
- A pyramid scheme is an MLM that pays its distributor based heavily, if not solely, on their recruitment.
- Multilevel marketing groups commonly have charismatic leaders who recruit others to join based on promises of making large amounts of money. Traits and characteristics of leaders overlap those of other groups relying on persuasive leadership, including charismatic, and at times narcissistic, individuals who use misleading and biased claims to draw in potential recruits seen in MLM leaders. Additionally, certain characteristics including the desire for an in-group, having unmet needs, and being psychologically immature can be found in MLM members or followers.
- Some of these groups use cult-like strategies to enhance member commitment such as alienation from those outside the group, maintaining an "us versus them" mentality, and creating feelings of emotional connectedness between members and leadership.

References

1. *Sperring v. LLR, Inc.* (2021) 995 F.3d 680 (9th Cir.).
2. H Liu. The behavioral economics of multilevel marketing. *Hastings Business Law Journal.* 2018;14(1):109–38. https://repository.uchastings.edu/hastings_business_law_journal/vol14/iss1/3
3. D Valentine. *Pyramid schemes: international monetary funds seminar on current legal issues affecting central banks.* Federal Trade Commission. 1998 May 13. https://perma.cc/W9E5-GL9J
4. A Coughlan. Multi-level marketing business opportunities: analyzing net economic return and avoidable economic loss to distributors. Kellogg School of

Management, Northwestern University. 2016 Jul 15. https://papers.ssrn.com/sol3/papers.cfm?abstract_id=2822402.

5. Federal Trade Commission. Multi-level marketing businesses and pyramid schemes. Federal Trade Consumer Advice. 2021 May. https://consumer.ftc.gov/articles/multi-level-marketing-businesses-pyramid-schemes
6. P Herbig, R Yelkurm. A review of the multilevel marketing phenomenon. *Journal of Marketing Channels* 1997;6(1):17–33.
7. Amway Corp. Amway founders: a history of entrepreneurship. 2023. www.amwayglobal.com/our-story/founders/
8. In the Matter of Amway Corporation, Inc., et al. (1979) 93 F.T.C. 618.
9. Amway. About Amway. 2022. www.amway.com/en_US/about-amway
10. P Felps. Inside ScAmway – the alluring life offered by the world's largest 'multi-marketing' business closely resembles a sham. Weekly Wire. 1998 Jul 13.
11. C Brunori. Amway – the impossible dream [publisher unknown]. 2002 Aug.
12. M Pratt. The good, the bad, and the ambivalent: managing identification among Amway distributors. *Administrative Science Quarterly* 2000;45:456–93.
13. Some factions of Amway use cult tactics. 2002 Mar. https://culteducation.com/group/815-amway/1740-some-factions-of-amway-use-cult-tacticss.html
14. Amway. Amway events. 2022. www.amway.com/en_US/events/npc
15. Alticor Inc. Amway 2021 U.S. income disclosure. 2022. www.amway.com/en_US/income-disclosure
16. Amway Corp. Amway Global Impact Report Summary 2022. 2023. AmwayGlobal.com/impact-report
17. LuLaRoe – become a fashion entrepreneur. 2022. www.lularoe.com/join-lularoe
18. S McNeil. Millennial women made LuLaRoe billions. Then they paid the price. BuzzFeed. 2020 Feb 22. www.buzzfeednews.com/article/stephaniemcneal/lularoe-millennial-women-entrepreneurship-lawsuits
19. *State of Washington* v. *LLR, Inc.* (2019).
20. *Stella Lemberg* v. *LuLaRoe, LLC.* (2017) 5:17-cv-02102.
21. Washington State Office of the Attorney General. LuLaRoe to pay $4.75 million to resolve AG Ferguson's lawsuit over pyramid scheme. 2021 Feb 2. www.atg.wa.gov/news/news-releases/lularoe-pay-475-million-resolve-ag-ferguson-s-lawsuit-over-pyramid-scheme
22. LuLaRoe 2021 Income Disclosure Statement. 2022. www.lularoe.com/lularoe-income-disclosure-statement
23. United States Department of Justice. NXIVM leader Keith Raniere sentenced to 120 years in prison for racketeering and sex trafficking offenses. 2020 Oct 27. www.justice.gov/usao-edny/pr/nxivm-leader-keith-raniere-sentenced-120-years-prison-racketeering-and-sex-trafficking
24. M Cutler. *Cults: inside the world's most notorious groups and understanding the people who joined them.* Gallery Books; 2022. p. 271–313.
25. *Rhodes* v. *Consumer Buyline* (1993) 868 F. Supp. 368 (D. Mass.).
26. *United States* v. *Raniere* (2019) 384 F. Supp. 3d 282 (E.D.N.Y.).
27. J Ax, B Pierson. Accused sex cult founder could face former 'slaves' at New York trial. 2019 May 7. www.insider.com/accused-sex-cult-founder-could-face-former-slaves-at-new-york-trial-2019-5
28. S Cohn. NXIVM's Keith Raniere used a common marketing technique to attract victims. 2021 Jan 22. www.cnbc.com/2021/01/22/nxivm-keith-raniere-used-multilevel-marketing-to-attract-victims.html
29. J Bloch. Escaping NXIVM. *CBC True Crime.* Sep 3, 2018 through Oct 27, 2020. https://podcasts.apple.com/us/podcast/escaping-nxivm/id1527772333
30. S Berman. *Don't call it a cult: the shocking story of Keith Raniere and the women of NXIVM.* Steerforth Press; 2021.

31. *The vow* [film]. HBO Documentary Films; 2020–2021.
32. L West. A psychiatric overview of cult-related phenomena. *Journal of the American Academy of Psychoanalysis.* 1993;21(1):1–19.
33. T Rose. *Collective illusions: conformity, complicity, and the science of why we make bad decisions.* Hachette Books; 2022.
34. I Begg, A Anas, S Farinacci. Dissociation of processes in belief: source recollection, statement familiarity, and the illusion of truth. *Journal of Experimental Psychology: General.* 1992;121(4):446–58.
35. J Sparks, J Schenk. Explaining the effects of transformational leadership: an investigation of the effects of higher-order motives in multilevel marketing organization. *Journal of Organizational Behavior.* 2001;22:849–69.
36. A Epstein. Multi-level marketing and its brethren: the legal and regulatory environment in the down economy. *Atlantic Law Journal.* 2010;12:91–121.
37. LLR Defective. *State of Washington v LuLaRoe – Deanne Brady (Stidham) Deposition 3/8* [video]. 2021. https://youtu.be/9-UGZPrWlxw
38. *LuLaRich* [film]. Directed by: Jenner Furst, Julia Willoughby Nason. Cinemart, Story Force Entertainment, Amazon Studios; 2021.
39. A Padilla, R Hogan, R Kaiser. The toxic triangle: destructive leaders, susceptible followers, and conducive environments. *The Leadership Quarterly.* 2007;18:176–94.
40. E Fromm. *The heart of man.* Harper and Row; 1964.
41. OF Kernberg. *Severe personality disorders.* Yale University Press; 1984.
42. American Psychiatric Association. *DSM-5-TR: diagnostic and statistical manual of mental disorders* (5th ed., Text revision). APA, 2022.
43. OF Kernberg. *Borderline conditions and pathological narcissism.* Jason Aronson; 1975.
44. T Lamoreaux. *Home is where the work is: women, direct sales, and technologies of gender.* Unpublished PhD dissertation. Arizona State University. 2013 May. https://core.ac.uk/download/pdf/79566618.pdf
45. J Busher, S Bremner, P Muljono. Freedom, family, hope, reward? Points of departure for development studies research on direct selling. School of International Development. 2009 Apr. https://ueaeprints.uea.ac.uk/id/eprint/18849/1/WP16.pdf
46. M Singer. *Cults in our midst: the continuing fight against their hidden menace.* Jossey-Bass; 2003.
47. *Oxford English dictionary*, 2nd ed. Oxford University Press; 1989.
48. F MacHovec. Cults, personality, and pathology. *Psychotherapy in Private Practice.* 1992;8(4):77–85.
49. T Judge, E Locke, C Durham, A Kluger. Dispositional effects on job and life satisfaction: the role of core evaluations. *Journal of Applied Psychology.* 1998;83(1):17–34.
50. F Luthans, S Peterson, E Ibrayeva. The potential for the “dark side” of leadership in post communist countries. *Journal of World Business.* 1998;33(2):185–201.
51. A Bandura. *Social foundations of thought and action: a social cognitive theory.* Prentice Hall; 1986.
52. D McClelland. *Power: the inner experience.* Irvington Publishers; 1975.
53. R Hogan. *Personality and the fate of organizations.* Psychology Press; 2015.
54. R Lord, D Brown. *Leadership processes and follower self-identity.* Lawrence Erlbaum Associates Publishers; 2004.
55. B Shamir, R House, M Arthur. The motivational effects of charismatic leadership: a self-concept based theory. *Organizational Science.* 1993;4:577–94.
56. E Choi, M Hogg. Self-uncertainty and group identification: a meta-analysis. *Group Processes and Intergroup Relations.* 2020;23(4):483–501.

Chapter 7

Family Cults

Ajay Nair and Amanie Salem

"What you need to believe in is what you can see . . . If you see me as your friend, I'll be your friend. If you see me as your father, I'll be your father, for those of you who don't have a father . . . If you see me as your savior, I'll be your savior. If you see me as your God, I'll be your God."
– *Jim Jones, leader of the Peoples Temple*

Introduction

Characteristics of Families

The Health Resources and Services Administration defines family as "a group of two or more persons related by birth, marriage, or adoption who live together" [1]. Structures of families differ increasingly, as the traditional conception of a child living with both biological parents and no half or step siblings is no longer the norm [2]. New definitions of family are becoming broader as societal structure changes, with some considering family to be any group of people who are "connected in love" [3]. For the purpose of this chapter, we will not be so broad in our definition, as then all cults could be considered families, but will rather think of a family as a unit that regularly spends time together, usually lives together, and is particularly focused on the relationships they maintain among each other above relationships they may hold with other members of society.

Characteristics of Cults

Definitions of cults generally include belief in a doctrine (often characterized as religious) that is not in line with the majority contemporary beliefs, and charismatic leadership [4]. It is not uncommon for cults to involve some sort of deviancy, including crimes of differing degrees or some sort of behavioral manipulation of followers.

It has been a long-held belief among experts that an attraction to cults can be linked to the cult providing a sense of structure that was lacking in an individual's life. Oftentimes that proposed missing structure is attributed to the lack of grounding in a strong family. Others contend that instead of contributing to cult membership, weak family ties are a result of an individual's involvement in cult membership and that cults are pulling people from their families and turning them against what could have been an adequate family structure [5]. In both scenarios, cults often provide many of the functions of a family for their members. Interestingly, having a strong family structure prior to cult membership has been shown to correlate with members' likelihood to defect from a cult [5].

Family Cults

For the purpose of this chapter, we will define a family cult as a cult that either mainly consists of one family or a cult whose doctrine specifically defines or exerts control over the family structures of its members. Though cults that do not meet either of these criteria may include family members and even children, they will not be considered family cults in this chapter.

Family cults are unique in that loyalties and ties between family members may create added complexity in cult dynamics. Cult leaders place importance on ensuring followers maintain loyalty to the cult, frequently at the expense of members' loyalty to their families. We will discuss six different family cults in this chapter, providing detail about the characteristics of leaders and followers of these cults and examining how the cults attempted to manage family dynamics and loyalty within their membership. The six cults will be briefly introduced in this section and then further discussed as the chapter progresses.

The Branch Davidians are an offshoot of the Davidian Seventh Day Adventist Church. They were founded by Benjamin Roden in 1955 after the passing of Davidian leader Victor Houteff. Roden was opposed to the proposed leadership of Houteff's wife, Florence, and gained control of the headquarters in Mount Carmel, near Waco, Texas. He remained the leader of the group until his passing in 1978. After a power struggle and the passing of Roden's wife in 1986, a convert named Vernon Howell took control of the Branch Davidians and changed his name to David Koresh [6]. Koresh and the Branch Davidians lived at Mount Carmel, where they had a large community comprised of several families. They awaited judgment day, considering Koresh to be the messiah. One of the roles that Koresh gave himself was to create a lineage of "God's children." He referred to his group of women as the "House of David" and had several children with members of the group [7]. He was known to separate members of families from each other when he felt that their loyalties were greater to each other than they were to him [8]. Koresh and 86 members of the Branch Davidians died in a fire that destroyed Mount Carmel, ending a 51-day standoff with the US government and Texas law enforcement.

The Children of God cult, later known as The Family International, was a group started by David Berg in 1968. He initially attracted a group of runaway teens by combining religious teaching with sexual promiscuity during the sexual revolution of the 1960s. The philosophy was called the Law of Love [9]. Members lived minimalist lives, giving up their belongings and living together in communes, awaiting the impending end of the world. Many families were members of the group, and they all lived isolated and simple lives. Ultimately, allegations of sexual abuse of minors forced Berg to escape to Portugal, where he died in 1994. More recently, in 2009, new leadership changed the message of the group, saying that they no longer needed to prepare for an impending apocalypse and could integrate more into society [9]. Famously, actor Joaquin Phoenix revealed his family were part of the Children of God until learning of Berg's involvement with grooming children.

The Manson Family, infamous for a string of murders in 1969 including that of actress Sharon Tate, also began during the sexual revolution of the 1960s. In 1967

Manson became a "guru" during the "Summer of Love" [10], living with 18 young women, who ultimately followed Manson's orders. Manson had sexual relationships with many, if not all, of the women he lived with, and the women were extremely motivated to please him with their actions [11]. Manson served nine life sentences in prison and passed away in prison in 2017.

The Peoples Temple was founded by Jim Jones in 1954, spreading a message of socialist and communist leanings, with a particular focus on racial equality [12]. Because of his progressive message in a time where social change was needed, he attracted a left-wing, predominantly Black, following and had the support of many progressive politicians. Jones ended up moving the Peoples Temple to Guyana amid questions about the dealings of the group. This was not his first move, having previously moved from Indiana to northern California. When controversy about the group's practices remained, United States Representative Leo Ryan took a trip to the Peoples Temple settlement, termed Jonestown, in Guyana. He and three journalists were ultimately killed by security from the Peoples Temple as they were leaving after the visit. That evening, Jim Jones ordered his followers to drink a cyanide-laced drink, leading to the deaths of 918 people [12].

The Fundamentalist Church of Jesus Christ and the Latter-Day Saints (FLDS) broke off from the Mormon Church when the latter abandoned polygamy in 1890. Groups have been mainly located on the Utah–Arizona border, though there are smaller groups in other locations. Initially the structure appeared to be more like a conventional church, but power has since been consolidated to one leader. Current leader Warren Jeffs is in prison serving a life sentence for crimes related to underage marriages [13]. He followed in the footsteps of his father, Rulon T. Jeffs, who established "One Man Rule" and controlled the marriages of members of the group [14], having immense power over the family dynamics of members of the FLDS. Even from prison, Jeffs appears to have at least some degree of influence over members.

The Church of the Lamb of God is another group that was created due to a disagreement with the mainstream Mormon Church's abandonment of polygamy as a practice. Alma Dayer LeBaron initially moved his family to Mexico to be able to practice their religion, including polygamy. When Alma died, his son Joel initially took the mantle of spiritual leader of the Christ of the Firstborn of the Fullness of Time. Joel's younger brother Ervil became a rival and was removed from the church in 1970. Ervil went on to found the Church of the Lamb of God. Ervil claimed that he was the sole leader of all polygamist offshoots from the Mormon Church. Until Ervil's eventual imprisonment in 1980, he and his family, consisting of 13 wives and at least 50 children, murdered rivals and dissenters in both the United States and Mexico. Even after Ervil's death in prison in 1981, murders were carried out through the 1980s based on a list he had provided to his family before his passing [15].

Characteristics of Leaders

Leaders of cults are frequently described as charismatic, articulate, and intelligent [16] and leaders of family cults are no exception. However, the draw of a leader of a family cult is particularly strong, as oftentimes a converted follower is either bringing family members along with them into the cult or creating an entirely new family and lifestyle in the cult. A few distinct characteristics have defined specific leaders of prominent family cults through history. Though many leaders of family cults possess several of the characteristics we will enumerate, the leaders' ability to recruit and retain followers can often be credited to one characteristic in particular.

Messianic Appeal

Many leaders of family cults see themselves as prophetic leaders and are similarly viewed as such by their followers. The devotion of the cult followers is primarily due to their reverence for the divine appointment of the leader. This high degree of faith in the leader allows followers to bring their families into cults and raise families within them, even changing their internal family dynamics at the request of cult leadership.

David Koresh, the leader of the Branch Davidians at Mount Carmel Center near Waco, Texas, was a messianic leader, holding a belief since he was young that he was divinely chosen. He was described by his followers as using various techniques to exert power and influence over them, including isolating them from the outside world, separating groups of people – including families – that were closer to each other than they were to him, and demanding obedience to his strict rules [8]. He had a magnetism that enticed followers to believe his prophetic claims and follow his strict guidelines. This belief in Koresh's prophetic claims was so strong that members joined Koresh in a standoff with the US government and Texas state officials that eventually killed 86 members of the Branch Davidians, including Koresh.

Appeals to Contemporary Beliefs and a Desire for a New Societal Structure

Another quality seen in leaders of family cults is the ability to sell a vision of a new way of living, appealing to contemporary trends in thinking and dissatisfaction that potential recruits may have with their experiences of societal structure. These leaders tap into the vulnerability of individuals who are dissatisfied with the status quo and are looking for something new and meaningful in their lives.

Revolutionary ideas about the family structure were a major draw for followers of David Berg's Children of God cult, later known as The Family International. Like David Koresh of the Branch Davidians, Berg saw himself as having prophetic visions regarding the end of the world, but it was his ability to combine traditional Christian teaching with contemporary beliefs of the sexual revolution in the 1960s that made him such a draw to followers of the cult. He advocated for a level of sexual promiscuity that ultimately led to allegations of sexual abuse against him shortly before his death in 1994 [9]. The unconventional nature of his teachings, as well as his ability to create a family structure within his cult that appealed to the contemporary prevailing rebellious beliefs, gave him a unique ability to appeal to youth and young families.

Charles Manson, the leader of the infamous Manson Family, also took advantage of the sexual revolution of the 1960s and particularly the "Summer of Love" in 1967 by recruiting young women to live with him in various rented and abandoned spaces, as well as traveling the country in a bus [10]. His ability to capture the contemporary dissatisfaction that many young women were having with their lives and their desire to find a new way of living contributed to his ability to recruit them and ultimately convince them to commit crimes at his behest [11]. Manson died in prison in 2017 while serving nine life sentences for orchestrating multiple murders in 1969, most famously the murder of actress Sharon Tate.

Jim Jones appealed to the desire for a better life, promising a utopia and attracting many Black followers by promising a racially integrated society starting in the 1950s [17]. His ability to sell a vision of a perfect society led his supporters to follow him to Guyana and ultimately participate in a mass suicide resulting in the "largest number of American civilian casualties in a single non-natural event" prior to September 11, 2001 [12].

Authoritarian Rule through Elimination of Competition

In order to gain the level of control needed to influence their followings, family cult leaders use a variety of tactics to consolidate power. One such tactic that proves very important for several leaders of family cults is the ability to convince their followings to remove competition as well as any checks and balances on their power. Because a competing power structure is the individual family, these leaders often work to exert control over families, including potential family composition, to ensure that the ultimate loyalty is to the cult leader.

When Rulon Jeffs took over the FLDS, there were seven priests who governed the church. Jeffs and his son Warren, who took over after his father's passing in 2002, ultimately transitioned to "One Man Rule," eliminating any checks on the ultimate authority of the appointed prophet [18]. Warren Jeffs had full control over family structure, determining which men would earn the right to marry and deciding who their wives would be. Men in Jeffs' favor would be assigned multiple wives while those who were not in his favor would remain unmarried. Women were used as rewards, assigned to marry men who were held in good standing. The lack of any checks to his power led all cult members to prioritize pleasing Jeffs, as he was in control of their futures. After facing various charges in Utah and Texas, he was ultimately convicted of sexual assault of a child and aggravated sexual assault against a child in 2011 and is currently serving a life sentence in prison [19].

Ervil LeBaron's creation of the Church of the Lamb of God started with the murder of his brother Joel, who had taken over the family church after the passing of their father, Alma. Alma had moved his family to Mexico due to their desire to continue the tradition of polygamy which had been outlawed by the Mormon Church in 1890 and was illegal in the United States. However, Joel LeBaron was just the first competitor who fell victim to Ervil LeBaron and his followers. The Church of the Lamb of God had several members charged and convicted of murdering rival polygamists as well as defectors from and critics of the church. Ervil himself was imprisoned in 1980 for ordering the killing of one such rival, Rulon Allred, in 1977 [20]. Ervil's charisma led cult members to continue their killings, even after he was imprisoned and after he passed away in 1981. They used a list he had made of people to target, and continued killings at least until 1988 [20].

Characteristics of Followers

Those who seek membership in a cult often feel that their current life is unpleasant and dissatisfying and are looking for something new to replace an increasingly intolerable existence [16]. While this is less relevant for members who are born into a cult, as happens in many family cults, people who are converts into a family cult are either looking for a new family or are looking for a new life for their existing family. Followers of the cults that have been discussed in this chapter often have characteristics that are directly related to the characteristics of the cults' leaders (Table 7.1).

Table 7.1 A sample of prominent family cults

Cult Name	Cult Founder/ Leader	Years Active	Description
Agapemonites	Reverend Harry James Prince	1846–1956	Fundamental belief involved a spirituality of the state of matrimony. Many members were unmarried wealthy women and cult leaders took many spiritual wives. They preached celibacy, though many leaders were known not to practice it.
Aggressive Christianity Missionary Training Corps	James and Deborah Green	1981–present	Started in Sacramento, CA. Ostensibly presenting itself as a Christian movement, but leaders have been accused of isolating members, refusing members' medical treatment, corporal punishment, child abuse, sexual assault, and rape.
Alamo Christian Foundation	Tony and Susan Alamo	1969–present	Started in Hollywood, where members would attract hippies and youth to an extreme form of Pentecostalism. Tony Alamo considered many underaged women his wives and ultimately went to prison for sexually abusing them.
Branch Davidians	Benjamin Roden formed an offshoot of the Davidians, an Adventist branch created by Victor Houteff in 1934. David Koresh took control in the 1980s	1955–present	David Koresh wanted to create a lineage of world leaders. He believed himself a prophet and created the "House of David" – women who were chosen to procreate with him.
Church of the First Born of the Lamb of God	Ervil LeBaron	1972–89	Initially an offshoot of Mormonism due to unwillingness to end the practice of polygamy, the group frequently murdered those who defected.
The Family International	David Berg	1968 (started as The Children of God)–present	The group combined Christian teachings with ideas from the sexual revolution of the 1960s, appealing to the views of the youth at the time. There were

Table 7.1 *(cont.)*

Cult Name	Cult Founder/ Leader	Years Active	Description
			many accusations of sexual abuse, including against Berg, who died in hiding in 1994. The Family rebranded and instituted overt rules against underage sex in the 1980s.
Fundamentalist Church of Jesus Christ of Latter-Day Saints	Founded by Lorin C. Woodley. Power consolidated by Rulon T. Jeffs, then taken over by his son Warren Jeffs	1929–present	Initially an offshoot of Mormonism due to unwillingness to end the practice of polygamy, it was ultimately run by Warren Jeffs, who determined family structure. Jeffs is now serving a life sentence in prison for marrying underage children.
The Manson Family	Charles Manson	1967–69	Started by Charles Manson, who built a following of young women during the "Summer of Love," and ended up directing them to commit a series of murders, including the murder of actress Sharon Tate.
Peoples Temple	Jim Jones	1955–78	Jim Jones used egalitarian teachings to sell a utopia. He gained a large Black following due to his promotion of racial equality. Ultimately he founded a settlement in Guyana that ended with a tragic mass suicide in 1978.

Followers of a messianic leader like David Koresh had an unwavering belief in his status as leader and messenger of God. They were obedient to his many demands, including how people dressed, how they disciplined their children, that they should remain celibate even with their spouses, and even that men should give their wives and children to him to join the "House of David" so they could help him procreate and continue his lineage [8].

Followers of leaders promoting a new societal structure fall within the subgroup of cult followers that are dissatisfied with the status quo and are looking for something new in their lives [16]. These people can be looking for a new family dynamic or structure, like the followers of The Family International and the members of the Manson Family. These two cults provided their followers with a new form of living and a new social dynamic within the family, which better matched their followers' perceptions of how life should be led. Others who are dissatisfied with the status quo may be looking for fundamental societal change, like the followers of the Peoples Temple. Jim Jones brought together followers who were looking for social, economic, and racial equality, selling a vision of a utopia that appealed to their sensibilities. The Church of the Lamb of God and the FLDS appealed to those who believed in the doctrine of polygamy and were searching for a society that would allow them to practice their religious beliefs.

Followers of autocratic leaders often have ties that bind them to the cult, making it difficult to leave. They end up following cult doctrine to protect themselves and their families from punishment. Ervil LeBaron's Church of the Lamb of God consisted mainly of his family members, which helped him indoctrinate and exert control over his followers. The complex family dynamics resulted in members feeling compelled to kill on LeBaron's behalf. Followers in the FLDS felt the same pressure under the rule of Rulon and Warren Jeffs. Their families were controlled by the church leader, and they could be separated from their spouses and married to someone else if they fell out of favor with the group. Even worse, sometimes, their sons and daughters could be chosen to be married when underage. To protect themselves and their families, members felt compelled to follow cult doctrine.

Future Considerations

The definitions of family are rapidly changing [3] for various reasons. The transition from the traditional model of one male parent and one female parent living with their biological children to the inclusion of all lifestyles is changing our conception of what constitutes a family. Additionally, increased connectivity, particularly in the age of the internet, allows people to maintain connections and forge deep bonds with other individuals living in any part of the world. People do not need to see each other in person on a regular basis, or even at all, to have strong relationships. As our concept of a family continues to change, and as our communities interact in different ways, it will be interesting to see how our conceptions of family cults change over time.

Key Points

- For the purposes of this chapter, a family is considered to be a unit that regularly spends time together, usually lives together, and is particularly focused on the relationships they maintain among each other, above relationships they may hold with other members of society.
- For the purposes of this chapter, a family cult is considered to be a cult that either mainly consists of one family or a cult whose doctrine specifically defines or exerts control over the family structures of its members. Several cults throughout history have fit this definition, and six of them are discussed in the chapter.
- Family cult leaders share characteristics with leaders of all cults but there is an added degree of complexity to maintain their influence because their members have family loyalties that have the potential to interfere with the leader's ability to exert control. Their strategies to maintain control often involve influencing or minimizing the dynamics of families within their cults.
- Family cult members are looking for a way to live that is outside of contemporary societal norms. While cult members generally commit to changing their way of life, members of family cults are making this commitment not only for themselves but also for their loved ones. Their convictions are so great that they are willing to put their family members in the position of having to abide by the rules of the cults as well.

References

1. Health Resources and Services Administration. Definition of family. 2022 Mar. www.hrsa.gov/get-health-care/affordable/hill-burton/family
2. LL Bumpass. Social change and the American family. *Annals of the New York Academy of Sciences*. 2006;1038(1):213–19.
3. LA Miller. Defining family. *Journal of Perinatal & Neonatal Nursing*. 2014;28(2):155–56.
4. B Holoyda, W Newman. Between belief and delusion: cult members and the insanity plea. *Journal of the American Academy of Psychiatry and the Law*. 2016;44(1):53–62.
5. SA Wright, ES Piper. Families and cults: familial factors related to youth leaving or remaining in deviant religious groups. *Journal of Marriage and Family*. 1986;48:15–25.
6. JG Melton. Branch Davidians. Encyclopedia Britannica. 2023 Aug 11. www.britannica.com/topic/Branch-Davidian
7. TM Kerstetter. Branch Davidians. Encyclopedia of the Great Plains. 2011. http://plainshumanities.unl.edu/encyclopedia/doc/egp.rel.007
8. M Pearson, S Wilking, L Effron. Who was David Koresh: ex-followers describe life inside apocalyptic religious sect involved in 1993 Waco siege. ABC News. 2018 Jan 2. https://abcnews.go.com/US/david-koresh-followers-describe-life-inside-apocalyptic-religious/story?id=52033937
9. S Tewa. Children of God Church: from sex cult to Texas-Mexico sect. *The Guardian*. 2017 Mar 11. https://bit.ly/3OhkUJn
10. S Almasy, B Griggs. Charles Manson, leader of murderous '60s cult, dead at 83. CNN. 2017 Nov 20. www.cnn.com/2017/11/20/us/charles-manson-dead/index.html
11. S Atkins. Grand Jury testimony. 1969 Dec 5. www.cielodrive.com/susan-atkins-grand-jury-testimony.php
12. D Chiu. Jonestown: 13 things you should know about the cult massacre. *Rolling Stone*. 2019 Nov 14. www.rollingstone.com/feature/jonestown-13-things-you-should-know-about-cult-massacre-121974/
13. B Winslow. New edict purportedly from FLDS leader Warren Jeffs raises alarm. Fox 13 Salt Lake City. 2022 Aug 1. www.fox13now.com/news/local-news/new-edict-purportedly-from-flds-leader-warren-jeffs-raises-alarm
14. Southern Poverty Law Center. Fundamentalist Church of Jesus Christ of Latter-Day Saints. www.splcenter.org/fighting-hate/extremist-files/group/fundamentalist-church-jesus-christ-latter-day-saints
15. B Wheeler. Anna LeBaron: How I escaped my father's murderous polygamous cult. BBC News. 2017 Feb 17. www.bbc.com/news/magazine-38526255
16. SV Levine, NE Salter. Youth and contemporary religious movements: psychosocial findings. *Canadian Psychiatric Association Journal*. 1976;21(6):411–20.
17. A Tikkanen. Jim Jones. Encyclopedia Britannica. 2023. www.britannica.com/biography/Jim-Jones
18. W Goodwyn, H Berkes, A Walters. Warren Jeffs and the FLDS. NPR. 2005 May 3. www.npr.org/2005/05/03/4629320/warren-jeffs-and-the-flds
19. M Mitchell. Where is Warren Jeffs now? Inside the FLDS "Keep Sweet, Pray, Obey" on Netflix. *Newsweek*. 2022 Jun 8. www.newsweek.com/where-warren-jeffs-now-flds-keep-sweet-pray-obey-netflix-1713380
20. G Abrams. A family's legacy of death: Ervil LeBaron said God told him to kill anyone who strayed from his polygamist cult. A tenacious Salt Lake investigator tracked the LeBarons for 15 years. Now, an anonymous tip may have helped him close a case that claimed as many as 30 lives. *Los Angeles Times*. 1992 Sep 20. www.latimes.com/archives/la-xpm-1992-09-20-vw-1753-story.html

Chapter 8

Adolescents and Cults

Amanie Salem

"These children that come at you with knives – they are your children. You taught them. I didn't teach them. I just tried to help them stand up."
– *Charles Manson, leader of the Manson Family*

Introduction

Adolescence is a period of time when many individuals engage in group-like activity. Because of biological, social, and psychological factors, individuals during this transitional time are increasingly susceptible to peer pressure and following the norms of a group. Peer influence during this phase of an individual's life is normative and may be positive or negative. A cult is on a continuum of a far range where influence extends beyond normal.

Adolescent Development

Adolescent development remains a popular topic of research. Erikson's theory of adolescent identity development was a dominant force in research (1968), followed by Piaget's theory of formal operations, an organizational framework for adolescent research in the early 1970s and 1980s. In the 1990s, cognitive development and informational-processing garnered interest as empirical studies elucidated further information regarding normative adolescent brain development [1].

Research regarding typical adolescent development has also assisted in describing problematic adolescent behavior. Studies indicate that the rate of occasional experimentation in adolescence exceeds the rates of enduring problems or dangerous behaviors. While some teenagers do fall into patterns of delinquent behavior during adolescence, other adolescent behaviors have their origins evident in early childhood. Many problems experienced by adolescents are resolved by the beginning of adulthood [1].

Until the maturation of cognitive control that develops during early adulthood, many adolescents engage in heightened reward-seeking behavior without adequate impulse control. Neuroscientific explanations of adolescent risk-taking behavior implicate increased dopaminergic activity in the limbic and paralimbic projections to the prefrontal cortex during puberty. Though the brain does improve its thinking processes during adolescence as well, primarily due to synaptic pruning affecting the frontal lobes and maturation of multiple cortical and subcortical regions, this occurs on a slower time course, resulting in adolescence being a time of inherently immature judgment for many youth [2].

Adolescence is also a time of self-exploration. During the transition from childhood to adolescence, developing youth explore characteristics of the self to discover their identity, who they really are, and how they fit into the social world around them. Early adolescents begin to develop abstract characterizations of themselves and start viewing themselves in terms of personal beliefs and standards [3]. While individuals developing through middle adolescence describe themselves in discrepant ways, adolescents form a more consistent view of themselves in later years.

There is evidence that adolescents view themselves differently across contexts. For example, when they are with peers, adolescents may behave differently than when they are with parents or teachers. During the transition into adolescence, an increasing amount of time is spent alone and with friends as compared to time spent with their parents. Research suggests that adolescents in less cohesive adaptive families are more influenced by peers than parents, with peers influencing adolescent development in both positive and negative ways [4].

Susceptibility to Cult Recruitment

The empirical evidence regarding adolescent development illuminates characteristics that make young people susceptible to cult recruitment. Individuals within the 18- to 30-year age range, and more specifically, the 18- to 23-year age range, are particularly susceptible to cult recruitment [5, 6]. There are many documented cases of adolescents leaving families, dropping out of education, and even venturing to remote communes to participate in cults [7]. One Canadian survey found that some cult members interviewed were former university students who dropped out to join cults, never returning to their studies [8]. Another survey of campus chaplains found that 77% of chaplains believed it was likely or probable that some students on their campus were currently in a cult. Moreover, 93% believed that students on their campus had, at some point, been involved in a cult, and 86% believed that college and university administrators across the nation should be concerned about cults on campus [9].

Characteristics of Normal Adolescent Life Predispose Adolescents for Recruitment

Characteristics of normal adolescent life may also contribute to stress that make adolescents particularly predisposed to cult recruitment. Firstly, adolescence is a time of searching for one's identity and questioning one's place in the world. According to Erikson's stages of development, adolescence is a time in which individuals are confronted with conflicting ideas and values as they develop a sense of self. Because adolescents find difficulty coping with new and unfamiliar scenarios as they navigate developing an identity, they draw from models found within their environment [10]. Although youth might struggle to cope with their existence due to their biological and psychosocial growth, as well as the constant changes of the social climate, they strive for a sense of belonging and self-identity that are crucial to their psychosocial development [11]. They often seek comfort in those who welcome them or reinforce a sense of belonging. Thus, feeling alienated and unwanted may compromise this psychosocial development and increase adolescent likelihood of involvement in cults, as cults fulfill needs of belonging and overcoming alienation, demoralization, and low-self-esteem [12,

13]. Within a few weeks, adolescents who join a cult may develop an identity made up of primarily cult doctrine, while suppressing further exploration of identity that they have been taught associates with an unacceptable world [7].

Secondly, adolescence is a time of heightened dissatisfaction with established ways of thinking and known institutions. As they continue to explore their world, adolescents start seeing the deficiencies present in institutions they have trusted. During this time, youth may be critical of established values and patterns of society, leading to feelings of frustration when the change they desire does not occur. Teens may view solutions as simple and believe that those in the power of established institutions have failed to meet the needs of various groups [10]. This increasing frailty of the belief systems that they have had throughout their childhoods provides a window for recruiters from cults to promise something better [7]. Joining a cult fulfills a conscious or unconscious search for a more satisfactory life for these individuals, reflected in how they answer questions regarding joining a cult, what they receive from membership, and why they continue to stay involved [13].

Thirdly, being in a "transitional phase of life" makes adolescents vulnerable to joining a cult. As part of the developmental transition discussed earlier, adolescents may experience job changes, moving, loss of romantic partners, or academic changes. For example, leaving home for college or a job after high school is a major life change that can precede cult membership [7]. Adolescents who joined cults agreed that their removal from the previous life that they experienced made it easier to convince them of the cult's doctrines [7].

Lastly, adolescents do not yet possess the maturity and sophistication that may be necessary to differentiate realistic goals and ideals from illusion and fantasy. Research indicates that cults are most successful in recruiting individuals between 18 and 23 years of age, when an individual is most likely seeking "perfect" answers to life's questions or problems [10].

Providing What Is Missing

Adolescent development and characteristics of normal adolescent life predispose some adolescents to cult recruitment and lead to cults providing much of what is often missing in their lives. Cults attract youths experiencing stress, loneliness, and identity confusion, and they offer respite from the psychological stress of adolescence, offering an environment to overcome alienation, demoralization, and low self-esteem. Because these characteristics are often seen in the normal adolescent experience, these youth come from all walks of life and society [10, 13]. Cults provide the basic needs of "believing" and "belonging." As described by Levine, "believing" refers to a coherent, meaningful system of values or a set of inspiring goals, and "belonging" refers to a sense of being part of an intense, communal experience, with explicit acceptance, shared aspirations, emotions, and experiences [13]. A sense of belief and belonging can be provided to adolescents by both destructive and constructive groups, including cults. Often because recruited individuals feel little purpose and control over their lives, cult members can make these individuals feel a sense of identity, belonging, and increased self-esteem [13, 14]. Teens seeking comfort from people who give them a sense of belonging and who welcome them are particularly susceptible to a cult's ability to satisfy the adolescent's need for approval, belonging, and self-worth. These groups may further provide adolescents with something akin to family, giving them companionship, loyalty, identity, and status [11].

As they look for answers to what is missing, cults meet adolescent needs that may include of a sense of belonging, mastery and structure, power and control, rebellion, curiosity and relief from boredom, self-esteem, and validation of anger and violence [14]. Membership in a cult can provide a community that seems certain about life, and it can lead to adolescents being able to cede decision-making power to cult leadership. Cults provide a structure dictating what is good and what is bad, and the structure appears to have a joint purpose [7]. By making life seemingly safe, predictable, and controllable, cults can be a place of respite, even providing therapeutic benefit to those with certain psychiatric or behavioral problems [13, 15].

Specific Considerations for Adolescents

As adolescents strive for social acceptance, school settings provide an opportunity for such an experience. Student cliques and social groups within schools have been popularized in teen-themed books, movies, and TV shows. These groups provide something for adolescents to attach to beyond the comfort zone of their childhood and family, serving as a safety zone for a feeling of belonging and acceptance [15]. However, it is also challenging for adolescents to find their identity and then find others who also reflect that identity. And while the purpose and value of social groups in school settings is not always negative, students who find it difficult to bond with cliques may seek more serious and vulnerable forms of bonding through cults [15].

Cult-like behavior in the school setting is often seen within groups of children and adolescents organizing to bully or harass other students, teachers, or even administrators. For example, a small group of bullies aligning to harass a peer with a disability or an organized group of peers harassing a student because of academic skill provide the basis for understanding cult behavior within a school setting [15]. With the expansion of internet access, this behavior can occur both in person and online.

Taking into account the common characteristics between cult membership and addictive disorders, specifically the symptom of persistence despite negative consequences and the proposed neurophysiological mechanisms, some research has drawn parallels between cult membership and addictive disorders, postulating that this could be an effective way to understand the behavior of cult members [14, 16]. Given that adolescents are susceptible to disorders of addiction, this may provide an understanding of adolescent recruitment into cults.

Case Vignette

The Slender Man, a fictional supernatural character, first emerged in 2009 on an online post and quickly appeared in numerous works of fan art and online fiction. Stories of the Slender Man describe a thin, unnaturally tall human with a featureless white face, and commonly center around his stalking, abducting, or traumatizing others, specifically children. As the Slender Man grew in popularity, many people began entertaining the possibility that he might be real. For adolescents in particular, the lines between legend and reality were blurred. In 2014, two 12-year-old girls in Wisconsin held down and stabbed a 12-year-old classmate 19 times. They reported to authorities that after reading about him online, the stabbing was a first step to becoming proxies for the Slender Man.

Characteristics of Leaders

Intelligence and Charisma

Research regarding characteristics of cult leaders of adolescents remains limited. However, studies of all cults indicate that compared to followers involved in cults, leaders of cults tended to be more "articulate" and "intelligent" [8]. Recruiters are often strong, intelligent, and convincing – convinced themselves and convincing others that they know what is best for an individual [7]. These traits can be harnessed by cult leaders with the aim of dominating members using pressure strategies or psychological manipulation [16]. They slowly aim to detach recruits from their prior identification objects and replace their earlier belief systems with that of cults. Through their determination and domination, these (often self-appointed) persuasive cult leaders may make adolescents feel for the first time that they are "like other people."

Through their intelligence and charisma, cult leaders are also able to identify and meet the needs of vulnerable adolescents. Leaders often try to recruit people who are vulnerable and have limited connections to outside influences [16]. They can target people whom they know need companionship, with recruiters focusing on adolescents who recently dropped out of classes or who recently attended counseling at universities. In one case, a recruiter infiltrated Bible study groups and used his superior knowledge of the Bible to gain trust of people who he eventually recruited into his cult, convincing others that he had the truth they were searching for [7].

Indoctrination and Isolation

Cult leaders use to their advantage the uncertainty experienced by many individuals during adolescent development to strategically indoctrinate and isolate new recruits. Leaders provide answers to existential questions and to identity-related concerns of followers. For adolescents, already in a developmentally vulnerable state of exploring these questions and concerns, answers provided by the leaders offer a new system of logic in which things that were confusing become comprehensible [8].

In their recruitment of adolescents and new members, leaders often start by giving importance and flattery to new recruits prior to isolating them from outside influences. They are then able to cultivate an unconditional adherence to the rules of the group and the rule of leadership [5]. The process of recruitment is aggressive, with a focus of leaders to obtain membership by separating individuals from people in their outside lives to change value systems and instill a dependence on the cult [10]. Leaders anticipate that families and friends of new members may counter their beliefs, and they preemptively prepare the new members for conversations with other members of their lives. Intimidation through force or threats may also occur and control the adolescent's behavior. Due to the power differential between adolescents and adults, the thoughts of the adolescents recruited tend to follow the behavior of the leader through rationalization, justification, and identification with the aggressor [5].

Personality Considerations

A number of studies have reported accounts of antisocial acts and behaviors by cult leaders. It has also been suggested that cult leaders display characteristics of narcissistic personality disorder [17]. More serious cult members can also originate from more dysfunctional families and have trouble maintaining healthy peer relationships [14]. Those in cults with a more fantastical basis – such as vampire cults – may have more schizotypal characteristics, and others, with more organization and intact reality testing, may have perverse or psychopathic tendencies. Leaders with more perverse tendencies may derive sexual satisfaction from the fantastical or grotesque, whereas the more psychopathic may enjoy the aspect of control over others [15].

Characteristics of Followers

Covering Deficiencies

As with characteristics of cult leaders who target adolescents, there is still research to be conducted regarding characteristics of adolescents who are followers in cults. People attracted to cults are often looking to cover for deficiencies within their own lives [12]. In general, followers may be individuals who are experiencing a level of internal pain prior to deciding to join a cult [13]. While they may not always be experiencing clinical disturbance, individuals who are attracted to cults are engaged in a search for more satisfaction in their lives [8, 13]. The search for satisfaction is frequently reflected in answers regarding why they joined cults, why they stayed as members, and what they gained from the experience [13]. In general, there is a theme that life was not pleasant for these individuals and that they were having difficulty coping with even minor stressors. Their sense of identity consolidation, a developmental milestone in adolescence, was not yet achieved and they were searching for something new prior to being recruited [8]. For this reason, cult activity very frequently starts after a significant life event, often something traumatic [11, 14]. Individuals finding no joy in work, no point to education, no reason to trust institutions, and no strong relationships to their lives are susceptible to cult recruitment [15].

Adolescents who feel particularly alienated, alone, angry, and desperate are more likely to be enticed by the promises of cults [14]. A teenager who feels empty and alienated may be searching for an identity and a place to belong. Because a sense of belonging and self-identity is central to the adolescent experience, alienation presents a serious impediment to adolescents resolving their identity crisis. Thus, in the absence of others who welcome and comfort them, they might find fulfillment by aligning with a cult.

Although specific characteristics of adolescents who become cult followers requires more research, there is some evidence in the literature of deficiencies individuals may exhibit prior to joining a cult. Rousselet et al found that a majority of ex-cult individuals who were recruited as adolescents surveyed had an anxiety disorder and just under half had a mood disorder in the year prior to cult commitment [16]. In another study, several respondents cited a lack of fulfillment with their spiritual lives and loosened ties with their churches as precursors to joining a cult. The same study reported individuals coming from a strict family where authority was followed without questioning provided an easy transition into cult lifestyle [7]. However, other studies note a lack of correlation between strictness or laxness of religious training or involvement as children [8].

Additionally, adolescents seeking an intimate form of communication that they have not been able to find elsewhere in their lives through family or peer experiences may be

Box 8.1 Factors Predisposing Adolescent Involvement in Cults

- A time of life transition
- Alienation from familiar environments and information
- A desire for belonging
- Dissatisfaction with current explanations of life
- Family difficulties

susceptible to cult membership [18]. People who felt a need for love and the desire to be a part of a good cause were often blinded to the manipulation of cult leaders and later can reflect on this being a factor in their recruitment [7]. They are often first attracted to these groups because of the promise to fulfill a need missing in their lives.

Demographic and Personality Considerations

The personality or demographic characteristics that predispose an adolescent to cult membership vary (Box 8.1). While the personality of an adolescent susceptible to cult recruitment might include identity confusion, alienation from family, limited cultural, religious, and community ties, and feelings of powerlessness, it is unclear that any specific personality characteristics definitively allow for being lured into cults [7]. Although many members cite being unhappy before they joined cults and a disproportionate number were manifesting psychiatric symptoms, psychiatric diagnoses could not be applied to most adolescent cult-involved cases [8]. Commonly, cult members also had previous exposure to cults, or even family members in cults, prior to joining [16].

Not all cult members come from dysfunctional families. One author notes that many members came from intact families [8]. Another author notes that a surprising number of members come from egalitarian homes and upper socioeconomic levels. Specifically, cults may attract gifted, creative youth experiencing some sort of psychological stress, emptiness, and identity confusion, and such experiences affect youth from every walk of life and class of society [10].

Initial Improvement after Joining a Cult

Joining a cult can result in initial improvement in how new recruits feel. Because individuals who join cults may have been searching for a feeling of security and sense of belonging, those individuals who joined cults initially found abrupt improvement in their lives. They reported initially being happier, more self-accepting, and improved in their psychological state. Members reported that joining the groups helped them both internally feel better about themselves and interpersonally have better relationships [8].

After Joining Cults

In contrast to the fulfillment members may report they felt after initially joining a cult, notable personality and philosophical changes happen to adolescents later in their experience of cult membership. Adolescents in cults often appear negative and seem hopeless about the future [14, 11]. Some adolescents withdraw, change friends, and start using a new vocabulary [11]. They express a bleak outlook on life and lack humor and spontaneity observed as part of normal adolescent development. These adolescents also tend to have difficulty maintaining flexibility in their relationships and relationships that they do maintain are frequently superficial and centered around the experience of cult activity [11].

As members become increasingly involved in cults, they struggle to balance their lives outside the cult with their life inside the cult, and their dependence on the cult increases. Adolescents involved in cults may find this balance increasingly difficult, and their active involvement in the cult could subsequently lead to dependence on the cult leader or the group [16]. The dysfunctional and manipulative culture of cults can induce temporary characteristics of dependent personality disorder in cult members [17].

Dynamics of Staying or Leaving

Various dynamics underlie whether cult members choose to remain in cults or to leave, and these dynamics may explain why people stay despite threats to their physical and psychological integrity. Protective factors that allow people to leave cults are difficult to predict and may seem surprising in the context of the constraints of a cult [16].

Once in a cult, membership can be reinforced by both positive emotions associated with membership and negative emotions associated with being pushed out of the group or rejection and abuse that could come from failing to meet the standards of the group [16]. This fluctuation may be conflicting, particularly for adolescents, as they are developmentally in a state of exploration and understanding of their identities and emotions. Individuals who remained in cults the longest were found to be those whose respective cults humiliated members who opposed leadership or those who displayed "social precariousness" (i.e., having limited job prospects and stability outside the cult). Individuals cited particular difficulty leaving a cult when they felt reassurance from being a part of the group, they had family members or romantic partners in the group, or they had connections with cult members [16]. A study examining the personality traits of ex-cult members as young as age 16 years found that individuals with higher levels of dependent personality traits were more likely to join cults and those with higher levels of autonomy were more likely to leave or be removed from cults [19]. This presents a challenge for younger members, as adolescence is a time when true autonomy is just being developed.

Future Considerations

Access in the Age of the Internet

With the emergence of increased access to technology, the internet, and social media, it is worth discussing how cults and adolescent membership in cults has changed. While access to cults may have previously required physical presence, the prevalence of the internet provides adolescents access to cults that requires much less effort to explore. Many adolescents have internet access through school, their homes, and personal electronics, all of which provide an opportunity for them to learn about cults and for cults to target and recruit them.

Additionally, adolescents continue to use social media at a significant rate. Surveys indicate that upwards of 90% of adolescents aged 13–17 reported using at least one social media platform [20] with users often engaging in social media as early as 10 years old [21]. Social media offers adolescents an opportunity to share information about themselves with others online whom they may or may not know. And because adolescents show a much greater susceptibility to peer influence than adults, as well as deficiencies in future orientation and the ability to consider long-term consequences of their actions, they are a considerably vulnerable population in online communities.

Rethinking Adolescents and Cults

How adolescents interact with the internet and how the internet and technology target adolescents offer an updated lens through which to define and consider adolescent involvement in cults. The cravings for belonging and purpose have likely existed since the beginning of humanity, but the present era of ubiquitous internet access and social media make the twenty-first century particularly ripe for groupthink. Modern groups with similar interests can now gather online, declaring themselves as part of a larger, global group such as "Swifties" (fans of the singer Taylor Swift) or "Potterheads" (fans of the Harry Potter book series). And while online communities made of fans referencing popular culture icons do not constitute "cults," these online communities are illustrative of society's shifting views regarding belonging and purpose. For new generations growing up in a digital age when one method of belonging means clicking "like" or "follow," finding and joining others who hold similar beliefs seems easier than ever.

For example, the case of the Slender Man presented earlier in the chapter features cult-like characteristics that originated online. Another example involves what is known as the Blue Whale or Blue Whale Challenge, a social networking "game" that seems to have first appeared online in 2015. The game is run on various social media platforms and consists of a series of tasks assigned to players by administrators over a 50-day period. These tasks start benignly before introducing elements of self-harm and a final challenge requiring the player to commit suicide. While first appearing in Russia, one investigation concluded that there had been 200 child and adolescent suicides traced back to the Blue Whale Challenge and numerous vulnerable children and adolescents affected by linked cyberbullying and online shaming.

Practical Implications

In today's digitally connected era, cults may provide vulnerable adolescents a perceived sense of guidance in a culture where there's pressure to create a persona that looks and thinks a certain way. Awareness of groups extending beyond the continuum of the normal adolescent experience may assist in preventing adolescents from engaging in potentially dangerous behavior (Table 8.1). Additionally, adults can adopt certain behaviors that may assist in preventing adolescents from engaging with cults (Box 8.2).

Key Points

- The stress and search for an identity inherent in adolescent development make teenagers prime targets for recruitment by cults.
- Cults present solutions to the many problems that adolescents face. Adolescents show deficiencies in future orientation and the ability to consider long-term consequences of their actions, and many members initially find improvement in their well-being in the short term.
- Beyond a desire to solve their existential problems, it is difficult to find many predictive characteristics that would predispose adolescents to cult membership.

Table 8.1 A sample of groups extending beyond normal adolescent experience

Name	Description
Tumple	– Described by its own leadership as a cult. – Attempted to subvert Western tradition and dismantle "white methodology" and replace it with a "black pleasure foundation." – Lifestyle included prioritizing pleasure, practicing sober leaving, learning antiracist education and mystical sex practices, and paying for a course through which to learn about this lifestyle. – Majority of members interacted with the organization over the internet.
Slender Man	– A fictional, supernatural character that originated on the internet. – Described as thin and unnaturally tall with a featureless white head and face, wearing a black suit. – The success of Slender Man is attributed to its collaborative nature. The character is viewed as mysterious and online users can adapt the imagery to create new stories. – Although users understand that Slender Man is not real, disbelief is suspended by users who become engrossed in the story, adding authenticity to the character.
The Blue Whale Challenge	– A social networking event. – Described as a "game" in which administrators assign individuals a series of tasks over a 50-day period. – Challenges are initially harmless before introducing self-harm and culminating into a final challenge requiring players to kill themselves.
Satanic	– Variety of groups that focus on worship of and service to Satan or the Devil. – Often connected to other antisocial behavior.
Vampire	– Contemporary subculture attributed as an offshoot of the Gothic movement of the 1980s. – Range of behaviors including only emerging at night, sleeping in coffins, and blood sharing. – One of the most notorious was a Kentucky group of 30–40 teenagers called the "Vampire Clan." They came to public attention in 1996, when four teenagers were charged with first-degree murder of two parents of one cult member.

Box 8.2 Preventing Adolescents from Engaging in Cults

- Connect with adolescents by knowing what their beliefs are, who their friends are, and what activities they are engaging in
- Strengthen adolescents' sense of self-esteem
- Encourage adolescents to express their views and ideas, ask questions, and foster discussion if they have questions about cults
- Empower adolescents' feelings of making differences in their own lives

- Leaving cults is a complex decision and is often multifactorial. Having characteristics of autonomy and having more of a life to go back to outside the cult can be factors that aid someone to leave cult membership.
- Increased access to the internet and social media has created additional vulnerabilities for adolescents and cult membership.
- Prevention of cult membership can be achieved by addressing the needs of adolescents and finding alternative avenues for them to have structure, feelings of accomplishment, self-esteem, and a sense of belonging.

References

1. L Steinberg, AS Morris. Adolescent development. *Annual Review of Psychology*. 2001;52:83–110.
2. L Steinberg. Adolescent development and juvenile justice. *Annual Review of Clinical Psychology*. 2009;5:459–85.
3. S Harter, S Bresnick, HA Bouchey, NR Whitesell. The development of multiple role-related selves during adolescence. *Development and Psychopathology*. 1997;9(4):835–53.
4. C Gauze, WM Bukowski, J Aquan-Assee, LK Sippola. Interactions between family environment and friendship and associations with self-perceived well-being during adolescence. *Child Development*. 1996;67:2201–16.
5. LJ West. Persuasive techniques in contemporary cults: a public health approach. *Cultic Studies Journal*. 1990;7(2):126–49.
6. SA Wright, ES Piper. Families and cults: familial factors related to youth leaving or remaining in deviant religious groups. *Journal of Marriage and Family*. 1986;48:15–25.
7. MA Venter. Susceptibility of adolescents to cults. *Southern African Journal of Child and Adolescent Mental Health*. 1998;10(2):93–106.
8. SV Levine, NE Salter. Youth and contemporary religious movements: psychosocial findings. *Canadian Psychiatric Association Journal*. 1976;21(6):411–20.
9. RK Elleven, KJ Greenhaw, J Allen. Campus chaplains: cult training and perceptions. *College Student Journal*. 2004;38(2):314–20.
10. E Hunter. Adolescent attraction to cults. *Adolescence*. 1998;33(131):709–14.
11. CM Clark. Deviant adolescent subcultures: assessment strategies and clinical interventions. *Adolescence*. 1992;27(106):283–93.
12. M White, H Omar. Vampirism, vampire cults, and the teenager of today. *International Journal of Adolescent Medicine and Health*. 2010;22(2):189–95.
13. S Levine. Cults and mental health: clinical conclusions. *Canadian Journal of Psychiatry*. 1981;26:534–39.
14. CM Clark. Clinical assessment of adolescents involved in Satanism. *Adolescence*. 1994;29(114):461–68.
15. TW Miller, TF Holcomb, RF Kraus. Cliques and cults as a contributor to violence in the school environment. In TW Miller, editor. *School violence and primary prevention*. Springer; 2008. p. 215–25.
16. M Rousselet, O Duretete, JB Hardouin, M Grall-Bronnec. Cult membership: what factors contribute to joining or leaving? *Psychiatry Research*. 2017;257:27–33.
17. J Burke. Antisocial personality disorder in cult leaders and induction of dependent personality disorder in cult members. *Cultic Studies Review*. 2006;5(3):390–410.
18. TW Miller, LJ Voltkamp, RF Kraus, T Lane, T Heister. An adolescent vampire cult in rural America: clinical issues and case study. *Child Psychiatry & Human Development*. 1999;29(3):209–19.
19. Y Walsh, RJH Russell, PA Wells. The personality of ex-cult members. *Personality and Individual Differences*. 1995;19(3):339–44.

20. M Anderson, J Jiang. *Teens, social media, and technology 2018*. Pew Research Center; 2018. file:///Users/amaniesalem/Downloads/PI_2018.05.31_TeensTech_FINAL.pdf

21. RB Mann, F Blumberg. Adolescents and social media: the effects of frequency of use, self-presentation, social comparison, and self esteem on possible self imagery. *Acta Psychologica*. 2022;228.

Chapter 9 Comorbid Major Mental Disorders

Ashley H. VanDercar, Ren Belcher, and Susan Hatters Friedman

"Every expert agrees that Ryan has grandiose, self-centered, paranoid, and hostile thought processes, that he professes a rigid and unusual religious belief in Yahweh, and that he claims to receive audible messages from Yahweh which control his actions. The experts disagree on whether mental illness is the cause."
[1, p. 1054]

Introduction

Any discussion of major mental disorders in cult populations must begin with an awareness of the inherent difficulties in obtaining data on this topic, as well as that clinicians may disagree on the role of mental illness in cult behavior in any particular case. Cults are, by definition, secretive. Neither their leaders nor their members are prone to seek psychiatric care. When cult members or leaders see a mental health professional, either voluntarily (e.g., a member who sees a psychiatrist after leaving the cult) or as part of a legal proceeding (e.g., a cult member or leader who sees a forensic psychiatrist while being prosecuted for murder), the circumstances themselves impact the data.

Some cults, such as the Unification Church [2, 3], the Divine Light Mission [4], and the Hare Krishna devotees [5], have voluntarily allowed the gathering of psychological data from active members. Their doing so raises questions as to their underlying objectives, and the potential desire of the cult to portray psychological wellness. Conversely, cult members who have left the cult and go on to seek psychiatric care have cut ties with the organization. This separation often either came about as a result of, or resulted in, a negative perception of the cult. Resulting data are prone to be tainted. To further confound the data, cult membership in and of itself can result in significant destabilization of its members' lives; separating out preexisting pathology from an adjustment-like response is challenging [6].

A review of the literature shows a similar problem when obtaining psychological data on cult leaders. Available data come from three primary sources: (1) collateral records (e.g., the audio recordings, videos, and cult member testimonies on David Koresh from Waco [7]); (2) forensic interviews of a specific subpopulation (e.g., competence to stand trial or sanity evaluations of cult leaders who are accused of criminal offenses and then have the prospect of mental illness brought forth as a pertinent issue in their case); and (3) psychiatric treatment of a subpopulation within the penal system. Each of these sources has its own limitations. Collateral information such as audio recordings must be interpreted in the context of a cult leader attempting to influence members; there can also be an overlay of substance use [8]. Forensic interviews are high-stakes situations where a cult leader has an incentive to feign or exaggerate mental illness in an attempt to reduce their potential punishment. Prison mental health records are hard to gain access to and include evaluations targeted more at symptomatic treatment than a forensic diagnosis; furthermore, as treating psychiatrists often change, this can result in an ex-cult leader having a wide variety of different diagnoses and clinical formulations over the years [9].

Despite the aforementioned problems, this chapter will discuss available literature on comorbid major mental disorders in cult leaders and their followers. Case vignettes are based on psychological and psychiatric evaluations from reported legal cases and the interpretation of those evaluations by the courts. The adversarial nature of the legal system and availability of opposing expert mental health opinions provide salient points for discussion.

Case Vignette of a Cult Leader: Jeffrey Don Lundgren – The Use of Psychiatric Evaluations in a Cult-Related Criminal Case [10, 11, 12, 13, 14]

The Reorganized Church of Jesus Christ of Latter Day Saints (RLDS) is headquartered in Missouri (in comparison to the Church of Jesus Christ of Latter-day Saints [LDS], or the Mormon Church, which is headquartered in Utah). Jeffrey Lundgren was raised as a member of the RLDS before ultimately forming a splinter group – a cult. Lundgren, together with some of his members, murdered five people in Kirtland, Ohio in 1989. Many of those followers received lengthy prison sentences; Lundgren was the only one sentenced to death (he was ultimately executed) [15]. Lundgren did not pursue an insanity defense at trial. After he was sentenced to death, his appellate attorneys, citing a forensic evaluation that had made a psychotic disorder diagnosis, argued that his trial attorneys should have pursued an insanity defense.

Lundgren had moved to Kirtland, Ohio, in 1984 with his wife Alice. For the next three years he worked and taught at the Kirtland Temple of the RDLS. He began to attract a following, including Ron Luff (whose case is described in the Characteristics of Followers section). In 1987, after various issues, including his soliciting and failing to turn over contributions from visitors, he was fired and evicted from the Kirtland Temple. In 1988 he was excommunicated. When Mr. Lundgren left the Kirtland Temple, his followers, and their monetary support, went with him. The Avery Family (Dennis, Cheryl, and their three minor daughters) later joined his group.

Mr. Lundgren told his followers that he was having visions and conversations with God. He began teaching about a need to recapture the temple and kill 10 followers in order for Christ to come and establish Zion. He said that the Averys had "failed to repent" and selected them as followers who would be killed. Accordingly, on April 17, 1989, Lundgren and several of his followers (including Ron Luff) shot and killed the Avery family. After the murders, Lundgren took one of his followers, Kathryn Johnson (who was already married to Larry Johnson, also a cult member), as a second wife. In December 1989, Larry Johnson contacted the authorities and disclosed the murders.

Prior to trial, Lundgren's attorneys retained two clinical psychologists to evaluate Mr. Lundgren; based on their evaluations, the trial attorneys opted not to pursue an insanity defense. Lundgren was convicted of five counts of aggravated murder and five counts of kidnapping. At sentencing, Lundgren admitted the murders but stated that he had been commanded by God to kill the Averys and that he was "even more than a prophet" [13, p. 321].

After being sentenced to death, Lundgren appealed; one of the grounds for appeal was that his trial attorneys had provided ineffective assistance of counsel due to a failure to put forth an insanity defense. At the time of his initial trial, in 1990, the Ohio insanity defense allowed either a moral incapacity or volitional incapacity defense. Specifically, that the defendant had a mental disease or defect that caused them to lack capacity either to (1) know the wrongfulness of their conduct or (2) conform their conduct to the law.

In deciding not to pursue an insanity defense, his trial attorneys had relied in part on the expert opinion of Nancy Schmidtgoessling, PhD. Dr. Schmidtgoessling had diagnosed Mr. Lundgren with "mixed personality disorder with the dominant features being narcissism, paranoia, and anti-social tendencies" [10, p. 773], and she tied this diagnosis to feelings of inadequacy. She opined that he did not have a mental disease or defect for purposes of an insanity defense.

In 1996, Mr. Lundgren's appellate attorneys, in attempting to argue for the viability of an insanity defense and thus ineffective assistance of trial counsel, cited a postconviction affidavit by psychologist Jeffrey Smalldon, PhD [16]. Dr. Smalldon opined that Mr. Lundgren had both a "severe character disorder and a psychotic disorder . . . best described as either Delusional Disorder, Mixed Type (with grandiose and persecutory themes) or Psychotic Disorder Not Otherwise Specified" [10, p. 791]. Dr. Smalldon opined that Mr. Lundgren, due to his psychotic disorder, had not been able to conform his conduct to the law.

The Sixth Circuit Court of Appeals rejected an ineffective assistance of counsel argument, agreeing that the trial attorneys' decision to not pursue an insanity defense was reasonable. One of the appellate judges, Judge Merritt, wrote separately in dissent. Although a dissenting opinion does not have a determinative legal impact, it provides an interesting perspective on legal considerations in the case. Judge Merritt cited evidence he viewed as supporting the possibility that Lundgren had a delusional belief (that God had commanded him to kill the Avery family) and therefore "probably [did] not have the capacity to conform his conduct to the law's requirements" [10, p. 792]. Judge Merritt pointed to various pieces of testimony he viewed as indicative of psychosis, including Mr. Lundgren's claims that he had been present at the time that Christ was crucified, had special powers to predict the future, could transcend time, could sense people, could trigger natural events, experienced visions, and had become divine and immortal as a result of having killed the Avery family.

Characteristics of Cult Leaders

As cult leaders tend not to seek treatment voluntarily, obtaining adequate data to separate between a primary mental illness (in particular one involving delusions), a personality disorder, and a manipulative use of extreme beliefs, is challenging. This chapter provides a number of case examples, such as that of Lundgren. It will not, however, attempt to make diagnoses. The goal in providing reported legal cases is to highlight the pertinent differential diagnoses considered in these cases and factors that can point in one direction or another.

Reported legal cases include cult leaders who have argued that they were incompetent to stand trial (stating that due to their mental condition they are either not able to understand the court process or to assist in their defense) or who have pleaded not guilty by reason of insanity (stating that they should not be held criminally responsible for their alleged offenses due to the effect of their mental disease at the time of the offense). They also, as in the case of Lundgren, include postconviction appeals based on the lack of use of an insanity defense at trial. Whether a cult leader's beliefs are simply eccentric, with behavior motivated by personality traits or disorders (especially narcissistic, paranoid, and/or antisocial) – as opposed to delusional – is of crucial legal significance.

The experts in the Lundgren case agreed that Lundgren evidenced grandiosity. They disagreed on whether his grandiosity was part of a delusional belief set or a personality disorder. Psychotic delusions can form the basis for an insanity defense; personal beliefs and personality disorders generally cannot. The expert (and judicial) disagreement in the Lundgren case highlights pertinent questions when assessing the basis for grandiose beliefs in cult leaders.

Grandiosity can be a result of a personality disorder, a delusion, or even a realistic appraisal of effective charisma. A self-appointed leader of a large group of people who convinces them to do their bidding will understandably feel superior to their followers. Lundgren convinced his followers to give him their paychecks and to commit five murders. The complicating factor in the Lundgren case was the claims that could appear psychotic – that he communicated with God and had special powers.

Cult leaders tend to be self-appointed as leaders, persuasive, charismatic, domineering, and determined [17]. The symptom of grandiosity is explicitly interwoven into these characteristics. Another especially relevant characteristic – which focuses in on the line between personality disorders and delusions – are cult leaders' tendency to claim that they have a special mission and/or knowledge [17]. Lundgren displayed this when he told his cult members that they had to kill followers in order for Zion to be created by Christ.

In cases such as Lundgren's, a pertinent question is assessing whether the leader's extreme beliefs were delusions. There are numerous factors that go into assessing whether a belief is psychotic, including both historical and behavioral collateral. For cult leaders, an assessment should include inquiries into (1) the personal relevance of the beliefs, as opposed to their instrumental use for manipulation and (2) whether the beliefs can be characterized as subcultural beliefs (and thus not delusional). These two issues are illustrated, respectively, in the cases of Brian David Mitchell and Michael Ryan, which we will discuss next.

Case Vignette of a Cult Leader: Brian David Mitchell – Psychosis or a Personality Disorder with Manipulative Behavior? [18]

As is discussed in Chapter 11, formally evaluated cult leaders are often found to have a personality disorder, such as a narcissistic [19] and/or antisocial personality disorder [20]. The diagnosis of a personality disorder was particularly relevant with Brian David Mitchell, who had kidnapped 14-year-old Elizabeth Smart in 2002. Whether Mitchell was a cult leader, as opposed to an attempted cult leader, is arguable. However, he was part of a fringe social group, with shared religious beliefs. Despite attempts to recruit members, his specific message did not gain traction beyond his codefendant (and wife) Wanda Barzee and the kidnapped Elizabeth Smart. Of note, Wanda Barzee, discussed later in this chapter, was later diagnosed as having a psychotic disorder, with one forensic evaluator opining her to have a "shared psychotic disorder" [21].

Brian David Mitchell and Wanda Barzee had met at an LDS divorce support group and married in 1985. Mitchell became dissatisfied with LDS teachings and sought exposure to various fringe LDS religious groups and the Patriot movement. Mitchell and Barzee moved around the country. Mitchell spoke and ministered about religion in various contexts. In 2000, after telling Barzee that he had "received the revelation that plural marriage was to be restored" [18, p. 1172], he attempted to solicit a second wife. When that failed, he "claimed to receive a revelation to 'plunder' girls ages 10 to 14 to be his wives because they were more malleable" [18, p. 1173]. The kidnapping of Elizabeth Smart followed.

Mitchell told Smart many things, among them that he was a prophet, a Davidic king, and would be taking her as a wife. He said that in seven years he would be stoned, die, rise up, and kill the Antichrist. He and Barzee attempted to indoctrinate Smart into their fringe beliefs; meanwhile, according to Elizabeth Smart's later testimony, Mitchell repeatedly raped her. In 2003, Mitchell and Barzee were arrested and charged with various state felony charges, including aggravated kidnapping [21].

Over the next six years, Mitchell's competence to stand trial was questioned in various contexts. Primary to this issue was the question of whether he had a psychotic disorder. Mitchell mostly declined to partake in formal competence evaluations. Nonetheless, numerous reports were written as to his diagnosis and competence to stand trial, including in the context of an inpatient forensic hospitalization in 2003. Opinions varied, both as to his competence, and his diagnosis. Diagnoses ranged from a personality disorder (e.g., a narcissistic personality disorder) to a psychotic disorder (e.g., a delusional disorder). In 2005, Mitchell was adjudicated incompetent to stand trial in state court and sent for inpatient restoration to competency. In 2008, after failed attempts to involuntarily medicate him in the state system, federal charges were filed for kidnapping and unlawful transportation of a minor. Mitchell was moved to a hospital in the federal system: Springfield Medical Center.

At Springfield, the assigned competence evaluator, Richart DeMier, PhD, "authored a report concluding that Mitchell is suffering from paranoid schizophrenia because his religious delusions are bizarre and such condition renders Mitchell incompetent to stand trial" [18, p. 1189]. The United States retained a private evaluator, Michael Welner, MD, for a second opinion. Dr. Welner opined that Mitchell was not psychotic and had the essential elements of competence; he diagnosed Mitchell with pedophilia, antisocial personality disorder, narcissistic personality disorder, malingering, and alcohol abuse [22].

Mitchell was ultimately adjudicated competent in the federal system. The court, relying on numerous pieces of data, including Dr. Welner's report, found that Mitchell's beliefs were not delusions and he was not psychotic. The court explained that Mitchell's beliefs were malleable, part of a subculture, and consistent with a personality disorder. The court noted how Mitchell "voluntarily use[d] his extreme beliefs in a manipulative, self-interested way to gain power and authority over a given situation and voluntarily denies his beliefs when it is in his own self-interest to do so" [18, p. 1194]. In other words, the court interpreted Mitchell as using "the concept that he was receiving revelations from God to establish control over his 'followers'" [18, p. 1194].

This case provides a good example of how ultimately, despite differing opinions as to whether a defendant is psychotic, it is up to the trier of fact (the judge or jury) to make such a determination. At the state court level, Mitchell was viewed as psychotic and adjudicated incompetent. This was in line with numerous of the clinicians over the years who had diagnosed Mitchell as psychotic – including his treating psychiatrist at Utah State Hospital: Paul Whitehead, MD (Dr. Whitehead diagnosed Mitchell with a delusional disorder) [23]. Noting this, Mitchell's attorneys heavily contested the admission of Dr. Welner's report; they argued that it constituted advocacy, misrepresented facts, and was methodologically deficient [23]. The court, however, while acknowledging the contradictions, found Dr. Welner's report to be admissible – noting that such contradictions were best dealt with through cross-examination. In later proceedings, Dr. Welner's opinion, that Mitchell was not psychotic, is the one the federal court found most credible, rather than that of the clinicians who believed him to have a psychotic disorder [18].

Case Vignette of a Cult Leader: Michael Ryan – Psychotic Delusions or Unusual Subcultural Beliefs? [24, 25]

Even if a cult leader's unusual religious beliefs are idiosyncratic personally held beliefs, rather than stated tenets utilized in an instrumental fashion, they are not necessarily a product of a major mental illness. This can be true despite comorbid symptoms of grandiosity and paranoia, which may instead be ascribed to a personality disorder. The question of credibility, regarding professed extreme beliefs (as opposed to manipulative lies), was also addressed in the case of Michael Ryan. For our purposes, we will focus our discussion on the other issue addressed in the case of Michael Ryan – the distinction between delusions and subcultural beliefs.

According to the *Diagnostic and Statistical Manual of Mental Disorders, Fifth Edition* (DSM-5), a delusion is a fixed false belief that is held despite incontrovertible evidence to the contrary [26]. The definition of a delusion specifically excludes those beliefs that are "ordinarily accepted by other members of the person's culture or subculture (i.e., it is not an article of faith)" [26, p. 819]. This becomes a complicated question with cult leaders, as they are often the creator of their own articles of faith and the very subculture that adopts them. This issue, and the associated concept of an extreme overvalued belief [27], is discussed in greater detail in Chapter 10 of this book.

In 1985, Michael Ryan, a cult leader, killed two of his members: 5-year-old Luke Stice and 26-year-old James Thimm. For the murder of James Thimm, Ryan put forth an insanity defense. That defense failed and Ryan was sentenced to death (though he died of natural causes before his execution [28]). After his sentencing there were a series of unsuccessful appeals, both regarding the initial insanity defense and adjudicative competence. A key question on appeal was whether Mr. Ryan had a psychotic disorder. Specifically, whether his odd religious beliefs, grandiosity, and claim to hear Yahweh's (God's) voice flowed from psychosis, as opposed to subcultural religious beliefs and perceptions.

Ryan was the leader of the Rulo group, characterized as both "a religious cult and a band of criminals" [24, p. 79]. Ryan's ideas were loosely based on the teachings of Reverend James Wickstrom, a leader of the Posse Comitatus. Ryan's teachings also included "a shared religious belief that Armageddon was imminent, that they were special and chosen by Yahweh, and that they were to prepare for the upcoming battle" [25, p. 1050].

Ryan took multiple wives within his cult. He gave directives to cult members that he described as coming from Yahweh. One of the cult members, James Thimm, verbalized doubt about the existence of Yahweh and Ryan's means of receiving commands from Yahweh. Ryan began to abuse Thimm and other members who had fallen out of favor – stating that it was at the direction of Yahweh. Thimm's limbs were broken, a shovel was inserted into his rectum, he was placed in a grave, shot in the head, and ultimately killed.

In 1986, Ryan was convicted of the first-degree murder of James Thimm. Numerous mental health professionals came in contact with Ryan between his arrest and death. William Logan, MD, evaluated Ryan in relation to the 1986 insanity defense. Dr. Logan diagnosed Ryan with paranoid schizophrenia, testifying that Ryan had auditory hallucinations and delusions. Ryan believed that the end of time was imminent, and Yahweh (God) had chosen him and his followers to be part of a group of warriors meant to fight Satan when the Battle of Armageddon came. Ryan reported that he had received a message from Yahweh telling him that James Thimm was "lacking in faith and must be punished" and that the farm the cult was living on had to be "purified to become a holy birthplace" [25, p. 1058]. Based on this information, Dr. Logan opined that Ryan was "obeying the commands of Yahweh in killing Thimm and could not distinguish between right and wrong" [25, p. 1059]. Conversely, Emmet Kenney, MD, testified for the state and opined that Ryan was not mentally ill or psychotic at the time of the offense and understood that his actions were wrong.

After the failed insanity defense, and issuance of a sentence for execution, Ryan had more mental health evaluations and appeals. Of particular note were the 2001 and 2002 evaluations based on an appeal retrospectively challenging Ryan's competence to stand trial, and also challenging his competence during federal suits (habeas corpus proceedings). Ryan's appellate attorneys, in alleging that Ryan was incompetent, relied again on opinions from Dr. Logan (who again diagnosed Ryan with schizophrenia) and Robert Schulman, PhD (who diagnosed Ryan with delusional disorder and paranoid personality disorder).

The state brought in their own expert, Daniel Martell, PhD, to support the contention that Ryan was competent. In addition to another Minnesota Multiphasic Personality Inventory (MMPI; several had been done prior to this point), Dr. Martell also administered a Personality Assessment Inventory (PAI). Dr. Martell described the PAI results as showing personality traits of hostility and suspiciousness, poor interpersonal skills, and a tendency to have unusual ideas. Dr. Martell rejected a psychotic disorder diagnosis, describing Ryan's hearing Yahweh as an illusion, part of Ryan's own self-described "wishful thinking," and "the product of a shared subcultural religious belief espoused by the Christian Identity Movement" [25, p. 1050]. Dr. Martell diagnosed Ryan with a personality disorder with narcissistic and schizotypal features.

The court's ultimate holding, that Ryan was competent, was also supported by the opinion of Christina Pietz, PhD. Dr. Pietz performed a court-ordered inpatient evaluation of Ryan at the Federal Medical Center in 2002 and diagnosed Ryan with a personality disorder not otherwise specified (with paranoid and grandiose traits). She rejected a psychotic disorder diagnosis, attributing his hearing voices, belief that he could communicate with God, and belief about the Battle of Armageddon to "cultural beliefs."

The court, in finding Ryan competent, noted that Ryan's unusual religious beliefs did not result from mental illness. Even though Ryan was "not a member of a mainstream religious denomination," his "rigid adherence" and "strict interpretation of the scriptures" were not delusional [25, pp. 1054–55]. The court, in explaining this finding, pointed to the shared nature of the beliefs and their religious tenor.

Characteristics of Followers

In the 1960s and 1970s, concern about the mental health of cult followers led courts across the country to grant conservatorship to parents who wished to have their adult children forcibly removed from cults they had joined [29]. Although most conservatorship laws at the time did not require adjudication of the cult followers as mentally ill (they needed simply be "gravely disabled"), the spirit of these judicial trends spoke to a commonly held belief that many people entering cults were incapacitated [5, 30, 31].

Indeed, early estimates suggested that a large number, maybe even a majority, of young adults entering cults had psychotic disorders or severe personality disorders. For example, John G. Clark, MD, a Boston psychiatrist, testified to the Special Investigating Committee of Vermont in 1978 that "58%" of cult members were mentally ill [5]. Around the same time, commentaries and case series published in the *Journal of the National Association of Private Psychiatric Hospitals* summarized psychiatrists' impressions of the mental health of cult followers. One case series of four patients admitted under guardianship revealed that two patients had "clear diagnoses of schizophrenic psychosis," consistent with that author's prior experience suggesting that "roughly half the people who join [cults] ... are clearly mentally ill before joining" [30, p. 21].

These case series lacked methodological rigor but illustrated apparent prototypes. For example, a patient in a different report "had recently become psychotic and had been approached by proselytizing cult members at the airport in her disturbed, hallucinating state. She was told by the cult that these hallucinations were true manifestations of the God that this particular cult worshiped and that she was being blessed with something very special and marvelous" [32, p. 28]. In another example, "[a] neurotrophic viral infection and LSD use preceded a psychotic episode, which was treated. A relapse, however, led the patient into joining a cult that served as a precipitating factor for his psychosis. When he was withdrawn from the cult, his psychosis reappeared, and the patient was hospitalized" [30, p. 21]. The doctors also described situations in which they rejected the application of hopeful parent-guardians: In one case, "after examining the individual, I suggest to the parent that he be allowed to return to the cult. His mental illness was not severe enough to warrant hospitalization" [32, p. 28].

In the late 1970s, academic psychiatrists and psychologists took a serious interest in the phenomenon of cult membership and published a series of higher-quality studies in mainstream scientific journals. These studies attempted to discern whether major mental illness was truly a common finding among cult followers. By and large, they revealed that severe pathology was rare.

A 1976 study by Levine and Salter analyzed the interviews of 106 followers of nine major cults, including Hare Krishna, Divine Light, Process, Foundation, 3HO, Jesus People, Unification Church, Children of God, and Scientology. The authors found that "a significant number of the members could have been described as neurotically anxious or depressed before their conversion, or less frequently, as borderline or personality disorders," but "no overtly psychotic individuals were seen" [33, p. 414]. They gathered a large amount of data on motivational factors relevant to the joining of cults (see Box 9.1) and concluded that "psychiatric diagnoses could not be applied to the majority of cases"

Box 9.1 Common, Nonspecific Motivations for Joining a Cult

- Friendship and community [29, 30]
- "Instant solution" to normal uncertainties of life [29]
- Direct, intense experience of religion [30, 33]
- Craving for external authority and control [5, 30]
- "Strong ideological hunger" [quoted in 31]
- Routine and constancy [5, 29]
- Approval of others [5, 34]
- Feeling lonely, rejected, sad, or not belonging [33]
- Feeling life had no meaning [33]
- Avoiding an unpleasant personal or family situation [33]
- Intense dependency needs [34]
- Moral idealism [34]

[33, p. 414]. One caveat was that the study recruited only volunteers, and as such did not include more anomalous cases of which the authors were anecdotally aware. In some of those anecdotal cases, "severe emotional problems" were apparent.

A 1979 study by Ungerleider and Wellisch set out "to report on certain psychosocial characteristics of 50 individuals who are or were members of several new religions" and to describe "their ability to make sound legal decisions about their choice of lifestyle" [31, p. 279]. Intellectual, personality, and mental status examinations revealed no major psychopathology, and the authors commented that "no evidence of insanity or mental illness in the legal sense was found" [31, p. 279].

Another 1979 study, by Galanter et al. [2], interviewed 237 members of the Unification Church ("Moonies"). Over a third (39%) self-reported that they had experienced "serious emotional problems in the past," leading 30% to have accepted treatment and 6% to have been psychiatrically hospitalized [2, p. 168]. In addition, scores on a neurotic distress scale were higher than a similar-aged comparison group. Details of their psychiatric histories were not available. The study indicated that joining cults typically had favorable impacts on depression and anxiety (as reported on standardized instruments) and the authors concluded that "affiliation with the Unification Church apparently provided considerable and sustained relief from neurotic distress" [2, p. 168].

A 1983 study by Ross [5] described personality and psychodiagnostic tests performed on the entire population of the Hare Krishna Temple in Melbourne, Australia (42 individuals). The MMPI was conducted on all participants and results were assessed by a blinded outside examiner. There was no evidence of pathology on any of the profiles. Ross commented, "these findings do not support the popular view that many members of the Hare Krishna are mentally disordered . . . one must consider devotees capable of rational judgment and, in a legal sense, sane" [5, p. 419].

Psychiatrists and psychologists interested in the treatment of cult followers have identified a pattern of young adults entering cults at times of transition or vulnerability, often coinciding with periods of depression [29, 34]. In particular, a "depressive episode secondary to the loss of a significant figure" may be a common precipitant [34, p. 204]. In general, however, the motivations for joining a cult are nonspecific and may be seen in both normal and abnormal mental states.

Case Vignette of a Cult Follower: Blaine Applin – A Psychotic Deific Decree? [35]

Blaine Applin was a follower of the Gatekeepers, led by Christopher Turgeon. When Turgeon learned that Child Protective Services planned to remove children from some of his followers' homes, he decided to relocate the movement from Washington to California. For expenses related to that move, Turgeon organized a number of fraudulent schemes. Dan Jess, a former Gatekeeper who had defected, was implicated in one of these scams. In an angry phone call after learning he had been involved, Jess called Turgeon a false prophet.

In response, Turgeon gathered all male members of the Gatekeepers, telling them God instructed Turgeon that Jess must be killed. Applin volunteered for the task and told Turgeon, "God told me that I must be the one who does it" [35, p. 1153]. Applin and Turgeon drove to Jess's home, knocked on the door, and Applin shot him. Both men were arrested and charged with first-degree murder.

Mr. Applin pleaded not guilty by reason of insanity, stating that his instructions from God were a deific decree that altered his ability to know right from wrong. The insanity defense was rejected by the jury and Mr. Applin was convicted of first-degree murder. He subsequently appealed, claiming that jury instructions did not specifically address moral wrongfulness, and expert testimony may have led the jury to errantly believe that they could only consider legal wrongfulness in evaluating Mr. Applin's insanity defense. The Court of Appeals of Washington found that the testimony on wrongfulness was not misleading and did not require a special jury instruction. The verdict was affirmed.

Case Vignette of a Cult Follower: Steven Fishman – A Coerced Delusion? [36]

Steven Fishman, a member of the Church of Scientology, was indicted on 11 counts of mail fraud. He pleaded not guilty by reason of insanity, stating that he had been brainwashed (subjected to "coercive persuasion") by the Scientology Church. Mr. Fishman sought to call a forensic psychologist and a sociologist in his defense.

Mr. Fishman indicated that the forensic psychologist, Margaret Thaler Singer, PhD, would opine that Mr. Fishman had been influenced to the point that he was delusional. The sociologist, Dr. Richard Ofshe, would opine that "the Church's influence process regularly leads people to believe that they have the power to control mental matter, energy, space and time … [and was] designed to lead Mr. Fishman to believe that participation in Scientology's fraud scheme was not a reprehensible act" [36, pp. 715–16].

In *United States* v. *Fishman*, the government moved to exclude the testimony of both experts. The motion was granted in part and denied in part. Dr. Ofshe was not allowed to testify, as he was not a mental health professional, and his testimony was not generally accepted within the scientific community. Dr. Singer, while allowed to testify as to the presence of a mental defect, was not permitted to testify as to volitional defects, or about thought reform (defined in the court's opinion as "the creation of a controlled environment that heightens the susceptibility of a subject to suggestion and manipulation through sensory deprivation, physiological depletion, cognitive dissonance, peer pressure, and a clear assertion of authority and dominion" [quoted in 36, p. 716]). Mr. Fishman subsequently pleaded guilty and was sentenced to five years in prison.

Case Vignette of a Cult Follower: Dennis Ryan – Shared Psychosis or a Familial Religious Belief? [37, 38]

Dennis Ryan was the 15-year-old son of Michael Ryan, discussed earlier in this chapter. In 1985, Dennis was charged with first-degree murder related to the death of James Thimm. At the initial trial, he pleaded not guilty by reason of insanity and presented testimony from four experts. Two of Dennis's defense experts – James Cole, PhD and William Logan, MD – diagnosed him with "shared paranoia" (Cole) or "shared psychosis" (Logan). Dr. Cole opined that this was related to a "systematized religious delusion" of a persecutorial nature and that Dennis was especially susceptible to this delusion because of his age and dependence upon his father. Both experts opined that the delusion impaired Dennis's ability to know right from wrong, but Dr. Logan conceded that Dennis would have known he was breaking the law and could be subject to punishment.

A prosecution expert, Emmet Kenney, MD, rebutted the diagnosis of shared psychotic disorder and emphasized that Dennis showed no signs of psychosis at the time of the crime. Dr. Kenney opined that Dennis's dependence on his father was age-appropriate rather than pathological, that his beliefs were religious rather than delusional, and that he knew right from wrong. Ultimately the jury agreed with Dr. Kenney. The insanity defense was rejected, and Dennis was convicted of second-degree murder. His conviction was later overturned based on faulty jury instructions, after which he pleaded guilty to manslaughter, and was sentenced to time served, and released [39].

Case Vignette of Two Cult Followers: David Molko and Tracy Leal – Psychological Damages from Coercive Persuasion? [40]

Mr. Molko and Ms. Leal, former members of the Unification Church (the "Moonies"), sought restitution and psychological damages from the Holy Spirit Association for the Unification of World Christianity after being deprogrammed from the church. They alleged that the organization had undue influence over their decisions as a result of coercive persuasion and sued for fraud, false imprisonment, and intentional infliction of emotional distress.

The plaintiffs (Molko and Leal) sought to introduce declarations by a psychologist, Margaret Thaler Singer, PhD, and a psychiatrist, Samuel Benson, MD, who opined that techniques used by the organization had psychological influence over susceptible members, so that they were "incapable of exercising their own will and judgment" [40, p. 1110]. Their declarations were found inadmissible. This holding, at the lower court level, was based on two things. First, the conflict between Molko and Leal's testimony as to why they had joined the church ("because it satisfied 'personal concerns and anxieties'" [40, p. 1110]) and that of the doctors (that Molko and Leal had been unaware of the identity of the Church). Second, that the doctors' testimony would raise "inquiries forbidden by the free exercise clause of the First Amendment" [40, p. 1110].

The case was resolved through a grant of summary judgment for the Church by a trial court; that was affirmed by the state appeals court. Summary judgment is a way of resolving a court case when there is no "triable issue as to any material fact" and the party asking for summary judgment is entitled to it as a "matter of law" [40, p. 1107]. The case was appealed to the California Supreme Court, who ruled partly in favor of Molko and Leal.

The California Supreme Court affirmed the summary judgment regarding false imprisonment but found that the lower court had erred by issuing summary judgment for fraud, intentional infliction of emotional distress, and restitution. Specifically, the court concluded that there were triable issues of fact (in other words, ones that a judge or jury needed to decide). These issues included "whether Molko and Leal were, by means of coercive persuasion, rendered unable to respond independently upon learning they had been deceived" [40, pp. 1119–20]. Of note, the court also disagreed with the lower court's rationale for excluding the doctors' testimony.

In its discussion, the court cited concerns about the deleterious impact of coercive persuasion on some followers: "While some individuals who experience coercive persuasion emerge unscathed, many others develop serious and sometimes irreversible physical and psychiatric disorders, up to and including schizophrenia, self-mutilation, and suicide . . . The state clearly has a compelling interest in preventing its citizens from being deceived into submitting unknowingly to such a potentially dangerous process" [40, p. 1118]. Interestingly, the court cited a law review article as its source for this. Meanwhile, the American Psychological Association (APA) had filed an amicus brief arguing that coercive persuasion was neither "accepted in the scientific community" [41, p. 16] nor a "meaningful scientific concept" [41, p. 9]. The APA thus argued that the doctors' declarations espousing the concept were appropriately excluded.

Case Vignette of a Cult Follower: Ronald Luff – Cult Influence Impacting Knowledge of Wrongfulness of a Murder?[42]

Ronald Luff was raised in the Reorganized Church of Jesus Christ of Latter Day Saints (RLDS), a Mormon denomination based in Mr. Luff's home state of Missouri. As a young adult, he sought to become a Church leader and wanted to influence the Church to become more fundamentalist. In this pursuit, he traveled to Kirtland, Ohio to meet with Jeffrey Lundgren, a self-proclaimed RLDS prophet described in the section on cult leaders in this chapter. When Lundgren was eventually asked to leave his position at the Kirtland Temple of RLDS for alleged ethics violations, he formed a religious cult of about 20 people, including Luff, and the group took up residence on a small farm. Lundgren was hypercritical of the members, limited their access to outside information, and threatened to kill them if they deviated from his rules.

In April 1989, Lundgren instructed Luff and others to "sacrifice" five members of the cult: Dennis and Cheryl Avery and their three daughters Trina (age 15), Rebecca (13), and Karen (7). Luff's role in the crime was to escort each member of the Avery family, in order from oldest to youngest, to a barn, where he would use a stun gun or other means to incapacitate them. Lundgren then shot each of them to death.

In December 1989, a defected follower informed authorities of the crime. Luff was indicted, among the others, on five counts of aggravated murder with death penalty specifications. He entered pleas of not guilty and not guilty by reason of insanity. He was found guilty and sentenced in 1991 to five consecutive life terms in prison.

Luff appealed his conviction to the Court of Appeals of Ohio, naming seven assignments of error. The first was that the trial court erred in its jury instructions regarding the insanity defense. The jury was given instructions closely resembling a new version of an Ohio statute that had gone into effect in July of 1990. This was a M'Naghten-like insanity rule, only allowing for an insanity defense if at the time of the offense the defendant, due to a severe mental illness, did not know the wrongfulness of their acts (moral incapacity). Prior to the enactment of that statute, the insanity defense was based on a Model Penal Code standard, allowing an insanity defense either due to a lack of knowledge of wrongfulness or a lack of capacity to "conform" conduct to the law (volitional incapacity). As the crime occurred in 1989, the Ohio appeals court found that the jury instructions violated the *ex post facto* clauses (prohibiting retroactive application of laws) of the Ohio and United States constitutions.

However, this error was found to be harmless, as the court commented that no reasonable jury would have found Mr. Luff to meet either insanity standard. The court emphasized that the insanity standard in effect in 1989, based on case law, referred only to legal wrongfulness, not moral wrongfulness. The defense's expert psychiatrist, Kurt A. Bertschinger, MD, had testified that Mr. Luff's "ability to reason was severely impaired" and, as a result, in his opinion, Mr. Luff had not recognized at the time of the offense that it was morally wrong [42, p. 499]. However, notably, Dr. Bertschinger had acknowledged that Mr. Luff did not have a "diagnosable mental illness or defect" [42, p. 499]. Dr. Bertschinger also acknowledged that, in his opinion, Mr. Luff had known the crime was legally wrong [42, p. 499]. Thus, on this assignment of error (and the six others), the trial court's judgment, and Mr. Luff's conviction, was affirmed.

Case Vignette of a Cult Follower: Wanda Barzee – Schizophrenia or a Shared Psychotic Disorder? [21]

Wanda Barzee was the wife of Brian David Mitchell, described in the section on cult leaders in this chapter. Related to the events involving victim Elizabeth Smart in 2003, also described in the section regarding Mitchell, Ms. Barzee was charged with aggravated burglary, aggravated sexual assault, aggravated kidnapping, attempted aggravated kidnapping (or, alternatively, conspiracy to commit aggravated kidnapping). The state moved for Ms. Barzee to be evaluated for her competency to stand trial, and two evaluators diagnosed her with a psychotic disorder. She was adjudicated incompetent and admitted to Utah State Hospital for the restoration of her competency.

After over a year in the hospital, Ms. Barzee remained incompetent, and the District Attorney's office filed a motion to compel medication, which was eventually granted. Ms. Barzee appealed the court order requiring her to take medications to the Utah Supreme Court.

The Utah Supreme Court performed *Harper* [43] and *Sell* [44] analyses regarding the constitutionality of forcing antipsychotic treatment on Ms. Barzee. The court noted that the *Harper* analysis was inapplicable, as it only applies "if the inmate is a danger to herself or others or if the inmate's refusal to take drugs poses grave risks to her health" [21, p. 55]. This was not the case with Ms. Barzee. They thus looked at the *Sell* criteria, which determines when a defendant can, from a constitutional standpoint, be involuntarily medicated solely to restore competence. Among other things, *Sell* requires that involuntary medications be medically appropriate and substantially unlikely to interfere with the fairness of the proceedings. *Sell* also requires that the medications be necessary to, and substantially likely to result in, the restoration of a defendant's competence.

Given the importance of diagnosis in determining the likelihood of a treatment response, a key discussion in the Utah Supreme Court's opinion was Ms. Barzee's diagnosis. The court reviewed testimony of eight mental health professionals who had been involved at various stages and hearings related to Ms. Barzee's competency restoration. All eight professionals had diagnosed Ms. Barzee with a psychotic disorder, but the specific diagnoses differed, including delusional disorder, schizophrenia, shared psychotic disorder (with her husband), and psychotic disorder not otherwise specified. All hinged on Ms. Barzee's nonbizarre grandiose delusions, some of which were related to Mr. Mitchell. Despite the differing opinions, and relevance to the likelihood of an adequate treatment response (e.g., schizophrenia as opposed to a shared psychotic disorder), the Utah Supreme Court concluded that the trial court had not erred in finding that involuntary medication treatment was warranted under *Sell.*

In 2009, Ms. Barzee was found competent to stand trial [45]. She pleaded guilty to reduced charges, agreed to cooperate in the investigation into Mr. Mitchell, and was sentenced to two concurrent 15-year prison terms [46].

Psychometric Instruments to Aid Assessment

Three decades ago, researchers sought to create scales for cultic abuse. The Group Psychological Abuse Scale (GPAS) was developed using the characterization by 308 former cult members and included four subscales: compliance, exploitation, mind control, and anxious dependency [47]. Compliance included such items as serving leaders and having one's intimacy dictated; exploitation included such items as threatening critics and approving the use of violence. Mind control included that people stay because of being deceived and manipulated. Authors envisioned many uses for the GPAS, given its reliability and validity, in characterizing types of abuse, as well as in determining whether a group was a cult or innocuous. Although there are references to the GPAS's use in research [48], a case-law search on Lexis Nexis does not show any cases referencing it.

Other articles have used the MMPI [29] and the Wechsler Adult Intelligence Scale [49, 50]. Still other articles have been based on evaluations without standardized measures, while still others have used esoteric scales, including the Comrey Personality Scales [51]; the Self-Consciousness Scale and Rosenberg Self-Esteem Scale [52]; and the California Psychological Inventory [53]. However, such rarefied scales may not have utility in individual evaluations.

Diagnostic considerations should lead to decision-making about whether and which psychometric instruments to utilize in the evaluation of persons who are cult followers or leaders. Common considerations regarding cult followers include both mood and anxiety disorders as well as yearning for acceptance and belonging. As we have noted, common diagnostic considerations regarding cult leaders include whether the person's beliefs are delusional and the leader is psychotic, whether they are consistent with a subculture, or whether they are grandiose due to a personality disorder.

As described in the aforementioned cases, individual forensic evaluations have included psychological testing including the MMPI and the PAI, both tests of personality. Other psychological testing may seek to explore depressive symptoms, such as utilizing a depression inventory.

Conclusion

In conclusion, when considering major mental disorders among persons involved in cults, there are differences between diagnoses that tend to be found among leaders and followers. Despite this, neither leaders nor followers often seek psychiatric care themselves. Rather, leaders or followers may be evaluated and receive care within the criminal justice system subsequent to arrest, while followers may be more likely to be encouraged to engage in psychiatric care by their family members. Due to the very nature of cults, it is difficult to ascertain rates of various mental illnesses. Review of cases indicates that after arrest of cult leaders related to violent crimes, forensic psychiatric or forensic psychological evaluations may occur. In these evaluations, it is important for evaluators to consider whether the grandiosity of a cult leader may be due to a personality disorder, whether it is due to delusional thinking of a mental illness, or whether it is consistent with their subculture. Careful assessment is critical in these cases, and experts have disagreed in high-profile cases.

Conversely, among followers, when mental illness exists, it may be more likely to be in the depressive spectrum. As well, the follower may have a sense that they lack belonging outside of the cult, or they may be experiencing grief after the loss of a significant figure in their life. Some followers may also experience delusional thinking, and cult leaders and organizations may have great psychological influence over susceptible members. Collateral information is critical in these cases. Psychological testing can be helpful in ferreting out diagnosis in some cases.

Key Points

- Due to the secrecy of cults, and the manner in which cult followers and leaders tend to enter psychiatric care, data on the prevalence and nature of major mental disorders are limited and confounded.
- When assessing whether there is a major mental disorder in a cult leader, it is important to carefully assess for, and distinguish between, subcultural religious beliefs, personality traits, and delusions.
- Most cult followers do not have a serious mental illness. Cult followers have been largely unsuccessful when alleging insanity for cult-associated crimes or seeking psychological damages from cult leaders.
- Psychological testing, if performed in cult leaders or followers, should consider the diagnosis and psychological factors of importance in the individual case. This may most commonly include personality testing or scales considering anxiety or depression.

References

1. *Ryan* v. *Kenney*, 281 F. Supp. 2d 1008 (D. Neb. 2003).
2. M Galanter, R Rabkin, J Rabkin, A Deutsch. The "Moonies": a psychological study of conversion and membership in a contemporary religious sect. *American Journal of Psychiatry*. 1979;136(2):165–70.
3. RA Dean. *Moonies: a psychological analysis of the unification church*. D Phil doctoral thesis. University of Michigan; 1981.
4. M Galanter, P Buckley. Evangelical religion and meditation: psychotherapeutic effects. *Journal of Nervous and Mental Disease*. 1978;166(10):685–91.
5. M Ross. Clinical profiles of Hare Krishna devotees. *American Journal of Psychiatry*. 1983;140(4):416–20.
6. JA Saliba. *Psychiatry and the cults: an annotated bibliography*. Routledge; 1987.
7. FBI. The Vault, WACO / Branch Davidian Compound. https://

vault.fbi.gov/waco-branch-davidian-compound

8. Jim Jones autopsy report. 1978. https://jonestown.sdsu.edu/wp-content/uploads/2013/10/JimJones.pdf
9. C Leonetti. Eye of the beholder: the wrongful conviction of Charles Milles Manson. *Southwest Law Review.* 2015;45(2):257–331.
10. *Lundgren* v. *Mitchell*, 440 F.3d 754 (6th Cir. 2006).
11. *State* v. *Lundgren*, 1993 Ohio App. LEXIS 4394 (Ct. App. Sep. 1, 1993).
12. *State* v. *Lundgren*, No. 90-L-15-140, 1993 WL 346444, at *1 (Ohio Ct. App. Sept. 14, 1993).
13. *State* v. *Lundgren*, 653 N.E.2d 304 (Ohio, 1995).
14. *State of Ohio, Respondent-Appellee,* v. *Jeffrey D. Lundgren, Petitioner-Appellant*, 1999 WL 33840275 (Ohio), 13.
15. SB McPherson. Death penalty mitigation and cult membership: the case of the Kirtland killings. *Behavioral Sciences & the Law.* 1992;10:65–74.
16. *State* v. *Lundgren*, CASE NO. 97-L-110, 1998 Ohio App. LEXIS 6164 (Ct. App. Dec. 18, 1998).
17. M Singer, J Lalich. *Cult in our midst: the continuing fight against the hidden menace.* Jossey-Bass; 2003.
18. *United States* v. *Mitchell*, 706 F. Supp. 2d 1148 (D. Utah 2010).
19. PA Olsson. *Malignant pied pipers: a psychological study of destructive cult leaders.* Strategic Book Publishing & Rights Agency; 2017.
20. J Burke. Antisocial personality disorder in cult leaders and induction of dependent personality disorder in cult members. *Cultic Studies Review.* 2006;5(3):390–410.
21. *State* v. *Barzee*, 177 P.3d 48 (Utah 2007).
22. Forensic panel report on Brian David Mitchell. 2009. https://archive.org/details/BDMCSTReport
23. *United States* v. *Mitchell*, 2009 U.S. Dist. LEXIS 106865 (D. Utah, 2009).
24. *State* v. *Ryan*, 233 Neb. 74 (1989).
25. *Ryan* v. *Kenney*, 281 F. Supp. 2d 1008 (D. Neb. 2003).
26. American Psychiatric Association. *Diagnostic and statistical manual of mental disorders.* 5th ed. American Psychiatric Association; 2013.
27. T Rahman, SM Hartz, W Xiong, JR Meloy, J Janofsky, B Harry, et al. Extreme overvalued beliefs. *Journal of American Academy of Psychiatry and the Law.* 2020;48(3):319–26.
28. N Kim. In the end, State never does kill Michael Ryan. *Falls City Journal.* 2015 May 27. https://fcjournal.net/2015/05/27/in-the-end-state-never-does-kill-michael-ryan/
29. MT Singer. Coming out of the cults. *Psychology Today.* 1979;72–82.
30. RP Hopkins. The hospital viewpoint: mental illness or social maladjustment? *Journal – National Association of Private Psychiatric Hospitals.* 1978;9(4):19–21.
31. JT Ungerleider, DK Wellisch. Coercive persuasion (brainwashing), religious cults, and deprogramming. *American Journal of Psychiatry.* 1979;136:279–82.
32. JG Clark. Problems in referral of cult members. *Journal – National Association of Private Psychiatric Hospitals.* 1978;9(4):27–29.
33. SV Levine, NE Salter. Youth and contemporary religious movements: psychosocial findings. *Canadian Psychiatric Association Journal.* 1976;21(6):411–20.
34. DA Halperin. Psychiatric perspectives on cult affiliation. *Psychiatric Annals.* 1990;20:204–13.
35. *State* v. *Applin*, 67 P.3d 1152 (Wash. Ct. App. 2003).
36. *United States* v. *Fishman*, 743 F. Supp. 713 (N.D. Cal. 1990).
37. *State* v. *Ryan*, 409 N.W.2d 579 (Neb. 1987).
38. *State* v. *Ryan*, 249 Neb. 218 (Neb. 1996).
39. J May. Discovery investigation to air Rulo-cult story on Dennis Ryan. Hiawatha World. 2017 Feb 16. www.hiawathaworldonline.com/news/

discovery-investigation-to-air-rulo-cult-story-on-dennis-ryan/article_b21dd661-9372-5223-a57d-bda3f2f6384b.html

40. *Molko* v. *Holy Spirit Association*, 46 Cal.3d 1092 (Calif. 1988).
41. *Molko* v. *Holy Spirit Association*. Brief amicus curiae of The American Psychological Association et al. 1987 10 Feb.
42. *State* v. *Luff*, 621 N.E.2d 493 (Ohio Ct. App. 1993).
43. *Washington* v. *Harper*, 494 U.S. 210 (1990).
44. *Sell* v. *United States*, 539 U.S. 166 (2003).
45. Minute Entry, Document 171. *United States* v. *Mitchell et al.*, Case No. 2:08-cr-00125-DAK-2 (D. Utah Nov. 17 2009).
46. P Reavy. Wanda Barzee sentenced to 15 years in federal prison, gets scolding from Elizabeth Smart's mother. Desert News. 2010 May 22. www.deseret.com/2010/5/22/20116683/wanda-barzee-sentenced-to-15-years-in-federal-prison-gets-scolding-from-elizabeth-smart-s-mother
47. WV Chambers, MD Langone, AA Dole, JW Grice. The Group Psychological Abuse Scale: a measure of the varieties of cultic abuse. *Cultic Studies Journal*. 1994;11(1):L88–117.
48. C Almendros, JA Carrobles, A Rodriguez-Carballeira, M Gamez-Guadix. Reasons for leaving: psychological abuse and distress reported by former members of cultic groups. *Cultic Studies Review*. 2009;8(2):118–38.
49. MH Spero. Psychotherapeutic procedure with religious cult devotees. *Journal of Nervous and Mental Disease*. 1982;170:332–44.
50. J Aronoff, SJ Lynn, P Malinoski. Are cultic environments psychologically harmful? *Clinical Psychology Review*. 2000;20(1):91–111.
51. AS Weiss, AL Comrey. Personality characteristics of Hare Krishnas. *Journal of Personality Assessment*. 1987;51(3):399–413.
52. CA Latkin. The self-concept of Rajneeshpuram commune members. *Journal for the Scientific Study of Religion*. 1990:91–98.
53. ND Sundberg, CA Latkin, RA Littman, RA Hagan. Personality in a religious commune: CPIs in Rajneeshpuram. *Journal of Personality Assessment*. 1990;55(1–2):7–17.

Chapter 10

Extreme Overvalued Beliefs

Tahir Rahman and Jason G. Roof

"While most people would not jeopardize their careers or lives for overvalued ideas, some will (and are secretly regarded as heroes by those less inclined to fight for an idea). This is to say that it is not the idea itself but the reckless (toward oneself and others) pursuit that causes isolation and suffering."
- *Oliver Freudenreich, psychiatrist*

Introduction

Fixation has been identified as an important proximal warning behavior seen in acts of terrorism. It is defined as a pathological preoccupation with a person or a cause, accompanied by a deterioration in social and occupational functioning [1, 2, 3]. There are three cognitive-affective drivers of fixations pertinent to the discussion of cults: delusions, obsessions, and *extreme overvalued beliefs* [4–7]. Media, the lay public, and even mental health professionals will often use the terms obsession and delusion loosely and interchangeably. This is of particular concern when discussing targeted attacks such as mass shootings or assassinations in a forensic context. For example, individuals might be described as being "obsessed with abortion laws" or as having "delusions about the election results." Such individuals are usually neither obsessional nor delusional. Instead, they harbor extreme overvalued beliefs. We will begin by discussing the classical description of overvalued ideas. Next, we will review concise definitions of delusions and obsessions. Finally, we will discuss extreme overvalued beliefs as a new concept that will be discussed in detail including its historical provenance and its demarcation from delusions and obsessions [8].

Definition

An extreme overvalued belief is one that is *shared* by others in a person's cultural, religious, or subcultural group. The belief is often relished, amplified, and defended by the possessor of the belief and should be differentiated from an obsession or a delusion. The belief grows more dominant over time, more refined, and more resistant to challenge. The individual has an intense emotional commitment to the belief and may carry out violent behavior in its service [5]. The term was first introduced as part of an analysis of Norwegian terrorist Anders Breivik's insanity trial at the American Academy of Psychiatry and the Law and is also regarded as an important aspect of threat assessment (discussed in detail later).

Overvalued Ideas

Note that the current *Diagnostic and Statistical Manual of Mental Disorders*, fifth edition (DSM-5) definition of *overvalued* idea differs from multiple reference volumes, including: Sims' guidebook, *Symptoms in the Mind*; the *Oxford Textbook of Psychiatry*; *Psychotic Disorders*; *Psychiatry and Clinical Neuroscience*; *The Medical Basis of Psychiatry*; and *Fish's Outline of Psychiatry*. All of these guides classify overvalued ideas as a major type of psychopathology [9–14]. These texts follow traditional British scholarship that views overvalued ideas as part of several key disorders: anorexia nervosa ("I feel fat"); paranoid state; querulous or litigious paranoid states ("they owe me damages for my accident"); morbid jealousy ("my wife is having an affair"); hypochondriasis ("my nose is too big"); body dysmorphic disorder ("my face is shaped ugly"); hoarding ("keep that, don't waste things"); and parasitophobia ("there are bugs in my house") [15]. Some of these conditions can have delusional variants (such as methamphetamines causing the belief that insects are burrowing under the skin).

Overvalued ideas are experienced as "normal" by individuals and held with an intense emotional commitment. As we shall discuss, the DSM-5 classifies many of these disorders into the category of "delusional disorder" (with subtypes of erotomanic, grandiose, jealous, persecutory, and somatic). Thus, major categorical disparities exist between US and British practice – something that we will strive to clarify in this chapter. We will begin by describing phenomenology in forensic psychiatry and then we will discuss the psychological factors that describe how "normal" beliefs become dangerously overvalued – often subsequent to intensive online interaction in digital subcultures [16].

Phenomenology in Forensic Psychiatry

Delusions are fixed, false, idiosyncratic beliefs out of keeping with the individual's background or culture [5]. When part of a syndrome with other cardinal symptoms, delusions are indicative of a psychotic mental disorder. Psychotic symptoms usually spring from brain diseases such as schizophrenia, severe mood disorders, delirium, or substance use disorders. As an example, Andrea Yates developed a delusional belief system within the context of postpartum psychosis that led her to drown her five young children in their home's bathtub. Her delusional belief system involved the need to take her children's lives while they were still "innocent" so that they might go to heaven. Additionally, she believed that Satan was "within her" and that when she was inevitably executed for killing her children, Satan would also be executed [4, 17, 18]. Even though themes such as heaven, hell, Satan, and the innocence of children are found in Christianity, Yates was alone in her odd belief system – making her beliefs fixed, false, and idiosyncratic.

Misidentification delusions such as Capgras delusions or persecutory delusions are commonly used in an insanity defense. In one case involving persecutory delusions, a 49-year-old man with schizoaffective disorder killed and dismembered his neighbor's body. He was seen hurling the victim's arms at witnesses. He was later recorded by police discussing delusional beliefs of serial killers that were "eating his son's liver." In reality, his son was safe at home with his family. He was alone in his beliefs that serial killers with cannibalistic behavior were living in his neighborhood, thus making his beliefs fixed, false, and idiosyncratic (delusions).

Folie à Deux

The French psychiatrists Lasegue and Falret were the first to describe delusions that can be shared by others (*folie à deux*, meaning "insanity of two"). This classically involves the transmission of delusional symptoms from a psychotic individual (the dominant or index case) to a more suggestible party (the secondary case). For example, the primary and secondary cases could be siblings who both suffer from schizophrenia and possess the same delusions. However, secondary cases are often not psychotic and tend to be gullible and passive, with dependent traits. The shared delusion is usually within the limits of possibility, and the degree of impairment is generally less severe in the secondary case. There may also be rare cases in which the secondary case is a child or has an intellectual disability – making it a great challenge to evaluate them. The term *extreme overvalued belief* is more concise than *folie à deux*, because it clarifies that the beliefs in secondary cases are not due to a delusion or obsession, an important distinction in cults [19].

Obsessions are "recurrent and persistent thoughts, urges, or images that are experienced, at some time during the disturbance, as intrusive and unwanted, and in most individuals cause marked anxiety or distress" [5, Table 3]. These individuals often attempt to ignore or suppress such thoughts, urges, or images or to neutralize them with some other thought or action (i.e., by performing a compulsion – say, ritualistic and repeated checking behavior). Advances in neuroimaging have identified brain structures involved in obsessive compulsive disorder (OCD), including the prefrontal cortex, the dorsal striatum (caudate), and associated neurocircuits modulating emotional, cognitive, and motor control – further delineating them from delusions [20, 21]. Treatment-resistant disorders can be treated with deep brain stimulation. In a forensic or threat assessment context, fixations driven by obsessional thoughts are very infrequent and generally do not pose a risk of violence [20].

Consider a young woman who is having intrusive and distressing thoughts of harming her baby. Her obsessions are ego-dystonic – she would never harm her baby – rather than ego-syntonic (compatible with the self and often an element of one's identity). By contrast, a member of a neo-Nazi group is not considered to be "obsessed" with it because they enjoy, amplify, and defend it – the complete opposite of an obsession. Obsessions rarely lead to violent behavior. However, there are rare cases of "catathymic homicides" in which an individual, such as a 37-year-old man with OCD who intentionally drowned his 13-month-old son and was later consumed with enormous guilt [22].

Extreme overvalued beliefs, the focus of this chapter, emphasize the *shared* nature of some types of rigidly held beliefs. They spring from strong affective experiences and are felt as "normal" by the individual, such as passionate political, religious, sexual, or ethical conviction. The term was first introduced as part of an analysis of Norwegian terrorist Anders Breivik's insanity trial. Breivik had bizarre and rigidly held beliefs that were found to be motives behind his bombing and mass shooting attack, which resulted in the deaths of 72 mostly young people in Norway. His insanity trial created confusion regarding the source of his beliefs. Prior to his attacks, Breivik released a compendium entitled "2083: A European Declaration of Independence," in which he opposed multiculturalism, Marxism, and the Norwegian Labor Party. He also referred to himself as a "Knight Templar," raising concerns that he held delusions from a possible diagnosis of schizophrenia [23]. In fact, a team of examining psychiatrists erroneously believed that he held delusions stemming from schizophrenia [23–29]. He was eventually determined to have extremist beliefs shared by other right-wing groups in Norway and not idiosyncratic, fixed, false beliefs from delusions. The finding of insanity was rejected by the Norwegian court. His tales of being a "Knight Templar" were later seen as dramatic, colorful, and fantastic stories of heroism to achieve admiration and sympathy [24–29].

Another example of an extreme overvalued belief is the case of Malik Hasan, a US Army major and psychiatrist, who committed a mass murder at Fort Hood, Texas, in 2009. He shot and killed 13 soldiers and injured 32 others at the time that his unit was being medically processed for deployment to Afghanistan. He was radicalized prior to the attack, as evidenced by emails he exchanged with a radical cleric, Anwar al-Awlaki. His fixations were also apparent to others in presentations he gave during his psychiatry residency and public health fellowship, which increasingly focused on convincing others that the West was at war with Islam – almost devoid of any references to psychiatry. After he was charged for the attack, he was examined by several military forensic psychiatrists who determined he did not have a mental disorder. Hasan was subsequently stripped of his military rank and, on August 28, 2013, jurors recommended he be sentenced to death for his heinous actions [4].

Cult Members' Extreme Overvalued Beliefs

Forensic research has identified beliefs held by members of cults or groups as extreme overvalued beliefs that may lead to violence, including terrorism and/ or suicide [6]. Examples include the suicides and homicides occurring in Jonestown, Guyana (over 900 deaths) and in California with the Heaven's Gate cult (39 deaths). On September 11, 2001, nearly 3,000 individuals perished in the deadliest terrorist attack in the history of the United States. Masterminded by Al-Qaeda's Osama bin Laden and Ayman al-Zawahiri, four passenger jets were hijacked with the plan to crash them into designated targets. Another example, which will be discussed in detail next, are the extreme overvalued beliefs leading to lethal violence during the 2021 United States Capitol attack, where over 2,000 rioters believed that the 2020 presidential election had been "stolen" [6, 16].

Case Vignette: US Capitol Attack

On January 6, 2021, a large group of supporters of President Donald Trump (including many members of antigovernment radicalized groups such as the Oath Keepers, Proud Boys, and Three Percenters) violently breached security and occupied the US Capitol. They attempted to prevent a joint session of Congress from counting Electoral College votes needed to certify the election of President-elect Joe Biden. Approximately 140 police officers – around 80 US Capitol Police and 60 from the Metropolitan Police Department – were assaulted. One person was shot by Capitol Police, another died of a drug overdose, and three died of natural causes. The rioters occupied the Capitol building, vandalizing and looting it. A gallows was erected west of the Capitol, and many rioters chanted "Hang Mike Pence" in response to the false claims that Vice President Pence could overturn the election results in favor of Trump. Pipe bombs were found at both Democratic and Republican National headquarters, and Molotov cocktails were discovered in a vehicle near the US Capitol. According to US government sources, more than 1,000 defendants were subsequently arrested in nearly every state and the District of Columbia. The attack caused extensive and in some instances incalculable losses to historic American infrastructure [16, 30, 31].

We acknowledge that there are ethics-related considerations regarding the controversial Goldwater rule, proclaiming that it is unethical for a psychiatrist to offer a professional opinion about an individual's mental condition unless that psychiatrist has conducted an examination of the individual and has been granted proper authorization (§ 7.3 of the American Psychiatric Association's Principles of Medical Ethics with Annotations Especially Applicable to Psychiatry). However, given the large volume of information that is publicly available about the US Capitol and the many defendants charged in the attack, including data from some of the professionals who examined one such charged individual (Jacob Chansley), and considering the professional and social interests that may be served by an analysis of his case and discussion of new perspectives on forensic assessment in cases such as his, we believe we are within the boundaries of ethics [32, 33].

Jacob Chansley (QAnon Shaman)

One prominently dressed insurrectionist, Jacob Chansley (aka Jacob Angeli) wore a Viking hat with fur and horns, a coyote tail, and red, white, and blue face paint. He climbed a media tower and a scaffolding to enter the Capitol grounds. He carried a six-foot-long spear and used a bullhorn to howl and claim that the Capitol was "our house" and that the insurrectionists were there to "take the Capitol" and to "take out" several members of Congress [34, 35]. Standing at the lectern of the US Senate dais, Chansley spoke to fellow rioters proclaiming:

> Thank you, Heavenly Father, for gracing us with this opportunity . . . to allow us to send a message to all the tyrants, the communists, and the globalists, that this is our nation, not theirs. That we will not allow America, the American way of the United States of America to go down . . . Thank you for filling this chamber with Patriots that love you . . . Thank you for allowing the United States of America to be reborn. Thank you for allowing us to get rid of the communists, the globalists, and the traitors within our government. [34, p. 2]

On January 7, 2021, Chansley called the Washington Field Office of the FBI and requested to speak with law enforcement. Chansley confessed that he was the man photographed at Vice President Pence's chair on the Senate dais. In the photograph, his face is painted, and he is clearly relishing being in the moment while carrying the spear and wearing the horned helmet. He said that he was able to get into the United States Senate in DC "by the grace of God." Chansley defended his action of sitting in the Vice President's chair, stating that Pence is a "child-trafficking traitor." However, Chansley said he did not mean his note to Vice President Pence – "it's only a matter of time, justice is coming" – as a threat. Chansley also relished the opportunity to return to Washington, DC for the inauguration, later telling the FBI: "I'll still go, you better believe it. For sure I'd want to be there, as a protestor, as a protestor, fuckin' A!" Prior to his arrest, Chansley was also interviewed by media and stated: "The fact that we had a bunch of our traitors in office hunker down, put on their gas masks and retreat into their underground bunker, I consider that a win" [34, p. 6]. Chansley stated that he drove to Washington, DC as part of a group effort, with other "patriots" from Arizona, at the request of the president that all "patriots" come to DC on January 6, 2021.

In the weeks leading up the attack, Chansley accrued thousands of followers across several social media platforms including Facebook, Rumble, Parler, and YouTube. In one Facebook post he wrote: "We shall have no real hope to survive the enemies arrayed against us until we hang the traitors lurking among us" [34, p. 13]. Chansley was part of QAnon, an umbrella term for a set of internet conspiracy theories. QAnon is constantly evolving but at its core stands a belief that a global pedophilic cabal exists for the purposes of child sex trafficking. QAnon adherents, at times in the past receiving updates from an individual or individuals referred to as "Q," have endorsed a wide variety of conspiracy theories involving popular figures or satanic blood sacrifices and have made allegations that others are conspiring against former President Donald Trump. QAnon followers include a wide following of liberals, conservatives, doctors, lawyers, and all education levels [34, 35, 36].

QAnon social media posts often involve anger, disgust, and contempt toward government leaders, Hollywood elites, and have antisemitic elements. Chansley's attorney Albert Watkins was interviewed with *Talking Points Memo*. Watkins stated that his client had Asperger's syndrome and added that "a lot of these defendants – and I'm going to use this colloquial term, perhaps disrespectfully – but they're all fucking short-bus people. These are people with brain damage, they're fucking retarded, they're on the goddamn spectrum" [37, p. 1).

Federal Legal Charges, Forensic Examination, and Sentencing

Chansley was arrested in Arizona on January 9, 2021 and charged with the following offenses: Civil Disorder; Obstruction of an Official Proceeding; Entering and Remaining in a Restricted Building; Disorderly and Disruptive Conduct in a Restricted Building; Violent Entry and Disorderly Conduct in a Capitol Building; Parading, Demonstrating, or Picketing in a Capitol Building. The insanity defense was not raised as an issue. Instead, he entered into a plea agreement on September 3, 2021, and was sentenced to 41 months in prison, followed by 36 months supervised release and ordered to pay restitution of $2,000. The diagnosis of autism or Asperger's was not mentioned in his agreement. During one of his hearings he stated: "I may be guilty of this crime, but I am in no way, shape, or form a dangerous criminal. I am not a violent man. I am not an insurrectionist. I am certainly not a domestic terrorist. I am a good man who broke the law" [34, p. 34].

The court ordered the US Bureau of Prisons to conduct a psychological examination of Mr. Chansley, which was completed by psychologist Angela J. Van der Walt. Dr. Van der Walt determined that he was competent to stand trial. The report was accompanied by a 2006 medical report from the US military while the defendant was serving on active duty in the US Navy aboard the *USS Kitty Hawk* in 2006–7. While serving aboard the *USS Kitty Hawk*, Mr. Chansley consulted with the ship's medical doctor seeking clarification as to whether he was "crazy." A series of consultations with the doctor ensued, resulting in a 2006 diagnosis of schizotypal personality disorder, and he was declared "fit for duty" [34, 35, 36].

Digital Subcultures and Gestalt Psychology

Messaging on social media platforms is well known to influence many people's opinions and decisions. This is highlighted by nefarious Russian activity during the 2016 US presidential election and false information regarding Covid-19 vaccinations. Prior to the US Capitol attack, several social networking services spread extreme overvalued beliefs posted by members of antisemitic groups, QAnon, and other extremist groups [38–43]. This was accomplished through mobilization and incitement. The mobilization was accomplished through the use of many hashtags like these:

> #Calmbeforethestorm #GetReadyPatriots #WomenForTrump #MagaMarchDC #MAGA2021 #TRUMP #TRUMP2021 #HoldTheLine #maga #donaldtrump #Marchfortrump #DC #whitehouse #stopthestealcaravan #ElectionFraud #HoldTheLinePatriots #WashingtonDC #trumptrain #Teamtrump #protest #4moreyears #mmmdc12 #stormtheCapitol #patriotsunited #patriots #magamarch #millionmagamarch2021 #trumprally #proudboys #ProudboysUSA #fuckAntifa #parler #parlerusa #trumpmarch #fakeelection #fakeelections #fakepolls #stopthesteal #millionmagamarch #dcprotest #dcprotests #rightwing #Stopthesteal2021 #jan6 #jan6th #wildprotest #MillionMAGA #theproudboys [42, p. 2]

Another highly popular post, with 25,000 impressions and 68 shares, urges attackers to "Hang traitors to the United States of America! #stopthesteal #prosecutethedeepstate" [42, p. 3].

The use of multiple hashtags amplified many messages across many platforms – essentially stitching together a subculture. How was it possible for so many individuals to believe something they read online? The answer may lie in the fact that these individuals literally saw an illusion of something that the rest of American society did not – something best explained by Gestalt psychological principles.

Gestalt Psychology

In 1912 Max Wertheimer introduced the term phi phenomenon (perception of apparent movement). He described the optical illusion of apparent movements when two optical stimuli are presented with alternating high frequency [44, 45]. This is why stick images appear to move in flipbooks. Gestalt laws showed how objects are perceptually grouped together by the brain to form patterns that are regular, simple, and orderly – but can sometimes be misleading. In another example, the laws describe how patterns in "connect the dots" images are perceived as figures. Gestalt theory suggests that the mind understands external stimuli as a whole rather than as the sum of parts – the brain fills in missing gaps. This concept is called isomorphism, and it also features in cognitive psychology, where insightful thinking about decisions and environmental experiences interact [46]. The internet has done much the same with internet cognitive isoforms – as a piece of information learned online that is used to connect the "cognitive dots."

As may be found in referencing the hashtags we listed, reinforcement of extreme overvalued belief can also occur when individuals limit the number of relevant informational sources. Groups that hold and maintain extreme overvalued belief systems actively work toward isolating individuals, discrediting outside information sources, and creating an "echo chamber" where extreme overvalued belief may be internally validated and uncritically accepted [47]. The brain is a hungry organ (high oxygen demand) and a lazy organ (relies on cognitive shortcuts) [12]. Social media, like the Gestalt concept of an optical illusion, allows for the rapid intake of information that, through cognitive shortcuts, saves the brain time and energy. Cognitive illusions can be weaponized during political movements or cultish recruitment efforts. Treading on moral codes is a matter worth fighting for and even dying for – the cognitive fuel for individuals who harbor extreme overvalued beliefs. A notable symbol of this is the Gadsden rattlesnake flag, which reads "Don't Tread on Me" [48].

Binary Bias and Emotional Tagging

As we have described, the brain takes very large amounts of data and boils it down to a smaller number of categories – often two. This is seen in everyday behavior where people consume their favorite foods, use the same routes to travel to work or school, etc. Humans also tend to treat evidence as "all or none." This is seen in courtrooms where jurors often judge a witness as "bad" or "good" to evaluate credibility. Many critical behavioral outputs such as "fight versus flight" and "sustenance versus poison" are binary decisions [49]. In other words, sometimes our very survival depends on being able to make a decision between two courses of action quickly – and humans are not always great at rapidly weighing all of the options and nuances.

Emotions have important relevance for survival because emotional stimuli capture human attention more quickly than nonemotional stimuli. Seeing and detecting potential threats, like poisonous snakes or spiders, and remembering where they are located (tagged) is important for survival [50, 51, 52]. The emotions of anger, contempt, and disgust (in our example, those that stole the election) also fuel violent rhetoric [53]. Schemas are cognitive frameworks that help the brain organize and interpret information. Putting this all together, the logic flows as seen here:

> Moral schema (Election Stolen) ⟶ Extreme Overvalued Beliefs ⟶ emotions such as anger, contempt and disgust "tagging "⟶ pathway to violence at US Capitol attack

It is critical to note that some people saw something the rest of Americans did not. To a select portion of the US population, an assumption was made that was shared by many others of the same ilk. In their eyes, a violent response was needed to cleanse the Capitol of traitors – even if the safety of oneself and others was compromised. Harvard psychiatrist Oliver Freudenreich notes: "While most people would not jeopardize their careers or lives for overvalued ideas, some will (and are secretly regarded as heroes by those less inclined to fight for an idea). This is to say that it is not the idea itself but the reckless (toward oneself and others) pursuit that causes isolation and suffering" [11, p. 6]. Indeed, some prominent individuals minimized the behavior of the insurrectionists as "tourists."

Discussion

A cult is defined as a social group that is defined by its philosophical beliefs and related behaviors, or its common interest in a particular individual, object, or goal outside of the generally accepted beliefs of their culture. English and American law developed the insanity defense to relieve the accused of legal responsibility when their thinking and behavior are so impaired at the time of the crime as a result of mental disorder that the defendant meets that jurisdiction's legal definition of insanity. Legal definitions of insanity vary, and some states do not even recognize the insanity defense. The fact that a defendant committed a crime because of a delusional belief is a common basis for an insanity defense. It is therefore critically important that forensic psychiatrists properly identify a defendant's belief as either a fixed false conviction (a delusion) or as an intense emotional commitment to a commonly held belief shared by other members of their cultural group (an extreme overvalued belief). Violent attacks stemming from shared ideologies in cults have generally been rejected by courts as a basis for the insanity defense [19].

Historical Origins of Extreme Overvalued Beliefs

Neuropsychiatrist Carl Wernicke (1848–1905) astutely observed that damage to the left posterior, superior temporal gyrus from strokes resulted in peculiar speech problems. He published the discovery in a book called *The Aphasic Symptom Complex.* Three years later Wernicke described another remarkable disease that he observed in two alcoholic men and a young woman with sulfuric acid poisoning as encephalopathic presentations with nystagmus, gaze palsy, delirium, and ataxia. The description now bears his name and that of another neurologist as Wernicke–Korsakoff syndrome to describe the nutritional deficiency and neurological findings seen in serious alcoholics [54].

Ueberwertige Idee

Wernicke first defined the term *Ueberwertige Idee* (overvalued idea) in an 1892 article in which he described it as a fixated belief that was neither delusional nor obsessional but could influence behavior to a pathological degree. As an example from literature, Wernicke described the acts of violence in Dostoevsky's novel, *Crime and Punishment*, as motivated by overvalued ideas. The novel's grandiose protagonist, Rodion Raskolnikov, writes a manifesto in which he identifies with individuals like Napoleon. He believes that he can make exceptional contributions to humanity and thus has the right to break the law, including murder, in pursuit of making such exceptional contributions [8]. Wernicke essentially captures the psychological nature of "spiritedness" or "passion," which Plato first described as *thumos* in the fifth century as one of three parts of the human psyche. The other two were reason and desires. Sigmund Freud and Carl Wernicke were both students of German-Austrian neuroscientist, Theodur Meynert. While Sigmund Freud studied human desire, it was his counterpart Carl Wernicke who captured the essence of spiritedness or passion in his seminal description of the overvalued idea. It should be pointed out that the current DSM-5-TR glossary definition of overvalued idea differs from Wernicke's original concept, in stating it is *a belief not shared by others.* Therefore, in keeping with Wernicke's historic description, the definition of *extreme overvalued belief* has been seen as making an important distinction for forensic cases and threat assessment [8, 55]. The term has been applied to well-known cases of targeted attacks, including Anders Breivik, Ted Kaczynski (Unabomber), assassins (John Wilkes Booth, John Hinckley, Jr., Lee Harvey Oswald, Charles Giteau), as well as online inspired violence seen in incels (a portmanteau of "involuntary celibate"), the US Capitol attack, anti-LGBTQ, sovereign citizens, violent jihadists (Osama bin Laden, the Boston Marathon bombers Dzhokhar "Jahar" Anzorovich Tsarnaev and Tamerlan Tsarnaev), and Adolf Hitler and neo-Nazis [5, 16, 23, 25, 28, 30, 43, 55]. Extreme overvalued beliefs spring from strong affective experiences and are felt as "normal" by the individual, such as passionate political, religious, sexual, or ethical conviction. They may be marked by several warning signs prior to an attack, such as a noticeable increase in perseveration, strident opinion, negative statements about the target(s), increasing anxiety or fear about the target, and an angry emotional undertone [1–4].

Morality and Psychodynamics

Violence seen in cults leading to targeted attack involves predation that is *morally* driven and is best understood as a superego-sanctioned homicidal act, not the valueless, self-absorbed cruelty seen in antisocial personality disorders. The individuals that attacked the US Capitol believed they were defending the US Constitution, while the 9/11 attackers believed they were defending the holy lands from Jews and Christians. Notable scholar Dr. Reid Meloy utilized object relations theory, and Kernberg's model of personality structural deficiencies, to explain such dynamics [56]. Individuals possessing extreme overvalued beliefs may regress to a borderline level of personality organization or, alternatively, may experience prolonged fixation at this level. This condition can lead to significant susceptibility in the individual and allow exploitation of their beliefs by others for their personal or ideological gains. Motivated by destructive intentions to harm others, or themselves, such beliefs may be further nurtured and lead to acts of violence perceived to be justified and sanctified. In some cases, the regression or fixation may be at a level wherein there is *identification* as a warrior or pseudocommando for a cause [57, 58]. There can also be the characterological defect of pathological narcissism. Splitting as a defense in adults is the psychopathological outcome of the normative infant and childhood needing to separate objects and pleasure/displeasure feeling states. The predominance of splitting in adulthood is signaled by the tendency, if not conviction, to view the world in stark black and white terms, to simplify reality, to eliminate the gray zones, to perceive the self and others as part objects, and a gross failure to empathize with, or understand, the inner lives of others – making extreme overvalued beliefs binary, simplistic, and absolute. Psychoanalytic terms are important in describing personality organizations seen in borderline or narcissistic traits, etc. They sometimes create confusion for psychiatric examiners because they traditionally use terms such as "psychotic" or "paranoid" to describe primitive personalities that feature rigidity, concreteness, simplicity, and certainty, where reflective capacity, symbolization, and mentalization are lacking. These personality characteristics should not imply a psychotic mental illness (e.g., with delusions) often seen in severe mental disorders such as schizophrenia. Instead, the DSM-5-TR can be used to describe persons with extreme overvalued beliefs as part of a modern comprehensive forensic assessment [3, 16, 56].

DSM-5-TR Alternative Model for Personality

Cult members should be carefully screened for evidence that they are suffering from severe psychopathology as seen in the traditional DSM-5-TR "disease category" disorders such as schizophrenia or serious mood (affective) disorder with psychosis. *Delusional disorder* is important to consider but should not be confused with extreme overvalued beliefs [15, 27, 28, 55]. Once the presence or absence of these disorders is clarified, a deeper biographical or life story will further inform diagnostic accuracy. The number of victims and severity of violence also should not determine the severity of psychopathology. DSM-5-TR character and temperamental traits can be applied to an assessment of a person's cultural background and identification of any pathological personality traits. Ideological framing, moral outrage, pathological narcissism, as well as changes in thinking and emotions can be discovered through information gathered with structured interviews and collateral information relying on cultural and subcultural formulation and assessment of personality traits, rather than only reliance on cardinal signs and symptoms of a serious mental disorder. Personality traits can generally be ascertained through the collection of biographical data from collateral sources as well as interviews with the individual [16].

Cultural Identity

The DSM-5 *Handbook on the Cultural Formulation Interview* has several sections pertinent to the discussion regarding extreme overvalued beliefs. It must be remembered that these beliefs are experienced by the individual as normal and justified, fully explained by the events that led to their formation, and may appear irrational, even delusional to outsiders. The cultural interview helps formulate cases such as Anders Breivik, Osama bin Laden, Ted Kaczynski (the Unabomber), or Malik Nidal Hassan (the Fort Hood shooter) where there is otherwise no clear mental disorder to describe [16, 27]. In these cases, we have argued that violence springing from their respective extreme overvalued (shared, subcultural beliefs) was initially misdiagnosed as schizophrenia. This is because beliefs that appear to be delusional in one culture or subculture (e.g., witchcraft) may be commonly held in another. In some cultures, visual and/or auditory hallucinations with a religious context (e.g., hearing God's or an angel's voice) are normal experiences. In fact, distressing hallucinations or pseudohallucinations along with overvalued ideas may present clinically similar to true psychosis but are normal in the subculture. A terrorist's subculture may sanction suicide bombings (Al-Qaeda), mailing package bombs (ecoterrorism), or targeting minorities (white supremacy groups). Therefore, in a forensic case, the DSM-5 cultural context is of critical importance. The guide states: "Understanding the cultural context of illness experience is essential for effective diagnostic assessment and clinical management." It goes on to explain:

> Culture refers to systems of knowledge concepts, rules and practices that are learned and transmitted across generations. Culture includes language, religion and spirituality, family structures, life-cycle stages, ceremonial rituals, and customs, as well as moral and legal customs. Cultures are open dynamic systems that undergo continuous change over time; in the contemporary world most individuals and groups are exposed to multiple cultures which they use to fashion their own identities and make sense of experience. These features of culture make it crucial not to overgeneralize cultural information or stereotype groups in terms of fixed cultural traits. [16, p. 5]

Subcultural Distinctions

It is critical to understand that a *subculture* can also exist that may differ to a large degree from a more mainstream culture (and we should avoid stereotyping them). For example, many mainstream cultures reject violence, while a subculture within it (e.g., Al-Qaeda, Islamic State, or white supremacy) may embrace it. The ideology of Al-Qaeda or neo-Nazis is a deviant strain of mainstream cultures, but like antiabortionist, pro-life, religious, political, and other "morally driven" movements, can become latched onto by others who develop a fixation driven by extreme overvalued beliefs. Al-Qaeda, like white supremacy groups (e.g., Boogaloo Bois, Rise Above Movement, Atomwaffen, Proud Boys) contain within them a subculture and can vary significantly from the more moderate mainstream racism, antisemitism, or antigovernment beliefs that are pernicious undercurrents in the culture. Fixations leading to violence seen in cults or terrorism require a deeper understanding of the individual's character and temperament, within the context of their subculture. They also contain psychoanalytic nuggets that are unique to each individual, and their personality – requiring a deeper person-centered probing [8, 16, 23, 27].

DSM-5-TR and Personality Traits

The DSM-5-TR alternative model for personality has Criteria A–F that include a) levels of personality functioning, b) pathological personality traits, c–d) pervasiveness and stability, and e–f) alternative explanations for personality pathology. The model includes two important domains: self and interpersonal. Self includes identity and self-directedness and interpersonal includes empathy and intimacy. Although a person may not meet the threshold for needing psychiatric medications, psychiatric hospitalization, or meeting the strict legal criteria for insanity, it is critical to include the above-mentioned sections of the DSM-5-TR for a proper diagnostic assessment in forensic cases. The examiner can then move away from signs and symptoms (e.g., mania or psychosis) and into the domains of emotions, life events, culture, subculture, personality traits, biography, character, and temperament [16].

Psychometric Instruments

The Terrorism Radicalization Assessment Protocol (TRAP-18), developed by psychologist and FBI consultant Dr. J. Reid Meloy, is a structured and validated assessment instrument for counterterrorism professionals. The TRAP-18 helps identify potential attackers before the violence starts. It is a professional model designed for prevention, not prediction, of an attack. It has two parts: distal characteristics (of which there are 10) and proximal warning signs (of which there are 8) (Table 10.1).

Another important structured professional judgment tool was recently proposed to separate delusional constructs from radicalized beliefs. Dr. Mark Cunningham developed the Model of Analysis for Differentiating Delusional Disorder from the Radicalization of Extreme Beliefs–17 Factor (MADDD-or-Rad-17) to inform this important differential.

Summary

The scenarios documented throughout this book all lead to a simple test for forensic examiners to consider in cases they encounter: Are fixed, false, idiosyncratic beliefs different from shared subcultural beliefs? Utilizing concise definitions of fixations holds the key to better understanding the motives behind targeted attacks. The next logical step is to think about causation. Psychotic symptoms such as delusions and hallucinations are likely due to defects in brain function. Extreme overvalued beliefs spring from a person's unique personality/culture/biography.

Key Points

- When encountering individuals with unusual or bizarre beliefs, forensic examiners should apply concise definitions of obsessions, delusions, and extreme overvalued beliefs to the case.
- Extreme overvalued beliefs are best formulated using the DSM-5 cultural formulation and the alternative model for personality. Delusions are best formulated utilizing

Table 10.1 The Terrorism Radicalization Assessment Protocol

Proximal Warning Signs	Distal Characteristics
Pathway	Personal Grievance and Moral Outrage
Fixation	Framed by an Ideology
Identification	Failure to Affiliate with a Group
Novel Aggression	Dependence on the Virtual Community
Energy Burst	Thwarting of Occupational Goals
Leakage	Changes in Thinking and Emotion
Last Resort	Failure of Sexually Intimate Pair Bonding
Directly Communicated Threat	Mental Disorder
	Creativity and Innovation
	Criminal Violence

criteria for mental disorders with psychotic symptoms (e.g., schizophrenia, mood disorders with psychotic features, substance-induced psychotic disorders).

- While shared beliefs seen in cults are not generally accepted as exculpatory for criminal responsibility (insanity), cooccurring issues can be considered as mitigating factors (e.g., intellectual disability, past abuse, genuine remorse, minor role in the offense) or aggravating factors (e.g., repeat offenses, drug-related offenses, lack of remorse, heinous acts).

References

1. JR Meloy, P Gill. The lone-actor terrorist and the TRAP-18. *Journal of Threat Assessment and Management.* 2016;3(1):37–52.
2. JR Meloy. The operational development and empirical testing of the Terrorist Radicalization Assessment Protocol (TRAP–18). *Journal of Personality Assessment.* 2018;100(5):483–92.
3. JR Meloy, J Hoffmann, editors. *International handbook of threat assessment.* 2nd ed. Oxford University Press; 2021.
4. JR Meloy, T Rahman. Cognitive-affective drivers of fixation in threat assessment. *Behavioral Sciences & the Law.* 2021;39(2):170–89.
5. T Rahman, SM Hartz, W Xiong, JR Meloy, J Janofsky, B Harry, PJ Resnick. Extreme overvalued beliefs. *Journal of the American Academy of Psychiatry and the Law.* 2020;48(3):319–26.
6. T Rahman. Extreme overvalued beliefs: how violent extremist beliefs become "normalized." *Behavioral Sciences.* 2018;8(1):10.
7. J Kupper, P Cotti, JR Meloy. The Hanau terror attack: unraveling the dynamics of mental disorder and extremist beliefs. *Journal of Threat Assessment and Management.* 2024;11(3):149–85.
8. T Rahman, JR Meloy, R Bauer. Extreme overvalued belief and the legacy of Carl Wernicke. *Journal of the American Academy of Psychiatry and the Law.* 2019:47(2):180–87.
9. F Oyebode. *Sims' symptoms in the mind: an introduction to descriptive psychopathology.* 4th ed. Elsevier Health Sciences; 2008.

10. Oxford Textbook of Psychiatry. 3rd ed. M Gelder, D Gath, R Mayou, P Cowan, editors. Oxford University Press; 1996.
11. O Freudenreich. *Psychotic disorders*. Springer International Publishing; 2020.
12. C Zorumski, E Rubin. *Psychiatry and clinical neuroscience: a primer*. Oxford University Press; 2011.
13. H Akiskal. Diagnosis in psychiatry and the mental status examination. In: G Winokur, P Clayton, editors. *The medical basis of psychiatry*. W. B. Saunders; 1986; p. Diagnosis in psychiatry and the mental status examinationW.B. Saunders Co.369–83.Akiskal H
14. FJ Fish. *An outline of psychiatry for students and practitioners*. 2nd ed. John Wright and Sons; 1968.
15. D Veale. Overvalued ideas: a conceptual analysis. *Behaviour Research and Therapy*. 2002;40(4):383–400.
16. T Rahman, L Zheng, JR Meloy. DSM-5 cultural and personality assessment of extreme overvalued beliefs. *Aggression and Violent Behavior*. 2021;60:101552.
17. PJ Resnick. The Andrea Yates case: insanity on trial. *Cleveland State Law Review*. 2007;55:147.
18. PJ Resnick. The Andrea Yates case: insanity on trial. Presented at University of New Mexico Department of Law; 2011 Mar 31.
19. T Rahman, KA Grellner, B Harry, N Beck, J Lauriello. Infanticide in a case of folie à deux. *American Journal of Psychiatry*. 2013;170(10):1110–12.
20. BD Booth, SH Friedman, S Curry, H Ward, SE Stewart. Obsessions of child murder: underrecognized manifestations of obsessive-compulsive disorder. *Journal of the American Academy of Psychiatry and the Law*. 2014;42(1): 66–74.
21. WC Drevets, JL Price, ML Furey. Brain structural and functional abnormalities in mood disorders: implications for neurocircuitry models of depression. *Brain Structure and Function*. 2008;213:93–118.
22. JR Meloy. A catathymic infanticide. *Journal of Forensic Sciences*. 2010;55(5):1393–96.
23. T Rahman, PJ Resnick, B Harry. Anders Breivik: extreme beliefs mistaken for psychosis. *Journal of the American Academy of Psychiatry and the Law*. 2016;44(1):28–35.
24. JR Meloy, E Habermeyer, A Guldimann. The warning behaviors of Anders Breivik. *Journal of Threat Assessment and Management*. 2015;2(3–4):164–175.
25. MH Logan. Hate crime perpetrators: the psychopath and the perseverator. *Violence and Gender*. 2018;5(1):42–44.
26. J Pobocha. Delusions in forensic examinations. *SVEIKATOS*. 2014;24(1):93–100.
27. KJ Weiss. At a loss for words: nosological impotence in the search for justice. *Journal of the American Academy of Psychiatry and the Law*. 2016;44(1):36–40.
28. MD Cunningham. Differentiating delusional disorder from the radicalization of extreme beliefs: a 17-factor model. *Journal of Threat Assessment and Management*. 2018;5(3):137–154.
29. RA Knudsen. Why terrorism researchers should care about criminal responsibility. *Perspectives on Terrorism*. 2023;17(1):50–57.
30. M Amman, JR Meloy. Stochastic terrorism. *Perspectives on Terrorism*. 2021;15(5):2–13.
31. DC Rapoport. The Capitol attack and the 5th terrorism wave. *Terrorism and Political Violence*. 2021;33(5):912–16.
32. PS Appelbaum. Reflections on the Goldwater rule. *Journal of the American Academy of Psychiatry and the Law*. 2017;45(2):228–32.
33. J Martin-Joy. Interpreting the Goldwater Rule. *Journal of the American Academy of Psychiatry and the Law*. 2017;45(2):233–40.
34. Government Brief in Support of Detention. *United States* v. *Jacob Anthony Chansley, a.k.a. "Jacob Angeli."* George

Washington University, Program on Extremism. 2021 Jan 14. https://extremism.gwu.edu/sites/g/files/zaxdzs5746/files/Jacob%20Chansley%20Detention%20Memo.pdf

35. K Balevic. Justice Department seeks a 4-year prison sentence for the QAnon Shaman, calling him the 'flagbearer' for insurrectionists. Business Insider. 2021 Nov 10. www.businessinsider.com/justice-department-seeks-4-year-prison-sentence-qanon-shaman-2021-11

36. *United States* v. *Jacob Anthony Chansley* (1:21-cr-00003), District Court, District of Columbia. 2021 Jan 11. www.courtlistener.com/docket/29100583/united-states-v-chansley/

37. B Levin. "They're all fucking short-bus people": Capitol Riot attorney manages to insult at least three different groups while defending 1/6 actions. *Vanity Fair*. 2021 May 18. www.vanityfair.com/news/2021/05/albert-watkins-jacob-chansley-capitol-attack

38. J Tollefson. How Trump turned conspiracy theory research upside down. *Nature*. 2021;590:192–93.

39. A Amarasingam, MA Argentino. The QAnon conspiracy theory: a security threat in the making. *CTC Sentinel*. 2020;13(7):37–44.

40. V Padinjaredath Suresh, G Nogara, F Cardoso, S Cresci, S Giordano, L Luceri. Tracking fringe and coordinated activity on Twitter leading up to the US Capitol attack. *arXiv e-prints*. 2023 Feb:arXiv-2302.

41. EL Wang, L Luceri, F Pierri, E Ferrara. Identifying and characterizing behavioral classes of radicalization within the QAnon conspiracy on Twitter. In *Proceedings of the International AAAI Conference on Web and Social Media*. 2023 Jun 2 (Vol. 17, pp. 890–901).

42. L Munn. More than a mob: Parler as preparatory media for the US Capitol storming. *First Monday*. 2021;26(3).

43. J Kupper, TK Christensen, D Wing, M Hurt, M Schumacher, R Meloy. The contagion and copycat effect in transnational far-right terrorism. *Perspectives on Terrorism*. 2022;16(4):4–26.

44. M Wertheimer. *Source book of Gestalt psychology*. Harcourt, Brace and Co.; 1938.

45. S Guberman. On Gestalt theory principles. *Gestalt Theory*. 2015:37(1):25–44.

46. I Rock, S Palmer. The legacy of Gestalt psychology. *Scientific American*. 1990;263(6):84–91.

47. L Terren, R Borge-Bravo. Echo chambers on social media: a systematic review of the literature. *Review of Communication Research*. 2021;15(9):99–118.

48. CD Barnes, RP Brown, LL Osterman. Don't tread on me: masculine honor ideology in the US and militant responses to terrorism. *Personality and Social Psychology Bulletin*. 2012;38(8):1018–29.

49. M Fisher, FC Keil. The binary bias: a systematic distortion in the integration of information. *Psychological Science*. 2018;29(11):1846–58.

50. A Öhman, A Flykt, F Esteves. Emotion drives attention: detecting the snake in the grass. *Journal of Experimental Psychology: General*. 2001;130(3):466–78.

51. JA Bergado, M Lucas, G Richter-Levin. Emotional tagging – a simple hypothesis in a complex reality. *Progress in Neurobiology*. 2011;94(1):64–76.

52. M Shabo. *Techniques of propaganda and persuasion*. Prestwick House Inc.; 2008.

53. D Matsumoto, HC Hwang, MG Frank. The effects of incidental anger, contempt, and disgust on hostile language and implicit behaviors. *Journal of Applied Social Psychology*. 2016;46(8):437–52.

54. JM Pearce. Wernicke-Korsakoff encephalopathy. *European Neurology*. 2007;59(1–2):101–4.

55. T Rahman, JR Meloy, R Bauer. Extreme overvalued belief and the legacy of Carl Wernicke. *Journal of the American Academy of Psychiatry and the Law*. 2019;47(2):180–87.

56. RJ Meloy. *Violent attachments*. Jason Aronson, Inc.; 1997.

57. JR Meloy, K Mohandie, JL Knoll, J Hoffmann. The concept of identification in threat assessment. *Behavioral Sciences & the Law*. 2015;33(2–3):213–37.

58. PE Dietz. Mass, serial and sensational homicides. *Bulletin of the New York Academy of Medicine*. 1986;62(5): 477–91.

59. MD Cunningham. Differentiating delusional disorder from the radicalization of extreme beliefs: a 17-factor model. *Journal of Threat Assessment and Management*. 2018;5(3):137–54.

Chapter 11

Psychopathy and Personality Disorders

Joslyn K. Wallenborn and J. Reid Meloy

"Remorse for what? You people have done everything in the world to me.

Doesn't that give me equal right? I can do anything I want to you people at any time I want to. Because that's what you've done to me."

– *Charles Manson [1]*

Introduction

Crazy, [2] demented, [3] evil, [4] insane, [5] remorseless, [6] deranged [4] – these psychologically loaded words have been used across time and media platforms to describe cult leaders and their followers. Given the exposure of cults' bizarre rituals, extreme overvalued beliefs, surreptitious nature, and unconventional and often outright criminal behavior, these characterizations are not surprising. Undoubtedly, the radically counternormative and innately destructive nature of cults invites meaningful scientific inquiry into the personality characteristics that underpin cultic leadership and engagement. In this chapter, we will illuminate the profile of the psychopathic cult leader, and the corresponding personality disorders that we have observed in cult followers, as well as the complementary and concordant ways in which such personalities interact. We conclude with a review of suggestive forensic instruments utilized for the clinical and forensic assessment of cult leaders and their followers.

Case Vignette: Charles Manson

In August 1969, Charles Manson (Figure 11.1) orchestrated the massacre of seven individuals, including the actor Sharon Tate, over the course of two nights in Los Angeles, California. Although he was not present during the killings, Manson was the leader of a cult referred to as "the family," and the subsequent trial and conviction of all the defendants in the case cemented the "Tate–LaBianca" murders as one of the most notorious crimes of the twentieth century. All of the Manson family members were initially sentenced to death, subsequently commuted to life in prison following a US Supreme Court decision in 1972 [7]. Manson served out his sentence until his natural death at the age of 83.

Manson's upbringing was traumagenic, including multiple abandonments by his mother, and he spent most of his adolescence and adulthood in some form of custody due to an extensive history of both violent and nonviolent crimes. When he was paroled in 1967, he gathered together his group of mostly young women on the streets of San Francisco, and with a combination of existing vulnerabilities, physiological deprivation, drug use, group pressure, isolation, the excitement of unbridled sexuality and aggression, and his charismatic leadership,

Figure 11.1 Mug shot of Charles Manson, 1968
Source: California Department of Corrections and Rehabilitation, public domain

created a cult that embraced a grandiose and violent "helter skelter" fantasy: the massacres would initiate a race war and eventually the family would emerge from the desert to lead the post-apocalyptic world disorder. On a more plebeian level, Manson had experienced a humiliating rejection of his music at the same house where the first five murders occurred; he had been befriended by Terry Melcher, a producer for the Beach Boys, who previously lived at the home at 10050 Cielo Drive but declined to record Manson and his songs.

A recent published analysis of a 1997 psychological evaluation of Manson, including multiple test results, indicated that he scored 36 on the Psychopathy Checklist-Revised (PCL-R) [8], placing him at the 98th percentile for severe psychopathy among inmates, and ruled out a historical diagnosis of schizophrenia [9]. Other testing indicated an additional mood dysregulation disorder such as mania or hypomania and personality *organization* at a borderline or psychotic level.

Clinical Profile of Cult Leaders

"Without me, life has no meaning."
Jim Jones [10], just before ordering the mass suicide and murder of over 900 Peoples Temple devotees and their children in Guyana

Cults are deliberate endeavors often orchestrated by psychopaths, which cannot be fully understood without first unraveling the psychopathology of their leader. As the brief passage earlier suggests, cult leaders present with distinctive personalities that enable them to exert inordinate influence over others and to exhibit highly manipulative and remarkably destructive conduct. Within the literature on cults, narcissistic and antisocial[1] personality

[1] Antisocial personality disorder will be discussed at length within the subsequent section concerning cult followers.

disorders [11] are among the most commonly identified character pathologies ascribed to cult leaders. However, psychopathy may be the most fitting yet least explored constellation of traits and behaviors observed in such individuals [8]. To disentangle the personality structure and functioning of cult leaders, we begin with examination of narcissistic personality disorder before proceeding to explore psychopathy. Next, we consider the role of histrionic and borderline personality disorders [11] among female cult leaders.

Narcissistic Personality Disorder

Cult leaders have been widely recognized across the literature as presenting with narcissistic personality disorder (NPD) or its relevant traits [12–21]. The DSM-5-TR [11] diagnostic criteria of NPD encompasses impairments in self-functioning (exaggerated self-appraisal or sense of entitlement) and deficits in interpersonal functioning (impaired ability to empathize or superficial relationships), along with grandiose and attention-seeking personality characteristics. These features are readily identifiable among some figures who present themselves as gurus, prophets, messiahs, and saviors. Beyond mere monikers that invite adulation, narcissistic cult leaders claim to possess prescient knowledge of things ordinary, spiritual, otherworldly, or exceptional to all others. With an insatiable need for attention and adoration, they are prone to be impatient and angry when they feel they are not receiving special treatment by their followers.

To illuminate the etiology of NPD among charismatic cult leaders, much of the literature [12, 17, 22, 23, 24] has leveraged Kernberg's [25, 26] and Kohut's [27, 28, 29] divergent psychoanalytic perspectives on early impairments in narcissistic development as antecedents to such pathology. While Kohut considers developmental arrest to be key to the narcissistic leader's grandiose self, Kernberg views the grandiose self as a pathological development. Its origins notwithstanding, NPD appears ubiquitous among cult leaders. In an in-depth case study, Clarke [13] illustrated the features of NPD[2] exhibited by self-proclaimed guru Bhagwan Shree Rajneesh to include grandiosity, fantasies of unlimited success, need for constant attention, interpersonal difficulties, and a preoccupation with grooming and lying. However, beyond these narcissistic traits and without explicit mention of psychopathy, Clarke [13] more aptly describes Rajneesh as a psychopath with his extensive discussion of the guru's impulsivity, contempt for others, lifelong pattern of manipulation and law-breaking, lack of empathy, disregard for the well-being of others, affective and predatory aggression [31] toward others, documented behavioral problems in childhood, as well as severe emotional detachment. Indeed, narcissistic personality traits and an avoidant attachment style of detachment may distinguish self-serving charismatic leaders from benevolent charismatic leaders [16], or as Volkan [24] terms them, destructive and reparative leaders, respectively.

Though NPD serves as a central component of charismatic personalities, narcissism alone belies the full psychopathological portrait of the cult leader. Indeed, the psychopathic process proves particularly pertinent to this population. Though psychopathy bears certain similarities to NPD [32, 33], each is considered a distinct clinical construct

[2] Utilizing the criteria set out in the *DSM-III* [30].

for both clinical and research purposes [34]. Specifically, NPD lacks the full constellation of affective, interpersonal, lifestyle, and antisocial features exuded by cult leaders that is more aptly captured by the construct of psychopathy.

Psychopathy

Psychopathy is a distinct clinical disorder characterized by affective and interpersonal deficits and a socially deviant lifestyle [8]. While not a diagnosis in the DSM series, most recently DSM-5-TR [11] – although highlighted in the companion treatment volume to DSM-5 [35], *Gabbard's Treatments of Psychiatric Disorders* [36] – psychopathy shares some personality traits and behavioral characteristics among the antisocial, borderline, histrionic, and narcissistic personality disorders [37, 38, 39], which have in common generally intact cognition and often primitive defenses. Many consider psychopathy a more biologically based and severe variant of antisocial personality disorder [40]. Absent genuine socialized emotion and compassion for others, the psychopath's distinguishing characteristic is an inability to form human attachments, a "fundamental disidentification with humanity" [41, p. 5]. Adept at camouflaging their profound emotional poverty with a superficial and deceptive veneer, the bright psychopath is at once charismatic, manipulative, callous, and exploitative, with the distinctive capacity to harm others without shame, guilt, or remorse. Psychopaths characteristically exhibit aggressive narcissism while engaging in a socially deviant lifestyle [42]. Since the construct's first measurement and validation over 30 years ago [8, 43], psychopathy is the most widely researched personality disorder, with several hundred scientific studies published each year in the world literature. There is also a small but substantial literature on psychopathy as an evolutionary adaptation, although this is a minority view [44].

Are cult leaders psychopaths? Indeed, many present as striking prototypical examples of the psychopathic personality. Yet there is scant literature that explores this connection. The smattering of research that tackles this query is largely comprised of idiographic case studies that are qualitatively rich but scientifically uninformative. A review of the extant literature provides a springboard upon which we will expand our understanding of the cult leader's psychopathy.

Anthropologist Weston La Barre [45, 46] was among the first scholars to recognize the construct of psychopathy among cult leaders. In his case study of a southern snake-handling cult, La Barre [45] describes in detail how psychopathic cult leader and spiritual con man Beauregard Barefoot insidiously exploited his parishioners for personal gain and routinely subjected them to venomous snake-handling rituals as a supreme test of faith – of which there were numerous fatalities. The etiology of Barefoot's psychopathic personality is traced back to deficiencies in parental attachment and the developmental psychodynamic underpinnings of "his father's passive sabotage … of his mother's hysteric religiosity" [45, p. 151]. In pioneering this novel perspective, La Barre [45] paved the way for subsequent studies of psychopathic cult leaders. Yet, in the next three decades of literature to follow, psychopathy was seldom associated with cult leaders despite an obvious nexus. The notion reemerged in a typology of youth who join satanic cults, in which Moriarty [47] contended that psychopathic delinquents opportunistically seek out cults as a means to acquire power. Shortly thereafter, Tobias and Lalich [48] were the first to systematically conceptualize the cult leader personality as psychopathic.

Drawing upon Hare's [49][3] seminal list of personality and behavioral markers, the authors performed an item-by-item examination of 15 psychopathic characteristics and their salience to cult leader affect and behavior, illustrated by a case study of David Koresh, the leader of the Branch Davidians in Waco, Texas, who perished in a conflagration in April 1993.

Efforts to study the psychopathic cult leader slowed yet again until Barbara [50] rendered a review of the abuse of religion by psychopathic leaders within cults. Meanwhile, Hassan [51] incorporated psychopathy into the cult leader segment of his continuum model of cult influence, as did Harms and colleagues [52] in their model of archetypal autocratic leader personality characteristics. Others have also drawn cursory connections between psychopathy and cult leaders over the years [49, 53–56). Most recently, Roy and colleagues [9] classified Charles Manson as a severe psychopath using the PCL-R in the first publication of Manson's psychological test data. Incidentally, research has also analogized the family unit to a cult when the household is run by a psychopathic parent [57]. As a whole, the scant extant literature forms a preliminary connection between psychopathy and such authoritative figures, but leaves the reader longing for a much more vivid and validated portrait of the psychopathic cult leader.

Psychopathy, much like cultism [58], exists on a continuum [40, 59–62]. Therefore, cult leaders may exhibit some or all of the psychopathic personality characteristics and behaviors; some may be more psychopathic than others (Table 11.1). Indeed, not all cult leaders are psychopaths, and certainly most psychopaths do not become cult leaders [49, 63]. As a clinical disorder, psychopathy is distinguished by distinct but interrelated pathological features and conduct that are readily observable among cult leaders. We use the well-validated four-facet model of the construct psychopathy as measured by the PCL-R to illustrate these findings [8, 64].

Affective Personality Traits

Spiritual cons, much like "corporate cons" [65], embody certain personality characteristics desirable in a leader. In fact, several core affective psychopathic traits masquerade as attractive leadership qualities. The psychopathic cult leader's compelling superficial charm and grandiose sense of self-worth serve to elevate their status and help them attain power and influence over others. For instance, as part of a myriad of fiction used to gain trust and compliance, sex cult leader Keith Raniere convinced countless women that he was the smartest man in the world with a self-reported IQ of 240 [18]. Though cult leaders are preoccupied with their own self-perceived exceptionalism and superiority, they are generally no more cunning or intelligent than the average person [66].

With a keen persuasive ability, cult leaders convincingly distinguish themselves from others as superior beings or agents of God who possess special knowledge, abilities, powers, spirituality, or immortality. Despite a wide array of self-adorned titles – guru [13], prophet [67], deity [68], and messiah [69] – the magnificence implied in such monikers remains homogeneously grandiose. Psychopaths opportunistically seek out cults as a means to acquire power, control, and superiority over others, often masking

[3] In *Without Conscience*, Hare [49] briefly mentions that psychopaths may be found operating in society as cult leaders among several other flourishing subcriminal vocations.

Table 11.1 Common manifestations of psychopathic traits in cult leaders

Facets	Psychopathic Traits	Common Manifestations in Cult Leaders
1. Interpersonal	Superficial charm	Uses superficial charm and charisma to captivate, impress, and recruit new members
	Grandiosity	Superiority of leader/guru/prophet/messiah to all others; has special knowledge, power, and/or spirituality; self-proclaimed as agent of God (or equivalent); members may have special status but not to same elevation as leader
	Pathological lying	Sustainability of cult depends on continual deception of members to advance goals of leader; elaborate fabricated explanations of childhood, education, and spiritual visions and experiences
	Manipulativeness	Deceit and defrauding of others for personal gain; elaborate coercion and thought reform techniques to gain trust and control of members
2. Affective	Lack of remorse	Exhibits cruelty to members in punishment for disobeying rules and to out-group
	Shallowness	Contrived and exaggerated displays of emotional, spiritual, and/or mystical experiences; sex conflated with "love"
	Callousness	Hostile and violent disregard for out-group, defectors, and followers who violate rules
	Failure to accept responsibility	Routine victim-blaming; hide out, flee the county, or commit suicide to evade authorities
3. Lifestyle	Need for stimulation	Engagement of self and followers in risky rituals, rites of passage, and/or tests of loyalty
	Parasitic lifestyle	Chronically unemployed; subsists off others; exploits members and their families financially and sexually; forced labor; sex trafficking
	Lack of long-term, realistic goals	Espouses short-term, lofty, fantastical, and unachievable aims and promises (e.g., immortality, salvation, reincarnation, absolute certainty)
	Impulsivity	Impetuous participation in murders without long-term plan
	Irresponsibility	Chronic failures to honor obligations and commitments to others
4. Antisocial	Poor behavioral controls	Highly reactive, lashes out at disobedient members; expels noncompliant members
	Early behavior problems	Acts out sexually; harms animals; persistent lying, violent behavior, cheating and truancy in school
	Juvenile delinquency	Adolescent antisocial behavior
	Revocation of conditional release	Escape from prison and violation of conditional release
	Criminal versatility	Physical and sexual abuse of adults and children, financial exploitation, fraud, drug offenses, homicide, mass homicide, coerced suicide

Table 11.1 *(cont.)*

Facets	Psychopathic Traits	Common Manifestations in Cult Leaders
Other	Many short-term marital relationships	Having numerous spouses or committed, live-in relationships over life course; may present as polygamy or polyamory
	Promiscuous sexual behavior	Sex with several partners, selects sexual partners indiscriminately, maintains several sexual relationships at once, or unfaithful to sexual partners; sexual activity that is mandated or coerced by the cult leader, including sex trafficking and sexual assault, is common

their own narcissism by proclaiming themselves an *agent* of an omnipotent power. Adept at expertly appraising individuals' wants, needs, and vulnerabilities, the psychopathic cult leader's skill for manipulation and effortless ability to lie enables them to masterfully gain the trust and control of others, levy their imposed reality, and assume an autocratic role over others, as shown in Table 11.1.

Interpersonal Style

Void of empathy, shame, and remorse, the solipsistic cult leader is able to accomplish their objectives (e.g., power, control, sex, money) at the expense of others without enduring the emotional toll of such endeavors. True to their shallow nature, the leader will employ convincing but contrived and exaggerated displays of emotional, spiritual, and mystical experiences to influence followers, such as speaking in tongues or delivering divine messages. The psychopath's inability to access the same emotional experience that is fundamental to others may prompt them to misattribute emotions to sensations. Cult leaders frequently conflate sexual activity (whether willing or coerced) with love [63]. For instance, in the Children of God cult, David Berg encouraged pedophilia and incest under the pretext of familial love in the name of God [67]. Beyond profound emotional deficits, psychopathic cult leaders express striking callousness toward outsiders, defectors, and, at times, devotees. There are many documented instances in which cult leaders have planned and orchestrated murders (typically carried out by proxy – Manson being a prime example) of such out-groups and opposition (see, e.g., [68–71]). Indeed, even loyal devotees are subjected to mental and physical punishment such as confessionals, isolation, extreme diets, beatings, and rape to prove their loyalty, atone for rule violations, or simply to serve their leader. Physiological deprivation is one of the keys to submission.

Predictably, the psychopathic cult leader is quick to avoid any personal responsibility for their destructive behavior. In accord, they routinely engage in victim-blaming as part of their coercive pattern of control and thought reform [71]. Additionally, they have been known to take extreme measures (e.g., going into hiding, fleeing the country, or committing suicide) to evade the legal and criminal implications of their actions. Suicidal attempts by psychopathic cult leaders, in particular, "are affectively triggered by the commingling of acute dysphoria and narcissistic rage, oftentimes precipitated by the psychopath's perception of being unjustly contained by a malevolent authority. This authority is commonly the criminal justice system, perhaps legal sanctions against the individual, or sudden, unexpected arrest and jailing" [72, p. 95]. We have likely seen a recent example of this in the suicide of Jeffrey Epstein following his imprisonment for several decades of child sexual abuse and sex trafficking [73].

Lifestyle Characteristics

To avoid the "zero state" [74], an inner state of worthlessness and emptiness, psychopaths seek continual excitement to assuage chronic boredom. To this end, cult leaders routinely engage themselves and their followers in risky rituals, rites of passage, and tests of loyalty. A few such practices include drinking one another's blood [54], amateur castration [75], venomous snake-handling rituals [45], and murder [70].

Beyond habitual thrill-seeking, the cult leader leads an intentionally parasitic lifestyle characterized by the psychological, physical, financial, social, and sexual exploitation of followers and cult outsiders. Opportunistic leaders demand that devotees finance the cult through extreme pressure to advance the cult's higher purpose; such carefully crafted schemes often involve personal disbursement of exorbitant amounts of money for tuition, rent, and living expenses, or bilking followers' family members through financial schemes or theft. Followers are often required to live austerely while they fund their chronically unemployed leader's more comfortable, even extravagant, way of life. As entrepreneurs of exploitation, cult leaders' persistent pattern of reliance on others may also involve labor or sex trafficking. In the Children of God, David Berg established a program called "Hookers for Jesus" in which female cult members were sex trafficked in servitude to the cult to generate income for the enterprise and to recruit new followers [67].

Yet another integral component of the psychopath's capricious existence is the lack of long-term, realistic goals. Cult leaders pursue short-term, lofty, fantastical, unachievable, and unsustainable ambitions. In doing so they make hollow promises to followers of immortality, salvation, reincarnation, or guarantees of absolute certainty about life's many unpredictabilities. Many fixate on imminent apocalyptic events or end-of-the-world inevitabilities wherein the cult will assume a position of secular power and dominance, or spiritual salvation [71].

In accomplishing their aims, a persistent pattern of impulsivity and irresponsibility is evident. For instance, David Berg's zealous endorsement of unprotected sex with numerous partners within the Children of God resulted in rampant spread of sexually transmitted diseases within the cult, which he explained was a necessary sacrifice to endure in order to save souls [67]. Another fundamental aspect of the cult leader's aberrant lifestyle is a corresponding pattern of destructive conduct that deliberately disregards the rights of others.

Antisocial Behavior

Cult leaders exhibit a lifelong pattern of antisocial behavior characterized by *both* affective (i.e., reactive, impulsive, emotional) and predatory (i.e., planned, instrumental) violence toward followers, defectors, and outsiders; these modes of violence are characteristic of psychopaths [31]. With the tendency to deliberately operate on the fringe of society, off the grid, and outside of the reach of the laws and institutions that hold individuals criminally accountable, these spiritual con artists may exhibit poor behavioral controls and engage in a wide array of crimes. The notion that criminal behavior is at once both universal and distinct [76] extends into the world of cults as well. Like many criminals, psychopathic cult leaders have a diverse criminal résumé. They have been known to commit violent crime (e.g., assault, sexual assault, child abuse, kidnapping, murder), organized and financial crime (e.g., fraud, theft, racketeering, tax evasion, money laundering, labor and sex trafficking), and crime against the state (e.g., treason, sedition, terrorism, hijacking). The cult leader's varied criminality as an adult is typically preceded by early behavioral problems and juvenile delinquency. In the case of Charles Manson, his adult criminal record was preceded by a long and storied history of juvenile misconduct and escape from institutions [71]. Correspondingly, when apprehended, cult leaders are prone to violate conditions of release or to attempt escape from custody. To name a few, polygamist Lyle Jeffs absconded from home confinement while on pretrial release [77]; "Black Jesus" Steven Tari absconded from conditional release and later escaped from prison in Papua New Guinea [78]; pedophilic cult leader George Feigley twice escaped from prison [79]; and, on the island of Réunion, false prophet Juliano Verbard escaped from prison via hijacked helicopter flown by his devotees [80].

Two additional indices of psychopathy, although they do not statistically cluster with the other four facets, entail many short-term and committed relationships, and promiscuous sexual behavior. Cult leaders may satisfy the first item by having several civil, religious, or common law marriages, or multiple committed live-in relationships over their life course. Among cult leaders this oftentimes presents in unconventional forms such as polygamy. It is common for cult leaders to acquire multiple spouses while at the helm of the cult [48]. Promiscuous sexual behavior, on the other hand, involves a variety of casual sexual activity. This component would be characteristic of cult leaders who have sex with several partners, select sexual partners indiscriminately, maintain several sexual relationships at once, or are unfaithful to their committed sexual partners. Additionally, sexual activity that is mandated or coerced by the cult leader, including sex trafficking and sexual assault, is common. Kent [67] describes how David Berg initiated a practice within the Children of God in which he granted himself full sexual access to all women and children in the cult, including his own daughters and granddaughters; a sinister and archaic *droit du seigneur* of sorts. Meloy [81] wrote about the polymorphous perversion within psychopathy, and subsequent research has validated the psychopathic sexual patterns of offending involving many acts and coerced objects [82].

Gender Considerations

The gendered notion of men as cult leaders and women who occupy subordinate roles is the dominant paradigm throughout the cult literature. Though less prevalent than their male counterparts [23, 83], women certainly lead cults as well. Some notable names include Anne Hamilton Byrne, "Archangel Uriel of Unarius" Ruth Norman, and "Mother God" Amy Carlson Stroud. Many female cult leaders assume a maternal or matriarchal role (à la Mother Earth or Mother Nature) that personifies creation, destruction, and healing; a siren or temptress archetype that exudes sexuality and lust; a goddess or high priestess persona that embraces magic and divinity; or an enmeshment of several such identities. Much like male cult leaders, female cult leaders may present with the clinical disorder of psychopathy and/or various personality disorders. Notably, psychopathy correlates moderately to strongly with antisocial, borderline, histrionic, and passive-aggressive personality disorders in women [84]. Coolidge and colleagues [85] reported that borderline and histrionic personality disorders are twice as prevalent among women than men, which can be attributed to a greater frequency of traumagenic histories in women, and may also be due, in part, to biases implicit in DSM nosology or the diagnostician [86, 87]. Indeed, female cult leaders may present with one or both of these disorders as defined in the DSM-5-TR [11].

Borderline Personality Disorder

Borderline personality disorder (BPD) involves a pervasive pattern of unstable relationships, frantic efforts to avoid real or perceived abandonment, an erratic self-image, impulsive behavior, actions of self-sabotage, suicidal threats or behavior, inappropriate anger, and temporary periods of paranoia (see [11]). Cult leaders with BPD will have severe difficulty recognizing and respecting the physical and psychological boundaries of their followers. They will attempt to exert intense control over followers by demanding extreme loyalty and will often create chaos in situations where none exists. Cult leaders with BPD will be overly sensitive to criticism and abandonment and prone to lash out explosively and unexpectedly. Other indicative behavior may include risky and impulsive behaviors such as hoarding, binge eating, spending sprees, self-injury, drug use, speeding, erratic driving, suddenly quitting jobs and terminating relationships, and instigating fights. BPD may also be found among cult followers [88].

Histrionic Personality Disorder

Histrionic personality disorder (HPD) is characterized by intense emotional instability, suggestibility, attention-seeking behavior, theatrical affective expressions, and a distorted self-image (see [11]). Cult leaders with HPD must be the constant center of their followers' attention and will perceive relationships as much closer than they actually are. They will exhibit provocative behavior and exaggerated emotions. Cult leaders with HPD are highly sensitive to criticism and view it as a form of rejection to which they may emotionally overreact. One such cult leader is "Archangel Uriel of Unarius" Ruth Norman, a self-proclaimed extraordinary being and flying saucer prophet who gilded herself in outrageous costumes, elaborate blue and purple wigs, extravagant tiaras, and carried a gaudy scepter [89, 90]. One of her prophecies foretold of aliens who were preparing an enormous closet to hold all of her beautiful dresses upon a spacecraft that was soon arriving to pick her up [91]. With a short-lived run on the talk show circuit and the routine self-reporting of her extraterrestrial prophecies to tabloids, she enlisted her devotees to make outlandish movies about (and starring) her, to create lifelike busts and oil portraits of her, and to sing songs about her [90, 91, 92]. Norman had zero tolerance for criticism and excommunicated two senior assistants who dared to question her [93]. Her noted capriciousness [90] may indicate features of BPD or a possible comorbidity of it.

Individual psychopathology notwithstanding, cult leaders leave a wake of harm and a trail of victims, and continue to warrant meaningful scientific analysis and discussion. Integral to the cult leader's psychological profile is that of the cult follower, since without devotees, a guru is nothing at all. In the following section, we describe in detail the psychological profile of the cult follower with attention to the personality disorders common among such individuals.

Clinical Profile of Cult Followers

"It was the most invigorating feeling that I had ever experienced. I suddenly knew what my life was about. And honestly, I don't know if I'll ever feel that much security, that much excitement again in my whole life."
– *Diane Benscoter, former follower of the "Moonies" cult [cited in 94]*

The nexus of cult membership, psychological characteristics, and personality disorders has been a topic of considerable attention but few definitive conclusions. Supposition abounds that cult followers are "crazy." This depiction is expected given their radical beliefs and bizarre behavior. Yet, far from this oversimplified and imprecise characterization, cult followers present a complex set of personality traits and mental disorders that are deeply enmeshed in their relationship with their psychopathic leader. As cult followers simultaneously engage in aggressive behavior toward others, yet are routinely victims themselves of psychological abuse by their cult leader, it is vitally important to assess their unique personality and psychopathology.

Prior to cult involvement, followers generally present without major mental disorder (see [95], for a full review). However, following indoctrination, cult followers tend to exhibit a myriad of severe psychopathology [12], illustrating the dynamic rather than deterministic nature of the latter. The distinct psychological profile that emerges for those ensnared within cults is typified by a noteworthy comorbidity of antisocial personality disorder, obsessive-compulsive personality disorder, and dependent personality disorder. The dimensional understanding of these psychological disorders is key to understanding the personality structure and functioning of cult followers.

Antisocial Personality Disorder

As specified by the DSM-5-TR, antisocial personality disorder (ASPD) is a "pervasive pattern of disregard for and violation of the rights of others" as indicated by a combination of the repeated nonconformity to lawfully prescribed social norms, a pattern of dishonesty, impulsivity, aggressiveness, irresponsibility, disregard for safety of self and others, and lack of remorse [11, p. 748]. Research indicates that only a minority of ASPD individuals will also meet the criteria for severe psychopathy [8, 96]. Applying the ASPD criteria, cult followers may abandon their careers and families to join the cult with no realistic plan for making a living; they may relinquish their financial assets and possessions to the cult; they may engage in psychological, physical, financial, social, and sexual exploitation of others while in the cult; they may engage in risky or exploitative sexual behavior (e.g., unprotected sex, frequent sex with multiple partners, sex as a recruitment tactic, sex trafficking); and they may neglect, endanger, and harm their own and others' children (e.g., child labor, corporal punishment, medical neglect, pervasive sexual abuse); they may commit ritualistic abuse, torture, murder, even mass murder of outsiders, defectors, government officials, and one another; and they may lie persistently to shield the cult from criticism and accountability. In conjunction with distinct behavioral markers, followers will likewise show affective indices of ASPD. These emotional deficits will present as indifference to the impact of their harmful behavior and, furthermore, a tendency to rationalize the consequences of their violent and aggressive behavior toward cult outsiders and defectors.

In a novel perspective that depended on the lived experience of one of the authors within al-Qaeda, Rahmani and colleagues [56] contend that incorporation of a group-based identity within cults can trigger an intrapsychic conflict or disturbance among cult followers that can manifest in the unusual comorbidity of ASPD and obsessive-compulsive personality disorder. These co-occuring personality impairments are uncommon outside of the cultic population but when linked with fervent zealotry can amount to a dangerous combination.

Obsessive-Compulsive Personality Disorder

Obsessive-compulsive personality disorder (OCPD)[4] is characterized by a pervasive preoccupation with orderliness, asceticism, perfectionism, and control expressed with such intensity and rigidity that it interferes with task completion and productivity (see [11]). In the context of zealous groups, this obdurate compulsiveness is sometimes referred to as "religious perfectionism" [97] in which devotees ambitiously strive to achieve exalted status by meticulously following the cult's rules no matter how strict, strange, or beyond reason. This is observed through adherence to extreme dietary restrictions (see [98]), rigid religious rituals, excessive devotional practices, and strong adherence to the in-group.

When OCPD and ASPD co-occur, a striking juxtaposition of complex, and at times contradictory, symptomology emerges. Drawing from a reservoir of righteousness affirmed through shared zealotry, OCPD behavior is apparent in the followers' extreme adherence to and defensiveness of the cult *in-group*, whereas ASPD is correspondingly revealed in the followers' harsh rejection of the *out-group* [56]. Such extreme identification with the in-group contributes to the potential for violent behavior associated with collective moral disengagement and dehumanization of outsiders [99–102] achieved through "a shared state of aggressive numbing" that can precipitate sadism, cruel aggression, and murder [103, p. 129]. Through the composite of OCPD and ASPD, cult in-group clinging is inextricably linked to out-group aggression. These maladaptive personality characteristics and behavioral patterns are normalized by the cult, which reinforces, even rewards, such conduct.

In an assessment of personality characteristics of 226 active Hare Krishna followers and 727 nonfollowers utilizing the Comrey Personality Scales [104], Weiss and Comrey [105, 106] found that Hare Krishna devotees of both genders were more compulsive,[5] hostile, suspicious, and distrustful of societal systems and values than nonfollowers. Indeed, compulsivity was strikingly 3.7 times more likely in cult followers than nonfollowers, rendering it "the hallmark characteristic of the Hare Krishna personality" [106, p. 406]. Overall, these findings lend convincing empirical support for the comorbidity of OCPD and ASPD among cult followers, with OCPD apparent in the fervent dogmatism and highly structured requirements of religious practice and ritual, and ASPD evident in the hostile attitudes toward and distrust of mainstream society that precipitate violent and unlawful behavior of devotees.[6] An obvious research priority is the extension of this work to include samples from a broader array of cults and a more widely validated instrument.

Dependent Personality Disorder

As individuals integrate into a cult, they become exceedingly reliant on their leader, particularly in their zealous adherence to the leader's thought system and their strict

[4] Not to be confused with obsessive compulsive disorder (OCD). OCPD is a personality disorder, whereas OCD is an anxiety disorder.

[5] This factor specifically measures compulsivity as it relates to obsessive compulsive personality traits, in which order, perfection, and rigidity become dominant aspects of one's identity, as described in the *Manual for the Comrey Personality Scales* [107].

[6] Several Hare Krishna cult leaders were later criminally charged with murder, murder-for-hire, physical and sexual abuse of children, prostitution, drug trafficking, and racketeering (see [108]).

obedience to the leader's control of all aspects of their lives (e.g., diet, sex, relationships, occupation). Whether developed prior or subsequent to cult affiliation, cult followers are likely to present with dependent personality disorder (DPD; see DSM-5-TR [11]) [53, 109, 111]. Given the retrospective nature of studies on cult followers, it can be difficult to discern when DPD precedes cult membership versus when it takes root through coercive cult indoctrination or a hybrid of the two. Nevertheless, in this actively submissive psychological state, followers may no longer exercise independent thought; they may be unable to disagree with the cult leader; they may allow the cult leader to take over their personal and financial affairs; and they may endure abuse, mistreatment, and participate in dangerous, unlawful, and violent activities at high personal cost in order to maintain closeness to the cult leader. Cults erode individuality of the followers, divesting them of their autonomy, as they are subsumed into the cultic dynamic.

As those with DPD characteristically struggle to define their individuality, routinely avoid being alone, and find it difficult to make even the most rudimentary autonomous decisions, cults offer an attractive environment for such individuals. With conformist ideals, intimate connections, and a self-assured leader, cults can relieve those with DPD of difficult decision-making and life's many uncertainties (particularly with respect to religion, spirituality, death, the meaning of life, and other existential ambiguities). Cult leaders actively target such universal fears and vulnerabilities. The follower's anxious awareness of the salience of mortality, or inevitability of death, is modulated through in-group clinging and out-group exclusion [112–115]. Harmony and unification are weaponized as mechanisms of control, while cohesion and cooperation are leveraged to accomplish the cult leader's messianic goals [9].

In the cult's dependency dynamic, the leader infantilizes followers by alleviating them of the responsibilities that accompany a mature societal existence. This relieves followers of the burden of reconciling the inevitable contradictions and multiplicities of the world. Schwartz and Kaslow aptly describe this as "the cocoon of perennial childhood offered by the cults" [116, p. 18]. In some instances, cult leaders will even don childlike names, as did Heaven's Gate's Marshall Applewhite and Bonnie Nettles when they insisted devotees call them "Bo and Peep" [117] and later "Do and Ti" [118]. For the DPD follower, such seemingly trivial eccentricities that, prima facie, appear to proffer guidance, reassurance, and a sense of belonging, belie insidious underlying mechanisms of power, control, and subjugation. Cult leaders create a social and psychological panopticon with an inbuilt system of ideological and behavioral control.

As the cult leader establishes an increasingly dominant role in their lives, followers with DPD may also become sexually submissive to the cult leader and other members [63]. While in the throes of this dependency dynamic, followers may willingly submit to coercive sex, arranged marriages and sexual partnerships, sexual sadism, sexual trafficking, reproductive controls, abstinence or celibacy, and even castration. In Heaven's Gate, followers submitted to castration in a quest for collective celibacy at the behest of leader Marshall Applewhite [75]. In fact, the first castration took place in a nonmedical setting in which one follower performed the surgery on another while the rest of the cult watched. After uncontrollable bleeding, the followers rushed the injured to the emergency room where he survived after undergoing lifesaving measures. Undeterred, seven other men in the cult, one as young as 21, traveled to Mexico where they too underwent surgical castration. As this disorder is undergirded by a deep fear of rejection, followers with DPD will often acquiesce to the cult leader's every demand without question, no matter how extreme or harmful.

As cult leaders frequently engage followers in the practice of self-blame, followers with DPD may not initially recognize their intense dependency on the cult leader and may have great difficulty seeing themselves as a victim in this relationship. Cult practices that intensify follower dependency include isolation, physiological deprivation (e.g., sleep and food), tests of loyalty, retention of damaging collateral data (e.g., compromising photos, knowledge or proof of unlawful behavior, and intimate or humiliating life details), and punishment, among others. In severe cases of DPD, cult followers will experience acute depressive symptoms following their exit from or the dissolution of the cult, or following any severance of their relationship with the cult leader – sometimes magnified with threats of death for doing so.

Group Dynamics

Though cults can vary in ethos, era, and locale, the psychological dynamics that underpin such groups appear to be universal. Through intensive thought reform practices [71] and by wielding near-complete control of the followers' daily lives, the psychopathic cult leader psychologically subjugates their followers by preying upon vulnerabilities and fears of uncertainties in order to satisfy narcissistic desires. Dazzled by the cult leader's charisma and swayed by their persuasively proselytized philosophy, cult followers adhere to the cult's rules with the aim of achieving the cult's purported greater purpose at any cost, even to the detriment of themselves and others. The erosion of individual personality dovetails with the indoctrination of group ideology. Together, cult leaders and followers ascribe to rigidly held shared extreme overvalued beliefs that can lead to violent behavior in their service [119–122]. Yet beyond the more generalized relationship between cult leaders and followers unveiled by the preceding analysis of the distinct psychopathology of each, it is possible to further identify relationships in which a follower forms an inordinately strong attachment to the emotionally detached psychopathic cult leader.

Psychopathic Pairings

Present in some cults are destructive dyads in which a follower (often a woman) forms an intense attachment to the psychopathic cult leader (often a man) and the two partner together to oversee control of the cult. In these pairings, the personality of the attached partner may be complementary (masochistic or histrionic/hysterical) or concordant (sadistic or psychopathic) to that of the psychopathic cult leader [42], as shown in Table 11.2. Complementary identifications are those dissimilar to the psychopathic cult leader (yet complete his pathology), whereas concordant identifications are similar to

Table 11.2 Complementary and concordant identifications with the psychopathic cult leader as love object

Complementary	Concordant
Masochistic	Sadistic
Histrionic/Hysterical	Psychopathic

Source: Adapted from *Violent Attachments* (Meloy, 1992) [42].

(and an extension of) the character of the psychopath. The attachment paradigm at play in these pairings can precipitate staggering violence and destruction. Popularized accounts of such relationships include Lori Vallow's murders of her two children with Chad Daybell [123], actress Allison Mack's mutilation and sexual abuse of women with Keith Raniere [124], Ma Anand Sheela's small-town reign of terror with Bhagwan Shree Rajneesh [125], vegan restauranteur Sarma Melngailis' investment fraud as a fugitive with Anthony Strangis [126], Isabella Pollok's conning of coeds with Larry Ray [127], and ex-socialite Ghislaine Maxwell's sophisticated child sexual exploitation endeavors with Jeffrey Epstein [73]. Alternatively, when the cult has a female leader at the helm (psychopathic or not), she may attach to a complementary or concordant male lieutenant in order to avoid power struggles with male followers [23].

Among complementary identifications, masochistic may be the most common attachment to the psychopathic cult leader [42]. This individual, whether she is the cult leader's wife, mistress, or lieutenant, seeks and experiences pleasure (often sexualized) through her suffering at the will of the psychopath. In the masochistic partner's submission to his omnipotent control, the psychopathic cult leader's grandiosity is exalted while his mate experiences gratification from the sensation of sharing in the control of the dominant-submissive interplay with him [42]. She feels exhilarated by his dangerous, violent, and debasing behavior toward her, whether psychological, physical, or both. Just as she is treated cruelly, cult followers will likewise be the target of his devaluation and control tactics.

In the concordant sadistic identification, the partner revels in the psychopathic cult leader's sadism toward others [42]. The sadistic mate vicariously participates with the psychopath in his humiliation of and violence toward others, typically, cult followers, defectors, and the out-group. The sadistic partner identifies with her mate and finds such experiences pleasurable, even erotic. Passive acts of sadistic voyeurism and fantasy hold a central role for this partner [42]. She may enforce his rules over cult followers, report back to him when they are not strictly obeyed, and in doing so, may precipitate and be present for his retaliatory cruelty and degradation. Throughout her relationship with the cult leader, she may alternate between sadistic and masochistic identifications due to the antipodal yet interrelated nature of the two [42].

In other instances, the psychopathic cult leader pairs with a complementary hysterical or histrionic personality [42, 45, 128]. This partner is provocative, exhibitionistic, impressionistic, mercurial, attention-seeking, and highly dependent [11]. Just as she is autonomically drawn to his volatile unpredictability, he is highly aroused by her eroticized naïveté [42]. In this destructive pairing, the histrionic partner idealizes the psychopathic cult leader, which in turn bolsters his own feelings of grandiosity and importance [42]. Though opposite personalities in many ways, the two complete one another's interpersonal pathology. Within this caustic relationship, the female counterpart psychodynamically represents the cult leader as a love object in her mind, typically to the gross neglect of herself and others [42]. The cult leader, on the other hand, views his histrionic partner as a part object or selfobject, a devalued extension of himself, as he distinctly lacks the capacity for mature and meaningful attachment to others. The dance is often sadomasochistic. Despite her shared participation, the cult leader ultimately retains control of the histrionic partner as she is desperate to please him. In this complementary role, she is acting at the behest of the cult leader to carry out his wishes and control others while she too is being manipulated by the psychopath all the while [42].

In the concordant psychopathic identification, albeit rare, a psychopathic partner attaches to a psychopathic cult leader [42]. Much like her male counterpart, she exhibits a myriad of affective and interpersonal deficits while living an antisocial lifestyle, as detailed in Table 11.1. Partnering with a fellow psychopath allows her, through transference, to fortify her own grandiose self-structure [42]. Just as he does, she can wield, at times, unbridled control and power over cult followers to gratify her own aggressive narcissism. Typically, she serves as his lieutenant, but may also acquire or even deliberately cultivate her own faction of followers who are expressly loyal to her. If this volatile concordant psychopathic attachment becomes unsustainable and she splits from him and the cult, these allied devotees are very likely to leave with her, perhaps to form their own breakoff group under her leadership.

In the wake of such violent attachments, the psychopathic cult leader's mate may take the fall for or with him or may otherwise meet her demise. In many instances, the chaotic reign of this terrible twosome ends in prison or violent death. The two case vignettes to follow illustrate in rich detail both complementary and concordant identifications with psychopathic cult leaders and the grim aftermath.

Histrionic–Psychopathic Dyad: Mack and Raniere

The complementary attachment of the histrionic individual to the psychopath is the classic pairing seen between Allison Mack and Keith Raniere. Soon after meeting 46-year-old NXIVM cult leader, the 24-year-old leading *Smallville* [129] television series actress, Mack, devoted herself to Raniere, referring to him as her mentor, lover, and master [130]. A consummate histrionic personality, Mack has been described as a bubbly and exuberant starlet who presents as insecure [124], naïve, impressionable, sensitive to criticism, and attention-seeking [131]. Of herself, she wrote: "I am insatiable. Greedy, in a way. I live with voracity and intensity … *voracitensity*" (cited in [131], emphasis in original). Captured even in this brief quote are the exaggerated, impressionistic, and self-centered expressions characteristic of the individual with HPD. Raniere, on the other hand, exhibits a myriad of psychopathic traits. As a longtime self-help and pyramid scheme con man, he presents as a narcissistic, coercive, callous, and exploitative pathological liar [18].

In this complementary coupling, the histrionic mate idealizes her psychopathic partner and seeks his attention through seductive, flirtatious, and approval-seeking behavior [42]. The psychopath welcomes this idealization as it elevates his own grandiosity. He unconsciously views her as a devalued and submissive extension of himself. To mitigate the impact of the psychopathic cult leader's aggression toward her, and to gratify his appetite for violence, the histrionic partner may invite others into their orbit onto which his violence can be displaced. In an overtly sadomasochistic scheme, Mack recruited women and underage teens to be Raniere's "sex slaves" and Mack's "slaves" [131, 132]. As a "master," she enforced sexual subservience to Raniere, also a "master." Other times, she and other women would engage in sex acts while Raniere watched. In these erotic acts, the histrionic partner's exhibitionism is stimulated by the psychopath's voyeurism – a prelude to aggression [42]. In a gesture of omnipotence, Mack and Raniere orchestrated the permanent physical branding of herself (submission to violence) and other female followers (displacement of violence) on their pelvic regions with a symbol comprised of Raniere's and Mack's initials using a cauterizing device to burn and scar their flesh.

In the obsessive concern with physical appearance characteristic of HPD, the already thin Mack adhered to a strict 500-calorie-a-day diet to lose more weight in a masochistic attempt to satisfy Raniere's penchant for underweight women and to continue to be gratified by his presence [132, 133]. She enforced the same restrictions with Raniere's other sexual partners – all were expected to weigh less than 100 pounds – their frailty and suffering a physical representation of their devotion and of his omnipotence. As collateral, she would take nude photos and sexually explicit videos of them, and forced one woman to write a falsified story about being sexually abused by her father, to be shared publicly if they attempted to exit the cult [134]. As their elaborate criminal enterprise, replete with sexual servitude and pyramid schemes, inevitably unraveled, both faced sex trafficking and racketeering charges. Raniere was sentenced to 120 years in federal prison, and Mack to only three after providing extensive assistance to federal prosecutors [133, 134].

Mack was one among 13 actors who were affiliated with NXIVM [135]. Histrionic personality disorder is prevalent among actors [136, 137], and actors appear to have held a notable presence in several high-profile cults. Indeed, Heaven's Gate, Scientology, Breatharianism, and NXIVM have all counted actors among their ranks. Curiously, there may be a mutual attraction for thespians and cultic groups. While cults can give performers a unique starring role, there appear to be clear benefits for cults too in having actors among their acolytes, as resident stardom may help cults appear legitimate to outsiders and aid in the recruitment of new members. In any event, the fringe and radical nature of cults provides fertile ground for volatile psychopathic personality pairings to take root.

Psychopathic–Psychopathic Dyad: Sheela and Rajneesh

Though concordant psychopathic identification with another psychopath is exceedingly uncommon, Ma Anand Sheela and Bhagwan Shree Rajneesh (aka "Osho") formed such a pairing. At 16, Sheela met 34-year-old Rajneesh. Immediately infatuated, she devoted her life to him, declaring, "it was a necessity to be near him" [125]. As a charismatic psychopathic guru, Rajneesh profited financially, emotionally, and sexually from his followers. Among other excesses, the wealth from the cult afforded him over 90 Rolls-Royces [13]. While amassing an arsenal of weapons and arranging sham marriages among his disciples, Rajneesh also enforced participation in abusive sexual practices, female sterilization, prostitution, and forced labor [125]. As his personal secretary, Sheela oversaw the cult's day-to-day operations. Charming and exploitative in her own right, Sheela was a provocative and ruthless lieutenant who exhibited an antisocial pseudo-masculine identity [138] often seen in the psychopathic female partner of the male psychopath [42], and in the erotomanic woman [139]. Sheela publicly gave the middle finger, cursed, open carried firearms, threatened violence, and infamously quipped "tough titties" in a national television interview [125]. Her relationship with Rajneesh allowed Sheela to experience a narcissistic twinship identification [27] in which her own grandiosity could compensate for internal feelings of worthlessness and disregard for self [42]. Through Rajneesh, she was able to solidify her own grandiose self-structure through transference. In this concordant psychopathic dyad, Sheela utilized Rajneesh as an idealized object image which she condensed with her own self-concept [42].

In an attempt to rig a local election, she orchestrated the first and largest bioterrorist attack in US history [140] and bussed in over 3,000 homeless individuals from across the country to outvote the locals [125]. By attacking the out-group, Sheela was managing her fear of annihilation through the vigilance of paranoia [42]. Abruptly, Rajneesh diminished Sheela's role and access to him as he promoted a new female aide. Sheela then wiretapped Rajneesh's home and discovered he had arranged a physician-assisted suicide [125]. Sheela instructed her secretary to murder Rajneesh's doctor. After the physician survived the attempted murder, Sheela left the cult with 20 followers who remained loyal to her, and publicly exposed Rajneesh as an exploitative mastermind [125]. Infuriated, Rajneesh held a press conference where he aired Sheela's criminal activity and invited law enforcement into the cult's commune to investigate. Ironically, Rajneesh's invitation to search his property for evidence of Sheela's crimes exposed his own illegal activity [125]. However, his assertion that he was in the midst of a years-long vow of silence and was therefore unaware of and uninvolved in the cult's illegal activities, allowed him to circumvent criminal accountability for the most serious charges, which ultimately fell on Sheela. Sheela pled guilty and served prison time for attempted murder, assault, wiretapping, arson, and immigration fraud. Rajneesh entered an Alford plea for two immigration fraud charges and was deported from the country [125].

According to both, they fell in love but never engaged in a sexual relationship. Of this, Sheela declared: "There was no sex with Osho. Our relationship was not sexual. The integrity mattered because I was already drowning in him" [141]. In this projective identification, Sheela simultaneously fears and attributes her own destructive omnipotence to Rajneesh, which he accepts/reflects, and she then fears as all-consuming ("drowning"). The absence of a sexual relationship between the two, which Sheela attributed to "integrity," may in fact be her unrequited sexual desire for Rajneesh [139]. In later statements, Rajneesh indicates that Sheela desired a sexual relationship with him, which he denied her, stating:

> I have never made love to her. That much is certain. Perhaps that is the jealousy. She always wanted [to] but I have made it a point to never make love to a secretary. Love affair never ends. It can turn into a hate affair. She did not prove to be a woman. She proved to be a perfect bitch. [125]

Unrequited sexual desire can provoke violence toward the love object [139]. When the deprivation of such desires is projectively identified onto others, it can lead to intense hatred and revenge [142]. To this end, Sheela orchestrated the attempted murder of Rajneesh's physician and confidante, and publicly exposed him as a manipulative and exploitative mastermind [125]. In retort, Rajneesh publicly threatened unspecified violence toward Sheela if law enforcement failed to take action against her. When the prosthesis of compensatory transference of grandiosity no longer served their partnership, only by annihilation of one another (through devaluation and violence) could each truly achieve omnipotence.

Object Relations

The cult dynamics and behavior suggest borderline personality *organization* for both leaders and followers. In Kernberg's [143] objects relations model, the level of development and integration of the ego and superego determines where one falls along a personality continuum (neurotic ↔ borderline ↔ psychotic). Across these levels there are differences in object relations, defenses, and reality testing. For example, at the borderline level of personality, there is no mental representation of self or others as whole, meaningful, and separate individuals; common psychological defenses are splitting, denial, projection, introjection, and projective identification; and reality testing impairments are evident in the person's confusion over the origin of stimuli – anger, for example, may be perceived as coming from others when in fact it is originating in the self. Cult members and leaders appear to both fall within the borderline or psychotic level of personality organization [144, 145]. Preliminary research even suggests those with OCPD may be organized at a borderline level [146, 147].

Cult followers often also suffer from narcissistic personality deficits, or a defective sense of self. Weakened ego functioning of followers may precede cult involvement, or as Salande and Perkins [148] contend, the cult experience itself may impair the follower's ego, which then elicits regression to borderline personality organization. Followers compensate for a fragmented and defective sense of self by seeking an idealized self-object, or extension of self. This extension of self is especially found in the cult leader through the mechanism of idealizing transference in which the follower views the cult leader as superior, God-like, or an agent of God – an ideal object [22]. This process is reciprocally reinforced through the intensive thought reform [71] and control practices of the leader, and the obsessive worshipping, idolatry, and fanaticism of the cult followers. In this sense, the cult superficially serves a reparative and substitutive function for the followers' narcissistic personality impairments [22]. In turn, the cult leader loves the followers as an idealized extension of self [23, 24]. Despite the outward presentation as omnipotent and superior to others, the narcissistic cult leader is what Volkan terms "object-hungry" [149, p. 132]. In other words, he is overly dependent on the continual attention and adulation of his worshippers to supplant his defective ego. Thus, in this complex identity integration and exchange, the follower serves as a narcissistic prosthetic of self-love for the psychopathic leader, while the leader provides compensatory fulfillment to the followers' impaired sense of selves; both maintained through antisocial hostility toward the out-group and obsessive compulsive tendencies within the group [51].

Forensic Psychological Instruments

A range of forensic psychological instruments can be utilized to effectively assess personality disorders and their risk among cult leaders and followers. Such tools offer systematic and dimensional measures to empirically and heuristically evaluate the psychopathology and mental mechanisms at work in such populations. As cult followers simultaneously engage in harmful behavior to self and others yet are routinely victims of psychological, physical, and sexual abuse by the cult leader, it is vitally important to assess their unique personality and psychopathology. In exposing the psychological underpinnings of such radical groups with well-validated instruments, the clinical or forensic psychiatrist or psychologist not only gains deeper insight into the complex dynamics and functioning of cults, but can also gauge competency, risk, dangerousness, and amenability to treatment in order to predict and prevent future catastrophic violence.

Psychopathy Checklist-Revised

The Psychopathy Checklist-Revised (PCL-R) [8] is considered the most valid and reliable standardized observational measure of psychopathy across research, clinical assessment, and criminal justice practice [8, 62, 150, 151, 152]. This unidimensional measure captures a comprehensive range of personality and behavioral features to quantify an individual's level of psychopathy. The PCL-R is administered through an in-depth interview and a review of the individual's institutional and other records. With scores ranging from 0 to 40, the PCL-R distinguishes the subject as severely psychopathic (PCL-R $\geq$ 30), moderately psychopathic (PCL-R = 20–29), or mildly psychopathic (PCL-R = 10–19), although use of each item's parameters will arrive at a more individualized understanding of the subject's psychopathy [153]. Within forensic and clinical practice, psychopathy is best understood dimensionally along a continuum [59, 60, 62]. Categorization (>30<) using a cutting score for psychopathy (psychopath/nonpsychopath) should only be used for group research studies.

Risk Assessment

Although not originally intended, the PCL-R also serves as a robust predictor of criminal behavior [154], violent recidivism [62, 155–161], dangerousness [162, 163], poor amenability to treatment [164, 165], and institutional misconduct [49, 166–169]. It is considered the "gold standard" for the measurement of psychopathy, and is widely used in forensic settings [170]. Across the spectrum of cult leaders, the PCL-R would prove valuable in predicting who are most prone to acts of violence and criminal behavior. Even more, PCL-R results indicative of severe psychopathy in cult leaders, taken together with the specific cult characteristics predictive of mass suicide and murder in cults offered by Bohm and Alison [171], may bolster the predictive power in estimating the most destructive cults. Such features entail physically preventing members from leaving the group, endorsing violence, engaging in drills, doomsday preparation, building defensive structures, collecting weapons, and a leader who claims to be an incarnation of a religious or historically significant figure. Within correctional facilities, psychopathy has been linked to institutional violence, infractions, and escape [49, 166–169]. Furthermore, psychopaths are less amenable to treatment [164]. Correctional facilities consider these factors when managing prison populations, and psychopathy measures are routinely utilized in decisions determining institutional classification, placement, housing restrictions, privileges, access to treatment, and release decisions.

Beyond prediction of risk and future behavior, the PCL-R carries important legal implications for cult leaders. Within the courts, expert testimony about psychopathy and forensic use of the PCL-R impacts decisions concerning competency, determination of guilt, sentencing, parole, and release [170, 172, 173]. Though psychopaths are considered cognitively intact, a group of mock jurors was more likely to find defendants labeled "a psychopath" not guilty by reason of insanity (NGRI) than those labeled "not mentally ill" [174]. However, a noteworthy review of appellate case law reveals that pleas of NGRI have proved unsuccessful for cult leaders and members in court [175]. Further, cult leaders may attempt to justify their actions under the guise of religion in such a way that conflates the legal protections afforded to the freedom of religion with that of their unlawful actions within the cult. In a review of expert testimony in cult-related litigation, Young and Griffith [176] emphasize the critical role of the forensic psychiatric and psychological expert in distinguishing religious belief from psychopathology for the judge and jury. Despite a dearth of recent literature regarding expert testimony in cult litigation, clinical and forensic

Table 11.3 Forensic assessment instruments for cult leaders and their followers

Forensic Instrument	Use With	Purpose	Format	Type
Psychopathy Checklist-Revised (PCL-R)	Cult leaders and followers	Psychopathy assessment, research, risk assessment	Semistructured interview and records review	Observational
Minnesota Multiphasic Personality Inventory 2 (MMPI-2)	Cult leaders and followers	Psychological assessment, research, risk assessment	Written Q&A	Self-report
Rorschach	Cult leaders and followers	Psychological assessment, research	Responses to ambiguous stimuli	Performance
Terrorist Radicalization Assessment Protocol (TRAP-18)	Cult leaders and followers	Threat assessment, risk assessment for violence	Structured professional judgment instrument (SPJ)	Observational

psychiatrists and psychologists continue to testify routinely in cult-related trials [177, 178]. Defensive strategy notwithstanding, a diagnosis of psychopathy can lead to more punitive and restrictive outcomes overall concerning sentencing, release, level of supervision, and access to treatment in prison. Nevertheless, as shown in Table 11.3, the PCL-R can benefit from the supplement of complementary forensic tools that illuminate dimensional aspects of psychopathy [179, 180, 181].

The Rorschach

The Rorschach inkblot test [182] contributes incremental validity to the dimensional assessment of psychopathy and personality disorders across cult leaders and followers (144, 179, 183]. As a valid and reliable measure of personality structure and functioning [184, 185], this performance-based psychological test can deepen the clinician's understanding of the internal architecture of the cult leader's personality and of the followers' personalities as well.

With the Rorschach, the subject is handed a series of ambiguous inkblots one by one and asked "what might this be?" Their perceptions are recorded and scored by the evaluator based on the subject's description of the perceived form of the inkblot including whether and how movement, color, texture, shading, and dimensions are described. Subsequent analysis of the recorded responses can open a dimensional window into the subject's personality traits and mental mechanisms. With cult leaders and followers, the Rorschach can be employed to detect thought processes, personality traits, and emotional functioning that underlie personality disorders, especially when subjects are reluctant or unable to express their thoughts openly or explicitly. Given the intrinsically insular and reticent nature of the cult involved this can be an effective way to supplement diagnostic data from other psychological assessment tools.

The test's namesake and creator, Hermann Rorschach, had a particular interest in cults and cult leaders himself [186], having published several in-depth psychoanalytic biographical case studies of Swiss cult leaders Johannes Binggeli and Anton Unternährer [187, 188, 189], which have been linked to his inkblot studies [190]. More recently, Roy and colleagues [9] analyzed Charles Manson's responses to a Rorschach test administered in 1997, which presented a preoccupation with sex, aggression, and other people; elevated features of narcissism and grandiosity; the presence of psychopathy; and the absence of disorganized thinking and cognitive impairment. Research by Gacono and colleagues [191] generally suggests the psychopathic cult leader would present on this measure with ambitent or extratensive style, narcissistic self-perception, moderate to severe levels of thought disorder and impaired reality testing, abnormal attachment patterns, affective avoidance, and low interest in human objects in any form. The psychopathic cult leader would tend to be unbothered by internal distractions such as fear, anxiety, empathy, or desire for dependency [191]. Rorschach data can yield abnormal structural features often present in the psychopathic personality and can also reveal features indicative of comorbidities and traits characteristic of other personality and mental disorders [183], such as a psychopathic cult leader with paranoia or delusions [192]. The examiner should look for consistencies in the subject's responses with their behavior and real-world histories. In some instances, the severe psychopath may malinger by constricting response frequency [193]. When assessing the psychopathic personality, Rorschach testing is best utilized as one of several forensic tools in the dimensional psychological assessment and diagnosis of cult leaders [179, 183, 191, 194].

Among Rorschach studies that have focused on cult followers [22, 111, 195, 196, 197], one found that Unification Church followers' Rorschach protocols were "rich in primary process features" (e.g., loose associations, illogical thought, and fusion of ideas and images) but that the degree of adaptiveness varied across subjects [198, p. 769]. A Rorschach analysis of former cult followers pre- and post-psychotherapeutic treatment found that they generally had "significant movement toward lessened constrictedness and greater perceptual accuracy" after treatment [197, p. 750]. This indicated that, through treatment, cult followers gained a stronger sense of self, and exercised greater independent thought compared to their initial passivity and muddled identities presented prior to treatment. In comparison to noncult followers, Kriegman and Solomon [22] found that Divine Light Mission followers scored significantly higher on fragmentation of self-experience, narcissistic disturbance in relationships with formative selfobjects, investment in objects that enhance the subject's self-experience, and general psychopathology. Overall, the literature suggests that Rorschach use with cult followers provides valuable insight into their internal psychological dynamics, and underscores the benefits of psychological treatment following cult involvement.

Rorschach data are commonly admissible in court [199, 200, 201] but care must be taken to ensure proper administration of the tool and presentation of the data in order to maintain the integrity of the forensic instrument. To this end, guidelines have been developed for the forensic psychological expert who testifies about Rorschach data in court (see [200, 202]).

The MMPI/MMPI-2 and Progeny

Much as with cult leaders, the MMPI/MMPI-2 are ideal self-report tests that can capture a broad spectrum of psychological problems and personality disorders among cult followers. As utilized in studies of cult members [203–9], early work with the MMPI/MMPI-2 demonstrated clinical and research utility for the diagnosis and treatment of this population. Moreover, resultant data provide a springboard for further examination with other tests, including the Rorschach, which has also seen application in cult research. Unlike the PCL-R and the Rorschach, however, the original MMPI has undergone a series of revisions over the decades, most recently the MMPI-RF shortened versions of the instrument, and the MMPI-3. Such changes, although good for business, often invalidate previous research and make generalizing previous empirical findings from the MMPI/MMPI-2 to the MMPI-3 invalid.

For professionals who do not have expertise to interpret the PCL-R, the Rorschach, and the MMPI suite, we recommend bringing in a psychologist who has such specialized training. Beyond these standard psychological measures, several nondiagnostic forensic psychological instruments have been developed specifically to assess the psychological problems and violent risks of former cult members and their leaders.

Nondiagnostic Research Instruments

In an effort to develop a standardized measure of the detrimental psychological effects experienced by cult followers, Chambers and colleagues [210] created the Group Psychological Abuse (GPA) scale. Grounded in theoretical bases furnished by cult scholars specializing in psychological abuse (see [211–15]), this 28-item self-report scale was derived from factorial analysis of responses to 112 descriptive items presented to 308 former cult members of 101 different groups of their accounts of their time in such groups. As a four-factor scale comprised of compliance, exploitation, mind control, and anxious dependency, the GPA has shown adequate internal consistency across factors (0.70–0.81) [210].

Rather than diagnosing specific psychological problems for clinicians, this measure primarily serves the cult research domain by empirically differentiating abusive cults from more benign groups based on individual experiences [95]. Nevertheless, this instrument can help uncover the specific cult practices and cult leader behavior that underpin associated individual psychological difficulties among followers. However, critiques leveled against the GPA draw attention to confusing wording, content that eclipses the domain, and muddled units of analyses, as some questions target behavior witnessed within the cult, generally, in addition to conduct that was personally experienced [14, 216]. A Spanish version with a modified factor structure, the Group Psychological Abuse-Spanish (GPA-S) [217] scale, has seen a marginal increase in reliability across factors (0.74–0.86) [218].

Beyond the GPA suite, myriad other instruments have emerged as measures of psychological abuse experienced by cult followers. The Individual Cult Experience Index (ICE) [219] serves as an empirical measure of individual postcult psychological distress. As a reliable measure with good internal consistency (0.89), the 47 items on this self-report survey are scored dichotomously. Next, the Across Groups Psychological Abuse and Control scale (AGPAC) [220] was developed to explore factors of psychological abuse and control across two groups: survivors of intimate partner violence and former members of cults. With good internal consistency (0.83–0.89) across three scales designed to measure emotional abuse, isolation/control of activity, and verbal abuse, this tool uncovered that the two groups similarly experience psychological abuse and control. A contemporary Spanish 18-item unidimensional measure of emotional disturbances in former cult members, the Emotional Distress Scale in Survivors of Abusive Groups (EDS-SAG) [221], appears to likewise be a reliable measure (0.86). Last, the Inventory of Psychosocial Difficulties in Survivors of Abusive Groups (IPD-AG) [222], a recently developed Spanish self-report survey with good internal consistency across scales (0.91–0.99) measures psychological and social difficulties experienced by former cult members.

That none of these standardized measures have been externally validated reveals a notable and significant limitation of each. Moreover, none (the GPA and GPA-S included) are suitable for active cult followers as they subjectively and retrospectively measure the cult experience in such a manner that could invite misperception and deception by those in the throes of the cult leader's coercive control. Although these measures are not designed for purposes of clinical diagnosis and treatment, they do offer promising application for cult research.

TRAP-18

The most applicable structured professional judgment instrument for assessment of targeted violence risk among cult leaders and their followers would be the Terrorist Radicalization Assessment Protocol (TRAP-18). The violence of cults invariably targets members of the out-group, often civilians, to advance their cause and is typically framed by the belief system, or ideology of the cult leader – the hallmarks of an act of terrorism. For cult leaders with messianic goals, certain pressures (e.g., the salience of mortality [whether by old age or serious illness], an imminent fall from power, and/or betrayal by followers) can prompt increased urgency to accomplish radical objectives [223]. In Meloy and colleagues' [224] typology of proximal warning behaviors, such stressors can lead to "last resort" warning behaviors: a call to action which contains within it both a violent action and time imperative.

The TRAP-18 is a reliable and valid assessment of risk of violence [225], and is composed of 8 proximal warning behaviors and 10 distal characteristics. It is widely used among counterterrorism professionals in North America, Europe, and Australia, and helps prioritize the most extreme and imminent risk cases. It also generalizes across ideologies [226], and has been shown to have excellent sensitivity and specificity [227]. Although originally developed for the assessment of lone actor terrorists, a recent study found that it could accurately postdict whether or not subjects were charged with violent or nonviolent crimes in the assault on the US Capitol on January 6, 2021 [228]. Preliminary research supports TRAP-18's robust face and content validity, and emphasized its utility to predict future violence of radical individuals [229]. As law enforcement, counterterrorism, and counterintelligence professionals have made concerted efforts to identify risk factors for cult violence [230, 231] and, thus, deal effectively with cult leaders and their followers, the TRAP-18 offers a structured professional judgment instrument for such professionals to help prevent and mitigate violence. The instrument is marketed by Multi-Health Systems, Inc. (mhs.com), and was developed by the second author who derives income from both the training and distribution [232].

Summary

This chapter sheds critical light on the salience of psychopathy and personality disorders observed among cult leaders and their followers. As illustrated by the psychological evaluation of Charles Manson, cult leaders often present with distinctive psychopathic personalities that enable them to exert inordinate influence over others and to exhibit highly manipulative and remarkably destructive conduct. Such leaders are nothing without their devotees, and this chapter illuminated the integral psychological profile that emerges for cult followers, which is often typified by a noteworthy comorbidity of antisocial, obsessive compulsive, and dependent personality traits and disorders. With this information in mind, forensic instruments, such as the PCL-R, Rorschach, MMPI-2, and TRAP-18, should be increasingly utilized to assess such individuals as they provide valuable clinical and forensic data as well as assessments of risk of targeted violence. Such tools can be leveraged to predict future violence, recidivism, risk, amenability to treatment, and institutional misconduct. Future research should more deeply explore the psychology of female cult leaders and the psychodynamic underpinnings of psychopathic dyads (of both the complementary and concordant type) at play within cults.

Key Points

- Psychopathy appears to be the most fitting yet least explored clinical disorder observed among cult leaders.
- Though psychopathy shares some personality traits and behavioral characteristics among the Cluster B personality disorders most commonly ascribed to cult leaders (ASPD and NPD), it is a distinct clinical construct characterized by affective and interpersonal deficits and a socially deviant lifestyle.
- With application of the well-validated four-facet model of the construct psychopathy (affective, interpersonal, lifestyle, and antisocial), the profile of the psychopathic cult leader presents as a charismatic and persuasive, yet aggressive, parasitic and impulsive figure who exhibits a lifelong pattern of antisocial behavior and distinctly lacks empathy, shame, and remorse.
- Despite the pervasive gendered notion of men as cult leaders, women certainly lead cults as well and may present with psychopathy, as well as Cluster B personality disorders, especially HPD and BPD.
- The corresponding psychological profile that emerges for cult followers is typified by a noteworthy comorbidity of ASPD, OCPD, and DPD.
- The psychopathic cult leader may pair with complementary (masochistic and/or histrionic/hysterical) and/or concordant (sadistic and/or psychopathic) personalities.
- Suggestive forensic instruments to utilize for the clinical, forensic, and risk assessment of cult leaders and their followers include the PCL-R, Rorschach, MMPI-2, and TRAP-18.

References

1. TODAY. Mass murderer Charles Manson's 1987 interview in San Quentin Prison [Web streaming video]. 1987. www.youtube.com/watch?v=3Edw-ftS2Jo
2. R Soll. 'Crazy cult' thrives on threats, past members say. *The Albuquerque Tribune.* 1983 Oct 8: A7.
3. N Dillon, N Hensley, L Greene. Say hi to Satan. New York Daily News. 2017 Nov 20: 3.

4. Daily Record. The cult lords. 1993 Apr 21: 4.
5. Associated Press. Attorney says mass suicides first step in insane cult plan. *The Tampa Times*. 1978 Nov 23: A19.
6. Associated Press. Cult leader: No remorse. *The Daily Spectrum*. 1990 Oct 18: 11, 325.
7. *Furman* v. *Georgia* [1972] 408 US 238.
8. PCL-R: RD Hare. *Psychopathy checklist-revised*. Multi-Health Systems; 1991, 2003.
9. TA Roy, LJ Mihura, AF Friedman, DS Nichols, JR Meloy. The last psychological evaluation of Charles Manson: implications for personality, psychopathology, and ideology. *Journal of Threat Assessment and Management*. 2023;10(3):127–50.
10. J Jones. The Jonestown death tape [Web streaming audio recording]. Federal Bureau of Investigation; 1978 Nov 18. https://archive.org/details/ptc1978-11-18.flac16.
11. American Psychiatric Association. *Diagnostic and statistical manual of mental disorders (DSM-5-TR)*. 5th ed. Text revision. APA; 2022.
12. SM Ash. Cult-induced psychopathology, part 1: clinical picture. *Cultic Studies Journal*. 1985;2:31–90.
13. RO Clarke. The narcissistic guru: a profile of Bhagwan Shree Rajneesh. *Free Inquiry*. 1988;8:33–45.
14. R Dubrow-Marshall, LJ Dubrow-Marshall. Cults and mental health. In: H Friedman, editor. *Encyclopedia of mental health*. 2nd ed. Academic Press; 2016. p. 393–401.
15. PA Olsson. Normal compared to abnormal leaders and groups. *Journal of Psychohistory*. 2013;41:39–43.
16. M Popper. Narcissism and attachment patterns of personalized and socialized charismatic leaders. *Journal of Social and Personal Relationships*. 2002;19:797–809.
17. JM Post. Narcissism and the charismatic leader-follower relationship. *Political Psychology*. 1986;7:675–688.
18. S Raine. Narcissistic sexual predation: Keith Raniere's grooming strategies in NXIVM. *International Journal of Coercion, Abuse, and Manipulation*. 2021;2:41–59.
19. DE Shaw. Traumatic abuse in cults: a psychoanalytic perspective. *Cultic Studies Review*. 2003;2:101–31.
20. DE Shaw. The relational system of the traumatizing narcissist. *International Journal of Cultic Studies*. 2014;5; 4–11.
21. A Storr. *Feet of clay: saints, sinners, and madmen: a study of gurus*. Harper Collins; 1996.
22. D Kriegman, L Solomon. Cult groups and the narcissistic personality: the offer to heal defects in the self. *International Journal of Group Psychotherapy*. 1985;35:239–61.
23. L Oakes. *Prophetic charisma: the psychology of revolutionary religious personalities*. 1st ed. Syracuse University Press; 1997.
24. V Volkan. Narcissistic personality organization and "reparative" leadership. *International Journal of Group Psychotherapy*. 1980;30:131–52.
25. OF Kernberg. Factors in the psychoanalytic treatment of narcissistic personalities. *Journal of the American Psychoanalytic Association*. 1970;18:51–85.
26. OF Kernberg. *Borderline conditions and pathological narcissism*. Jason Aronson; 1975.
27. H Kohut. *The analysis of the self*. International Universities Press; 1971.
28. H Kohut. Thoughts on narcissism and narcissistic rage. *Psychoanalytic Study of the Child*. 1972;27:360–400.
29. H Kohut. *The restoration of the self*. International Universities Press; 1977.
30. American Psychiatric Association. *Diagnostic and statistical manual of mental disorders (DSM-III)*. 3rd ed. APA; 1980.
31. JR Meloy. The empirical basis and forensic application of affective and predatory violence. *Australian & New*

Zealand Journal of Psychiatry. 2006;40:539–47.

32. SB Gustafson, DR Ritzer. The dark side of normal: a psychopathy-linked pattern called aberrant self-promotion. *European Journal of Personality*. 1995;9:147–83.
33. S Hart, RD Hare. Association between psychopathy and narcissism: theoretical views and empirical evidence. In: EF Ronningstam, editor. *Disorders of narcissism: diagnostic, clinical, and empirical implications*. American Psychiatric Press; 1998. p. 415–36.
34. DL Paulhus, KM Williams. The dark triad of personality: narcissism, Machiavellianism, and psychopathy. *Journal of Research in Personality*. 2002;36:556–63.
35. American Psychiatric Association. *Diagnostic and statistical manual of mental disorders (DSM-5)*. 5th ed. APA; 2013.
36. G Gabbard. *Treatments of psychiatric disorders*. 5th ed. American Psychiatric Publishing; 2014.
37. R Blackburn. Personality disorder and psychopathy: conceptual and empirical integration. *Psychology, Crime & Law*. 2007;13:7–18.
38. TH McGlashan, RK Heinssen. Narcissistic, antisocial, and noncomorbid subgroups of borderline disorder: are they distinct entities by long term clinical profile? *Psychiatric Clinics of North America*. 1989;12:653–70.
39. JS Wulach. The criminal personality as a DSM-III-R antisocial, narcissistic, borderline, and histrionic personality disorder. *International Journal of Offender Therapy and Comparative Criminology*. 1988;32:185–99.
40. JR Meloy, ed. *The mark of Cain: psychoanalytic insight and the psychopath*. The Analytic Press; 2001.
41. JR Meloy. *The psychopathic mind: origin, dynamics, and treatment*. Jason Aronson; 1988.
42. JR Meloy. *Violent attachments*. Jason Aronson; 1992.
43. RD Hare, TJ Harpur, AR Hakstian, AE Forth, SD Hart, JP Newman. The revised Psychopathy Checklist: reliability and factor structure. *Psychological Assessment: A Journal of Consulting and Clinical Psychology*. 1990;2:338–41.
44. JR Meloy, A Book, A Hosker-Field, T Methot-Jones, J Roters. Social, sexual and violent predation: are psychopathic traits evolutionarily adaptive? *Violence and Gender*. 2018;5:153–65.
45. W La Barre. *They shall take up serpents: psychology of the Southern snake-handling cult*. University of Minnesota Press; 1962.
46. W La Barre. *The ghost dance: the origins of religion*. Dell Publishing; 1970.
47. AR Moriarty. Adolescent satanic cult dabblers: a differential diagnosis. *Journal of Mental Health*. 1991;13:393–404.
48. ML Tobias, J Lalich. *Captive hearts, captive minds: freedom and recovery from cults and other abusive relationships*. Hunter House; 1994.
49. RD Hare. *Without conscience: the disturbing world of psychopaths among us*. Pocket Books; 1993.
50. L Barbara. The psychopath: untangling the dark mind. *Counselling and Spirituality*. 2015;34:77–100.
51. SA Hassan. *Combating cult mind control*. Freedom of Mind Press; 2015.
52. PD Harms, D Wood, K Landay, PB Lester, LG Vogelgesang. Autocratic leaders and authoritarian followers revisited: a review and agenda for the future. *Leadership Quarterly*. 2018;29:105–22.
53. J Burke. Antisocial personality disorder in cult leaders and induction of dependent personality disorder in cult members. *Cultic Studies Review*. 2006;5:390–410.
54. TW Miller, J Lane, RF Veltkamp, TL Kraus, H Tag. An adolescent vampire cult in rural America: clinical issues and case study. *Child Psychiatry & Human Development*. 1999;29:209–19.
55. S Porter, M Woodsworth. "I'm sorry I did it. . .but he started it": a comparison of the

official and self-reported homicide descriptions of psychopaths and non-psychopaths. *Law and Human Behavior.* 2007;31:91–107.

56. F Rahmani, A Hemmati, SJ Cohen, JR Meloy. The interplay between antisocial and obsessive-compulsive personality characteristics in cult-like religious groups: a psychodynamic decoding of the DSM-5. *International Journal of Applied Psychoanalytic Studies.* 2019;16:258–73.
57. LJ Leedom, A Bass, L Almas. The problem of parental psychopathy. *Journal of Child Custody.* 2013;10: 154–84.
58. H Rosedale, M Langone. On using the term "cult." *International Cultic Studies Association Today.* 2015;6:2–7.
59. JP Guay, J Ruscio, RA Knight, RD Hare. A taxometric analysis of the latent structure of psychopathy: evidence for dimensionality. *Journal of Abnormal Psychology.* 2007;116:701–16.
60. DK Marcus, SL John, JF Edens. A taxometric analysis of psychopathic personality. *Journal of Abnormal Psychology.* 2004;113:626–35.
61. JR Meloy. *The psychopathic mind: origin, dynamics, and treatment.* Jason Aronson; 1988.
62. CJ Patrick, ed. *Handbook of psychopathy.* Guilford Press; 2018.
63. J Lalich. Dominance and submission: the psychosexual exploitation of women in cults. *Women and Therapy.* 1996;19:37–52.
64. P Marques, M Paulino, L Alho, editors. *Psychopathy and criminal behavior: current trends and challenges.* Elsevier; 2022.
65. P Babiak, RD Hare. *Snakes in suits: when psychopaths go to work.* Regan; 2006.
66. O Sánchez de Ribera, N Kavish, IM Katz, BB Boutwell. Untangling intelligence, psychopathy, antisocial personality disorder, and conduct problems: a meta-analytic review. *European Journal of Personality.* 2019;33:529–64.
67. SA Kent. Lustful prophet: a psychosexual historical study of the Children of God's leader, David Berg. *Cultic Studies Journal.* 1994;11:135–88.
68. M Pehanick. Revolutionary suicide: a rhetorical examination of Jim Jones' "Death Tape." Alternative Considerations of Jonestown & Peoples Temple. 2013. https://jonestown.sdsu.edu/?page_id=30321
69. JE Wood. The Branch Davidian standoff: an American tragedy. *Journal of Church and State.* 1993;35:233–40.
70. V Bugliosi, C Gentry. *Helter skelter: the true story of the Manson murders.* Norton; 1974.
71. RJ Lifton. *Losing reality: on cults, cultism, and the mindset of political and religious zealotry.* The New Press; 2019.
72. JR Meloy. *The psychopathic mind: origin, dynamics, and treatment.* Jason Aronson; 1988.
73. J Patterson. *Filthy rich.* Penguin Random House; 2016.
74. SE Yochelson, SE Samenow. *The criminal personality.* Jason Aronson; 1976.
75. *The cult next door: the mystery and madness of Heaven's Gate* [TV series episode]. 20/20. ABC News. 2022 Mar 11.
76. JB Helfgott, JK Wallenborn. History of forensic psychology. In: C Garofalo, JJ Sijtsema, editors. *Clinical forensic psychology: introductory perspectives on offending.* Palgrave Macmillan; 2022. p. 1–26.
77. CR Wootson, Jr. Where is fugitive polygamist Lyle Jeffs? Possibly swept away in the rapture, his lawyer says. *The Washington Post.* 2016 Aug 30. www.washingtonpost.com/news/acts-of-faith/wp/2016/08/30/where-is-fugitive-polygamist-lyle-jeffs-possibly-swept-away-in-the-rapture-his-lawyer-says/
78. K Marks. 'Black Jesus' Steven Tari is hacked to death. *The Independent.* 2013 Aug 30. www.independent.co.uk/news/world/australasia/black-jesus-steven-tari-is-hacked-to-death-8792287.html

79. L Goldwert, T Whitcraft. Child sex 'cult' leader freed from prison. ABC News. 2008 Aug 14. https://abcnews.go.com/TheLaw/story?id=5575131&page=1

80. RFI. Cult leader jailed for prison escape by helicopter. 2012 Feb 6. www.rfi.fr/en/africa/20120602-cult-leader-jailed-prison-escape-helicopter

81. JR Meloy. The "polymorphously perverse" psychopath: understanding a strong empirical relationship. *Bulletin of the Menninger Clinic.* 2002;66:273–89.

82. E McCuish, P Lussier, R Corrado. Psychopathy and sexual offending over the life course: an exploratory longitudinal investigation. In: P Marques, M Paulino, L Alho, editors. *Psychopathy and criminal behavior: current trends and challenges.* Elsevier; 2022. p. 333–56.

83. B Zablocki. *Alienation and charisma: a study of contemporary American communes.* Free Press; 1980.

84. MJ Rutherford, JS Cacciola, AI Alterman, JR McKay. Reliability and validity of the Revised Psychopathy Checklist in women methadone patients. *Assessment.* 1996;3:145–56.

85. FL Coolidge, PD Marle, SA Van Horn, DL Segal. Clinical syndromes, personality disorders, and neurocognitive differences in male and female inmates. *Behavioral Sciences & the Law.* 2011;29:741–51.

86. W Braamhorst, J Lobbestael, WH Emons, A Arntz, CL Witteman, MH Bekker. Sex bias in classifying borderline and narcissistic personality disorder. *Journal of Nervous and Mental Disease.* 2015;203:804–8.

87. S Chun, A Harris, M Carrion, E Rojas, S Stark, C Lejuez, WV Lechner, MA Bornovalova. A psychometric investigation of gender differences and common processes across borderline and antisocial personality disorders. *Journal of Abnormal Psychology.* 2017;126:76–88.

88. M Miller. The treatment of a borderline patient complicated by involvement with a charismatic religious cult: a case report. *Jefferson Journal of Psychiatry.* 1984;2:25–31.

89. RG Kirkpatrick, DG Tumminia. Unarius: emergent aspects of an American flying saucer group. In: JR Lewis, editor. *The gods have landed: new religions from other worlds.* SUNY Press; 1995. p. 85–136.

90. DG Tumminia. When the Archangel died: from revelation to routinization of charisma in Unarius. In: C Partridge, editor. *UFO religions.* Psychology Press; 2003. p. 62–83.

91. DG Tumminia. How prophecy never fails: interpretive reason in a flying-saucer group. *Sociology of Religion.* 1998;59:157–70.

92. B Perrine [Director]. *Children of the stars: a documentary* [Documentary film]. Billingsgate Media; Backyard Green Films; 2012.

93. DG Tumminia. *When prophecy never fails: myth and reality in a flying-saucer group.* Oxford University Press; 2005.

94. K Campbell, A King. This former cult member is helping 'deprogram' QAnon believers. KUOW. 2022 Mar 18. www.kuow.org/stories/this-former-cult-member-is-helping-deprogram-qanon-believers

95. J Aronoff, SJ Lynn, P Malinoski. Are cultic environments psychologically harmful? *Clinical Psychology Review.* 2000;20:91–111.

96. JR Meloy, J Yakeley. Antisocial personality disorder. In: G Gabbard, editor. *Gabbard's treatments of psychiatric disorders.* 5th ed. American Psychiatric Publishing; 2014. p. 1015–34.

97. B Sorotzkin. Understanding and treating perfectionism in religious adolescents. *Psychotherapy: Theory, Research, Practice, Training.* 1998;35:87–95.

98. J Meikle. Imposed anorexia: a model of dietary restriction in four ideological groups. *Cultic Studies Review.* 2005;4:41–61.

99. JM Berger. *Extremism.* MIT Press; 2018.

100. B Doosje, A Loseman, K van den Bos. Determinants of radicalization of Islamic youth in the Netherlands: personal uncertainty, perceived injustice, and

perceived group threat. *Journal of Social Issues*. 2013;69:586–604.

101. B Doosje, K van den Bos, A Loseman, AR Feddes, L Mann. "My in-group is superior!": susceptibility for radical right-wing attitudes and behaviors in Dutch youth. *Negotiation and Conflict Management Research*. 2012;5:253–68.
102. B Leidner, E Castano, E Zaiser, R Giner-Sorolla. Ingroup glorification, moral disengagement, and justice in the context of collective violence. *Personality and Social Psychology Bulletin*. 2010;36:1115–29.
103. RJ Lifton. *Losing reality: on cults, cultism, and the mindset of political and religious zealotry*. The New Press; 2019.
104. CPS: AL Comrey. *Comrey personality scales*. Educational and Industrial Testing Service; 1970.
105. AS Weiss, AL Comrey. Personality and mental health of Hare Krishnas compared with psychiatric outpatients and 'normals.' *Personality and Individual Differences*. 1987;8:721–30.
106. AS Weiss, AL Comrey. Personality characteristics of Hare Krishnas. *Journal of Personality Assessment*. 1987;51:399–413.
107. AL Comrey. *Manual for the Comrey personality scales*. Educational and Industrial Testing Service; 1970.
108. R Formanek, Jr. Hare Krishna leader indicted on federal racketeering charges. Associated Press. 1990 May 25. https://apnews.com/article/da220a69ef18c05309a263a26bb7e3b4
109. SA Hassan, MJ Shah. The anatomy of undue influence used by terrorist cults and traffickers to induce helplessness and trauma, so creating false identities. *Ethics, Medicine and Public Health*. 2019;8:97–107.
110. M Rousselet, O Duretete, JB Hardouin, M Grall-Bronnec. Cult membership: what factors contribute to joining or leaving? *Psychiatry Research*. 2017;257:27–33.
111. MH Spero. Psychotherapeutic procedure with religious cult devotees. *Journal of Nervous and Mental Disease*. 1982;170:332–44.
112. E Castano. In case of death, cling to the ingroup. *European Journal of Social Psychology*. 2004;34:375–84.
113. M Herrera, F Sani. Why does ingroup identification shield people from death anxiety? The role of perceived collective continuity and group entitativity. *Social Psychology*. 2013;44:320–28.
114. ZP Hohman, MA Hogg. Fear and uncertainty in the face of death: the role of life after death in group identification. *European Journal of Social Psychology*. 2011;41:751–60.
115. F Sani, M Herrera, M Bowe. Perceived collective continuity and ingroup identification as defence against death awareness. *Journal of Experimental Social Psychology*. 2009;45:242–45.
116. LL Schwartz, FW Kaslow. Religious cults, the individual and the family. *Journal of Marital and Family Therapy*. 1979;5:15–26.
117. RW Balch, D Taylor. Seekers and saucers: the role of the cultic milieu in joining a UFO cult. *American Behavioral Scientist*. 1977;20:839–60.
118. RW Balch, D Taylor. Making sense of the Heaven's Gate suicides. In: DG Bromley, JG Melton, editors. *Cults, religion, and violence*. Cambridge University Press; 2004. p. 209–28.
119. JR Meloy, T Rahman. Cognitive-affective drivers of fixation in threat assessment. *Behavioral Sciences & the Law*. 2020;39:170–89.
120. T Rahman. Extreme overvalued beliefs: how violent extremist beliefs become "normalized." *Behavioral Sciences & the Law*. 2018;8:10–21.
121. T Rahman, S Hartz, W Xiong, JR Meloy, J Janofsky, B Harry, P Resnick. Extreme overvalued beliefs. *Journal of the American Academy of Child & Adolescent Psychiatry*. 2020;48:319–26.
122. T Rahman, L Zheng, JR Meloy. DSM-5 cultural and personality assessment of extreme overvalued beliefs. *Aggression*

and Violent Behavior. 2021;60: Article 101552.

123. T Palmer. Expert: doomsday cult leveraged control over Lori Vallow. NewsNation. 2023 Apr 6. www.newsnationnow.com/crime/lori-vallow/lori-vallow-doomsday-cult/

124. C Harris. 'Cruel and punitive': Allison Mack allegedly told NXIVM women 'They were worth nothing,' report says. People. 2018 May 21. https://people.com/crime/allison-mack-nxivm-sex-trafficking-charges-allegedly-cruel-punitive/

125. *Wild wild country* [Documentary TV mini series]. C Way, M Way, directors. Duplass Brothers Productions; 2018.

126. A Salkin. How Sarma Melngailis, queen of vegan cuisine, became a runaway fugitive. *Vanity Fair*. 2016 Nov 3. www.vanityfair.com/style/2016/11/how-sarma-melngailis-became-a-runaway-fugitive

127. C Moynihan. Sex cult's 'Lieutenant' gets over 4 years in prison for abetting abuse. *The New York Times*. 2023 Feb 22. www.nytimes.com/2023/02/22/nyregion/sarah-lawrence-sex-cult-pollok-sentencing.html

128. H Racker. *Transference and countertransference*. International Universities Press; 1968.

129. *Smallville* [TV series]. Tollin/Robbins Productions; Millar Gough Ink; DC Comics; Warner Bros. Television; 2001 Oct 16.

130. R Gavin. NXIVM defector Allison Mack now calls Keith Raniere a 'twisted man.' Times Union. 2021 Jun 26. www.timesunion.com/nxivm/article/NXIVM-defector-Allison-Mack-now-calls-Keith-16276677.php

131. C Knoll. From 'Smallville' to a sex cult: the fall of the actress Allison Mack. *The New York Times*. 2019 May 13. www.nytimes.com/2019/05/13/nyregion/nxivm-cult-allison-mack.html

132. N Hong, S Piccoli. Keith Raniere, leader of NXIVM sex cult, is sentenced to 120 years in prison. *The New York Times*. 2020 Oct 27. www.nytimes.com/2020/10/27/nyregion/nxivm-cult-keith-raniere-sentenced.html

133. *NXIVM* [TV series episode]. 20/20. EJ Dickson, director. ABC News. 2018 Apr 27.

134. Rolling Stone. Former slave describes Allison Mack's alleged abusive, terrifying behavior in detail. 2019 Jun 10. www.rollingstone.com/culture/culture-features/nxivm-trial-allison-mack-sex-slave-nicole-abuse-keith-raniere-845830/

135. S Lambe. NXIVM: Allison Mack, Grace Park and other actors recruited by the cult. Entertainment Tonight. 2022 Oct 17. www.etonline.com/nxivm-allison-mack-grace-park-and-other-actors-recruited-by-the-cult-152562

136. EM Cale, SO Lilienfeld. Sex differences in psychopathy and antisocial personality disorder: a review and integration. *Clinical Psychology Review*. 2002;22:1179–1207.

137. M Davison, A Furnham. The personality disorder profile of professional actors. *Psychology of Popular Media Culture*. 2018;7:33–46.

138. K Blacker, J Tupin. Hysteria and hysterical structures: developmental and social theories. In: M Horowitz, editor. *Hysterical personality style and the histrionic personality disorder*. Jason Aronson; 1991. p. 17–66.

139. JR Meloy. Unrequited love and the wish to kill: diagnosis and treatment of borderline erotomania. *Bulletin of the Menninger Clinic*. 1989;53:477–92.

140. News Desk. Netflix documentary series recounts salad bar bioterror attack. Food Safety News. 2018 Mar 2. www.foodsafetynews.com/2018/03/netflix-to-premiere-series-on-bhagwan-shree-rajneesh-and-the-largest-bioterror-attack-in-u-s-history/

141. M Sachdeva. Ma Anand Sheela opens up about her relationship with Osho in an interview with Karan Johar. *Vogue*. 2019 Sept 30. www.vogue.in/news/content/ma-anand-sheela-interview-relationship-with-osho-sexuality-rajneeshpuram-karan-johar

142. JF Clarkin, FE Yeomans, OF Kernberg. *Psychotherapy for borderline personality: focusing on object relations*. American Psychiatric Publishing, Inc.; 2006.

143. OF Kernberg. *Object relations theory and clinical psychoanalysis*. Jason Aronson; 1976.

144. CB Gacono, JR Meloy, JL Berg. Object relations, defensive operations, and affective states in narcissistic, borderline, and antisocial personality disorder. *Journal of Personality Assessment*. 1992;59:32–49.

145. OF Kernberg. *Aggression in personality disorders and perversions*. Yale University Press; 1992.

146. C De Panfilis, G Schito, S Riccardi, F Roscigno, C Marchesi. Obsessive-compulsive personality disorder and personality organization: implications for psychosocial functioning. *Clinical Neuropsychiatry: Journal of Treatment Evaluation*. 2018;15:251–57.

147. FF Giynaş, M Yazici Güleç, Ö Kazan Kizilkurt, Y Yilmaz, H Güleç, S Çitak. Personality organization in patients with obsessive-compulsive disorder and its relationship with functionality. *Anatolian Journal of Psychiatry*. 2019;20:38–46.

148. JD Salande, DR Perkins. An object relations approach to cult membership. *American Journal of Psychotherapy*. 2011;65:381–91.

149. V Volkan. Narcissistic personality organization and "reparative" leadership. *International Journal of Group Psychotherapy*. 1980;30:131–52.

150. AR Felthous, H Sass. *The international handbook of psychopathic disorders and the law*. John Wiley & Sons; 2007.

151. CB Gacono, editor. *The clinical and forensic assessment of psychopathy: a practitioner's guide*. 2nd ed. Routledge; 2016.

152. KA Kiehl, W Sinnott-Armstrong, editors. *Handbook on psychopathy and law*. Oxford University Press; 2013.

153. S Balsis, A Busch, K Wilfong, J Newman, J Edens. A statistical consideration regarding the threshold of the Psychopathy Checklist-Revised. *Journal of Personality Assessment*. 2017;99: 494–502.

154. RD Hare, CS Neumann, A Mokros. The PCL-R assessment of psychopathy: development, properties, debate, and new directions. In: CJ Patrick, editor. *Handbook of psychopathy*. 2nd ed. Guilford Press; 2018. p. 39–79.

155. J Blair, D Mitchell, K Blair. *The psychopathy: emotion and the brain*. Blackwell; 2005.

156. CB Gacono, editor. *The clinical and forensic assessment of psychopathy*. Erlbaum; 2000.

157. H Häkkänen-Nyholm, J Nyholm, editors. *Psychopathy and the law*. Wiley-Blackwell; 2012.

158. RD Hare. Forty years aren't enough: recollections, prognostications, and random musings. In: H Herve, J Yuille, editors. *The psychopath: theory, research, and practice*. Erlbaum; 2007. p. 3–28.

159. GT Harris, ME Rice, CA Cormier. Psychopathy and violent recidivism. *Law and Human Behavior*. 1991;15:625–37.

160. JF Hemphill, RD Hare, S Wong. Psychopathy and recidivism: a review. *Legal and Criminological Psychology*. 1998;3:139–70.

161. KS Douglas, GM Vincent, JF Edens. Risk for criminal recidivism: the role of psychopathy. In: CJ Patrick, editor. *Handbook of psychopathy*. 2nd ed. Guilford Press; 2018. p. 682–709.

162. SD Hart. The role of psychopathy in assessing risk for violence: conceptual and methodological issues. *Psychology, Crime & Law*. 1998;3:121–37.

163. S Porter, S Porter. Psychopathy and violent crime. In: H Herve, JC Yuille, editors. *The psychopath: theory, research, and practice*. Erlbaum; 2007. p. 287–300.

164. GT Harris, ME Rice. Treatment of psychopathy: a review of empirical findings. In: CJ Patrick, editor. *Handbook of psychopathy*. Guilford Press; 2006. p. 555–72.

165. JRP Ogloff, S Wong, A Greenwood. Treating criminal psychopaths in a therapeutic community program. *Behavioral Sciences & the Law.* 1990;8:181–90.

166. JF Edens, JS Campbell. Identifying youths at risk for institutional misconduct: a meta-analytic investigation of the psychopathy checklist measures. *Psychological Services.* 2007;4:13–27.

167. JF Edens, NG Poythress, SO Lilienfeld, CJ Patrick. A prospective comparison of two measures of psychopathy in the prediction of institutional misconduct. *Behavioral Sciences & the Law.* 2008;26:529–41.

168. AE Forth, SD Hart, RD Hare. Assessment of psychopathy in male young offenders. *Psychological Assessment.* 1990;2:342–44.

169. LS Guy, JF Edens, C Anthony, KS Douglas. Does psychopathy predict institutional misconduct among adults? A meta-analytic investigation. *Journal of Consulting and Clinical Psychology.* 2005;73:1056–64.

170. D DeMatteo, ME Olver. Use of the Psychopathy Checklist-Revised in legal contexts: validity, reliability, admissibility, and evidentiary issues. *Journal of Personal Assessment.* 2022;104:234–51.

171. J Bohm, L Alison. An exploratory study in methods of distinguishing destructive cults. *Psychology, Crime & Law.* 2001;7:133–65.

172. D Lyon, JRP Ogloff. Legal and ethical issues in psychopathy assessment. In: CB Gacono, editor. *The clinical and forensic assessment of psychopathy.* Erlbaum; 2000. p. 139–73.

173. T Walsh, Z Walsh. The evidentiary introduction of Psychopathy Checklist-Revised assessed psychopathy in U.S. courts: extent and appropriateness. *Law and Human Behavior.* 2006;30:493–507.

174. JA Rendell, MT Huss, ML Jensen. Expert testimony and the effects of a biological approach, psychopathy, and juror attitudes in cases of insanity. *Behavioral Sciences & the Law.* 2010;28:411–25.

175. B Holoyda, W Newman. Between belief and delusion: cult members and the insanity plea. *Journal of the American Academy of Psychiatry and the Law.* 2016;44:53–62.

176. JL Young, EEH Griffith. Expert testimony in cult-related litigation. *Bulletin of American Academy of Psychiatry and the Law.* 1989;17:257–67.

177. EJ Dickson. Expert witness at NXIVM trial describes how abusers 'gaslight' their victims. *Rolling Stone.* 2019 Jun 6. www.rollingstone.com/culture/culture-news/kieth-raniere-nxivm-trial-abuse-gaslight-expert-witness-845304/

178. A Klasfeld. Accused Sarah Lawrence sex cult leader suffered from a seizure, his lawyer said. He was whisked from court in a stretcher hours later. Law & Crime. 2022 Mar 15. https://lawandcrime.com/live-trials/larry-ray/accused-sarah-lawrence-sex-cult-leader-suffered-from-a-seizure-his-lawyer-said-he-was-whisked-from-court-in-a-stretcher-hours-later/

179. CB Gacono, JR Meloy. *The Rorschach assessment of aggressive and psychopathic personalities.* Erlbaum; 1994.

180. CB Gacono, JR Meloy. Assessing psychopathic personalities. In: JN Butcher, editor. *Clinical personality assessment: practical approaches.* Oxford University Press; 2002. p. 361–75.

181. JR Meloy, CB Gacono. Assessing psychopathy: psychological testing and report writing. In: CB Gacono, editor. *The clinical and forensic assessment of psychopathy.* 2nd ed. Routledge; 2016. p. 276–92.

182. H Rorschach. *Psychodiagnostics.* Hans Huber; 1942.

183. CB Gacono, JR Meloy. Assessing antisocial and psychopathic personalities. In: JN Butcher, editor. *The Oxford handbook of personality assessment.* Oxford University Press; 2009. p. 567–81.

184. JE Exner, Jr. *The Rorschach: a comprehensive system: Vol. 1. Basic foundations.* 2nd ed. Wiley; 1986.

185. G Meyer, D Viglion, J Mihura, R Erard, P Erdberg. *Rorschach performance*

assessment system administration, coding, interpretation and technical manual. Allegra Printing Services; 2011.

186. W Schwarz. Hermann Rorschach, M.D.: his life and work. *Rorschachiana* 1996;21:6–17.
187. H Rorschach. Einiges über schweizerische Sekten und Sektengründer [On Swiss sects and sect founders]. *Swiss Archives of Neurology, Psychiatry and Psychotherapy.* 1917;1:254–58.
188. H Rorschach. Weiteres über schweizerisch sektenbildungen [Further studies on Swiss sect founders]. *Swiss Archives of Neurology, Psychiatry and Psychotherapy.* 1919;2:385–88.
189. H Rorschach. Zwei schweizerische sektenstifter: Binggeli und Unternährer [Two Swiss sect founders: Binggeli und Unternährer]. *Imago: Journal for the Application of Psychoanalysis to the Humanities.* 1927;13:395–441.
190. DE Jonte-Pace. From prophets to perception: the origins of Rorschach's psychology. *Annual of Psychoanalysis.* 1986;14:179–203.
191. CB Gacono, JR Meloy, MR Bridges. A Rorschach comparison of psychopaths, sexual homicide perpetrators, and nonviolent pedophiles: where angels fear to tread. *Journal of Clinical Psychology.* 2000;56:757–77.
192. JR Meloy, CB Gacono. Assessing psychopathy: psychological testing and report writing. In: CB Gacono, editor. *The clinical and forensic assessment of psychopathy.* 2nd ed. Routledge; 2016. p. 276–92.
193. GG Perry, BN Kinder. The susceptibility of the Rorschach to malingering: a critical review. *Journal of Personality Assessment.* 1990;54:47–57.
194. TB Cunliffe, CB Gacono, JR Meloy, JM Smith, EE Taylor, D Landry. Psychopathy and Rorschach: a response to Wood et al. (2010). *Archives of Assessment Psychology.* 2012;2:1–31.
195. MS Cerney. The Rorschach and traumatic loss: can the presence of traumatic loss be detected from the Rorschach? *Journal of Personality Assessment.* 1990;55:781–89.
196. A Deutsch, MJ Miller. A clinical study of four Unification church members. *American Journal of Psychiatry.* 1983;140:767–70.
197. MH Spero. Some pre- and post-treatment characteristics of cult devotees. *Perceptual and Motor Skills.* 1984;58:749–50.
198. A Deutsch, MJ Miller. A clinical study of four Unification church members. *American Journal of Psychiatry.* 1983;140:767–70.
199. JR Meloy, TL Hansen, IB Weiner. Authority of the Rorschach: legal citations during the past 50 years. *Journal of Personality Assessment.* 1997;69:53–62.
200. D Viglione, C de Ruiter, C King, G Meyer, A Kivisto, B Rubin, J Hunsley. Legal admissibility of the Rorschach and R-PAS: a review of research, practice, and case law. *Journal of Personality Assessment.* 2022;104:137–61.
201. IB Weiner, JE Exner Jr., A Sciara. Is the Rorschach welcome in the courtroom? *Journal of Personality Assessment.* 1996;67:422–24.
202. JR Meloy. Rorschach testimony. *Journal of Psychiatry & Law.* 1991;19:221–35.
203. M Di Fiorino, E Fizzotti, M Miniati. Psychometric profiles in Italian Hare Krishna movement: affiliation and membership. *Archives of Psychiatry and Psychotherapy.* 2002;4:53–61.
204. W Kuner. New religious movements and mental health. In: E Barker, editor. *Of gods and men: new religious movements in the West.* Mercer University Press; 1984. p. 255–65.
205. CA Latkin. Coping after the fall: the mental health of former members of the Rajneeshpuram commune. *International Journal for the Psychology of Religion.* 1993;3:97–109.
206. M Ross. Clinical profiles of Hare Krishna devotees. *American Journal of Psychiatry.* 1983;140:416–20.

207. M Ross. Mental health in Hare Krishna devotees. *American Journal of Social Psychiatry*. 1985;4:65–67.

208. JT Ungerleider, DK Wellisch. Coercive persuasion (brainwashing), religious cults, and deprogramming. *American Journal of Psychiatry*. 1979;136:279–82.

209. JM van der Lans, F Derks, F Mertens. Personality correlates of religious attitudes: the case of Campus Crusade and Unification Church. *Psychologica Belgica*. 1986;26:147–59.

210. WV Chambers, MD Langone, AA Dole, JW Grice. The Group Psychological Abuse Scale: a measure of the varieties of cultic abuse. *Cultic Studies Journal*. 1994;11:88–117.

211. MD Langone. Psychological abuse. *Cultic Studies Journal*. 1992;9:206–18.

212. RJ Lifton. *Thought reform and the psychology of totalism: a study of "brainwashing" in China*. 1st ed. W. W. Norton; 1961.

213. RJ Lifton. *Thought reform and the psychology of totalism: a study of "brainwashing" in China*. University of North Carolina Press; 1989.

214. R Ofshe, MT Singer. Attacks on peripheral versus central elements of self and the impact of thought reforming techniques. *Cultic Studies Journal*. 1986;3:3–24.

215. MT Singer, M Temerlin, MD Langone. Psychotherapy cults. *Cultic Studies Journal*. 1990;7:101–25.

216. C Almendros, M Gamez-Guadix, Á Rodríguez-Carballeira, JA Carrobles. Assessment of psychological abuse in manipulative groups. *International Cultic Studies Review*. 2011;2:61–76.

217. C Almendros, JA Carrobles, Á Rodríguez-Carballeira, JM Jansà. Psychometric properties of the Spanish version of the Group Psychological Abuse Scale. *Cultic Studies Review*. 2003;2:203–4.

218. C Almendros, JA Carrobles, Á Rodríguez-Carballeira, JM Jansà. Propiedades psicométricas de la versión Española de la Group Psychological Abuse Scale para la medida de abuso psicológico en contextos grupales [Psychometric properties of the Spanish version of the Group Psychological Abuse Scale for measuring psychological abuse in group contexts]. *Psicothema*. 2004;16:132–38.

219. N Winocur, J Whitney, C Sorensen, P Vaughn, D Foy. The Individual Cult Experience Index: the assessment of cult involvement and its relationship to postcult distress. *Cultic Studies Journal*. 1997;14:290–306.

220. LB Wolfson. *A study of the factors of psychological abuse and control in two relationships: domestic violence and cultic systems*. D Edu Psychol doctoral thesis. School of Education, University of Connecticut; 2002.

221. O Saldaña, E Antelo, C Almendros, Á Rodríguez-Carballeira. Development and validation of a measure of emotional distress in survivors of group psychological abuse. *The Spanish Journal of Psychology*. 2019;22:1–11.

222 E Antelo, O Saldaña, G Guilera, Á Rodríguez-Carballeira. Psychosocial difficulties in survivors of group psychological abuse: development and validation of a new measure using classical test theory and item response theory. *Psychology of Violence*. 2021;11:286–95.

223. JM Post. Dreams of glory and the life cycle: reflections on the life course of narcissistic leaders. *Journal of Political & Military Sociology*. 1984;12:49–60.

224. JR Meloy, J Hoffman, A Guldimann, D James. The role of warning behaviors in threat assessment: an exploration and suggested typology. *Behavioral Sciences & the Law*. 2012;30:256–79.

225. CS Allely, SJ Wicks. The feasibility and utility of the Terrorist Radicalization Assessment Protocol (TRAP-18): a review and recommendations. *Journal of Threat Assessment and Management*. 2022;9:218–59.

226. JR Meloy, P Gill. The lone-actor terrorist and the TRAP-18. *Journal of Threat Assessment and Management*. 2016;3:37–52.

227. N Böckler, M Allwinn, C Metwaly, B Wypych, J Hoffmann, A Zick. Islamist terrorists in Germany and their warning behaviors: a comparative assessment of attackers and other convicts using the TRAP-18. *Journal of Threat Assessment and Management*. 2020;7:157–72.

228. DJ Challacombe, CL Patrick. The January 6th insurrection at the U.S. Capitol: what the TRAP-18 can tell us about the participants. *Journal of Threat Assessment and Management*. 2023;10:220–28.

229. E Corner, N Pyszora. The Terrorist Radicalization Assessment Protocol-18 (TRAP-18) in Australia: face validity, content validity, and utility in the Australian context. *Journal of Policing, Intelligence and Counter Terrorism*. 2022;3:246–68.

230. A Szubin, CJ Jensen, R Gregg. Interacting with "cults": a policing model. *FBI Law Enforcement Bulletin*. 2000;69:16–24.

231. JR Meloy. Violent true believers. *FBI Law Enforcement Bulletin*. 2011;80:24–32.

232. JR Meloy. *User's manual for the terrorist radicalization assessment protocol 1.0*. Multi-Health Systems, Inc.; 2017.

Chapter 12

Drug Use in Cults

Chris Sterwald and Jason G. Roof

"If God can be found through the medium of any drug, God is not worthy of being God."
– *Meher Baba [1]*

Introduction

In Greco-Roman antiquity, "cults" were often viewed differently than those of modern conception. Historically, cultist groups were often defined by their supernatural rituals and practices pledging devotion to religious deities, rather than the beliefs of any one individual or group of individuals in the physical realm. Many such groups relied on the use of medicines and other psychotropic substances in their rituals [2, 3]. This element of practice has however been carried forward into the modern world and has been seen in contemporary civilizations across the globe [4].

The colloquial use of the term "cult" carries with it implicit bias and inherent limitations, including the labeling of such by outsiders and those who might be ignorant about the groups' practices. The liberal use of the term may be reductive in as much as it may not fully or accurately reflect the nuances of the group's practices. For example, the ritualistic use of peyote by Native Americans led to historical mischaracterization as involvement as "peyote" cults, despite not fitting with contemporary characterizations [5, 6, 7]. Examples such as this bear little resemblance to the modern conception of cult-like groups that are in large part defined by the potential for undue influence by one or more leaders for personal gain. Drugs may in fact be used to further the beliefs and indoctrination of followers but may also be inconsequential or secondary to the aims of such groups.

Although the characterization of the ritualized uses of substances as cultic may be reductive, there may be also some validity to this characterization in certain contexts. Indeed, research has identified some similarities between drug addiction and cult membership. Cult membership and devotion has been compared to an addictive experience, with altered states of consciousness and withdrawal having been consistently identified as pivotal to the cult experience [8, 9, 10]. Nonetheless, the provisional shared use of substances should not be interpreted as wholly explanatory or as a defining trait of cultist groups but rather one potential element of their practices.

Within the more modern conception of cults and charismatic groups, different patterns of drug use exist, ranging from complete abstinence and discouragement of substance use to the active encouragement of extensive drug use to promote indoctrination. Groups that discourage drug use include many new religious movements.

Table 12.1 Example patterns of use and example cults

Patterns of Drug Use within Cults	Examples
Antidrug	Divine Light Mission, Unification Church
Pro-drug	Aum Shinrikyo, The Family
Incidental drug use	Nigerian college campus cults
Drug-centric	Timothy Leary and the psychedelic movement

Additionally, and perhaps controversially, some publications describe Alcoholics Anonymous as having certain cult-like traits [11]. However, other new religious movements do incorporate substance use, either as part of their rituals or as a form of control or coercion of members. At the extreme, cultic groups that have participated in mass poisoning events have utilized drugs for their toxic effects in order to instigate suicide and mass casualties [12, 13]. The majority of directive drug use in cultist groups exists in between these extremes. Outside of new religious movements, other groups with cultic traits utilize substances. Members of terrorist groups with cult-like features may use drugs. Relatedly, some criminal groups involved in drug trafficking have coopted spiritual and mystical tradition beliefs and practices, which have been referred to as *narcocults* [14].

The aim of this chapter is to outline different patterns of drug use within cultic groups, ranging from those with "antidrug" to "pro-drug" attitudes, as illustrated in Table 12.1.

Research on antidrug-oriented cults has generally shown that cult membership may reduce drug use, even among those who had a high incidence of drug use upon joining [15–18]. Pro-drug orientations, on the other hand, are sometimes reflected as a central part of cult practices or are sometimes incidental with inconsistent effects on group membership and following. Groups that are solely focused on drug use will be discussed. Finally, instruments used to measure and quantify drug use will be reviewed.

Antidrug

Characteristics of Leaders

Divine Light Mission

The leader of the contemporary religious cult known as the Divine Light Mission was a man named Prem Pal Singh Rawat, better known as the Guru Maharaj Ji [15, 19]. He was the son of a religious leader in India named Sri Hans Ji Maharaj, who founded the Divine Light Mission in 1960 [20]. Although the formal organization of the Divine Light Mission started in 1960, Sri Hans Ji Maharaj had been informally preaching for much longer [19]. Sri Hans Ji Maharaj had been a member of a Sikh group in India called the Radhasoami Satsang Beas, whose leader guided them along a path to God. Sri Hans Ji Maharaj had four sons, the youngest of whom was Maharaj Ji, who even at a young age engaged in the family's public religious practices. As a result of his participation, he received attention from followers of his father. When his father died, he ascended to lead the group at age 8 – chosen due to his charismatic skill in religious oration [20]. He reportedly had received instruction from "a voice" instructing him to take his spiritual knowledge to the world and inform his followers that he had inherited the role of "perfect master" when his father died [19]. By age 11, Maharaj Ji had spent time in London to spread the word of the Divine Light Mission. In 1971, at the age of 13, he came to the United States following an invitation from some of his devotees [15, 19, 20]. As he traveled and spread his message throughout the United States, he attracted a following from the youth counterculture. After a year-long trip to India, he returned to the United States and established a headquarters for the Divine Light Mission in Denver, Colorado [20].

Being so young, Maharaj Ji became known for his "playful" public behavior and lavish lifestyle, including moving into a mansion and being transported in a limousine [20]. He was sometimes seen as immature and had been criticized for allegedly diverting funds from the Mission for his own use [19]. He also began wearing American-style clothing, such as business suits, rather than his traditional Indian attire [19, 20]. He eventually married his secretary, who was older than him, effectively rupturing his ties with his family, with the Indian branch of the Divine Light Mission, and many of his American followers, who saw the union as a violation of the vow of celibacy that the Guru himself preached. His mother seized control of the Indian branch of the Divine Light Mission and handed the reins to his eldest brother. In response, he returned to India in 1975 and took his family to court, where he was granted control of the movement everywhere except India. He had declared that his new wife was the incarnation of an Indian goddess [20]. He abruptly moved the cult's headquarters to Miami without explanation, with many of his remaining followers accompanying him. His public appearances dwindled, and the group became less cohesive. When he moved again, this time to Malibu, he did not call for his devotees to follow, and his activity in the group continued to wither [20]. With regards to his personality traits, Maharaj Ji has been described as "eloquent and shrewd" [21, p. 179]. Some have noted that he may have been comparatively less charismatic than similar cult leaders [22]. There exists a paucity of information in the literature detailing whether Maharaj Ji engaged in any drug use himself or how that may have influenced his practices.

Unification Church

Reverend Sun Myung Moon, leader of the members of the Unification Church, also known as Moonies, was born in 1920. He stated that, starting at a young age, he had fostered psychic abilities. He claimed that in his childhood he saw Jesus Christ in a vision, who told him to carry out his unfinished work; he similarly declared seeing Moses and Buddha. Early in his life, he was arrested on three occasions. Differing accounts of these arrests have been suggested; more favorable views claim that he was experiencing religious persecution, while more critical viewpoints indicate they were related to sexual indiscretions [23]. Information regarding these past indiscretions is scarce in the literature, as is information concerning whether Moon engaged in drug use in his youth.

By 1954, he had self-appointed himself a minister, had moved to South Korea, and started the Holy Spirit Association for the Unification of World Christianity [23]. He was an expelled member of the Presbyterian Church of Korea [24]. However, Moon maintained good standing with the South Korean regime and developed many business ventures. Moon's involvement in commercial fishing was one such "mystical commitment" [25, p. 105]. With growing wealth and acclaim, he soon spread his religious sect to Japan [23].

In 1959, Moon sent representatives to the United States; however, growth remained limited at that time. He himself came to the United States from Korea in the early 1970s [23]. Moon proselytized that his travel was guided by the need to restore morality to America, which he viewed as suffering from a degradation of morals, family values, and drug problems [26]. Although his new followers had commonalities with the youth counterculture movement, drugs and alcohol were forbidden. However, within Moon's own family, there were struggles with drugs. His eldest son began using drugs in his school years and, according to revelations from his son's wife, would spend much of his time alone in his room doing cocaine [27]. These experiences, to the extent they are true, may have informed Moon's hard stance against drug and alcohol use within the Unification Church. Moon was aided by a man named Neil Salonen, who became the president of the Unification Church in the US. Moon showed stronger and longer-lasting ties to his followers than Maharaj Ji and was known for his political and financial ventures. He even became involved politically, in supporting President Richard Nixon during the Watergate scandal. With regards to foreign political involvement, he was accused of having ties with the Korean CIA. He put forth the idea that he was a messiah, even testifying in a federal court case regarding deprogramming that he was a messiah [23]. His followers also believed him to have a divine mission [15]. Further, they believed that he embodied all of their "emotional and spiritual satisfactions" [24]. He has been described as charismatic [22].

However, he continued to lose credibility in the eyes of the press regarding his fundraising and spending, receiving attention for his own expensive residence and other lavish real estate purchases. To maintain a positive image in the eyes of the American population, Moon began hosting large rallies. His first big appearance in the US occurred in 1976 in Yankee Stadium. In 1982, shortly after he was convicted of tax fraud, he married off 1,410 followers in a mass ceremony. This happened after having matched and engaged them in 1979. He served 11 months in federal prison and was released in 1985. Despite his conviction, his followers maintained his innocence and that he was merely being subject to religious persecution [23].

Around the time of the new millennium, Moon dissolved the Unification Church but started a new organization called the Family Federation for World Peace and Unification, which allied with other religions to spread a pro-family message. He cultivated ties with American conservative politicians and continued to spread a conservative message through *The Washington Times*. He continued to claim he was a reincarnation of Jesus Christ in a 2002 tour and has also stated that he had children without original sin, although they were noted to have struggled with substance use problems and suicide, both of which he sermonized against [28].

Meher Baba

Meher Baba was an Indian spiritual leader. His trajectory as a spiritual leader began at age 19, when he allegedly had a transcendent experience after an encounter with a venerable spiritual leader [29]. In 1925, he began a period of silence that would last until the end of his life. He died in 1969. He claimed to be the latest reincarnation of a lineage that included Buddha, Christ, and Mohammed [30]. He took care of people whom he referred to as "God-intoxicated" in India, many of who exhibited signs of mental illness [29]. He had many followers in India and though he traveled to the US on occasion, it was not until the last few years of his life that he found a substantial

American following. He opposed the use of psychedelic drugs as dangerous and pointless from a spiritual perspective. Meher Baba found an audience of American youths in the counterculture movement who decided to reject drug use [30, 31].

Meher Baba's views on drugs are summarized in a 1966 pamphlet he wrote entitled *God in a Pill*. In it, he contends that the spiritual experiences espoused by those who take hallucinogens are shallow and false compared to those that can be obtained through work and religious pursuit with the Perfect Master. However, he did acknowledge that there were legitimate medical uses of LSD; for example, he suggested that using it as a treatment for alcoholism, depression, and other mental illnesses may be acceptable. Using LSD for other uses, however, was viewed as harmful to one's body, mind, and spirit. Meher Baba also included cannabis in his discussion of drugs that could be harmful. Rather than using drugs, he suggested that people instead look to him for spiritual ascendance and love. He famously stated: "If God can be found through the medium of any drug, God is not worthy of being God" [1].

Synanon

Synanon was a therapeutic community started in 1958 that aimed at rehabilitating drug users. Its founder was a man named Charles Dederich [11]. Dederich was born in Ohio in 1913 and lost his father and younger brother at an early age. As an adult, he struggled with alcohol after two marriages ended. He eventually moved to California and found Alcoholics Anonymous (AA) [32]. After joining AA and benefitting himself, he began to adapt the organization's principles for use with drug addicts. He altered AA's framework by including a residential component and removing the religious aspects of the group's practices [33]. He began giving confrontational seminars that he identified as "attack therapy" or "the game" [32, p. 7]. In "the game," participants would surround the subject of the therapy and criticize them aggressively, until they submitted to changing to conform to the group's norms [32, 33].

His beliefs and therefore Synanon's practices became increasingly extreme; for example, he eventually forbade members from having children and ordered couples to divorce [32]. However, at one point the group's coercive persuasion began being used to incite group members into sexual acts. He began employing his members at Synanon-owned and -operated small businesses and manufacturing jobs and subjecting them to close monitoring [33].

Dederich has been criticized for being arrogant and controlling [33]. Marc Galanter, an American psychiatrist who has researched drug use and cults, suggests that Synanon's eventual rebranding as a religion afforded him more power in the group. Galanter suggests that he became grandiose, paranoid, and unstable over time, citing Dederich's statements such as that he was "more famous than Santa Claus" [33]. He also filed libel and conspiracy suits against the media in the 1970s as part of his "Holy War" [34, p. 232]. Paul Morantz, a journalist who wrote about Synanon and who the group eventually tried to have killed, has noted that Dederich was "a cheap bastard" in relation to his reliance on group members to execute violence rather than hiring hitmen [35]. In contrast, Walker Winslow, an American writer who became known for chronicling his experience with the mental healthcare system, noted that Dederich had "the carriage of a gladiator, and his features are square and aggressive . . . he exudes an aura of power . . . he has the toughness that he knows is needed to control dope fiends." He notes that due to his "obsessive personality," he committed wholly to the work of AA. With regards to his use of LSD, he notes "he experienced no regression, no sensory enhancement or hallucinations . . . his normal traits appeared merely in a sort of caricature." Winslow adds that while Dederich attributed his personal growth and well-being to those early uses of LSD, he did not think it was safe or effective for all alcoholics and addicts [36, p. 2].

Like the other cults mentioned in this section, Synanon also comprised a substantial business operation; it has been estimated that their holdings were worth tens of millions of dollars [32]. Members of Synanon were employed by Dederich in the operation of these ventures [33]. Dederich himself profited by claiming tax-exempt status and buying himself a large mansion in California [32]. Dederich would sometimes expunge members from the group; at one point former members of the group attempted to sue him, and their lawyer Paul Morantz found a rattlesnake in his mailbox in return in 1978 [32, 37]. In 1980 he plead no contest to charges related to this attempt at murder, and he was ordered to cease his participation with Synanon, which was sanctioned by the government by losing its status as a tax-exempt entity. Dederich died in 1997 [32].

Characteristics of Followers

Members of cults that carry strong antidrug messages, such as those we have outlined, have been described extensively in the literature. Along with emotional vulnerability, tendency toward dissociation, poor social and family supports, poor coping skills, history of childhood abuse or neglect, unusual family patterns, and socioeconomic and situational stress, a tendency to abuse substances has been suggested as a factor that could make individuals more susceptible to being recruited into a cult [16]. Galanter suggests that experiences with drug-induced altered consciousness may prime cult members to be more accepting of alternative or unusual beliefs [38].

A study of the characteristics of members of the Unification Church was undertaken by Galanter, Rabkin, Rabkin, and Deutsch [39]. Using a questionnaire developed based on their prior research, Galanter et al. assessed psychological characteristics of members of the Unification Church, with special focus on how these characteristics influenced their joining and continued membership to the Church. They found that most members were unmarried (91%), white (89%), and most often young, with a mean age of around 24 years old. Additionally, males had a slight predominance, forming just over 60% of the members. Of the sample, two-thirds had identified as having at least a moderate investment in their family's religion as a child, and nearly all eventually developed at least some commitment to Eastern religious sects. More than half had started college but generally started to drop out before and during conversion to the group. Many reported some element of psychological distress before joining the group, and about a quarter had "serious drug problems in the past." Galanter et al. noted that the proportion of members surveyed that had ever used drugs was higher than a comparable national sample, citing that 45% had tried hallucinogens as opposed to 14% in the comparison group. With regards to changes that occurred during continued group membership, Galanter et al. reported that an increased commitment to avoiding alcohol was associated with an increase in neurotic stress after conversion.

In a follow-up study, Galanter, Buckley, Deutsch, Rabkin, and Rabkin specifically examined the ability for cults to diminish drug use among their members [15]. Their sample included members of the Divine Light Mission and the Unification Church. They noted that these groups and indeed many religious cults of that era discouraged drug use.

The study took place over five years and consisted of interviews and self-report research instruments. In addition to studying long-term members of both groups, Galanter et al. also studied individuals who were currently being recruited into the Unification Church.

With regards to the Divine Light Mission, Galanter et al. noted that while its organizing philosophy was opposed to drug use and members were thus expected to attain enlightenment through religious means instead, strict limitations on drug use were only enforced on those who lived in their organized communities. With regards to their research findings, Galanter et al. reported that members of the Divine Light Mission tended to be in their mid-twenties, white, and slightly more often male. Most had attended college, though of those that attended college, only about half graduated. At the time of the study, individuals had been members of the Divine Light Mission for nearly two years. Some 27% reported that they had had "serious problems with drugs" [15].

With regards to the drug use within Divine Light Mission, in comparing the two-month period immediately prior to joining the sect and the two-month period immediately after, they found a 43% decrease in usage of marijuana and 32% decrease in the use of alcohol. Divine Light Mission members also reported a decline of any caffeine use over the course of joining the cult; daily use of caffeine also declined but trended toward its original incidence over the course of time studied. The usage of more socially acceptable drugs such as marijuana and alcohol dropped less than the usage of less socially acceptable drugs such as depressants (i.e., sedative-hypnotic agents) and stimulants. They note, for example, that stimulant usage decreased from 21% to 5% and depressant use decreased from 23% to 5%, whereas the decrease in marijuana usage was proportionally lower, from 82% to 44%. Additionally, heavy drug use dropped more than lighter drug usage; after joining, heavy usage of any drug was less than 1% [15].

In discussing the Unification Church, Galanter et al. reported that members' self-reported use of marijuana, alcohol, hallucinogens, stimulants, depressants, and heroin decreased over time after having joined the cult. They examined both any use of the substance at all and heavy use of the substance; both patterns decreased over time. Marijuana usage decreased from 79% to 3% and alcohol fell from 90% to 13% [15].

In addition, Galanter et al. compared the frequencies of having ever used drugs among members of the Divine Light Mission to comparison data from a sample of college students. They noted that the comparison group's incidence of drug use was a third to a half less than that of the Divine Light Mission members. However, they do also note that the frequency of having ever used alcohol was similar between the comparison group and the religious sects. Galanter et al. suggest that members of the Divine Light Mission, as well as members of the Unification Church, had been associated with the youth counterculture movement prior to joining the cult. They state that this was even more so the case for Divine Light Mission members than Unification Church members, and they expectedly had higher drug use prior to joining [15].

Galanter describes a member of the Divine Light Mission named Ellen who he met while attending a festival, as a case example of how cult membership impacted drug use. She had started abusing barbiturates before joining the cult and eventually progressed to LSD and then opioids, the latter of which led to an addiction resulting in her participating in prostitution as well as suicide attempts and psychiatric hospitalization. She failed methadone maintenance and eventually relapsed, but she soon met members of the Divine Light Mission and found herself joining their group. After joining the group, she was reportedly able to stop using heroin, which Galanter attributed to group cohesion [40].

Box 12.1 Proposed Mechanisms for Reduction in Drug Use by Cults

Various mechanisms for which cult membership may reduce drug use have been described, including replacing drug use with other forms of altered consciousness and group cohesion and conformity. Joining a cult may also entail living in an environment in which access to drugs is reduced. Some have suggested cult membership may, albeit temporarily, reduce emotional distress, which may in turn reduce the desire to use drugs.

Galanter et al. speculate that reasons for decreased drug usage after joining may be due to members having a predisposition to addictive behaviors such that they substituted drug usage with affiliation with a cult [15, 38]. Curtis and Curtis support this notion, suggesting that a tendency to abuse substances is a risk factor for susceptibility to cults. They posit that the use of substances hinders decision-making and reasoning, which in turn may make individuals more suggestible and able to be influenced into group conformity. Curtis and Curtis suggest that meditation and other "transcendental experiences" might supplant the usage of drugs in these religious sects [16]. Galanter notes that members of the youth counterculture may have found it easy to transition from one form of altered consciousness (i.e., drug use) to another in the form of meditation, despite psychedelic drug use not being a central component of the religious cults emphasizing meditation [38]. Additionally, Galanter has suggested that Christian mysticism has not been tied to the use of psychedelics because Christianity had been associated with rejection of bodily pleasures rather than embracing them; this may explain why Christian-influenced religious cults are associated with reduced drug use [38].

However, they also suggest that the decrease in drug usage may be due to group norms and influence on behaviors. Galanter et al. utilized an instrument designed to assess members' feelings of group cohesion and found that the degree of experienced group cohesion was a significant predictor of diminished drug usage and diminished mental distress. These possible mechanisms for the reduction of drug use by cult membership are summarized in Box 12.1.

By examining drug usage at multiple time points, they were also able to determine when the decline in drug usage occurred, which appeared to have occurred right after converting rather than over time [40]. Additionally, Galanter reported that, in the Unification Church, although only 42% agreed with the statement "I should avoid getting high from alcohol" before joining the cult, 89% felt that way right after joining, indicating that their beliefs changed to conform with the group [41, p. 85].

Levine and Salter also describe the characteristics of members of some of these religious cults as well as their patterns of drug use. In their study, they interviewed 106 members across 9 different fringe religious groups, which they defined as groups that identified a godlike figure and were novel, small in comparison to mainstream religions, and not accepted as legitimate by society at large. The groups studied included both the Divine Light Mission and the Unification Church, but also the Hare Krishnas, Process, Foundation, 3HO, Jesus People, Children of God, and Scientology. Across their sample, the median age of those interviewed was 21.5, and males and females were relatively evenly divided. They tended to be educated and from a middle-class background, with almost all having at least completed high school and most having some college education. Levine and Salter noted that a large number of subjects had left college after being drawn to their religious group. Most were single and were engaged in part-time or occasional work or worked for their religion. The majority of them came from large, intact families and thought their relationship with their parents was at least average. Regarding their previous religious background, no one had been very committed to any religion before joining the cult. However, they did note that among members who had joined an Eastern-derived cult, there were more individuals who had come from Catholic or Jewish families [17].

Concerning their drug usage histories, the drug most frequently used by members of the cults studied was alcohol. They reported that the members of the Eastern-derived cult had a much greater history of using "softer" drugs such as marijuana and that they had also tried other drugs like MDMA and LSD. The Western-derived groups, in contrast, had more history with "harder" drugs such as amphetamines and heroin, though they had also used alcohol and marijuana. Levine and Salter also noted that if drug use had been a problem, it had stopped after joining the cult, though since they did not serially interview their subjects, this finding may be subjected to reporting bias [17].

Levine and Salter also randomly selected 11 members to subject to a more detailed psychological examination. They noted that through these more in-depth interviews and their regular interviews, they encountered no grossly psychotic individuals. However, they did report having found that many were anxious or depressed before joining their cult, and some met diagnostic criteria for borderline or other personality disorder features. They described a small group that was more well-defended, utilizing defense mechanisms such as denial and intellectualization, as well as chanting and engaging in ritual. Despite these findings of psychiatric symptoms, however, they concluded that in most cases, no clear psychiatric diagnosis could be made. As this research was undertaken before DSM-III and the rise of modern, structured approaches to psychiatric diagnosis, the finding that no psychiatric diagnosis could be made, even in an era in which diagnoses were less distinct and formalized, is impressive. Although Levine and Salter did not serially interview their subjects, they do note that their subjects reported diminished symptoms of anxiety or depression after having joined the group, though this statement might be influenced by biased reporting [17].

Levine published a follow-up paper further examining the mental health and substance use of cult members. Rather than reflecting new research, Levine's conclusions therein were based on his prior studies, a review of contemporaneous literature, and clinical and professional work with cult members, their families, and other cult experts. He reported quite strongly that "in not one instance" did cult members' former drug use continue while they were in the cult, basing this on the reported "extensive drug" histories of 14 cult members out of the total 453 studied. He similarly wrote that their psychiatric symptoms had improved [18]. However, while Levine acknowledges improvement in these areas during cult membership, he also notes that cults do often contribute to emotional distress, particularly after individuals leave. Additionally, he indicates that cults can foster concerning cognitive and behavioral traits in their members [18].

Pro-Drug

Religious Groups: Drugs as a Means of Control

The Family

"The Family" was an Australian cult led by Anne Hamilton-Byrne and founded in 1963. Hamilton-Byrne, who was born as Evelyn Edwards in 1921, was raised by her mother and absentee father. Hamilton-Byrne's mother suffered from schizophrenia and was frequently hospitalized during her upbringing. Cusack, the author of one of the only scholarly works on Hamilton-Byrne and The Family to date, suggests that Hamilton-Byrne's tumultuous family life acted as a motivator for her later founding the cult known as The Family. After the death of her first husband Don Harris, with whom she had had one child, in 1955, she moved to Victoria and became a yoga instructor. During this time, she became acquainted with New Age religious traditions and drew followers from Australia's middle class with her teachings blending Western, Eastern, and occult ideas. Cusack suggests that Hamilton-Byrne's charisma helped support an image of her as an enlightened guru (and eventually a reincarnation of Christ) and further speculates that the use of psychoactive drugs at this stage helped cement that characterization [42].

Hamilton-Byrne's Family grew as she formed ties with academics and psychiatrists. One particularly notable acquaintance was Raymor Johnson, a physicist at the University of Melbourne with an interest in the spiritual and paranormal, who met Hamilton-Byrne through his gardener. Johnson had been planning on visiting ashrams in India with his wife, and Hamilton-Byrne warned him that if he went, his wife would become sick; when this indeed happened, he and his family committed themselves to Hamilton-Byrne through a ritual in which they consumed hallucinogenic mushrooms and came to see her as Christ reincarnate. He became known as Hamilton-Byrne's "John the Baptist" [42, 43].

Among The Family's other early members was Howard Whitaker, a psychiatrist who had experimented with using LSD on patients at a clinic called Newhaven. He eventually began experimenting with using LSD himself and when he met Hamilton-Byrne through Johnson, would join The Family and help supply her with hallucinogenic drugs. The Newhaven clinic became a source for Family initiates, including more medical personnel. Newhaven doctors would target and recruit patients by giving them LSD [44]. Cusack notes that the initiation process involved ingesting LSD or hallucinogenic mushrooms, known as sacred manna, at Hamilton-Byrne's behest [42]. One of the detectives who investigated Hamilton-Byrne and The Family has stated that followers were given LSD in a dark room during the initiation process, and Hamilton-Byrne would appear before them in a white gown with evaporating dry ice behind her, giving off an otherworldly image and helping convince others she was Christ [45]. These initiation rites were known as clearings, and initiates were encouraged to look back into past lives to better understand their present existence [45]. Once LSD was banned in Australia, the clearings continued using other drugs [46]. During these early years, Hamilton-Byrne met her second husband, Bill Byrne, and took his name. The Family established its base of operations in a rural area where Hamilton-Byrne would sermonize to members while they took LSD [42].

By the end of the 1960s, members' children began to move into The Family's headquarters to be raised by Hamilton-Byrne as their mother. Hamilton-Byrne would procure children from patients and from single mothers [44]. These children would be routinely given a number of psychoactive drugs [42]. One person who grew up as a child in The Family stated that Hamilton-Byrne had a "vision" under the influence of LSD that she was supposed to gather children, as the end of the world was approaching and she had to repopulate the earth with them [45]. Drugs were also used in order to procure the children; one victim recounts that their mother was given tranquilizers while giving birth and had her child taken from her before seeing them. When children reached 14 years old, they were administered LSD in large quantities to initiate them into The Family [45]. The LSD would either be given orally or parenterally, and afterwards the child would be left in the dark for up to days at a time, until they accepted Hamilton-Byrne as Christ [47]. Afterwards, they would receive doses of tranquilizing drugs to keep them calm throughout their days living under Hamilton-Byrne's influence [44, 48].

Eventually, in the 1980s, Australian police investigated Hamilton-Byrne and her cult. In 1987, they raided the compound where she was keeping the children and found LSD and other drugs [46]. Hamilton-Byrne and her husband evaded arrest for many years but eventually were caught and brought to trial in 1993 where they received only minor convictions and a $5,000 fine. She would eventually die in a nursing home, where she spent her final years suffering with dementia [42].

Jonestown

James Warren Jones was born May 13, 1931, to a father ailing from exposure to poison gas during his service in World War I and to a factory-employed mother. Jones, at 21 years old, was a husband, father to an adopted daughter, student at Indiana University, and a pastor at Somerset Methodist church. He would later credit his mother and her care for a "tramp" during his early childhood as fundamental to his ministry work [49].

In 1954, Jones and his wife Marceline, a nurse, began the Community Unity Church in Indianapolis. In 1955, Jones established a Pentecostal church named Wings of Deliverance. One of its fundamental tenets was "[t]otal absence of narcotics, alcohol and every other habit forming substance" [50, p. 5]. Wings of Deliverance would soon be renamed the Peoples Temple. Around this time of his life, Jones began to inject himself with a material he described to others as vitamin B12 or insulin; however, those close to him believed that he had begun to regularly use a variety of other substances. His substance use, which included amphetamines, benzodiazepines, methaqualone, barbiturates, and other recreational substances, would continue to increase throughout the 1970s with an observed surge of use following the death of his mother in December 1977 [51].

Already a popular evangelist prior to starting his own church, he remained in Indianapolis until 1965 where he visited Redwood Valley, California and would later establish the Temple there with his followers. One prior follower indicated that Jones chose the location because he felt it would be a safer location should a nuclear war occur [50]. Another recalls that at this time he began wearing his iconic sunglasses at all times, no matter the weather. While unclear to many of his followers why this had started one member indicated that it was likely to hide his eyes from those who might detect that he had been using drugs [50].

Temple members became increasingly unable to tolerate living in Redwood Valley, citing racial incidents involving local residents targeting their black constituents. In 1972, Peoples Temple purchased a former Scottish Rite temple in San Francisco and property in Los Angeles where regular services were provided. The organization was looked upon favorably in these more urbanized areas in part due to their inclusivity, social activism, and the establishment of health and welfare systems to care for those who were otherwise unable to care for themselves. Models of communal living were established within the Peoples Temple allowing for individuals to receive room and board in exchange for their outside paychecks or their direct work for the temple [51]. Further condemnation of substance use in participants was marked with punishment to include demands to pay fines to the Peoples Temple [52].

Jones, becoming increasingly paranoid and frustrated by the repressive political situation in the United States, sought a location where a larger communal experience could occur with less interference. In 1974, members met with officials from the Government of Guyana to lease acreage for a "branch church and agricultural mission" and construction of what would be known as Jonestown began. In 1977, a mass migration of followers numbering around 700, Jones among them, arrived to begin their collective social experiment. Jones and his followers sought a communal environment where property and resources were shared equally, one based on the practices of Jesus Christ and the apostles in the Bible – a kind of "Christian apostolic socialism." In the Bible, early Christian living was described as communal, and egalitarian [53].

Jones' troubling substance use increased while living in Jonestown and the death of his mother in December 1977 was a catalyst for further increased use. Jones' utopian vision for his project was ill prepared for the influx of new followers and struggled to feed and house followers. Punishments for infractions of Jonestown rules might result in work details, physical punishment, or periodic drugging and placement in a designated Intensive Care Unit in Jonestown [52]. Approximately a month after Jones' arrival to Jamestown, the first "white night" occurred. While survivors have defined "white nights" in a variety of ways, the term was utilized to spur followers into action because of various concerns or perceived threats and could involve stimulant-fueled overnight speeches. A primary theme involved Jones' concern that outside forces sought to compromise or end the Peoples Temple project. His concerns were exacerbated by the escape of one of their members (Leon Broussard), the contested fatherhood of one of the children living in Jonestown (John Stoen), and increasing concern from participants' family members and governmental officials. In the first "white night" he instilled a sense of urgency and fear in followers by telling them that he had survived an assassination attempt and that they must help defend their camp from hostile armed forces hiding in the words. In truth, no such assassination attempt had occurred and there were no individuals seeking to harm anyone. What followed would be known by followers as "the six-day siege" and would be heavily referenced in the future by Jones [50]. During these and other events, talk of "revolutionary suicide" would be discussed and later simulated as Jones became increasingly paranoid and intoxicated.

Another example of Jones' increasing paranoia includes an initiative to move to an even more remote location. In 1978, the Russian attaché to Guyana visited Jonestown to explore Jones' desire to move to Russia as he, and his followers, believed that they were no longer safe. Further fueling his paranoia, an organization known as Concerned Relatives began an initiative to rescue friends and family members from Peoples Temple and requested help from governmental officials and reporters to save them.

A month after the visit with the Russian attaché, US Congressman Leo J. Ryan visited Jonestown uninvited with a group of reporters and members of the Concerned Relatives. Though denied access to Jonestown on the first day of their visit, they returned the second day and found at least 16 individuals who secretly wanted to leave with them. As the group left Jonestown, Ryan was attacked by a Jonestown member who held a knife to his throat and threatened to kill him. Jonestown residents intervened and Ryan was uninjured. It was clear all needed to leave Jonestown quickly and return to the United States. After arriving at Port Kaituma airstrip, a short delay occurred as a second plane had to be chartered to facilitate the increased size of travelers. As the passengers began to board the planes, several members of Jonestown arrived and began firing. Ryan and four others were killed and nine others wounded before the attackers drove away. The injured survivors remained overnight with responding Guyanese troops [54, 55].

Under Jones' direction, Jonestown's medical team brainstormed methods to kill Jonestown residents en masse. Suggestions included starvation, slitting residents' throats, or use of carbon monoxide. Jonestown's physician, Larry Schacht, would come up with the idea and the formula that would ultimately be used [56]. A mixture of various substances, including cyanide, was added to a Flavor Aid mixture and consumed by Jonestown members. Over 900 Jonestown residents died that day. Jim Jones was later found to have died by gunshot wound.

Jones' sermons over time transformed from spiritual matters, social justice, and communal ways of living based on "Christian apostolic socialism" to those heavily themed by paranoia. He became increasingly focused on forces outside that would compromise or end the movement itself or himself specifically. A transition from outward advocacy therefore shifted to one where the group was to isolate and protect itself from the increasingly threatening world [57]. What began as a fundamentalist Pentecostal church, driven by racial equality, would transform over 25 years into a communal experiment steeped in substance-influenced paranoia deep in the jungles of Guyana in South America [51].

Manson Family

Born to a 16-year-old girl named Kathleen Maddox, who was incarcerated for five years of her young son's life, Charles Milles Manson spent most of his life in custody. His criminal history stretches back to the age of 12 with convictions for a variety of criminal activities including auto theft, burglary, forgery, and pimping [58].

Manson arrived in San Francisco in 1967 soon after his most recent release from prison and found an environment rich with impressionable youth seeking direction. Marijuana and hashish were available and, despite the recent criminalization in California of LSD use, it was increasingly known to be available in the Haight-Ashbury district of San Francisco, California [59]. The term "hippies" came into creation to pejoratively describe a counterculture movement from the Beats who were also described as hipsters [60]. Haight-Ashbury was becoming increasingly popular and attracted an increasing number of counterculture youth. Paul McCartney referred to the area and the hippies that lived there as "colorful and fun," further popularizing the area and growing social movement [59, p. 92].

Manson noted that street preachers had a distinctive delivery style and commanded groups of individuals. Inspired by his own experiences in prison as well as the dynamism of those he watched performing, he began to generate his own message built to attract followers. Manson's initial street philosophy was an amalgamation, dramatically presented, that combined elements from Beatles' song lyrics, biblical texts, musical performance, promises of freedom, spirituality, dedication to Earth's ecology, and Scientology [61, 62]. Additionally, while in prison, he appears to have been heavily influenced by the Dale Carnegie textbook, *How to Win Friends and Influence People*, as well as Scientology and integrated both into his message [58, 59].

Manson began to assemble a number of followers who were referred to as "the Family." He and his growing group of followers led a transient lifestyle over the next months, often traveling in a black school bus until settling in August of 1968 at the Spahn Movie Ranch in Chatsworth, California. Lynnette "Squeaky" Fromme was appointed to act as George Spahn's private attendant. Fromme had been one of the first recruited by Manson after a chance meeting and was known to have a history of emotional disturbance suicide attempts and a dysfunctional relationship with her parents [59]. Strained family relationships were one of the most common aspects of the Family [63]. Though Fromme would not be found to be involved in the murders to come, she would point a gun at President Gerald Ford in 1975, resulting in her imprisonment until 2009.

Manson utilized seduction and drugs to integrate followers into the family. Women were often seduced or asked to imagine Manson as a father figure or as Christ. Men joining the group would often be given LSD "to open [their] mind." While in the suggestible state, Manson would emphasize the importance of losing one's individuality in order to become one with all things [58]. He would administer specific amounts of various substances including marijuana, peyote, and LSD during orgies. Manson in effect utilized substances to "eradicate hang-ups" and to bond members to one another and to him as the primary leader. He utilized LSD to instill his philosophy and to manipulate his followers to do his bidding [58]. Shared substance-induced experiences and the breakdown of individuality in favor of group unity and loyalty among his followers were fundamental in establishing a distorted reality based in Manson's ideology.

Violence and distribution of illegal substances were known to have occurred within the Family in an effort to preserve the group and promote their shared vision of reality. On July 1, 1969, Bernard "Lotsapoppa" Crowe, who had allegedly threatened to kill members of the Family at Spahn Ranch, was shot and killed by Manson. Later that same month, on July 25, Gary Hinman, who Manson believed to be wealthy, was held hostage for two days in an effort to get him to hand over his wealth. Manson cut him with a sword and by Manson's command he was killed by another member of the Family, Bobby Beausoleil. Beausoleil was arrested for the murder on August 6, 1969.

Approximately a year later, and only two years after Manson's arrival in San Francisco, the first of two mass murders would occur by members of the Family. On August 9, 1969, Tex Watson, Linda Kasabian, Patricia "Katie" Krenwinkle, and Susan Atkins killed Sharon Tate, eight months pregnant at the time and the wife of the director Roman Polanski, as well her friends Abigail Folger, Wojtek Frykowski, and Jay Sebring. The following night, Manson joined Watson, Atkins, Krenwinkle, Kasabian, Leslie Van Houten, and Steven "Clem" Grogan near the home of Leno and Rosemary LaBianca. Manson is not believed to have participated directly in the murders of Leno and Rosemary LaBianca; however, he was determined to be the mastermind behind the murders by prosecutors. The murders went unsolved for a number of months until Atkins, in jail for another reason, bragged of her involvement to a cellmate [64].

At the trial of Manson and his followers, Dr. Joel Forte, psychiatrist and founder of a free clinic in Haight-Ashbury, offered testimony in the penalty phase of the Tate–LaBianca murder trials. He is reported to have said that it was "possible to program chronic drug users, under certain conditions, to commit murder." He clarified that whether a user is greatly changed by LSD use depends on "her underlying personality, the influence of the environment subculture or peer group and the leader or guru." Dr. Forte suggested that LSD had been used in the Manson family to create a "totally neutral system. . . to brainwash or to produce a new form of thinking, a new pattern of behavior for the girls living in this group with Mr. Manson" [65, p. 3].

Susan Atkins testified during her trial that she was "stoned on acid" and could not recall how many times she had stabbed Tate [64, p. 1]. Krenwinkel testified that she had twice attempted to leave the Family but followers brought her back and "kept her high on drugs" [64]. While both would have sufficient reason to be deceptive about the effects of substances on their behaviors during their time with the Manson Family, it is clear that illicit substances played a significant role in the group's creation and establishment.

Aum Shinrikyo

Aum Shinrikyo was formed in 1984 by Shoko Asahara (formerly known as Chizuo Matsumoto) and started as a yoga school but went on to become a religious group fusing Buddhist, Hindu, Taoist, and Christian ideas [66, 67]. By 1986, Asahara would state that he had been sent on a divine mission by the Dalai Lama, which the Dalai Lama himself would deny (although he did meet with Asahara and members of the Aum early in the group's lifespan). Asahara would also claim that he had psychic powers and could float in the air [67]. He has been characterized by Japanese psychiatry professor Haruo Akimoto as meeting the criteria for the psychiatric syndrome pseudologia fantastica owing to his improbable claims, grandiosity, and lack of empathy [68]. He has also been characterized as a psychopath by Tareq Albhlal, a professor of religious studies in Saudi Arabia [69]. He was blinded by infantile glaucoma and his blindness has been suggested as a contributing factor his mystic appeal [70]. Early in the 1980s, he opened a shop to sell Chinese medicines and was arrested and fined for selling drugs with uncertain benefit [71].

The members of Aum Shinrikyo tended to be well-educated and most were younger than 40 years old [67]. By 1989 they gained recognition as an officially recognized religious group, despite concern over their tenets that members had to renounce ties with the outside world [66]. Before they disbanded in 1995, they were involved in a number of criminal activities. While they are best known for using sarin nerve gas in terrorist attacks that killed several people and injured thousands, they were also charged with manufacturing truth serum and LSD [67, 72]. Although they came to be known as a terrorist group, Aum Shinrikyo preferred to stylize itself as a religious group [72]. By 1991, Asahara prophesized that a global war would occur in 1997 and that only members of Aum would survive. The group began manufacturing and acquiring large amounts of weapons, bombs, and tanks at that time. The leaders of Aum adopted the view that anyone who opposed them needed to be killed in order to purify their bad karma [67].

The cult attempted to emulate the Japanese government by setting up an organized internal system of ministries [72]. It also had ties with organized crime and was involved in trafficking in illegal hallucinogens. The members manufactured explosives, firearms, and biological weapons [66, 72]. Aum scientists were found to have been involved in the manufacture of illegal drugs [73]. Aum also collected large amounts of money from its members [67]. Christopher W. Hughes, a professor of international politics and Japanese studies, estimates that the group had assets of around US$200 million [72]. The influence and power of Aum transcended its financial implications. Asahara himself ran for election in the Lower House of the Japanese Diet in 1992 [72].

Following its first sarin gas attack on Matsumoto, Aum Shinrikyo was involved in a kidnapping event that drew the attention of the police. The group was alerted to the planned police raid on its facilities, and Asahara, as well as several other leaders, went into hiding. The group then carried out its attack on the Tokyo subway system approximately nine months after the first attack on Matsumoto. The attack was targeted toward the government district during commuting rush hour, presumably to target government employees and police [74]. Police raids after this attack resulted in the discovery of the large weapons cache and arrest of many of Aum's members [66]. Asahara was eventually sentenced to death in 2004 and executed in 2018. The group itself lost its religious status following the attacks [66, 69].

In addition to selling and manufacturing drugs, Aum Shinrikyo also encouraged its members to use hallucinogens such as LSD to help achieve spiritual enlightenment, along with excessive physical activity. Aum members adopted intense exercise regimens where they would engage in physical activity 15–20 hours a day, hoping to achieve psychic powers. With regards to drug use, sometimes LSD was forced upon members with little to no preparation, which made it a fearful and overwhelming experience and served to make them more dependent on the protective cult. Those who did have positive experiences with drugs, however, would also attribute them to the benevolence of the cult [67]. Hallucinations were framed as holy images to inspire members [75]. Robert Jay Lifton, an American psychiatrist who studies cults, describes the different rituals of Aum Shinrikyo that involved drugs. First, a "Christ initiation" where LSD was given to produce visions; second, a "narcotic initiation" where the member ingested a drug and was instructed to chant their present inability to comprehend Aum's message and resolve to try to improve their understanding [76]. Galanter adds that sometimes during these drug initiation rituals, members would also be starved whereby the psychogenic effects of the substances might be enhanced [72].

La Santa Muerte: A Narcocult?

Narcos, Mexican drug cartels, have been known to worship folk saints such as Santa Muerte ("Saint Death"), who is an object of worship by so-called death cults [77]. They appeal to her to evade arrest, ensure their drugs move from place to place safely, and for their enemies to be unharmed. Her scythe is believed to deflect bullets fired at them by their enemies [78]. Folk saints differ from traditional Catholic saints in that they have no official recognition and are believed to have supernatural influence [79]. Offerings are made to Santa Muerte, who is depicted as a skeletal woman (sometimes a man, but most often female), including alcohol and tobacco, in order to ask for protection from death and, if death is unavoidable, a good death [77]. Certain Santa Muerte rituals also incorporate the blowing of tobacco smoke [77]. Mirroring her appeal to those addicted to drugs and the drug cartels, she is sometimes depicted smoking a joint [80]. It has been estimated that 40% of those in jails in Mexico are followers of Santa Muerte [77]. Although most narco violence is secular in nature, a small proportion seems to have adopted ritualistic fashions. Beyond La Santa Muerte, other folk saints coopted by narcos include Jesus Malverde (who has a beer named after him) [14]. Additionally, narcos have engaged in corrupted forms of other religions, such as Santeria, voodoo, and Christianity [81].

However, Santa Muerte's influence extends beyond the narcos; her worship has been described as the fastest-growing new religious movement across the Americas [82]. Her followers number 10–12 million [83]. Narcos form only a minority of the cult's worshippers [82]. Narco use of religious imagery has been described as a misappropriation of faith and religious elements [84]. Worship of Santa Muerte, while not sanctioned by the Catholic Church, uses Catholic imagery and icons, including rosaries, and is engaged in by participants who otherwise identify as Catholic [77]. Santa Muerte worship is not as formalized as some of the other cults that have been discussed, as the religion possesses more than a thousand different groups with tens of thousands of members [78]. However, there has been some organization of her followers; in response to government destruction of Santa Muerte shrines, David Romo Guillén, the founder of the first church to Santa Muerte in Mexico City, called for mass demonstrations at Catholic sites in Mexico City [77, 78]. Similarly, in 2005, Santa Muerte followers responded in mass protest after they did not receive legal recognition as a church [77]. Scholars have suggested that labeling worship of La Santa Muerte as a dangerous religion is warranted due to its disenfranchised membership and its perceived challenges to the dominant established church and state. As we will detail further, the government's view of La Santa Muerte as a narcocult exemplifies its supposed threat to the state's power; with regards to threats to organized religion, Pope Francis has warned against the adoption of death symbols as an object of worship, despite most Santa Muerte worshippers viewing Catholicism and Santa Muerte worship as compatible [85].

One organized expression of Santa Muerte worship is found in Santa Muerte Internacional (SMI), founded by Enriqueta Vargas, which represents a linked network of shrines to Santa Muerte. The SMI organization has helped Santa Muerte worship propagate within Mexican prisons, where she is worshipped by prisoners setting out offerings of drugs and alcohol and covertly by prison guards [78]. Although Santa Muerte worship dates to the 1940s to 1950s, its growth in prisons began in the 1990s and a second wave of public interest began in 2000 when more public altars appeared in Mexico City [86]. Its growth was sparked by Doña Queta, a Mexican woman from Tepito, Mexico City, who famously set up an altar in her house where she sold food to locals in 2001 and is thus credited with starting the first public shrine to Santa Muerte [82]. Part of Santa Muerte worship includes lighting different symbolically colored candles, which is similar to the worship of other Mexican folk saints; however, Santa Muerte is unique in that black candles may be lit to wish for death against one's enemies. This "Santa Muerte Negra" is the form preferred by the narcos, though may also be used by police to shield themselves from death [78].

Although narcos may only form a small amount of the followers of La Santa Muerte, their misappropriation of her symbols (and those symbols of other religions) bears examining. Much as her law-abiding followers do, narcos may seek the help of La Santa Muerte for protection. However, additional functions that religious cultism may bring to narcos include providing a semblance of structure and helping to indoctrinate new members. It can also help alleviate the stress and anxiety of engaging in drug warfare [87].

The Mexican government and Catholic Church have resisted Santa Muerte's attempts to organize, saying that her worship is connected with drug cartels, a claim that her followers have denied as some of those who fight the drug cartels even ask for Santa Muerte to bless their weapons [80]. Scholars studying the Santa Muerte cult have depicted it as multifaceted, rather than monolithic, saying her relationship between good and evil is more ambiguous [80, 86]. The portrayal of Santa Muerte as a "narco-saint" by the Mexican government, Catholic Church, and media has been characterized as racist and sexist (in that her worship has been alleged to be tied to violent men and women's role in propagating the religion has been diminished). One author notes that in Oaxaca, female followers outnumber male followers twofold [82]. As both narcos and those who fight them (prison guards, lawyers, and police) worship Santa Muerte, it has been proposed that she be considered the saint of the drug war, rather than a saint of any one side in that war [78]. The first mentions of her in the media were in 1989, when a group of Mexican narcos who engaged in a fusion of Palo Mayombe (an Afro-Cuban religion) and Mexican occultism were found to have ritually burned more than a dozen people in Matamoros, and the media associated Santa Muerte with the killings. This association of Santa Muerte with drug traffickers has been enduring [78]. However, in the United States, a 2014 court case *United States* v. *Medina-Copete* established that the connection between Santa Muerte worship and drug traffickers was "not a straightforward matter" [88].

Nigerian College Campus Cults

Nigerian institutions of higher education have been afflicted by violence and crime perpetuated by so-called secret campus cults [89]. They are referred to as such due to their initiation rituals and intense dedication of members [90]. There are estimated to be over 40 groups across Nigeria who are responsible for at least 10,000 killings between 1996 and 2019 [91]. These cults, or confraternities, were not originally characterized by violence; in fact, the first known secret cult, the Pyrates Confraternity, was founded by Nobel Laureate Wole Soyinka in the 1950s. Rather than perpetuating crime, the goals of these early organizations were to rebel against colonialist attitudes and corruption while emphasizing attributes of positive citizenship including charity work [89]. Later, when faced with social turmoil, several groups splintered off from the Pyrates Confraternity and the Pyrates Confraternity removed itself from college campuses in the 1980s shortly before the government outlawed campus cults. Over the years, campus cults proliferated and began engaging in crime and violence [89, 92]. Popoola and Alao suggest that campus cults engage in this type of behavior due to poor university infrastructure and resources, a decline in the strength of the family unit, economic pressures and poverty, and due to the decreasing average age of matriculating students (making them more susceptible to peer pressure) [89]. Other causes of cultism that have been suggested include youth unemployment, unwillingness or unreadiness to work, socioeconomic deprivation and injustice, and political affiliations [93]. Campus cult membership is often familial and is seen as a way to obtain social elite status [92]. Campus cults' descent into violence mirrors the increase in violence in Nigerian society in general. Additionally, campus officials themselves may often be members [89]. Positive attitudes toward cultism among Nigerian students have been found to be associated with violence, as has psychopathy, though psychopathy and cultic attitudes have not been found to be related. Violence due to campus cults has been disruptive to the function of academic institutions, leading to closure and interruption of the academic calendar in some instances [94]. In addition to engaging in violence and crime at the university level, some cults have also become involved in militia conflict in the Niger River Delta [93, 95]. Ultimately, campus secret cults are no longer restricted to academic institutions, and count members among the general public and prison inmates [91]. One such campus cult, the Black Axe cult, has been suggested to be one of the largest organized crime groups in the world, with internet fraud being its largest money-making enterprise [90].

One activity that campus secret cults engage in is the use of drugs [89]. Cult members have been characterized as addicted to drugs including cocaine and marijuana and heavy users of alcohol [92, 96]. These cults have also been characterized as selling drugs as part of their criminal enterprise [91, 96]. Within prisons, they are known to traffic in marijuana, cigarettes, and alcohol [91]. During their group gatherings, they are said to smoke cannabis, use heroin, and drink alcohol [95].

Terrorist Groups

Terrorist groups can be defined as those that employ violent and coercive tactics to contest, rival, assault, or offer alternatives to the political power held by governmental bodies. In the post–Cold War era state sponsorship from the Soviet Union and its allies of terrorist groups has decreased requiring these organizations to seek funding elsewhere [97]. Funding group activities may take a variety of forms but in rare circumstances drug trafficking may be utilized [98]. Terrorist groups that are centralized and have an explicit ethnopolitical ideology increases the likelihood that they will utilize drug trafficking while religious ideology has no significant effect [98].

Drug trafficking has increased in the past several decades and is believed to be the single-largest source of income for terrorist groups [99]. Examples of terrorist groups that have utilized drug trafficking to fund their organizations include the Kosovo Liberation Army during the Kosovo conflict, as well as guerrilla groups in Spain, Sri Lanka, Turkey, and Lebanon, the Islamic Movement of Uzbekistan, and Hezbollah. The Taliban's sale of opium has allowed profits of approximately US$100 million annually and the Revolutionary Armed Forces of Colombia (FARC) has profited by trafficking cocaine [97].

In 1998, Egyptian Islamic Jihad member Muhammad Abed Abd al-Aal was apprehended in Colombia due to his participation in drug trafficking, weapons smuggling, and money laundering in collaboration with FARC. Additionally, he employed similar techniques to generate funds for al-Qaeda [100]. Though the Taliban government in Afghanistan has banned drug cultivation it has justified distribution for funding because sales are made only to non-Muslims and may serve to both bring in finances as well as harm potential enemies by use of their products [97, 98].

While predominantly a source of funding for many terrorist groups, substance use may also be supported and encouraged in violent extremism groups. For instance, white supremacist groups may allow members to engage in heavy use of alcohol, methamphetamine, and other illegal recreational substances to facilitate group bonding, manage coping with social stigma from outside forces, and balance cognitive dissonance they experience [101, 102]. Stimulants, such as fenethylline (Captagon), have been utilized to increase combat effectiveness in ISIS members [103]. Substance use within a terrorist group may also reinforce membership and compound the difficulties of leaving the group and risking both social alienation as well as substance withdrawal [104].

Drug-Centric Groups

Timothy Leary and the Popularization of Psychedelics

Timothy Leary, an American psychologist who championed the use of psychoactive substances, emerged as a prominent icon of the 1960s counterculture movement. His persuasive advocacy influenced a multitude of individuals during this era. His slogan "Turn on, tune in, drop out" became a counterculture slogan as he explored ways that psychoactive substances might be used therapeutically for their capacity to alter human consciousness.

Aldus Huxley (1894–1963), a British writer best known for his dystopian novel *Brave New World* that explored use of technology and mind-altering substances to control citizens, was also a powerful figure in the counterculture movement of the 1960s and 1970s. His experimentation with mescaline, described in his text *The Doors of Perception* (1954), suggested the powerful capacity of psychedelic substances to change consciousness could allow for spiritual experiences and growth. Huxley's work influenced Leary's exploration and positive endorsement of such substances which in turn helped inspire others to consider using psychedelic substances for purposes of spiritual and personal growth.

Huxley would later be one of the founding members of the Harvard Psilocybin Project (also known as the Harvard Psychedelic Project) that, along with Timothy Leary and Richard Alpert as cofounders, would seek to perform various psychological experiments involving psychedelics. This project was short-lived and closed after two years in 1962 after other Harvard professors, government officials, and the American Medical Association expressed concern related to the safety of their work [105]. One such project, titled the Good Friday Experiment, suggested that use of psilocybin in student volunteers greatly enhanced their spiritual experience of a religious ceremony. Though concerns were raised related to the soundness of the experiment, subsequent research yielded similar results and forms a connection between psychedelic use and intensity of spiritual and mystical experiences [106].

Leary was inspired by the Native American Church's successful petition to the US federal government for religious use of peyote in 1965. Leary founded the League for Spiritual Discovery (LSD) in 1966, a purported religious movement utilizing LSD instead of peyote as its sacrament. This short-lived organization was created in part to test the legality of utilizing an otherwise illegal drug as a religious right and to obtain tax-free status as other religion-based organizations had in the past [107]. It was one of a number of "Acid Churches" arising in New York during the 1960s where psychoactive substances were central to their practice [108]. Ultimately the LSD and other "Acid Churches" would be disbanded by 1970, succumbing to the increased legal scrutiny over their provocative stance on psychedelic use [108].

Psychedelics and significant cultural change led to the formation of several groups seeking to disrupt societal norms. One such organization, The Brotherhood of Eternal Love, which was also referred to as the "Hippie Mafia," would engage in a variety of illegal activities with substance use and distribution at their core. Founded in Laguna Beach, The Brotherhood was known to have engaged in international drug trafficking in Pakistan and Afghanistan and had ties with the Hell's Angels that facilitated movement of illegal substances throughout southern California [105]. The Brotherhood was heavily influenced by Leary and hoped to emulate a utopian society as described in Huxley's final book, *Island* (1962). The group would later facilitate Leary's escape from jail and his being smuggled to Afghanistan.

Many members of The Brotherhood had criminal histories including their leader, John Griggs, who attributed use of LSD as being fundamental in his renouncing his prior history of violence. The Brotherhood adopted religious terminology, describing themselves as "disciples" and, like Leary's League for Spiritual Discovery model, sought religious exemption to legally utilize LSD. Seeking additional privacy, the group moved to a ranch in California to create a couples-only commune led by Leary. Leary indicated that he and Griggs were "agents of God" and that they would lead "a new breed." Griggs would soon die of a psilocybin crystal overdose but The Brotherhood continued in its effort to mass produce its own LSD referred to as "Orange Sunshine" [106].

Folk Medicine

In antiquity, ceremonial substance use often accompanied rituals to allow for perceived closer connections with and appreciation of deities. Cults of antiquity were better characterized as groups or movements that venerated a particular figure or object as opposed to more modern definitions of a cult that often take on a more negative connotation involving the manipulation, exploitation, and isolation of their members. Greek and Romans would enhance religious experience through use of substances known to alter or enhance consciousness [2]. Frankincense when burned and inhaled was discovered to induce or enhance altered states for purposes of ceremonies and found use in early Christian and Shia Islamic faiths [4]. Medieval Islamic sects utilized hashish to "offer a taste of the paradise to come" [109, p. 452]. Prior to Columbus' arrival to the Americas, Native Americans utilized peyote and mescaline in religious ceremonies [109]. Indigenous groups of the Western Amazon utilized ayahuasca to make contact with supernatural beings [110].

These entheogens were found to be mind-altering compounds that create changes in perception, emotion, awareness, thought, or actions [111]. They were used to promote spiritual growth or serve other sacred purposes within ancient religious ceremonies. Synchronization of emotions, behaviors, and experiences, as may occur with mind-altering substances taken together, may act as very powerful catalysts to bond participants to one another, their collective causes and beliefs, and to consolidate their identity within a group [110].

In antiquity, fermentation of grains, honey, and fruit led to beer, mead, and wine. Ancient wine may have had a variety of other materials added to it to increase the potency and mind-altering qualities. Toxins extracted from various plants and animals include snake and salamander venom, opium, hemlock, cannabis, wormwood, ergot, and other psychoactive resins [111]. Grecian ceremonies celebrating Dionysus, also known as Bacchus in Roman mythology, would heavily rely on these substances in their ceremonies. An ancient Roman Senate decree termed the *Senatus consultum de Bacchanalibus* written in 186 BC goes into significant detail regarding Rome's concern about worrisome practices spreading deeper into their territory from Greek colonies that included heavy substance use and concerning sexual activities connected to the festivals of Bacchus [111].

While some religious ceremonies involve use of mind-altering substances by participants others involve use of mind-altering substances by a central figure. First recorded in 1672, the term "shaman" was utilized to describe an individual who dramatically performed in public to help or harm others. A shaman is generally defined as an individual who interfaces with worlds beyond reach of others and may facilitate interactions between our world and others. Performances may include theatrical spiritual ceremonies where the shaman utilizes mind-altering substances to alter their own state of consciousness and dialogue or be possessed by otherwise unreachable entities. Such individuals would not be limited to any one kind of religion and the term has been expanded to include a variety of spiritual practices where the practitioner would undergo altered states of consciousness and may be characterized by a state of ecstatic excitement [3].

One such religious group based out of Bronze Age Crete is known as the Minoan cult or religion and is believed through consumption of psychoactive substances to have facilitated ritual possession. While specific substances utilized are unclear, opium and alcohol would have been available to them at the time [3].

Psychometric Instruments

Mental health evaluators may be tasked with evaluating individuals with connections to cult involvement for a variety of reasons. Perhaps they are conducting a general mental health evaluation to provide a review of possible mental health symptoms or disorders, exploring family dynamics and relationships, risk assessment, and personality assessment, or answering questions posed by criminal or civil courts. For purposes of substance use, mental health professionals may utilize a variety of instruments to help inform their clinical evaluations. Frequently utilized screening instruments for substance use include those we list next.

Addiction Severity Index

The Addiction Severity Index is a semistructured interview that assesses medical status, employment and support, drug use, alcohol use, legal status, family/social status, and psychiatric status. Administration of the index takes approximately one hour and helps administrators better understand potential problems with substance use in the evaluee [112].

Alcohol Use Disorders Identification Test

The Alcohol Use Disorder Identification Test is a 10-item screening questionnaire developed by the World Health Organization to help determine whether alcohol drinking habits may negatively affect an individual's health [113].

CAGE Substance Abuse Screening Tool

The CAGE tool screens for potential problems with alcohol use by asking four questions. The acronym is derived from four questions that ask whether the individual felt that they should Cut down on their use, whether others' criticism of use has Annoyed them, whether they have felt Guilty about their drinking, or if they have ever had a drink in the morning to steady their nerves or get rid of a hangover (Eye-opener) [114]. The CAGE-AID is an adapted screening version that explores problematic alcohol and other drugs of abuse.

Substance Use Brief Screen

The Substance Use Brief Screen is a brief, self-administered tool that may help to screen for and identify problematic use of a variety of substances including tobacco, alcohol, and illicit and prescription drugs [115].

Drug Abuse Screening Test

The Drug Abuse Screening Test (DAST) is a 28-item screening instrument that may be completed by the evaluee on their own or administered in an interview format. A shorter version, the DAST-10, is a self-report instrument derived from the lengthier DAST [116].

Summary

Many different patterns of substance use exist between different group factions including those that may or may not be considered "cults." As has been illustrated in this chapter, some new religious movements such as the Divine Light Mission and the Unification Church have attitudes opposed to the use of drugs. While members of such groups may have had high drug use upon joining, the cultic environment appeared to have a protective effect on drug use in certain instances. Conversely, other religious cults, such as Anne Hamilton-Byrne's The Family, may utilize drugs as a central part of their practices. On the extreme end, as in The Family, Jonestown, and the Manson Family, drugs may be used as a form of control and coercion. Drug use is also common among terrorist groups and some drug traffickers have coopted religious imagery from folk religions, such as Santa Muerte worship, in their group practices. Taken together, cult membership alone cannot be used to predict whether a given individual abuses psychoactive substances, nor can the downstream effects of promoting abstinence or drug use be encompassed in any one generalized narrative. When assessing a cult member in a clinical or forensic context then, careful attention should be paid to collecting a full and detailed substance use history and inquiring about their particular cult's practices and attitudes concerning substance use. The examples illustrated in this chapter depict the wide range of possible orientations to drug use that may appear in cults and cult members.

Key Points

- There are many different patterns of drug use within cults.
- Membership in a cult does not in and of itself predict drug use.
- Few groups are organized exclusively around the use of a drug as their central tenet, though their use may be incidental or incorporated in certain practices.
- Drug use is common in nonreligious cult-like organizations.
- Drugs can be used as a method of controlling or coercing cult members.

1. M Baba. God in a pill? Sufism Reoriented. 1966. Reproduced online (2020) by Avatar Meher Baba Trust. https://avatarmeherbabatrust.org/wp-content/uploads/2021/12/God-in-a-Pill.pdf
2. D Hillman. Drugs, suppositories, and cult worship in antiquity. In: P Wexler, editor. *Toxicology in antiquity*. 2nd ed. Academic Press; 2019. p. 335–42.
3. CJ Tully, S Crooks. Dropping ecstasy? Minoan cult and the tropes of shamanism. *Time and Mind*. 2015;8:129–58.
4. FR Dannaway. Strange fires, weird smokes and psychoactive combustibles: entheogens and incense in ancient traditions. *Journal of Psychoactive Drugs*. 2010;42:485–97.
5. W La Barre. Primitive psychotherapy in Native American cultures: peyotism and confession. *Journal of Abnormal and Social Psychology*. 1947;42:294–309.

6. W La Barre. A cultist drug-addiction in an Indian alcoholic. *Bulletin of the Menninger Clinic.* 1941;5:40–46.
7. WN Pahnke. Drugs and mysticism. *International Journal of Parapsychology.* 1966;8:295–313.
8. KH Berger. *Similarities between chemical or psychological addiction and cult membership: treatment for cult exit.* Master of Arts Counseling Psychology. Pacifica Graduate Institute; 2022.
9. M Rousselet, O Duretete, JB Hardouin, M Grall-Bronnec. Cult membership: what factors contribute to joining or leaving? *Psychiatry Research.* 2017;257:27–33.
10. RB Simmonds. Conversion or addiction: consequences of joining a Jesus movement group. *American Behavioral Scientist.* 1977;20:909–24.
11. PL Myers. Cult and cult-like pathways out of adolescent addiction. *Journal of Child and Adolescent Substance Abuse.* 1991;1:115–37.
12. M Farrell. Mass suicide using poison. In: *Criminology of poisoning contexts: warfare, terrorism, assassination and other homicides.* Palgrave MacMillan; 2020. p. 147–70.
13. JE Dimsdale. Heaven's Gate: beliefs or delusions? In: *Dark persuasion: a history of brainwashing from Pavlov to social media.* Yale University Press; 2021. p. 184–201.
14. PL Bunker, LJ Campbell, RJ Bunker. Torture, beheadings, and narcocultos. *Small Wars & Insurgencies.* 2010;21:145–78.
15. M Galanter, P Buckley, A Deutsch, R Rabkin, J Rabkin. Large group influence for decreased drug use: findings from two contemporary religious sects. *American Journal of Drug and Alcohol Abuse.* 1980;7:291–304.
16. JM Curtis, MJ Curtis. Factors related to susceptibility and recruitment by cults. *Psychological Reports.* 1993;73:451–60.
17. SV Levine, NE Salter. Youth and contemporary religious movements: psychosocial findings. *Canadian Psychiatric Association Journal.* 1976;21:411–20.
18. SV Levine. Cults and mental health: clinical conclusions. *Canadian Journal of Psychiatry.* 1981;26:534–39.
19. JG Melton. Divine Light Mission. In: *Encyclopedic handbook of cults in America.* Garland Publishing; 1986. p. 141–46.
20. M Galanter. A charismatic religious sect: the Divine Light Mission. In: *Cults: faith, healing, and coercion.* Oxford University Press; 1999. p. 19–33.
21. M Galanter. An elaborated folie à deux. In: *Cults: faith, healing, and coercion.* Oxford University Press; 1999. p. 178–79.
22. SV Levine. Role of psychiatry in the phenomenon of cults. *Canadian Journal of Psychiatry.* 1979;24:593–603.
23. M Galanter. A religious sect: the Unification Church. In: *Cults: faith, healing, and coercion.* Oxford University Press; 1999. p. 122–66.
24. GH Stephenson. Medicine and contemporary cultism. *Canadian Medical Association Journal.* 1978;118:1326–28.
25. M Galanter. The cult as a social system. In: *Cults: faith, healing, and coercion.* Oxford University Press; 1999. p. 92–109.
26. F Sontag. The author's questions and replies of Sun Myung Moon. In: *Sun Myung Moon and the Unification Church.* Abingdon; 1977. p. 127–59.
27. M Blake. The fall of the House of Moon. The New Republic. 2013 Nov 12. https://newrepublic.com/article/115512/unification-church-profile-fall-house-moon
28. MT Singer. The "Moonie" makeover. In: *Cults in our midst: the continuing fight against their hidden menace.* Jossey Bass; 2003. p. 345–48.
29. S Sovatsky. Clinical forms of love inspired by Meher Baba's mast work and the awe of infinite consciousness. *Journal of Transpersonal Psychology.* 2004;36:134–49.
30. T Robbins. Eastern mysticism and the resocialization of drug users: the Meher

Baba cult. *Journal for the Scientific Study of Religion*. 1969;8:308–17.

31. T Robbins, D Anthony. Getting straight with Meher Baba: a study of mysticism, drug rehabilitation and postadolescent role conflict. *Journal for the Scientific Study of Religion*. 1972;11:122–40.
32. RA Ross. Growing cult awareness. In: *Cults inside out: how people get in and can get out*. CreateSpace Independent Publishing Platform; 2014. p. 1–56.
33. M Galanter. AA offshoots and Synanon. In: *Cults: faith, healing, and coercion*. Oxford University Press; 1999. p. 222–25.
34. MT Singer. Threatening legal suits. In: *Cults in our midst: the continuing fight against their hidden menace*. Jossey Bass; 2003. p. 209–40.
35. M Novak. The man who fought the Synanon cult and won. Gizmodo. 2014 Sep 27. https://gizmodo.com/the-man-who-fought-cults-and-won-1634267961
36. W Winslow. Synanon revisited. *MANAS Journal*. 1961;14:1–6.
37. MT Singer. Persecuting therapists and lawyers. In: *Cults in our midst: the continuing fight against their hidden menace*. Jossey Bass; 2003. p. 229–31.
38. M Galanter. Altered consciousness. In: *Cults: faith, healing, and coercion*. Oxford University Press; 1999. p. 60–76.
39. M Galanter, R Rabkin, J Rabkin, A Deutsch. The "Moonies": a psychological study of conversion and membership in a contemporary religious sect. *American Journal of Psychiatry*. 1979;136:165–70.
40. M Galanter. Group cohesiveness. In: *Cults: faith, healing, and coercion*. Oxford University Press; 1999. p. 15–33.
41. M Galanter. Biology and behavior. In: *Cults: faith, healing, and coercion*. Oxford University Press; 1999. p. 79–91.
42. CM Cusack. Anne Hamilton-Byrne and the Family: charisma, criminality, and media in the construction of an Australian "cult" leader. *Nova Religio*. 2020;24:31–54.
43. C Johnston. Family ties. *Sydney Morning Herald*. 2017 Feb 9. www.smh.com.au/interactive/2017/family-ties
44. N Jolly. 'I was raised in Australia's most violent and depraved cult.' News.com.au. 2019 Feb 24. www.news.com.au/lifestyle/real-life/true-stories/i-was-raised-in-australias-most-violent-and-depraved-cult/news-story/dbe5b9ea8d14f1b8ffb8ed223b32c122
45. P Van Sant. The Family: a cult revealed. CBS News. 2018 Feb 24. www.cbsnews.com/news/48-hours-inside-the-family-cult-australia-anne-hamilton-byrne
46. E David. From the archives, 1987: police raid on secretive sect "The Family." *The Age*. 2019 Jun 14. www.theage.com.au/national/victoria/from-the-archives-1987-police-raid-on-secretive-sect-the-family-20190614-p51xtp.html
47. C Sutton. Children of the damned: how my mother gave me to a sinister cult as a baby. *The Daily Telegraph*. 2018 Aug 21. www.dailytelegraph.com.au/lifestyle/children-of-the-damned-how-my-mother-gave-me-to-a-sinister-cult-as-a-baby/news-story/3b01ba73c3d7ba80e7b8d2be35a883df
48. A Haworth. Growing up with The Family: inside Anne Hamilton Byrne's sinister cult. *The Guardian*. 2016 Nov 20. www.theguardian.com/film/2016/nov/20/growing-up-with-the-family-inside-anne-hamilton-byrnes-sinister-cult
49. WB Treml. Mom's help for ragged tramp leads son to dedicate his life to others. *Richmond Palladium*. 1953. https://digitaljonestown.library.drake.edu/son-dedicates-life-to-others-transcript/
50. DJ Flynn. *Cult city: Jim Jones, Harvey Milk, and 10 days that shook San Francisco*. ISI Books; 2018.
51. R Moore. Peoples Temple. https://wrldrels.org/2016/10/08/peoples-temple
52. L Fondakowski. *Stories from Jonestown*. University of Minnesota Press; 2013.
53. D Chidester. *Salvation and suicide: Jim Jones, the Peoples Temple, and Jonestown*. Indiana University Press; 1991.

54. T Reiterman. Reporter's 1978 account of deadly ambush, Jonestown tragedy. AP News. 2018 Nov 14. https://apnews.com/article/north-america-us-news-south-america-in-state-wire-ca-state-wire-eda81af2599d485ab09eb39d72754ade

55. Jonestown: The Life and Death of Peoples Temple, November 18, 1978. PBS. n.d. www.pbs.org/wgbh/americanexperience/features/jonestown-nov-18-1978

56. J Scheeres. Jonestown doctor works out how to kill everyone with cyanide. Newsweek. 2021 Nov 8. www.newsweek.com/jonestown-revisited-part-8-doctor-pig-cyanide-1646809

57. R Moore, AB Pinn, MR Sawyer. *Peoples Temple and Black religion in America.* Indiana University Press; 2004.

58. V Bugliosi, C Gentry. *Helter skelter.* W. W. Norton & Company, Incorporated; 2001.

59. J Guinn. *Manson: the life and times of Charles Manson.* Simon & Schuster; 2013.

60. M Petruzzello. Where did the word hippie come from? www.britannica.com/story/where-did-the-word-hippie-come-from

61. LB Bosky. *The Scribner encyclopedia of American lives: the 1960s.* Thematic Series. American Library Association; 2003. p. 43–45.

62. BS Woodard. *The Scribner encyclopedia of American lives: the 1960s.* Thematic Series, 92–93. American Library Association; 2003.

63. AJ Atchison, KM Heide. Charles Manson and the family: the application of sociological theories to multiple murder. *International Journal of Offender Therapy and Comparative Criminology.* 2011;55:771–98.

64. G Brich. Key figures in Manson case: cult disciples, rich and famous. *The Telegraph.* 2019 Aug 6. www.telegraph.co.uk/news/2019/08/06/key-figures-manson-case-cult-disciples-rich-famous

65. J Kendall. Addict can be programmed to kill, witness tells Manson jury: MANSON TRIAL. *Los Angeles Times* (1923–1995). 1971 Mar 5. www.proquest.com/historical-newspapers/addict-can-be-programmed-kill-witness-tells/docview/156685389/se-2

66. E Simons. Faith, fanaticism, and fear: Aum Shinrikyo – the birth and death of a terrorist organization. *Forensic Examiner.* 2006;15:37–45.

67. Y Kogo. Aum shinrikyo. *Self & Society.* 2003;31:25–41.

68. H Akimoto. The Aum cult leader Asahara's mental deviation and its social relations. *Psychiatry and Clinical Neurosciences.* 2006;60:3–8.

69. TS Albhlal. Terrorism and contemporary religious cults: Jim Jones, Shoko Asahara and Abu Bakr Al-Baghdadi. *Journal of Politics and Law.* 2021;14.

70. M Juergensmeyer, M Kitts. Shoko Asahara. In: *Princeton readings in religion and violence.* Princeton University Press; 2011. p. 75–81.

71. M Galanter. Aum Shinrikyo. In: *Cults: faith, healing, and coercion.* Oxford University Press; 1999. p. 172–76.

72. CW Hughes. Japan's Aum Shinrikyo, the changing nature of terrorism, and the post-cold war security agenda. *Global Change, Peace & Security.* 1998;10:39–60.

73. A Spaeth, M Kunii. Engineer of doom. *Time.* 1995;145:57.

74. I Reader. Murder on the Tokyo subway: nerve centres, religion and violence. *Space & Polity.* 2013;17:377–92.

75. K Kiyoyasu. Aum Shinrikyō: society begets an aberration. *Japan Quarterly.* 1995;42:376–83.

76. RJ Lifton. Aum Shinrikyo. In: *Losing reality: on cults, cultism, and the mindset of political and religious zealotry.* The New Press; 2019. N.p.

77. BT Davies. In Mexico, a death cult thrives. In: D Henningfield, editor. *Death and dying.* Greenhaven Press; 2010. p. 175–80.

78. K Kingsbury, A Chesnut. Not just a narcosaint: Santa Muerte as matron saint of the Mexican drug war. *International Journal of Latin American Religions.* 2020;4:25–47.

79. K Kingsbury, RA Chesnut. Holy death in the time of coronavirus: Santa Muerte, the salubrious saint. *International Journal of Latin American Religions.* 2020;4:194–217.

80. Anonymous. Death in holy orders: a Mexican cult. *The Economist.* 2010;394:46.

81. TM Kail. Types of narco-cults. In: *Narco-cults: understanding the use of Afro-Caribbean and Mexican religious cultures in the drug wars.* CRC Press; 2015. p. 43–60.

82. K Kingsbury. Death is women's work: Santa Muerte, a folk saint and her female followers. *International Journal of Latin American Religions.* 2020;5:43–63.

83. K Kingsbury. At death's door in Cancun: sun, sea, and Santa Muerte. *Anthropology and Humanism.* 2021;46:244–65.

84. TM Kail. Preface. In: *Narco-cults: understanding the use of Afro-Caribbean and Mexican religious cultures in the drug wars.* CRC Press; 2015. p. xvii–xviii.

85. D Bromley. Santa Muerte as emerging dangerous religion? *Religions.* 2016;7:65–78.

86. RA Kristensen. La Santa Muerte in Mexico City: the cult and its ambiguities. *Journal of Latin American Studies.* 2015;47:543–66.

87. TM Kail. Narco-cults. In: *Narco-cults: understanding the use of Afro-Caribbean and Mexican religious cultures in the drug wars.* CRC Press; 2015. p. 43–59.

88. *United States* v. *Medina-Copete* (2014) 757 F3d 1092.

89. BI Popoola, KA Alao. Secret cults in Nigerian institutions of higher learning. *Journal of School Violence.* 2008;5:73–85.

90. Africa Eye. The ultra-violent cult that became a global mafia. BBC News. 2021 Dec 13. www.bbc.com/news/world-africa-59614595

91. MU Nnam, EJ Owan, MS Otu, G-P Okechukwu, MJ Eteng, P Offu, et al. '. . .Even correctional institutions are not safe': a qualitative study of campus secret cults/cultism among selected inmates in a custodial centre. *International Journal of Law, Crime and Justice.* 2022;68.

92. I Eguavoen. Killer cults on campus: secrets, security and services among Nigerian students. *Sociologus.* 2008;58:1–25.

93. GC Nche. Cultism in Rivers State: causes, faith-based organizations' role and the setbacks. *Transformation: An International Journal of Holistic Mission Studies.* 2020;37:18–36.

94. AS Olanrewaju, OB Dominic, OA Julius, A Funmilola. Influence of psychopathy and cultic disposition on attitude toward violence among students of tertiary institutions in Ekiti State. *Asian Social Science.* 2014;10:258.

95. I Alumona, L Amusan. Youth cultism, crime and lethal violence in Nigerian cities. *African Renaissance.* 2019;16:11–29.

96. FG Paulley. Secret cult and drug abuse as social problems in Nigerian education system: the way forward. *Journal of Education and Practice.* 2014;5:173–84.

97. S Hutchinson, P O'Malley. A crime-terror nexus? Thinking on some of the links between terrorism and criminality. *Studies in Conflict and Terrorism.* 2007;30:1095–107.

98. V Asal, HB Milward, EW Schoon. When terrorists go bad: analyzing terrorist organizations' involvement in drug smuggling. *International Studies Quarterly.* 2015;59:112–23.

99. LI Shelley, JT Picarelli. Methods not motives: implications of the convergence of international organized crime and terrorism. *Police Practice & Research.* 2002;3:305–18.

100. R Ehrenfeld. *Funding evil: how terrorism is financed – and how to stop it.* Bonus Books, Inc.; 2005.

101. BF Bubolz, P Simi. The problem of overgeneralization: the case of mental health problems and U.S. violent white supremacists. *American Behavioral Scientist.* 2019.

102. P Simi, R Futrell. Negotiating white power activist stigma. *Social Problems.* 2009;56:89–110.

103. M Katselou, I Papoutsis, P Nikolaou, S Qammaz, C Spiliopoulou, S Athanaselis. Fenethylline (captagon) abuse – local problems from an old drug become universal. *Basic & Clinical Pharmacology & Toxicology*. 2016;119:133–40.

104. D Koehler. Violent extremism, mental health and substance abuse among adolescents: towards a trauma psychological perspective on violent radicalization and deradicalization. *Journal of Forensic Psychiatry & Psychology*. 2020;31:455–72.

105. RC Cottrell. *Sex, drugs, and rock 'n' roll: the rise of America's 1960s counterculture*. Rowman & Littlefield; 2015.

106. B Ramm. The LSD cult that transformed America. BBC.com. 2017 Jan 12. www.bbc.com/culture/article/20170112-the-lsd-cult-that-terrified-america

107. R Dallos. Dr. Leary starts new 'religion' with 'sacramental' use of LSD. *The New York Times*. 1966 Sep 20. www.nytimes.com/1966/09/20/archives/dr-leary-starts-new-religion-with-sacramental-use-of-lsd.html

108. DR Lander. Start your own religion: New York State's acid churches. *Nova Religio*. 2011;14:64–80.

109. DA Halperin. Cults and drug use. In: R Carson-DeWitt, editor. *Encyclopedia of drugs, alcohol & addictive behavior*. 3rd ed. Macmillan Reference USA; 2009. p. 377–79.

110. D Dupuis. Psychedelics as tools for belief transmission: set, setting, suggestibility, and persuasion in the ritual use of hallucinogens. *Frontiers in Psychology*. 2021;12:730031.

111. P Wexler. *Entheogens in ancient times: wine and the rituals of Dionysus*. Elsevier Science & Technology; 2018.

112. AT McLellan, L Luborsky, GE Woody, CP O'Brien. An improved diagnostic evaluation instrument for substance abuse patients: the Addiction Severity Index. *The Journal of Nervous and Mental Disease*. 1980;168:26–33.

113. TF Babor, JC Higgins-Biddle, JB Saunders, MG Monteiro. AUDIT: the Alcohol Use Disorders Identification Test. In: *Guidelines for use in primary care*. World Health Organization; 2001. p. 17.

114. JA Ewing. Detecting alcoholism: the CAGE questionnaire. *JAMA: The Journal of the American Medical Association*. 1984;252:1905–7.

115. J McNeely, SM Strauss, R Saitz, CM Cleland, JJ Palamar, J Rotrosen, MN Gourevitch. A brief patient self-administered substance use screening tool for primary care: two-site validation study of the Substance Use Brief Screen (SUBS). *The American Journal of Medicine*. 2015;128:784.e9–.e19.

116. HA Skinner. The drug abuse screening test. *Addictive Behaviors*. 1982;7:363–71.

Chapter 13

Treatment

Steven Hassan, Zachary Schwartz, and Austin Blum

"When you meet the friendliest people you have ever known, who introduce you to the most loving group of people you have ever encountered, and you find the leader to be the most inspired, caring, compassionate and understanding person you have ever met, and then you learn the cause of the group is something you never dared hope could be accomplished, and all of this sounds too good to be true, it probably is too good to be true! Don't give up your education, your hopes and ambitions to follow a rainbow."
– *Jeanne Mills, Peoples Temple survivor*

Introduction

This chapter explores the psychological impact of cult involvement and the therapeutic strategies beneficial for recovery. Cults often employ intense coercive persuasion, resulting in significant psychological distress, including anxiety, depression, dissociation, and, in some cases, psychosis. Central to the discussion are theoretical models of authoritarian control and the concept of undue influence [1, 2]. These concepts provide critical insights into the mechanisms of cult control and offer a framework for therapeutic intervention. As models, they aid in understanding the identity disturbances and dissociative reactions often experienced by former cult members.

The chapter also highlights the importance of psychoeducation and learning about the nature and tactics of cults as a crucial component of treatment. Some fundamental psychotherapeutic approaches and strategies are briefly reviewed while calling for further research to identify the most effective interventions specific to affected individuals. There are unique challenges in treating former cult members – those born into or raised in one as well as those recruited. Extrinsic and intrinsic barriers to treatment including availability of resources, limited understanding and appreciation of cultist phenomena among clinicians, and indoctrinated distrust of mental health professionals are explored.

The chapter concludes that while cult involvement can lead to severe psychological distress, therapeutic interventions have the potential to support recovery.

Case Vignette: Laura

After 13 years of leadership in a Bible cult, Laura was admitted in and out of psychiatric hospitals for the next 11 years. She engaged in self-harm and attempted suicide multiple times. Laura contacted one author of this chapter (Hassan) after reading his book, *Combating Cult Mind Control* [3], because the name of her former church was described in the book as an authoritarian cult. After consulting with her treatment providers, Hassan was asked to do whatever he could to assist. The referring psychiatrist told Hassan that Laura was the most functional and least functional patient in her 30-year career.

Over those 11 years, Laura underwent multiple medication trials and had been given multiple diagnoses, including borderline personality disorder, bipolar disorder, and schizoaffective disorder. Her treating providers had scantily asked her details about her "church," even though she had described it as a cult that had significantly impacted her mental health. Nor had they researched the group independently. Had they researched the group, they would have found scores of articles, television exposés, and websites describing many of the group's exploits and concerning behaviors. Additionally, these professionals lacked training regarding dissociative responses potentially caused by involvement in such a group.

After approximately 24 hours of intensive counseling, Laura better understood the source of her suicidal and self-harm ideations largely resulted from her "cult identity," that was programmed with phobias and cult beliefs which operated in an unconscious manner. Generally, the cult had programmed her to believe that by leaving the cult, she had lost her ability to be saved and would remain in "Satan's world."

Appropriate psychoeducation around thought reform, brainwashing, and how cults stereotypically operate, provided a foundation for her to recover. Having an intellectual toolbox based on understanding Chinese Communist thought reform programs, Laura was able to reclaim her personal power and help herself heal. Further, psychoeducation involved learning how to trust herself by being back in one's own body and being present. By taking this approach, one can better recognize how one's younger self could have been exploited to prevent the person from accessing their authentic self. This process of exploitation, if the person was unequipped with psychoeducation, would enable one to be deceived and incrementally indoctrinated into the cult. In Laura's case, she was told her group's members were the only real Christians who understood the Bible. In their ideology, there was no other legitimate Church on Earth. In this approach of psychoeducation, Laura proceeded to access her cult identity by reimagining and redoing traumatic experiences. For example, she reimagined being forcibly raped by her cult-approved husband, being told she needed to submit to his desires.

Laura learned how to trust her own self by being back in her body and present. She learned a vital processing technique of imagining "if she knew then what she knows now," her younger self would have never allowed her authentic self to be deceived and incrementally indoctrinated into the cult. Laura understood why her previous dialectical behavioral therapy program was helping with symptom management, but ultimately was a negative as it would trigger her cult self, due to the rules that mirrored cult-shunning behavior. A number of years later, she no longer required medication, earned a graduate degree, married, and had children. She later assisted in providing a course to inform clinicians about the follies of her early treatment and the later approaches that were more beneficial.

Background and Precedent

Historically, psychologists, sociologists, and clinicians have debated the degree to which cultic environments are psychologically harmful and whether former members are likely to require psychiatric treatment.

Psychologists Margaret Singer and Edgard Schein and psychiatrists Robert Jay Lifton and Louis Jolyon West were among the first to observe, based on their experience treating former cult members and studies on Chinese Communist thought reform, that cultic environments could result in significant psychopathology [4, 5]. Lifton and Schein each published books in 1961, *Thought Reform and the Psychology of Totalism: A Study of Brainwashing in China* [6] and *Coercive Persuasion: A Socio-psychological analysis of the "Brainwashing" of American Civilian Prisoners by the Chinese Communists* [7], respectively. West later coauthored an article with psychologist and former cult member Paul Martin: "Pseudo-identity and the treatment of personality change in victims of captivity and cults" [8]. Martin founded Wellspring, a rehabilitation facility in Ohio where his team offered a two-week program to help former cult members learn about social psychology and mind control, process their former therapies, and access former members and other educational resources. Meadowhaven, based in Massachusetts, was a second facility for former cult members. Most people who leave cults they were born into have no one to turn to for help and have little formal education or life skills to interact in society. The founders, Reverend Bob and Judy Pardon, were willing to help former members for much longer periods of time.

However, during this same period, so-called cult-sympathizers such as Galanter et al. argued for the potential benefits of membership in – as they called them – "new religious movements," suggesting that these movements could provide healthy social bonding, protection against negative behaviors such as substance use, and ultimately lead to an improved emotional state [9, 10, 11]. According to these cult sympathizer studies, the incidence of psychopathology among individuals who had left such movements was estimated to be relatively low, with little need for formal treatment [12].

Over the following decades, evidence for the inherent harmfulness of cultic environments would continue to mount, with larger and higher-quality studies suggesting a high incidence of anxiety, depression, dissociation, and even psychotic symptoms among former members [13, 14]. In 2000, in the most well-conducted review of the available evidence to date, Aronoff et al. argued that psychiatric symptoms among former cult members are common and often severe [15]. Furthermore, they attributed these symptoms directly to cults, as they found little evidence to suggest that psychiatric symptomatology is initially more prevalent among individuals recruited into cults. Most manifested psychiatric illnesses seem to occur in individuals who have left or are leaving cults rather than active members. However, cult members, when they have problems, are often asked to leave the group if they can no longer function to recruit, make money, or perform cult chores.

Dennis Tourish, an esteemed scholar in dysfunctional leadership and cult phenomena, draws parallels between the operations of Elizabeth Holmes and her company Theranos, and dynamics typically observed in cult-like organizations [16]. We highlight this, as it drives home the point that cult phenomena are not limited to religious environments and may be shared in corporate and other environments. For Tourish, the corporate environment was imbued with elements of cult practices, including stringent surveillance, compliance enforcement, and grueling working conditions. Manipulative techniques, such as grandiose displays and an authoritarian hold on power, are seen in a variety of environments. While the collapse of Theranos underscores the need for effective corporate governance in various settings, it also exemplifies a cult-like tale of power concentration, highlights the imperative to combat unethical influence, and shows how many, rather than simply the desperate and vulnerable, can fall prey to such coercion [2].

"Malignant narcissism," a term coined by social psychologist Erich Fromm in 1964, refers to a severe form of narcissism often seen in authoritarian leaders and destructive cult figures [17]. It exhibits grandiose self-perception, fantasies of power, constant need for praise, entitlement, lack of empathy, exploitative behavior, and antisocial tendencies, including lying, sadism, harassment, violence, paranoia, and distrust. Malignant narcissism is evident in leaders and its effects pervade the group. It is one major aspect of what makes leaving these groups so difficult. Recognizing these behaviors has helped people escape abusive relationships. Though not officially recognized in the *Diagnostic and Statistical Manual of Mental Disorders* [18], the concept has been used by researchers and scholars to explain and understand destructive leadership and cult dynamics.

When we discuss treating former cult members, we focus on groups with leaders possessing the quality of malignant narcissism. This authoritarian leadership quality does not recognize followers as individuals but rather wishes to create them in their own image. The motivation of these cult leaders conflicts with a person's natural desire to connect mind and body and then to control both. However, overcoming the grips of malignant narcissism is challenging for many.

Still, recognizing that not every individual leaving cultic environments will develop psychiatric illness in the same manner or to the same degree is important. Just as a continuum of authoritarianism and undue influence exists, not all cults or involvement in differing cultic environments carry the same risk of provoking psychological harm. Likewise, not all individuals who enter cults will be equally predisposed to develop psychiatric symptoms, as is the case with any population exposed to a traumatic stressor [19].

Finally, individuals presenting for medical or psychological treatment may not always be aware that they have been in a cultic environment. In other cases, they are aware that they have been in a cultic environment in the past but may not grasp the psychological significance of this and the degree to which it contributes to their current distress. Making this connection explicit through psychoeducation can be profoundly important for treatment and is, in a sense, the backbone of the many different psychotherapeutic treatments discussed in this chapter.

Our goal in this chapter is to discuss psychotherapeutic techniques clinicians can use to help survivors of cults empower themselves to overcome the destructive influence of these leaders and the organizations they have created.

Models of Influence and Control

BITE Model of Authoritarian Control

The BITE Model of Authoritarian Control and the Influence Continuum offer the first scientific model for evaluating the granular details of coercion. Based on Festinger's (1957) cognitive dissonance model, Hassan created a model that examines behavior, information, thought, and emotion control aimed at its extreme toward creating a cult pseudo-identity in the image of the cult leader or its ideology [1, 20]. This paradigm was based on the models of Lifton, Singer, and Schein that described the process of brainwashing and offers a theoretical framework to discriminate between ethical, healthy influence and destructive authoritarian control aimed at creating dependency and blind obedience.

- *Behavior control* includes sleep deprivation, control of food, and clothing, rigid rules and regulations – with punishment for infractions. In some cases, physical harm may be threatened against individuals or their family members.
- *Information control* includes deceptive recruitment such as outright lying and withholding or distorting vital information. There is no informed consent – therefore people "join" a group but have no appreciation of what the group represents. Excessive propaganda, censorship of former members, and critical information are just some of the tactics commonly employed. Common strategies of information control are monitoring and controlling individuals' time, along with the encouragement of spying and reporting on fellow believers. Further, personal information is manipulated to exert control, for instance, by exploiting past indiscretions or legal violations. Vulnerability to undue influence lies on the dissemination of propaganda, indoctrination, blackmail, and the restriction of access to critical information and former members who may challenge the group's leader, doctrine, or policies.
- *Thought control* involves teaching members thought-stopping techniques, the use of "thought-terminating cliches," a belief system of black/white, all/nothing, good/evil, and us versus them. Some groups change the names of their members to reinforce a sense of cult identity. Hypnotic methods are also often employed to internalize the group's belief system and behavioral norms.
- *Emotion control* aims to cultivate a sense of specialness and belonging, such as elitism, within a privileged group, while simultaneously utilizing guilt and fear techniques to motivate, indoctrinate, and control individuals. Initial attraction to such groups often capitalizes on awe and fervor, but over time, irrational fears and phobias are induced, often through hypnotic manipulation, leading to psychological entrapment. Emotional-stopping techniques are taught to suppress negative emotions, such as doubt, unhappiness, homesickness, pain, and suffering. Emotion control is largely centered around programming in guilt and fear to keep individuals obedient.

The Influence Continuum

The Influence Continuum builds on the BITE model, serving as a visualization tool to assess the spectrum of influence [2]. Emphasis is placed on respecting individuals' self-identity, autonomy, conscience, and informed consent. It promotes an internal locus of control, encouraging individuals to ask difficult questions and seek critical information. Furthermore, it values positive qualities such as creativity, compassion, love, and a sense of humor.

On the unethical and unhealthy side of the Continuum, there exists a dissociated self, molded by cult leaders or rigid ideologies, driven by concepts of fear, hate, dependency, dogma, and blind obedience. Individuals are instilled with fears that make it challenging for them to imagine leaving the group without adverse consequences. The dissociated self operates with an external locus of control. Ongoing research seeks to quantitatively analyze these factors. Figure 13.1 offers criteria to ascertain this range of influence.

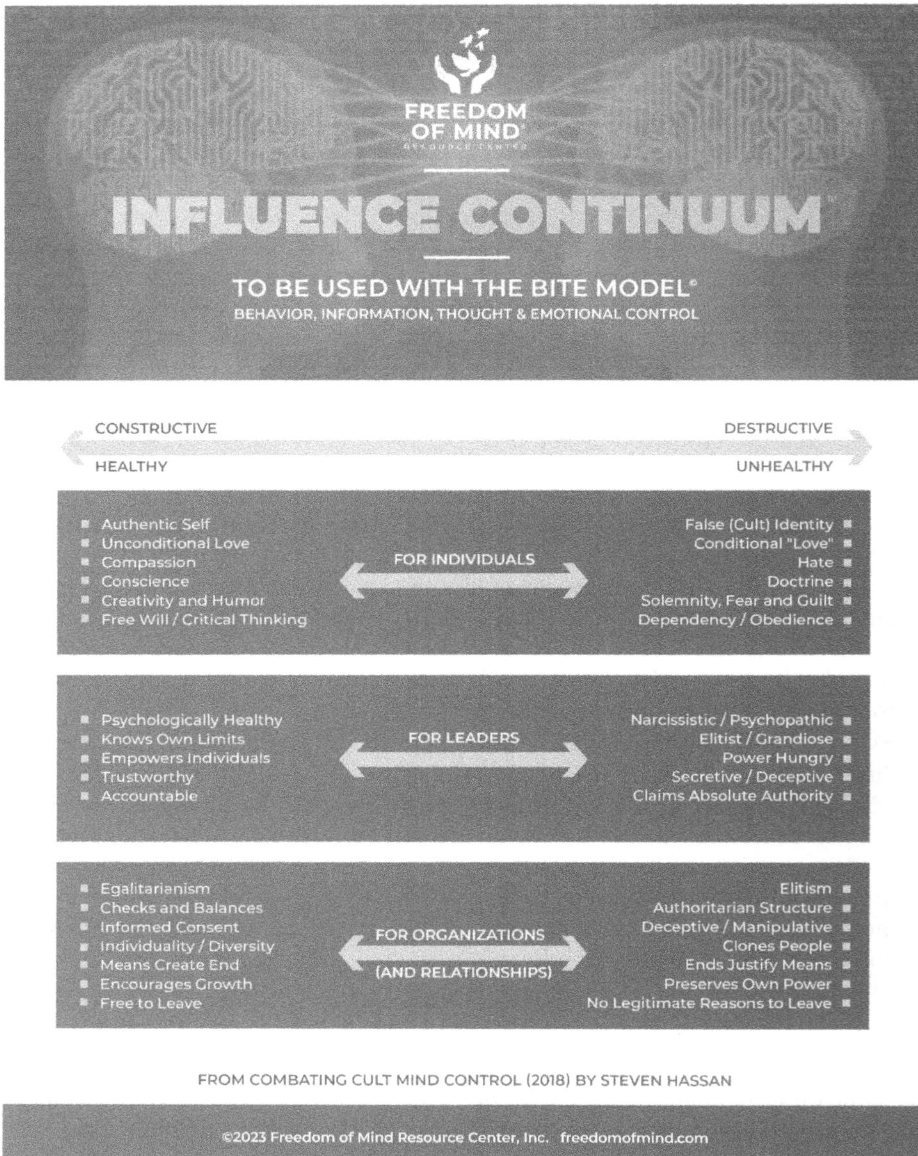

Figure 13.1 Influence Continuum

Indications for Treatment

Clinicians must understand that very few patients will present as clearly as Laura in the case vignette did, in specifically volunteering former membership in a cult. Many have not slept or cared for themselves for long periods of time. Many also have phobias about getting mental health assistance. Some groups program members to believe they will be raped, lobotomized, drugged, and incarcerated indefinitely. Clinicians must also realize that undue influence comes in many different forms: from an authoritarian parent that used corporal punishment, to an abusive and narcissistic partner, or a large group awareness training program or multilevel marketing group, to religious or political cults. It is vital when doing an intake to get a clear picture of the patient's current situation beyond just a family of origin inquiry. Open-ended and non-judgmental questions are often helpful. Questions that invite the person to maximally share as rapport and trust are developed are of the greatest use.

As background, we present some potential issues associated with cult involvement that may prompt treatment:

1. Extreme identity confusion
2. Dissociative states – "floating" (e.g., getting triggered back into cult mode)
3. Panic and anxiety attacks
4. Depression
5. Post-traumatic stress disorder (PTSD)
6. Psychosomatic symptoms (headaches, backaches, asthma, skin problems)
7. Problems with decision-making dependency
8. Impaired psychological development – loss of psychological power
9. Guilt
10. Fear and phobias
11. Sleep disorders/nightmares
12. Eating disorders
13. Sexual problems
14. Lack of trust/fear of intimacy and commitment with people/work
15. Harassment and threats
16. Grieving loss of friends and family especially in cults that have a shunning policy

The Challenge of Evidence-Based Treatment

Since the initial case reports by Singer and Clark, clinicians have been offering treatment to former cult members seeking relief from psychological distress. The challenge – for a textbook that seeks to take an evidence-based approach – is that few studies have systematically sought to evaluate these treatments for safety, efficacy, scalability, or other relevant treatment goals. Existing studies of treatments for cult-associated distress are dated and lack the methodological rigor now expected in the evaluation of medical or psychological interventions.

Still, it would be incorrect to say that *no* evidence exists whatsoever for the treatment of cult-associated distress. Consider, first, that cult-associated distress represents an *etiological* category rather than a *descriptive* category and is, as such, orthogonal to the symptom-based classifications of contemporary psychiatry (e.g., the DSM-5-TR). In other words, to the extent that cult-associated distress can be understood in terms of standard descriptive psychopathology, a large body of evidence already exists for treatment practices that are likely to be effective and safe. Furthermore, within the sparse early literature on cult treatment that does exist [3, 21, 22], recommended treatment practices often have considerable overlap with established evidence-based treatments for recognized psychiatric disorders – albeit using a different terminology and theoretical framework. For clinicians who wish to develop expertise in the field of distress stemming from cult involvement, we consider this early literature – by authors with years of direct experience working with cult victims – to be essential reading.

In summary, the approach will be to discuss the treatment of cult-associated distress in terms of standard descriptive psychopathology and its related evidence-based treatments. We will focus largely on psychotherapy since this is considered by most cult experts to be an essential part of treatment, and at least some evidence suggests that psychotherapy is effective in this context [14, 21, 22]. We will also provide recommendations on psychopharmacology, but as there are currently no controlled studies regarding the psychopharmacological treatment of cult-associated distress, these recommendations are bound to remain general.

Treatment

Before discussing intervention techniques, it is critical to note the key distinction between being born into a cult (second-generation members) and joining one later in life (first-generation members).

First-generation cult members are those who join a cult or religious group later in their lives. These individuals often have a precult identity that becomes suppressed or altered as they integrate into the cult environment [3]. Upon leaving the cult, first-generation members face the challenge of recovering their original, precult identity [3]. This process can be complicated by feelings of anger and betrayal as they come to realize the extent of the manipulation and control that they were subjected to within the cult.

Second-generation cult members, or those who were born into a cult or religious group, face a different set of challenges. Unlike first-generation members, these individuals do not have a precult identity to return to. Their religious identity is often their only identity, as it is all they have known from the beginning. Upon leaving a cult, second-generation members face the immense challenge of creating their identity from scratch – one that has little or nothing to do with their cult identity. This process involves not only distancing themselves from the beliefs and practices of the cult but also learning how to navigate relationships and societal norms outside of the cult environment.

Psychoeducation

It is important to note that virtually all psychotherapeutic modalities rely on some degree of psychoeducation, that is, imparting knowledge to clients/patients about how the mind works. A fundamental aspect of psychoeducation is understanding the mechanisms of psychological manipulation.

Indeed, we take the position that since it is *your* mind, you should control it. Psychoeducation is not about steering one toward this or that view. Conducting psychotherapy with cult victims should involve education not only about the mind itself – as an internal system – but also about the nature of cults and undue influence. For individuals experiencing cult-associated distress, the cultic environment has played an important causal role in the development of psychopathology; thus, knowledge of that environment also entails a kind of self-insight, which may prove highly therapeutic. This puts the responsibility on clinicians to gain more in-depth knowledge about cults – how they recruit, how they maintain control, and how they interact with members who have left or are attempting to leave – to share this knowledge with their clients.

Another related theme in psychoeducation is the development of self-awareness as it applies to critical thinking skills. Psychoeducation involves a process of self-reflection, encouraging individuals to reflect on their initial exposure to the group and evaluate their experiences through the lens of a given model (e.g., the BITE model). This process helps individuals regain control over their minds and lives. Aspects to consider include: (1) disconnecting from the group; (2) learning about mind control techniques; (3) seeking out critics and ex-members of the group; and (4) engaging in honest self-reflection.

Through psychoeducation, individuals are not only equipped with the knowledge and tools to resist cult indoctrination and recover from their experiences; they are also empowered to advocate for themselves and others who may be vulnerable to cult influence. Part of psychoeducation is teaching the healing power in encouraging those who have experienced cult involvement to share their stories, reach out to their family and friends, and contribute to the broader understanding and awareness of cult dynamics.

Sugarman discusses the benefits of hypnosis for individuals leaving cults and seeking empowerment [23]. He shows how hypnosis assists in being present and avoiding the resurgence of past phobias and indoctrination. To be clear, Sugarman emphasizes *ethical* hypnosis (not its unethical cousin), performed by experienced (not inexperienced) professionals, as a powerful tool for emotional well-being, concentration, and effectiveness in life.

Social work and counseling are two fields that often intersect due to their shared goal of helping individuals improve their well-being and functioning in society. While social work is a broad field that encompasses a wide range of services, counseling is a profession that focuses more specifically on helping individuals, couples, and families navigate mental health and life challenges.

Psychotherapy

The role of counseling in assisting former cult members is a complex and multifaceted one. It involves not only helping individuals understand and resist the manipulative tactics used by cults but also helping them heal from the emotional trauma of their cult experience and navigating the challenges of reintegration into society. As such, it requires a comprehensive understanding of cult dynamics, a compassionate and patient approach, and a commitment to supporting individuals in their journey toward healing and freedom.

As mentioned, undue influence refers to the manipulation of individuals' thoughts and behaviors. This culture often involves a complex system of beliefs, rituals, and norms that further entrench the individual in the cult's worldview. Counseling, in this context, can play a crucial role in helping former cult members navigate their way out of this manipulated reality. Through therapeutic techniques such as cognitive behavioral therapy, counselors can help individuals recognize the manipulative tactics used by the cult, challenge the cult's belief system, and develop healthier ways of thinking and behaving.

The manipulation of emotions can lead to a profound sense of confusion and disorientation, making it difficult for individuals to leave the cult and maintain their decision to stay away. Counseling can help individuals understand these emotional dynamics and develop healthier emotional patterns. Through techniques such as emotion-focused therapy, counselors can help individuals explore and process their emotions, develop emotional resilience, and build healthier relationships [24]. This emotional work can be particularly important in helping individuals heal from the trauma of their cult experience and build a sense of self-worth and autonomy.

By understanding the dynamics of undue influence, emotional manipulation, and power dynamics, counselors can provide effective support to individuals transitioning out of cults. This process includes helping them reconnect with their precult identity, building healthy relationships, and reintegrating into society. It also involves helping them process the trauma of their cult experience, deal with feelings of guilt and shame, and build a sense of hope and optimism for the future.

As society continues to grapple with the impact of cults, the role of counseling remains crucial in helping individuals regain their freedom of mind. It is through the therapeutic process that former cult members can heal from their experiences, regain their autonomy, and build a fulfilling life outside the cult.

Eye Movement Desensitization and Reprocessing

Eye movement desensitization and reprocessing (EMDR) is a psychotherapy treatment method developed by psychologist Francine Shapiro in the late 1980s [25]. Shapiro hypothesized that certain eye movements can reduce the intensity of disturbing thoughts under specific conditions. This led her to develop EMDR, a structured therapy that encourages the patient to briefly focus on a trauma memory while simultaneously experiencing bilateral stimulation, typically in the form of eye movements. Today, Shapiro's work has been instrumental in EMDR's recognition as an effective treatment for PTSD by organizations such as the American Psychiatric Association and the World Health Organization.

The therapy is based on the premise that the mind can heal from psychological trauma much as the body recovers from physical trauma. When traumatic memories are unprocessed, they can cause intense psychological symptoms. The therapy helps patients process these memories and, as a result, symptoms can decrease or disappear.

Expressive Therapies

Expressive therapies can be beneficial in the context of cult recovery, providing an avenue for individuals to articulate their experiences, process traumas, and regain control over their emotions and cognition. Furthermore, they offer an avenue for cult survivors to explore and rebuild their identities, a critical aspect of recovery given the extensive identity erosion experienced within cultic environments. As mentioned, cult survivors may experience dissociation, a coping mechanism during extreme stress or trauma involving detachment from thoughts, feelings, or identity [26]. Expressive therapies can aid in grounding individuals in the present moment and reintegrating dissociated experiences, which is essential for the healing process [27].

Dr. Laurence Sugarman's work shares the common theme of using self-regulatory therapies to promote healing and well-being. His work focuses on using hypnosis and biofeedback [23]. This approach aligns with the broader field of trauma therapy in emphasizing the power of the mind–body connection and the ability of individuals to tap into their own internal resources to promote healing.

As mentioned earlier, another type of expressive method includes asking former members to imagine how they might act differently if they knew *now* what they knew *then*. What would they have said to the recruiter? How would they have reacted to a certain feeling in the pit of their stomach? Who might have called to discuss something strange they observed?

Additional Counseling Resources

Counseling resources designed specifically for former cult members exist. We point the reader to two recent resources: the State of Israel's Ministry of Welfare and Social Services [27] and Gillie Jenkinson's *Walking Free from the Trauma of Coercive, Cultic and Spiritual Abuse: A Workbook for Recovery and Growth* [28], focused on identity and personal development; understanding cult dynamics; and recovery and healing.

Dissociative Disorders

Available data suggest an unusually high prevalence of dissociative symptoms among individuals who have left cult environments [15]. These symptoms may include depersonalization, derealization, selective amnesia, or even the sense of a separate self-identity. The latter should be distinguished from the development of "full-blown" dissociative identity disorder (DID), which is thought to arise almost exclusively in the setting of severe and sustained childhood trauma [29]. One particularly common dissociative symptom, estimated to occur in up to 75% of former cult members presenting for treatment [21], is referred to in cult literature as "floating." With "floating," individuals may find themselves, with certain triggers, suddenly reverting to the thoughts, feelings, and behaviors of their prior identity within the cult in a depersonalized manner. Although the concept of "floating" has been poorly operationalized and has not been assessed for construct validity, it is widely reported in early studies of cult psychopathology.

The available research does not clarify whether the high incidence of dissociative symptoms in former cult members is due to the overall high prevalence of psychiatric distress, or whether these symptoms have a unique causal link with cultic environments. A number of cult treatment experts favor the latter view, in which the stresses of the cultic environment necessitate the development of a separate "cult self." The separation between this cult self and the noncult self is, in this view, the cause of dissociative symptoms such as "floating." Interestingly, the only explicit mention of cults in DSM-5-TR occurs in the dissociative disorder subsection, under *Other Specified Dissociative Disorder, identity disturbance due to prolonged and intense coercive persuasion*. This diagnosis is further elaborated, wherein the text states: "Individuals who have been subjected to intense coercive persuasion (e.g., brainwashing, thought reform, indoctrination while captive, torture, long-term political imprisonment, recruitment by sects/cults or by terror organizations) may present with prolonged changes in, or conscious questioning of, their identity" [18]. Unfortunately, the DSM provides little else in terms of descriptive phenomenology of dissociative symptoms in cult members; however, the inclusion of this diagnosis speaks to the significance of dissociative symptoms in the presentation of cult-associated distress.

Perhaps because of the controversial position dissociative disorders have historically held in mainstream psychiatry [30], there is far less evidence regarding their treatment compared to anxiety, depression, psychosis, or even personality disorders. The long-term goal in the treatment of dissociative disorders is often referred to as *integration* (or *fusion* or *unification*), that is, the merging of disparate sensations, experiences, and identities. Although DID is considered to be comparatively rare and not necessarily a direct outcome of cultic environments, the psychotherapeutic approach for dissociative disorders is largely shaped by treatment guidelines for DID. These treatment guidelines recommend a stepwise approach in working through dissociative symptoms, including [29, 31]: establishing safety, stabilization, and symptom reduction; confronting, working through, and integrating traumatic memories; and identity integration and rehabilitation. Safety is often an overriding concern, as the co-occurrence of self-harm behaviors and suicide is high with dissociative symptoms [29]. Grounding techniques are considered central as a way of relieving distress and are also thought to contribute toward progress with the goal of identity integration.

Currently, no studies support pharmacotherapy as directly beneficial in the management of dissociative symptoms. There is weak evidence to support the use of selective serotonin reuptake inhibitors (SSRIs) and opioid antagonists in cases where dissociative symptoms are comorbid with PTSD, generalized anxiety, or depressive symptoms [30, 31, 32].

Anxiety Disorders

Available studies suggest that anxiety symptoms are extremely common among former cult members. Of those populations that have been sampled, up to 83% of former members have been estimated to experience excessive worry, panic attacks, or other clinical symptoms of anxiety [15]. The high prevalence of these symptoms is reported across a number of early studies of cult psychopathology.

Anxiety in cult victims can be theorized in different ways. At one level of explanation, anxiety disorders are typically conceived as a dysfunction of fear circuitry [33], and fear is among the primary means by which cults exert undue influence [1, 2, 3]. At another level of explanation, cults provide an authoritarian structure with rules that, in some cases, guide nearly every aspect of the cult member's life, including the kinds of thoughts they are permitted to have. When an individual has left the cultic environment, these rules may persist as internalized beliefs, which conflict with noncult life and hence generate a state of anxious distress [3].

Anxiety is, of course, a broad term that denotes a variety of psychological and physiological phenomena. Anxiety symptoms may include anything from pervasive multifocal worry to specific phobias to panic attacks and autonomic hyperarousal. Studies of former cult members have found a high incidence of all of these symptoms, but these studies have not always been conducted with the nosology of contemporary psychiatry in mind. Still, the data they report are highly suggestive of the criteria for various anxiety disorders, as described in more recent editions of the DSM, including generalized anxiety disorder, panic disorder, and phobias. A subset of these individuals likely also meet the current criteria for PTSD – reporting nightmares, flashbacks, avoidance, heightened startle reaction, and hypervigilance – although not all individuals leaving cultic environments should be considered a priori to have PTSD, and exposure to cults alone should not be considered to meet criterion A for diagnosing PTSD in the DSM-V-TR [18].

The psychological intervention with the greatest evidence for the treatment of anxiety disorders, in adults and youths, is cognitive behavioral therapy (CBT) [34, 35]. In short, CBT is a psychotherapeutic modality that aims to help individuals revise thought distortions, replace avoidant behaviors with more effective coping mechanisms, and calm excessive autonomic arousal. It has multiple forms, each entailing its own treatment structure and set of techniques, often directed by the specific concern at hand (e.g., CBT-I for insomnia). One specific form of CBT that warrants mentioning here, as it is particularly relevant to the treatment of anxiety disorders – including those brought about by cultic environments – is exposure therapy. In essence, exposure therapy involves repeated and progressively intense exposure to stimuli that are (pathologically) perceived as threatening, with the goal of the eventual extinction of inappropriate anxiety response. As with CBT, exposure therapy has different subtypes, which may be more or less appropriate depending on the specific anxiety disorder a clinician is treating. Exposure therapy typically involves different levels of exposure (imagined, virtual, in vivo) matched to the severity of an anxious focus and other practical concerns.

No studies so far have specifically evaluated the use of CBT (with or without exposure therapy) for individuals who have left cultic environments. However, the basic techniques and principles of CBT can be found woven throughout descriptions of cult victim psychotherapy by many of the first clinicians in this field, including Singer and Clark, even if these are not always described as such [3, 4, 5, 21, 22, 36]. Our own anecdotal experience with former cult members also supports the use of CBT principles – often involving components of exposure therapy – as effective, safe, and relatively easy to implement. Although CBT is not the only possible approach to the treatment of anxiety symptoms in former cult members, it is the modality with the greatest evidence base overall for the treatment of anxiety, and the modality that aligns most closely with the descriptions of psychotherapeutic technique by many of those experienced with cult victims.

Of note, clinicians ought to take special caution where violence or sexual trauma has occurred in the setting of cult membership and where specific symptoms of PTSD are present. Referral to a provider specializing in trauma therapy is often recommended in such cases, as the effective treatment of PTSD symptoms can require more specialized forms of CBT, such as cognitive processing therapy or prolonged exposure therapy, as well as other novel psychotherapeutic modalities therapies such as EMDR [37, 38, 39]. An elevated risk for symptom exacerbation also exists in the psychotherapeutic treatment of PTSD, even when therapy is conducted appropriately [40].

The consensus first-line psychopharmacological treatment for moderate-to-severe anxiety disorders – including generalized anxiety disorder, panic disorder, or PTSD – is with SSRIs or serotonin-norepinephrine reuptake inhibitors (SNRIs) [41, 42]. For intermittent or situation-specific anxiety, as-needed anxiolytic medications such as benzodiazepines or antihistamines may provide sufficient relief. However, some of these as-needed medications (e.g., benzodiazepines) involve risks, such as dependence and tolerance [43]. A common refrain in psychiatry – regarding anxiety disorders as well as other disorders that we will discuss – is that the most effective treatment involves a combination of psychotherapy and medications [44]. However, the truth of this adage remains unclear in the case of cult-associated distress, which involves known psychological causes, and may conceivably be better targeted by psychological interventions.

Depressive Disorders

Depressive symptoms are also commonly reported in individuals who have left cults [15, 45, 46]. These symptoms – at times meeting the criteria for major depressive disorder – may include pervasive low mood, anhedonia, poor energy, irrational guilt and shame, sleep disturbances (either insomnia or hypersomnia), and appetite changes. The theorized reasons for the development of depression, in the setting of former cult membership, could include (but are not limited to) a loss of structure/meaning, newfound social isolation, and shame over former membership [45]. While evidence suggests a greatly elevated occurrence of (unipolar) depressive symptoms in cult victims, no evidence so far suggests an increased incidence of manic/hypomanic episodes or bipolar disorder in this population.

The assessment of depressive symptoms in any population should include explicit assessment for suicidality, as depression is the most common risk factor for suicide [47]. In cases where the patient is deemed to be an imminent risk to themselves (or others), the standard of care is stabilization in an acute inpatient unit or other controlled setting, where means of harm can be restricted [48].

Where depressed individuals are sufficiently stable to continue outpatient treatment, a number of different psychotherapeutic modalities are well supported by current evidence. The evidence base for the treatment of depressive disorders is considerably broader, in terms of the variety of effective treatments, than that for other kinds of disorders discussed in this chapter. In addition to CBT, other evidence-based psychotherapeutic modalities for the treatment of depression include interpersonal therapy [49], psychodynamic therapy [50], behavioral activation therapy [51], and mindfulness-based therapies [52]. A full description of these diverse therapeutic techniques would go beyond the scope of the chapter, but, as with CBT, they may all be shaped by concerns specific to cult membership and the individual seeking treatment. Although the evidence for classic psychoanalytic psychotherapy in the treatment of most psychiatric disorders is mixed [53], psychoanalytic theory has historically informed many clinicians in their approach to understanding and treating cult-associated distress [54–57].

Evidence-based guidelines for the psychopharmacological management of depressive disorders are similar to those for anxiety disorders, with SSRIs/SNRIs and related medications considered first-line treatments [58, 59]. Extensive research has been conducted into the best approach toward treatment-resistant depression – that is, symptoms that do not respond to multiple consecutive trials of these first-line medications, which is relatively common – however, this goes beyond the scope of this chapter. In severe cases of depression, psychiatrists may employ neuromodulatory treatments such as electroconvulsive therapy (ECT) or transcranial magnetic stimulation. Although neuromodulatory treatments can be highly effective for treating depression, the amnestic effects of ECT, in particular, may limit the benefits of concurrent psychotherapy.

Personality Disorders

The relationship of cults to personality disorders (or pathological personality traits) is complex, and we refer the reader to Chapter 11 for more discussion on this topic. One common view holds that personality disorders are developed and manifested in childhood, although they may be shaped into adulthood by environmental factors [60]. Under this view, cult membership ought not to be viewed as directly *causing* personality disorder but rather as enhancing or unmasking traits that are already present (the exception, perhaps, in cases where an individual is born or adopted into a cult from a young age). However, this is not the only view, and other authors have suggested that cultic environments may be so influential as to lead to the development of new personality traits [57, 61, 62]. One notable challenge with research in this area – as opposed to other disorders discussed in this chapter – is that there is considerably more uncertainty around the validity of personality disorders as a diagnostic category in general [63].

Nevertheless, there seems to be widespread acknowledgment of an important link between cult membership/leadership and pathological personality traits. Some of the relevant diagnostic categories, in contemporary psychiatric nosology, would include dependent or borderline personality disorder (for current or former members) and narcissistic or antisocial personality disorder (for leaders). However, the epidemiology of these conditions is not clear from the available research.

The features of various personality disorders are discussed in greater detail in Chapter 11. Briefly, it is worth noting that both dependent personality disorder and borderline personality disorder share an overlapping set of features, including a motivating fear of abandonment and associated affective instability in the wake of perceived abandonment, and instability of individual identity. Intuitively, one can see how these traits might manifest after leaving a cultic environment, regardless of whether they were present from an early age. Our recommendation, fitting with our general approach in this chapter, is to recognize these personality features as part of an overall descriptive pattern, regardless of the supposed etiology.

The treatment strategy with the greatest evidence in the management of personality disorders is, as a rule, psychotherapy. The most studied personality disorder is borderline personality disorder, and the treatment with the greatest evidence for improving suffering in borderline personality disorder is dialectical behavioral therapy (DBT), which combines elements of CBT and mindfulness with practical skills for managing emotional reactivity [64]. Little research is available regarding the effective treatment of dependent personality disorder, although anecdotally, some clinicians will employ CBT or DBT. There is substantial controversy surrounding the question of whether antisocial personality disorder is a treatable condition; in a recent systematic review by Cochrane, only 3 of 19 studies demonstrated any benefit from psychotherapy, and none of these demonstrated compelling evidence of a change in antisocial behavior itself [65]. Similarly little evidence is available for the effective treatment of narcissistic personality disorder, although clinicians tend to be more optimistic regarding the possibility of effective treatment as compared to antisocial personality disorder [66].

To date, no trials have established the benefit of pharmacotherapy for the core modification of personality disorders, although medications may nevertheless be useful for treating comorbid depression, anxiety, PTSD, and other conditions [64].

Psychotic Disorders

Although cult beliefs may appear strange or unusual to outsiders, they do not necessarily indicate delusional or otherwise psychotic thinking. While some cult leaders may show signs of psychopathy or narcissism, cult members (whether leaders or followers) are generally not considered psychotic. In fact, the insanity defense has repeatedly been rejected for cult members who have committed violent crimes [67], demonstrating that unconventional beliefs alone are not typically considered delusional under the law.

An alternative framework for understanding the beliefs of cult members is the concept of *overvalued ideas* [68]. Overvalued ideas refer to rigidly held beliefs or convictions that are shared by others in a particular culture or subculture. Unlike delusions, which are fixed, false beliefs that are not shared by others, overvalued ideas are part of a larger belief system held by a group. While this concept acknowledges that individuals in cults may hold extreme beliefs and engage in harmful behaviors, it recognizes that these beliefs are not necessarily indicative of a psychotic illness.

However, there are limitations to the concept of overvalued ideas. The boundary between overvalued ideas and delusions may be unclear, making it difficult to distinguish between the two [69]. Additionally, the concept does not fully account for the coercive and manipulative tactics often used by cult leaders to control their followers, which may influence their behavior beyond their beliefs. Therefore, the concept of overvalued ideas should be applied with caution and in conjunction with an understanding of the social and psychological dynamics within the cult.

While there have been no studies specifically addressing the treatment of overvalued ideas in cult members, CBT has been shown to be effective in treating overvalued ideas in other contexts, such as obsessive-compulsive disorder [70]. However, treatment with antipsychotic medications is generally not helpful [71]. Although there are no clinical trials investigating this hypothesis, serotonin reuptake inhibitors may play a role in reducing the severity of depression and anxiety symptoms in individuals with overvalued ideas [72].

Psychometric Testing

Psychometric testing may, at times, be useful in diagnosing or tracking cult-associated distress. To our knowledge, no psychometric instruments are validated specifically for evaluating cult-associated distress. In everyday clinical practice, simple rating scales such as the Patient Health Questionnaire (PHQ-9) or General Anxiety Disorder-7 (GAD-7) may be helpful for tracking symptoms of anxiety and depression. More involved psychometric testing, administered by a trained psychologist, may be diagnostically helpful in complex cases involving dissociation, psychotic features, or personality disorders. The Structured Clinical Interview for DSM Dissociative Disorders (SCID-D) has long been considered the gold standard in the evaluation of dissociative symptoms, although the Dissociative Disorders Interview Schedule (DDIS) and the Dissociative Experiences Scale (DES) are simpler to administer and also validated [73, 74]. The Minnesota Multiphasic Personality Inventory (MMPI-2) is widely used in the evaluation of personality disorders. Where there is concern for an underlying psychotic disorder, with ambiguous psychotic symptoms, Rorschach testing or neurocognitive assessment may enhance diagnostic clarity [75].

The Challenge of Locating Effective Treatment

The vast majority of treatment for cult-related distress will occur on a voluntary, outpatient basis. This work entails a number of challenges that distinguish it from typical outpatient psychotherapy or medication management. First, many cult ideologies disparage and reject mainstream mental health treatment. Even after an individual has left the group, they may retain distrust or fear (to the point of phobia) of mental health professionals. It is crucial to assess and address this with individuals who have left cultic environments, as one would with other sources of anxiety, to the extent that this is possible.

Second, some concerns remain regarding recapitulating the cult dynamic within the context of a psychotherapeutic relationship. This concern is manifested in the historical literature on "psychotherapy cults" [76]. Indeed, the concerns about undue influence by mental health professionals are understandable: individuals leaving cults are often psychologically vulnerable, habituated to dependent relationships, and socially isolated outside of psychotherapy. These factors necessitate strict adherence to the basic ethical guidelines, including informed consent and appropriate boundary setting, as recognized by most psychotherapy organizations [77]. The goals of therapy ought to be developing emotional independence and autonomous thought rather than allegiance with the therapist's own view of a client's experience in a cult.

Occasionally, inpatient psychiatric treatment for cult-related distress may be necessary for the sake of physical safety. We agree with the widely held standard whereby a patient ought to be admitted if they pose a significant risk of physical danger to themselves or others or demonstrate a gross inability to care for themselves. Although inpatient psychiatric admission is necessary in some cases, psychiatric hospitalization may also lead to harm [78], and lengths of stay should be kept to the minimum time required until safety can be re-established, and autonomy can be restored. As autonomy is often a primary goal of psychotherapy with former cult members, there is reason to be uniquely cautious in the hospitalization of this group of patients.

Lastly, most of the recommendations in this chapter have been directed toward cult members rather than leaders. However, at times, cult leaders will also present for evaluation or treatment, particularly in forensic settings. Even leaders who demonstrate antisocial traits, and potentially are only participating in treatment as part of a court order, may experience comorbid psychiatric conditions such as those we have described. These individuals also deserve treatment under the medico-ethical principles of beneficence and justice. Furthermore, it must be noted that the line between membership and leadership is often blurred. Many former cult members may have acted in ways that are more characteristic of leaders, sometimes harming others in the process. Assuming that all such individuals have antisocial or narcissistic personality disorder would be inaccurate and harmful, rendering them unlikely to benefit from further treatment with psychotherapy or pharmacotherapy. This necessitates careful diagnostic work as a prerequisite for any treatment program.

Summary

The available research to date supports the idea that cults are psychologically harmful to cult members, commonly resulting in symptoms of anxiety, depression, dissociation, and, in some cases, psychosis. Although clinicians have been offering treatment for former cult members for decades, evidence regarding the most effective interventions specific to this population is scarce, and current practice is based largely on expert opinion. Treatment studies that do exist are generally dated and of low quality, but broadly suggest psychotherapy as safe and effective. We recommend assessment and treatment grounded in the descriptive nosology of mainstream psychology and psychiatry (e.g., the use of CBT and exposure therapy for anxiety symptoms). A crucial component of any treatment program in this context is education about the nature and tactics of cults. Evidence regarding the use of psychotropic medications in cult-specific contexts is virtually zero, although this does not mean that medications cannot help alleviate certain psychiatric symptoms. The vast majority of care is likely to take place in the outpatient setting, although inpatient settings (in cases of danger to self or others) and forensic settings (in the case of criminal charges or convictions stemming from cult involvement) are also possible. The treatment of former cult members can involve unique challenges, as cult ideologies commonly espouse distrust of mental health professionals, and these beliefs may persist even after an individual has left the cult.

Key Points

- The incidence of psychiatric symptoms, including anxiety, depression, dissociation, and potentially psychosis, in individuals who have left cults is high.
- Little high-quality evidence exists regarding specific treatments for individuals experiencing cult-associated distress, although psychotherapy is thought to be beneficial.
- At this time, most evidence-based practices are guided by symptomatology, in line with the approach of mainstream psychiatry and psychology (e.g., CBT and exposure therapy for anxiety disorders).
- Psychoeducation is a crucial component of any treatment program. In the case of cult-associated distress, it entails education about the nature of cults themselves.
- Most clinical encounters with former cult members are likely to be in the outpatient setting. These encounters can pose unique challenges, as cults often instill distrust and suspicion of mental health professionals, which may persist even after an individual has left the cult.
- Inpatient psychiatric hospitalization should be reserved for cases where an individual poses a significant threat to themselves or others.

References

1. SA Hassan. The BITE Model of Authoritarian Control: undue influence, thought reform, brainwashing, mind control, trafficking and the law. *ProQuest*. 2020. www.proquest.com/docview/2476570146
2. Influence Continuum. Freedom of Mind Resource Center. 2023. https://freedomofmind.com/cult-mind-control/influence-continuum/
3. S Hassan. *Combating cult mind control*. Park Street Press; 1990.
4. MT Singer. Therapy with ex-cult members. *Journal – National Association of Private Psychiatric Hospitals*. 1978;9(4):14–18.
5. JG Clark Jr. Cults. *JAMA*. 1979;242(3):279–81.
6. RJ Lifton. *Thought reform and the psychology of totalism: a study of "brainwashing" in China*. University of North Carolina Press; 1989.
7. EH Schein, I Schneier, CH Barker. *Coercive persuasion: a socio-psychological analysis of the "brainwashing" of American civilian prisoners by the Chinese communists*. Norton; 1971.
8. LJ West, PR Martin. Pseudo-identity and the treatment of personality change in victims of captivity and cults. *Cultic Studies Journal*. 1996;13(2):125–52.
9. M Galanter, R Rabkin, J Rabkin, A Deutsch. The "Moonies": a psychological

study of conversion and membership in a contemporary religious sect. *American Journal of Psychiatry*. 1979;136(2):165–70.

10. M Galanter, P Buckley, A Deutsch, R Rabkin, J Rabkin. Large group influence for decreased drug use: findings from two contemporary religious sects. *American Journal of Drug and Alcohol Abuse*. 1980;7(3–4):291–304.
11. M Galanter. Engaged members of the Unification Church: impact of a charismatic large group on adaptation and behavior. *Archives of General Psychiatry*. 1983;40(11):1197–202.
12. M Galanter. Unification Church ("Moonie") dropouts: psychological readjustment after leaving a charismatic religious group. *American Journal of Psychiatry*. 1983;140(8):984–89.
13. G Swartling, PG Swartling. Psychiatric problems in ex-members of Word of Life. *Cultic Studies Journal*. 1992;9: 78–88.
14. PR Martin, MD Langone, AA Dole, J Wiltrout. Post-cult symptoms as measured by the MCMI before and after residential treatment. *Cultic Studies Journal*. 1992;9(2):219–50.
15. J Aronoff, SJ Lynn, P Malinoski. Are cultic environments psychologically harmful? *Clinical Psychology Review*. 2000;20(1):91–111.
16. S Hassan. Elizabeth Holmes' Theranos corporate cult with Dr. Dennis Tourish. Freedom of Mind Resource Center. 2023. https://freedomofmind.com/elizabeth-holmes-theranos-corporate-cult-with-dr-dennis-tourish/
17. E Fromm. *The heart of man: its genius for good and evil*. American Mental Health Foundation Books; 2010.
18. American Psychiatric Association, editor. *Diagnostic and statistical manual of mental disorders: DSM-5-TR*. Fifth ed., text revision. American Psychiatric Association Publishing; 2022.
19. C Martin-Soelch, U Schnyder. Editorial: resilience and vulnerability factors in response to stress. *Frontiers in Psychiatry*. 2019;10:732.
20. L Festinger. *A theory of cognitive dissonance*. Stanford University Press; 2001.
21. MH Spero. Psychotherapeutic procedure with religious cult devotees. *Journal of Nervous and Mental Disease*. 1982;170(6):332–44.
22. JC Morse, EL Morse. Toward a theory of therapy with cultic victims. *American Journal of Psychotherapy*. 1987;41(4):563–70.
23. S Hassan. The therapeutic use of hypnosis to improve health and recover from trauma with Laurence Sugarman M.D. Freedom of Mind Resource Center. 2020. https://freedomofmind.com/the-therapeutic-use-of-hypnosis-to-improve-health-and-recover-from-trauma-with-laurence-sugarman-m-d/
24. D Whitsett, SA Kent. Cults and families. *Families in Society: The Journal of Contemporary Social Services*. 2003;84(4):491–502.
25. F Shapiro. Eye movement desensitization: a new treatment for post-traumatic stress disorder. *Journal of Behavior Therapy and Experimental Psychiatry*. 1989;20(3):211–17.
26. BA Van der Kolk. *The body keeps the score: brain, mind and body in the healing of trauma*. Penguin Books; 2015.
27. State of Israel Ministry of Welfare and Social Services. An examination of the phenomenon of cults in Israel. www.religionnewsblog.com/docs/Examination_Of_The_Phenomenon_Of_Cults_In_Israel.pdf
28. G Jenkinson, C Charnock. *Walking free from the trauma of coercive, cultic and spiritual abuse: a workbook for recovery and growth*. Routledge; 2023.
29. International Society for the Study of Trauma and Dissociation. Guidelines for treating dissociative identity disorder in adults, third revision. *Journal of Trauma & Dissociation*. 2011;12(2):115–87.
30. RJ Loewenstein. Dissociation debates: everything you know is wrong. *Dialogues in Clinical Neuroscience*. 2018;20(3):229–42.

31. BL Brand, CC Classen, SW McNary, P Zaveri. A review of dissociative disorders treatment studies. *Journal of Nervous and Mental Disease*. 2009;197(9):646–54.
32. BL Brand, R Lanius, E Vermetten, RJ Loewenstein, D Spiegel. Where are we going? An update on assessment, treatment, and neurobiological research in dissociative disorders as we move toward the DSM-5. *Journal of Trauma & Dissociation*. 2012;13(1):9–31.
33. LM Shin, I Liberzon. The neurocircuitry of fear, stress, and anxiety disorders. *Neuropsychopharmacology*. 2010;35(1):169–91.
34. MG Craske, MB Stein. Anxiety. *Lancet*. 2016;388(10063):3048–59.
35. MG Craske, MB Stein, TC Eley, MR Milad, A Holmes, RM Rapee, et al. Anxiety disorders. *Nature Reviews Disease Primer*. 2017;3:17024.
36. PR Martin, MD Langone, AA Dole, J Wiltrout. Post-cult symptoms as measured by the MCMI before and after residential treatment. *Cultic Studies Journal*. 1992;9(2):219–50.
37. CL Lancaster, JB Teeters, DF Gros, SE Back. Posttraumatic stress disorder: overview of evidence-based assessment and treatment. *Journal of Clinical Medicine*. 2016;5(11).
38. LE Watkins, KR Sprang, BO Rothbaum. Treating PTSD: a review of evidence-based psychotherapy interventions. *Frontiers in Behavioral Neuroscience*. 2018;12:258.
39. P Cuijpers, SCV Veen, M Sijbrandij, W Yoder, IA Cristea. Eye movement desensitization and reprocessing for mental health problems: a systematic review and meta-analysis. *Cognitive Behaviour Therapy*. 2020;49(3):165–80.
40. EB Foa, LA Zoellner, NC Feeny, EA Hembree, J Alvarez-Conrad. Does imaginal exposure exacerbate PTSD symptoms? *Journal of Consulting and Clinical Psychology*. 2002;70:1022–28.
41. MA Katzman, P Bleau, P Blier, P Chokka, K Kjernisted, M Van Ameringen, et al. Canadian clinical practice guidelines for the management of anxiety, posttraumatic stress and obsessive-compulsive disorders. *BMC Psychiatry*. 2014;14(1):S1.
42. AJ Melaragno. Pharmacotherapy for anxiety disorders: from first-line options to treatment resistance. *FOCUS*. 2021;19(2):145–60.
43. AN Edinoff, CA Nix, J Hollier, CE Sagrera, BM Delacroix, T Abubakar, et al. Benzodiazepines: uses, dangers, and clinical considerations. *Neurology International*. 2021;13(4):594–607.
44. P Cuijpers, M Sijbrandij, SL Koole, G Andersson, AT Beekman, CF Reynolds. Adding psychotherapy to antidepressant medication in depression and anxiety disorders: a meta-analysis. *World Psychiatry*. 2014;13(1):56–67.
45. M Rousselet, O Duretete, JB Hardouin, M Grall-Bronnec. Cult membership: what factors contribute to joining or leaving? *Psychiatry Research*. 2017;257:27–33.
46. C Buxant, V Saroglou, S Casalfiore, LL Christians. Cognitive and emotional characteristics of new religious movement members: new questions and data on the mental health issue. *Mental Health Religion & Culture*. 2007;10(3):219–38.
47. L Brådvik. Suicide risk and mental disorders. *International Journal of Environmental Research and Public Health*. 2018;15(9):2028.
48. Practice guideline for the assessment and treatment of patients with suicidal behaviors. *American Journal of Psychiatry*. 2003;160(11 Suppl):1–60.
49. P Cuijpers, AS Geraedts, P van Oppen, G Andersson, JC Markowitz, A van Straten. Interpersonal psychotherapy for depression: a meta-analysis. *American Journal of Psychiatry*. 2011;168(6): 581–92.
50. C Steinert, T Munder, S Rabung, J Hoyer, F Leichsenring. Psychodynamic therapy: as efficacious as other empirically supported treatments? A meta-analysis testing equivalence of outcomes. *American Journal of Psychiatry*. 2017;174(10):943–53.

51. E Uphoff, D Ekers, L Robertson, S Dawson, E Sanger, E South, et al. Behavioural activation therapy for depression in adults. *Cochrane Database of Systematic Reviews.* 2020;7(7): CD013305.

52. KT Sverre, ER Nissen, I Farver-Vestergaard, M Johannsen, R Zachariae. Comparing the efficacy of mindfulness-based therapy and cognitive-behavioral therapy for depression in head-to-head randomized controlled trials: a systematic review and meta-analysis of equivalence. *Clinical Psychology Review.* 2023;100:102234.

53. J Paris. Is psychoanalysis still relevant to psychiatry? *The Canadian Journal of Psychiatry.* 2017;62(5):308–12.

54. L Goldberg. Guidelines for therapists. In: MD Langone, editor. *Recovery from cults: help for victims of psychological and spiritual abuse.* W.W. Norton; 1993. p. 232–50.

55. L Goldberg. A psychoanalytic look at recovered memories, therapists, cult leaders, and undue influence. *Clinical Social Work Journal.* 1997;25(1): 71–86.

56. DE Shaw, CS Wan. Traumatic abuse in cults: a psychoanalytic perspective. *Cultic Studies Review.* 2006;2(2):101–32.

57. JD Salande, DR Perkins. An object relations approach to cult membership. *American Journal of Psychotherapy.* 2011;65(4):381–91.

58. SH Kennedy, RW Lam, RS McIntyre, SV Tourjman, V Bhat, P Blier, et al. Canadian Network for Mood and Anxiety Treatments (CANMAT) 2016 clinical guidelines for the management of adults with major depressive disorder. *Canadian Journal of Psychiatry.* 2016;61(9):540–60.

59. American Psychological Assocation. Clinical practice guideline for the treatment of depression across three age cohorts. 2019. www.apa.org/depression-guideline

60. G Newton-Howes, LA Clark, A Chanen. Personality disorder across the life course. *Lancet.* 2015;385(9969):727–34.

61. J Burke. Antisocial personality disorder in cult leaders and induction of dependent personality disorder in cult members. *Cultic Studies Review.* 2006;5(3):390–410.

62. Y Walsh, RJ Russell, PA Wells. The personality of ex-cult members. *Personality and Individual Differences.* 1995;19(3):339–44.

63. P Zachar, RF Krueger. Personality disorder and validity: a history of controversy. In: KWM Fulford, M Davies, R Gipps, et al., editors. *The Oxford handbook of philosophy and psychiatry.* Oxford University Press; 2013. p. 889–910.

64. LW Choi-Kain, EF Finch, SR Masland, JA Jenkins, BT Unruh. What works in the treatment of borderline personality disorder. *Current Behavioral Neuroscience Reports.* 2017;4(1):21–30.

65. S Gibbon, NR Khalifa, NHY Cheung, BA Völlm, L McCarthy. Psychological interventions for antisocial personality disorder. *Cochrane Database of Systematic Reviews.* 2020;9(9):CD007668.

66. I Weinberg, E Ronningstam. Dos and don'ts in treatments of patients with narcissistic personality disorder. *Journal of Personality Disorders.* 2020;34(Suppl):122–42.

67. B Holoyda, W Newman. Between belief and delusion: cult members and the insanity plea. *Journal of the American Academy of Psychiatry and the Law.* 2016;44(1):53–62.

68. T Rahman, JR Meloy, R Bauer. Extreme overvalued belief and the legacy of Carl Wernicke. *Journal of the American Academy of Psychiatry and the Law.* 2019;47(2):180–87.

69. KG Joshi, RL Frierson, TD Gunter. Shared psychotic disorder and criminal responsibility: a review and case report of folie à trois. *Journal of the American Academy of Psychiatry and the Law.* 2006;34(4):511–17.

70. F Aardema, S Bouchard, D Koszycki, ME Lavoie, JS Audet, K O'Connor. Evaluation of inference-based cognitive-behavioral therapy for obsessive-compulsive

disorder: a multicenter randomized controlled trial with three treatment modalities. *Psychotherapy and Psychosomatics*. 2022;91(5):348–59.

71. T Rahman, SM Hartz, W Xiong, JR Meloy, J Janofsky, B Harry, et al. Extreme overvalued beliefs. *Journal of the American Academy of Psychiatry and the Law*. 2020;48(3):319–26.
72. D Veale. Over-valued ideas: a conceptual analysis. *Behaviour Research and Therapy*. 2002;40(4):383–400.
73. MJ Dorahy, BL Brand, V Şar, C Krüger, P Stavropoulos, A Martínez-Taboas, et al. Dissociative identity disorder: an empirical overview. *Australian & New Zealand Journal of Psychiatry*. 2014;48(5):402–17.
74. L Lyssenko, C Schmahl, L Bockhacker, R Vonderlin, M Bohus, N Kleindienst. Dissociation in psychiatric disorders: a meta-analysis of studies using the dissociative experiences scale. *American Journal of Psychiatry*. 2018;175(1):37–46.
75. JL Mihura, GJ Meyer, N Dumitrascu, G Bombel. The validity of individual Rorschach variables: systematic reviews and meta-analyses of the comprehensive system. *Psychological Bulletin*. 2013;139(3):548–605.
76. MK Temerlin, JW Temerlin. Psychotherapy cults: an iatrogenic perversion. *Psychotherapy: Theory, Research & Practice*. 1982;19:131–41.
77. American Psychological Association. Ethical principles of psychologists and code of conduct. 2017. www.apa.org/ethics/code
78. A Borecky, C Thomsen, A Dubov. Reweighing the ethical tradeoffs in the involuntary hospitalization of suicidal patients. *American Journal of Bioethics*. 2019;19(10):71–83.

Chapter 14

Legal Implications of Cults

Eric Y. Drogin and Thomas G. Gutheil

"Many litigants articulate beliefs that have no legal support . . . sometimes these beliefs are sincerely held, sometimes they are advanced only to annoy the other side, but in neither event do they imply mental instability or concrete intellect . . . so deficient that trial is impossible."
– *Timothy Tymkovich, 10th Circuit Court Judge*

Introduction

Drawing on the authors' experience and the literature, this chapter will describe the legal repercussions for various parties in the civil and criminal justice systems, with particular emphasis on tort law, criminal law, and administrative procedure. Core questions to be addressed include: What is society's stake in these systems, and who are the stakeholders (cult members, attorneys, clinical and forensic evaluators, cult commentators, and the courts) involved? To what extent do the existence and imposition of legal repercussions for cults represent unconstitutional or otherwise illegally discriminatory actions?

Cults and Cult Leaders

Cults may be deemed to be criminal organizations and as such can be characterized in some cases as subject to the Racketeer Influenced and Corruption Organizations Act of 1970 (RICO). The purpose of RICO is to prevent patterns of criminal activity that may include "any act or threat involving murder, kidnapping, gambling, arson, robbery, bribery, extortion, dealing in obscene matter, or dealing in a controlled substance or listed chemical" [1]. In some cases, at least one of these elements might arguably apply.

Although generally understood to be a prime example of the criminal justice system's most complex and navigationally challenging statutes [2, p. 1279], RICO's value as a federal prosecution tool is greatly enhanced by its applicability to members of the organization en masse, and to all of the crimes that allegedly were committed, without the need to address each suspected incident in separate proceedings [3]. This may seem *too* convenient when one considers, for example, how easy it might be to employ RICO "against activists in an attempt to equate advocacy work to organized crime" [4, p. 59].

When it comes to civil lawsuits and to criminal charges that may be lodged against cults, these organizations might best be advised to incorporate, in order to shield their assets and otherwise perpetuate their viability with the sorts of legal protections typically afforded large business concerns as a matter of policy [5]; the most high-profile example of this approach in recent years has been the case of *Burley* v. *Hobby Lobby Stores, Inc.*, in which the Supreme Court of the United States determined that a corporation can avail itself of privileges based upon its collective religious orientation [6].

This having been noted, cults with their often chaotic and idiosyncratically managed affairs may not represent the type of business most suited to incorporation, since it is necessary in every jurisdiction to observe not only those requirements necessary for establishment as a corporate entity but also those factors involved in maintaining corporate status in a fashion that comports with codified legal requirements [7]. Depriving cults of the immunities and other perquisites of incorporated status is commonly known as piercing the corporate veil [8], which, among other options, "permits courts to hold shareholders personally liable for the debts of their corporation" [9, p. 1799].

Jurisdictionally bound rules vary, but in the United States, for example, courts will tend to look for the following occasionally overlapping potential veil-piercing factors [10, p. 160], as annotated here for use in the context of cult liability determination:

1. *The failure to observe corporate formalities.* Did a board of directors with clearly designated roles and named electees meet when it was supposed to meet? Were minutes of those meetings taken, and reports distributed to shareholders, along the lines described in the articles of incorporation? Were all necessary forms filed with the proper authorities, in the jurisdiction in which incorporation occurred?
2. *The commingling of individual and corporate assets.* Corporate protections are designed and prized, perhaps more than anything else, for their ability to protect the working capital of the enterprise and to refrain from keeping the personal property of the business from becoming subject to seizure in the event of an adverse legal decision. A mockery is made of this critical distinction when, for example, moneys are all kept in a cult leader's personal bank account and spent on luxury items that are without apparent business use or relevance; and are reserved exclusively for the individual in question.
3. *The absence of separate offices.* Corporations are often – albeit certainly not exclusively – multijurisdictional in nature. Business is typically conducted in offices, where corporate officers, employees, and business associates may meet in order to fulfill their duties. It is true that these days there is a decreasing emphasis on "bricks and mortar" operations, but in any event it would be considered good form for the cult-as-corporation to maintain distinct, identifiable technology for business transactions, as opposed to entertainment systems and other recreational applications.
4. *The treatment of the corporation as a mere shell without employees or assets.* Here one finds perhaps the most cynical and even reckless departure from the acknowledged purposes and agreed-upon strictures of incorporation. This process is not meant to function as some sort of "safe harbor," by means of which simply qualifying for corporate status, without maintenance, serves as a permanent shield against liability.
5. *The stripping of essential assets from the corporation by dividends, or excessive salaries or other payments for services.* From the court's perspective, to run a business is to run it *like* a business. Much is made of what some consider unduly high corporate leadership salaries, but eventually there may be a distinct difference to be observed between what may be greedy and what is outright fraudulent. Excessive payments to

external vendors are often presumed to be indicia of kickbacks, creative accounting, or both.

6. *The undercapitalization of the corporation at the outset so that it could not pay its foreseeable debts.* This particular approach may smack less of fraud than of inadvertence – at least until one realizes that incorporation maneuvers are typically contemplated and ultimately executed with the advice of counsel. Businesses can run into trouble, which courts are willing to accept; however, the standard here concerns what would reasonably be predictable, not what slings and arrows might happen to erode the corporation's bottom line along the way.

Whether due to alleged criminal activity or alleged civilly contextualized malfeasance, cults can be characterized as entities that would be as liable as any other group, be it as a result of violations of the law or of failure to adhere to business practices that would ensure insulating corporate status. Additional statutory innovations have lent support to those attempting to sue alleged cults at the organizational level, but so far with no particular success. For example, the Trafficking Victims Protection Act of 2018 (TVPA) [11] was recently the focus of a federal plaintiff's lawsuit [12], but the Ninth Circuit Court of Appeals "adopted a narrow interpretation" of the TVPA, in part because of its conclusion that "the couple could have left the church at any time despite their fear of repercussions" [13, p. 284].

Allegations of cultlike status and cultlike machinations have not been reserved for the most recognizably religious and quasi-religious of organizations. For example, multilevel marketing companies (MLMs) – sometimes characterized as "pyramid schemes" – have come under increasing scrutiny in this regard. Employing "both subtle and overt religious tones" at times, "recruitment methods for at least some MLMs have often been compared to recruitment into religious organizations" [14, p. 128].

The typical cult leader is a charismatic individual who may or may not claim divine authority; if the former is claimed, such individuals may try to assert First Amendment freedom of religious rights to excuse their activities; if the latter, such persons may be judged against the usual legal standards. A challenge in the latter case is the difficulty of convincing cult members, past or present, to testify against the leader. This is even more difficult when the cult activities have featured coercive control, which – in addition to instilling extreme commitment to the cult values – militates against challenging the cult's principles by means of weakening rational thinking through sleep deprivation, food restriction, and required group loyalty exercises such as rallies. Note that the charisma of the cult leader may, strangely, be undimmed by exposure of venality, criminal convictions, or other discoveries of "feet of clay."

Cult Members

Cult members who have been induced by the leader or senior figures in the cult to participate in illegal or harmful activities (such as theft, violence, fraud, and the like) may attempt to distance themselves from the cult and its principles by claiming, in essence, external control of their behavior in various forms, including "brainwashing" and duress. Brainwashing has long been associated with cult induction and retention [15]. Beyond its role as a social scientific phenomenon, brainwashing has been recognized in recent decades as forensically relevant in matters of criminal defense [16]. Immersion in cult "principles" may, at times, result in what is essentially an incapacity to deal with financial decisions (e.g., giving life savings or trusts to the cult) and with capacity to appreciate the wrongfulness of a cult-mandated extralegal act. Overall, attorneys seeking to rely upon brainwashing in establishing a defense may fare better by referring to the presence of coercive control and specific incidents of resulting incapacity, given admissibility concerns that attach to the notion of "brainwashing" as a free-standing scientific phenomenon [17].

Duress has long been entrenched as one of the so-called excuse defenses, along with "insanity," in attempts to "deny that the defendant should be held criminally liable to the same extent they might be found otherwise, because they lacked the capacity or (fair) opportunity to avoid committing the offense" [18, p. 521]. Duress might also be invoked when direct threats (e.g., of retaliation) are leveled against cult members who are, or seem, unwilling to perform cult-mandated activities, even those recognizably illegal. This pressure may also be exerted by leaders if the member seems to wish to leave the cult. The effect of this assessment may sidestep the capacity component of duress-based defenses.

An outright defense of "insanity," in those jurisdictions that allow for such defenses, may prove an exceptionally high hurdle for defense counsel to clear, given the typical requirement that there exist a discernible substrate of confirmed mental illness. Despite the fact that "mental health professionals may diagnose any number of psychiatric diagnoses in these individuals, from personality disorders to psychotic disorders," a recent review regarding "cases reaching the appellate level" found that as a general matter the testimony of defense experts in such matters "did not serve to promote a successful NGRI [not guilty by reason of insanity] plea" [19, p. 62].

Even after receiving some form of "deprogramming," former cult members may still feel pressure from the cult's principles or policies to avoid realistic analysis of their behavior or situation ("I still had the leader's voice in my head"), due to fears of legal, social, or physical retaliation. This may constitute a considerable challenge for defense counsel in attempts to avoid legal repercussions for their clients. Compounding this problem is the fact that many legal actors (judges, attorneys) may be unaware of the dynamics of cults in general (especially those that are presented as religious), and the specific effects of cults on mental capacities, competence, and freedom of choice.

Defamation law "shields reputation from harm" and exists as a legal concern because "offensive, pejorative, and vituperative comments cause harm to the victim's standing in society" [20, p. 456]. The two core subsets of defamation are "libel," involving all manner of "methods of publication" [21, p. 162], including, for example, documentaries on the cult, and "slander," which occurs specifically "by spoken word" [22, p. 35]. The essential elements of these torts are the same, involving "an assertion of fact that is false and damages the plaintiff's reputation" [23, p. 330]. Cult members who defame the cult in writing or verbally, who do so inaccurately, and who harm the cult as a result may be sued in civil court. The outcome of such litigation may be that cult members are forced to retract their remarks in a widely publicized forum, or that they become liable for "damages" typically leading to monetary compensation [24], or perhaps both. The same concerns exist in those situations when the allegedly false statements of cult members are disseminated via the press; potential defamers are unlikely to avail themselves of a safe harbor in instances where remarks are an aspect of media coverage, and reporters themselves are increasingly likely to face legal scrutiny for poorly substantiated allegations [25].

One increasingly implemented and occasionally controversial legal mechanism for controlling the public statements of current and prior cult members is the “nondisparagement” clause. These legal provisions “commit one contracting party to refrain from derogatory comment about the other,” by means of “exacting a threshold pledge of no adverse comment both during and after the relationship” [26, p. 97]. When cult induction involves a written contract that specifies mutual obligations, the cult may seek to prevent its members from writing or publicly proclaiming negative information about, for example, the cult’s mission, goals, practices, structure, activities, leadership, or interaction with persons both within and outside the organization.

As with any legal provision, greater specificity – as long as it does not run afoul of a given jurisdiction’s stated policy concerns – is likely to lead to greater enforceability. A clause that refers, for example, to “nothing untoward” may have the advantage of being sweeping and virtually all-inclusive in nature, but could be deemed later by a court to be impermissibly broad or uninterpretably vague. By contrast, a clause prohibiting, among other violations, “any public statement referring to the organization’s actions in a fashion that is negative, critical, or otherwise likely to damage the organization’s reputation” may offer a plaintiff’s attorney a considerably more effective means of squelching an article prior to publication, demanding a well-publicized detraction, or contextualizing and quantifying damages sustained by the cult as a result of impermissible commentary.

Although nondisparagement clauses may serve to chill the speech of current or prior cult members who were signatories to a written contract while entering or still enrolled in the organization, or who even more generally affirmed at that time their adherence to stated policies that were provided to them in writing or to which they were directed in an accessible online format, they cannot newly be imposed upon persons who by then are no longer affiliated. In addition, the most pointedly detailed and iron-clad of nondisparagement clauses will not aid the cult in those jurisdictions where such clauses are explicitly disfavored.

Lawyers

The template for addressing legal repercussions for lawyers themselves exists in regard to the practices of what are commonly described as “mob lawyers,” who may defend their clients literally “to a fault,” and whose “stigma and reputation,” it has been argued, will “continue to hang over the profession” [27, p. 114]. When legal representation strays over the line from appropriately zealous advocacy to “aiding and abetting” ongoing or potential illegal activities on the behalf of the cult as legal client, counsel may themselves wind up facing stiff legal penalties. The elements of aiding and abetting [28, pp. 245–60] include elements, as annotated here, for use in the context of cult representation:

1. *The accused lent practical assistance, encouragement, or moral support to the principal offender in committing an offense.* The primary distinction here is one of timing. Attorneys are commonly observed – indeed, expected – to help their clients, to urge them to do better any number of ways, and to assist them in seeing themselves in a proper light. This is quite a different matter, of course, when the analysis shifts to new offenses that are currently or subsequently being contemplated. A gray area involves determining whether legal assistance is being rendered in order to cover up a previously committed offense as opposed to fashioning a valid, effective defense and ensuring that such events do not occur again.

2. *The act or omission had a substantial effect on the commission of the crime.* Counsel's own potential liability here becomes a matter of degree. Policies that seek to criminalize every conceivable aspect of support open the floodgates to endless litigation and may ultimately have a deleterious effect on the well-meant and ethically oriented provision of legal services. Failing, for example, to provide explicit discouragement regarding certain potential causes of action is unlikely to be confused by the courts with incitement or participatory plotting of a specific illegal act. Similarly, when counsel instructs cult leadership on how to conduct legitimate day-to-day business matters in a fashion that does not incur legal scrutiny, it would be unfair to blame counsel consequentially if the client uses that information to undertake, on its own, illegal activities that previously would have been considered "too risky."
3. *The accused acted intentionally, or refrained from acting, with knowledge or awareness that their act or omission would lend assistance, encouragement, or moral support to the principal offender.* Standing in contrast to the "substantial effect" reservation addressed in the preceding examples, attorneys are likely to have a considerably more difficult time establishing that they did not act "intentionally" with respect to their professional interactions with clients. An exception could be stray remarks that are overinterpreted or misinterpreted by cult leadership as opposed to the provision of direct, experience-informed legal advice. Even more to this point, attorneys are far less likely to make a creditable case for their own activities when it becomes "knowledge or awareness" of the likely effects of the advice they proffer.
4. *The accused must have been aware of the essential elements of the principal offender's crime, including the principal's mental state.* This last element offers an intriguing mix of concerns. On the one hand, attorneys are hardly in a position to assert their ignorance of the elements of a crime – this, after all, is their stock in trade. On the other hand, they might successfully argue that despite their professionally honed knowledge of what constitutes a particular offense, they possessed no insight into the practical recourses or logistical capacities at the disposal of subsequently misbehaving clients. This might be especially true in the latter instance, given counsel's likely inclination to explain that they are used to relying upon expert witness services – although no duty exists to do so – to gauge "mental state" as opposed to undertaking this form of discernment on their own.

Defense counsel are not the only ones who would do well to consider the legal repercussions of various courses of action when engaging with cults on a professional basis. As addressed in detail throughout the rest of this book, the notion, nature, and activities of cults have captured the popular imagination and, it would appear, the professional imagination as well. Such considerations might reasonably be expected to affect the judgment of criminal prosecutors, whose otherwise ethically oriented approach could be impeded by what they believe was done by cults and cult members in general, or in particularly egregious instances.

"Malicious prosecution" is embodied by "an action that is initiated or continued with malice, is without probable cause, and is terminated favorably to the defendant in the action" [29, p. 227], whereas "selective prosecution" reflects an unconstitutional focus on a particular targeted group [30]. Well-represented cults might conceivably prevail if they were able to establish that prosecutors pushed the envelope a bit too aggressively in convicting them, or in singling them out for allegedly special attention in the first place.

Cult Member Treatment Providers: Clinical Issues

In reaction to notable increases in malpractice actions, in board complaints, and in patient aggressivity in general, clinical treatment providers around the world are more and more likely to engage in "defensive practice" [31], which may unfortunately result not only in an avoidance of certain patient populations but also in a potentially problematic deviation from normally accepted standards of practice on the part of doctors who *do* elect to engage [32]. Deciding abruptly to discontinue treatment, when aspects of the patient's cult membership make the treater anxious or threatened, may lead to charges of abandonment. It is easy to see how cult members in need of service might inspire either avoidance or a sharply limited scope and depth of care on the part of clinicians at all levels of experience.

When it comes to the genesis of negative responses on the part of treatment recipients, "the watchwords here are *too much treatment, too little treatment*, or the *wrong treatment*" [33, p. 19]. When practice is *not* defensive, too much treatment may be a byproduct of the treater's overidentification with the patient – due perhaps, to a shared identity as a cult survivor. Too little treatment is, as already telegraphed here, a classic manifestation of defensive practice. The wrong treatment can play out in the context of addressing several disparate, potential maladies simultaneously, secondary to an inability to identify a specific disease entity; the patient's true needs may spring from the urgency of physically and psychologically differentiating from the cult; this urgency may differ considerably from familiar conditions normally seen as clinically "treatable."

It may not be the treatment recipient who is the formally declared, practical source of legal repercussions for the cult member's treatment providers. Since a number of cults attempt to persuade members to avoid or abandon their families of origin in favor of the cult, aggrieved family members may, for example, sue civilly on the basis of "alienation of affection" [34] when it is alleged that the doctors have spirited patients away from their loved ones for capricious, unfounded reasons, thus depriving all involved of the emotional benefits of intimate, legally sanctioned relationships. In other instances, a criminal charge of kidnapping might ensue when patients are physically transported from their abodes with some measurable degree of participation on the part of the doctor – as part and parcel, for example, of a deprogramming intervention.

In the event that cult members eventually act on their own – or in concert with other cult members, and perhaps at the direction of cult leaders – to harm other individuals, treatment providers may find themselves facing malpractice actions based upon a failure to adhere to a given jurisdiction's imposition of a "duty to warn." Pursuant to this doctrine, the doctor can be sued, reflecting requirements that can vary substantially from jurisdiction to jurisdiction, for failure to alert a potential victim who is "readily identifiable" that harmful intent has been expressed by one's patient [35, p. 265]. Liability has at times been extended in instances in which risk was foreseeable but potential victims were not readily identifiable, as exemplified by such classic cases as *Lipari* v. *Sears* (1980) [36] and *Naidu* v. *Laird* (1988) [37], in the wake of which it was posited that without suitable juridical oversight "there will exist no impediment to promiscuous assignment of liability whenever injury occurs" [38, p. 274] as a means of punishing bad care rather than a miscarried duty to protect.

Cult members may decide that they want to terminate treatment, and they may also conclude upon reflection that they never wished to be the focus of clinical intervention in the first place. Should treatment providers not agree, or should they be perceived as failing to wrap up service with suitable alacrity, then they may find themselves to be the focus of criminal charges of harassment or even stalking. As with other such concerns, doctors may eventually determine that the identified treatment recipients were not the source of such charges and, in fact, may not even have known that these charges were going to be filed.

Situations like those we have noted drive home the importance of forming a positive working relationship with psychiatrically savvy counsel early in one's career, and maintaining that relationship throughout the clinically active phase of one's professional career. Whether one treats cult members or members of any other definable patient population, it can be exceptionally helpful to have recourse to a friendly attorney colleague for both "personal consultation" and "reality testing" [33, p. 53].

Cult Member Evaluators: Forensic Issues

A distinction should be made here between those who are seeking to evaluate cult members for *clinical* reasons (e.g., in order to determine a need and/or suitability for deprogramming or to treat the negative psychological effects of cult membership) and those addressing *forensic* issues, such as seeking to evaluate cult members for purposes of determining compensable damages or criminal liability. In the clinical context the possibility of charges for psychiatric malpractice may apply, even if brought by the cult organization in an effort to protect itself from vicarious liability.

Although the forensic context is somewhat more protected from such matters, liability for forensic practice may yet occur, not as malpractice, but as accusations of perjury, malfeasance, or inadequate forensic functioning; since these issues may not constitute malpractice in the clinical sense, they are not covered by traditional malpractice insurance alone but would require administrative insurance to be covered: absent the latter, the accused practitioner may face the considerable financial resources of some cults without insurance protection. The same administrative insurance may also cover, at least in part, two legal liabilities more common in forensic work where arguably the patient–clinician relationship does not fit within malpractice parameters: ethics complaints and complaints to local boards of registration/licensing. The religious claims cloaking some cults may complicate the forensic assessor's task in attempting to avoid seeming to discriminate against – or, even worse, to persecute – a religious group.

Conclusions

In addition to how these parties may experience legal repercussions on the basis of existing legal provisions and principles, in what ways does – or should – the civil and criminal justice systems evolve to meet novel challenges presented in the contexts that we have noted? How might we foster the ability to distinguish benign cults from noxious ones – those that use coercive control to overcome members' wills, rather than providing a means of expressing beliefs with groups of like-minded citizens? This chapter has outlined a number of relevant issues and questions, identifying the various stakeholders in this matter, together with suggestions as to where such evolution may be most necessary. With the expansion of what might be called political cults, the subject has gained in both complexity and potential partisan attitudes and interpretations.

Key Points

- Cults and their leadership may be criminally and civilly liable for their activities, although the legal issues involved are highly complex, and prosecutors and plaintiffs are by no means guaranteed to succeed in their pursuit of just outcomes.
- Cult members must take especial care not to run afoul of defamation strictures in civil matters, and may find it exceedingly difficult to assert defenses of duress, brainwashing, and insanity in the context of criminal proceedings.
- Legal representatives, treatment providers, and forensic evaluators may incur professional liability when failing to observe boundaries or to maintain adherence to appropriately standardized procedures.

References

1. Racketeer Influenced and Corrupt Organizations Act of 1970, 18 U.S.C. §§ 1961–68 (1970).
2. AM Sood. Reaching a verdict: empirical evidence of the crumbling conventional wisdom on criminal verdict format. *NYU Law Review*. 2023;98:1265–1357.
3. D Keenan. The game of RICO: a powerful prosecutorial tool versus strict legislative limitations. *DePaul Law Review*. 2020;69:827–50.
4. LL Prather. SLAPP suits: an encroachment on human rights of a global proportion and what can be done about it. *Northwestern Journal of Human Rights*. 2023;22:49–100.
5. GM Gilchrist. The expressive cost of corporate immunity. *Hastings Law Journal*. 2012;64:1–57.
6. *Burley* v. *Hobby Lobby Stores, Inc.*, 573 U.S. 682 (2014).
7. DL Chen. Judicial compliance in district courts. *International Review of Law & Economics*. 2022;74:1–16.
8. KF Tsang, K Fan. The proper role of agency in corporate group. *The International Lawyer*. 2023;56:333–76.
9. S Haward. Procedure at the intersection of law and equity: veil piercing and the seventh amendment. *Notre Dame Law Review*. 2023;98:1799–821.
10. T Chang-Han, J Wang, C Hoffman. Piercing the corporate veil: historical, theoretical and comparative perspectives. *Berkeley Business Law Journal*. 2019;16:140–204.
11. Trafficking Victims Protection Act of 2000, 22 U.S.C. §§ 7101–14 (2018).
12. *Headley* v. *Church of Scientology Int'l*, 687 F.3d 1173 (9th Circ. 2012).
13. CM Weigel. Trafficking cults: why courts should adopt a broad reading of the Trafficking Victims Protection Act to ensure protection of cult victims. *George Mason University Civil Rights Law Journal*. 2020;30:269–305.
14. H Liu. The behavioral economics of multilevel marketing. *Hastings Business Law Journal*. 2018;14:109–38.
15. A Stein. *Terror, love and brainwashing: attachment in cults and totalitarian systems*. 2nd ed. Taylor & Francis; 2021.
16. JT Richardson. "Brainwashing" as forensic evidence. In: SJ Morewitz, ML Goldstein, editors. *Handbook of forensic sociology and psychology*. Springer; 2014. p. 77–85.
17. J Reichert, JT Richardson, R Thomas. "Brainwashing": diffusion of a questionable concept in legal systems. *International Journal for the Study of New Religions*. 2015;6(1):3–26.
18. E Tiffany. Inclusive blameworthiness and the wrongfulness of causing harm. *Journal of Ethics & Social Philosophy*. 2023;25:516–44.
19. B Holoyda, W Newman. Between belief and delusion: cult members and the insanity plea. *Journal of the American*

Academy of Psychiatry and the Law. 2016;44:53–62.

20. YA Arbel, M Mungan. The case against expanding defamation law. *Alabama Law Review.* 2019;71:454–97.
21. JM Koffler. The pre-Sullivan common law web of protection against political defamation suits. *Hofstra Law Review.* 2018;47:153–229.
22. LY Garfield. The death of slander. *Columbia Journal of Law & the Arts.* 2011;35:17–53.
23. LYG Tenzer. Destroying defamation. *Harvard Journal of Sports & Entertainment Law.* 2023;14:329–63.
24. AL Nielsen, CJ Walker. Qualified immunity's 51 imperfect solutions. *Duke Journal of Constitutional Law & Public Policy.* 2022;17:321–46.
25. B Skorup, J Huddleston. The erosion of publisher liability in American Law, Section 230, and the future of online curation. *Oklahoma Law Review.* 2020;72:635–73.
26. AJ Kraus. Speak nice or else: the evolving law of non-disparagement provisions in the workplace. *Labor Law Journal.* 2019;70(2):97–102.
27. J Steinberg. Arbitrating with the Mafia: why civil RICO statutes are improperly used and how class action arbitration may provide just compensation for forgotten victims. *Cardozo Journal of Conflict Resolution.* 2020;22: 97–125.
28. G Dawson, R Boynton. Reconciling complicity in genocide and aiding and abetting genocide in the jurisprudence of the United Nations ad hoc tribunals. *Harvard Human Rights Journal.* 2008;21:241–79.
29. T Tymkovich, H Stillwell. Malicious prosecution as undue process: a Fourteenth Amendment theory of malicious prosecution. *The Georgetown Journal of Law & Public Policy.* 2022;20:255–81.
30. ASD Burdette, J Carruthers. Judicial review of prosecutorial blanket declination policies. *Ohio State Journal of Criminal Law.* 2023;20:179–207.
31. A Whittaker, T Havard. Defensive practice as "fear-based" practice: social work's open secret? *British Journal of Social Work.* 2016;46(5):1158–74.
32. O Ortashi, J Virdee, R Hassan, T Mutrynowski, F Abu-Zidan. The practice of defensive medicine among hospital doctors in the United Kingdom. *BMC Medical Ethics.* 2013;14:Article 42.
33. TG Gutheil, EY Drogin. *The mental health professional in court: a survival guide.* American Psychiatric Publishing; 2013.
34. S Schaus. Wrongs to us. *Michigan Law Review.* 2023;121:1185–1233.
35. T Ruutiainen, J Northrop. Defining the scope of duty to warn readily identifiable individuals. *Journal of the American Academy of Psychiatry and the Law.* 2021;49:265–67.
36. *Lipari* v. *Sears*, 497 F. Supp. 185 (1980).
37. *Naidu* v. *Laird*, 539 A.2d 1064 (1988).
38. R Pettis, TG Gutheil. Misapplication of the Tarasoff duty to driving cases: a call for the reframing of theory. *Bulletin of the American Academy of Psychiatry and the Law.* 1993;21:263–75.

Index

For EU product safety concerns, contact us at Calle de José Abascal, 56–1°,
28003 Madrid, Spain or eugpsr@cambridge.org.

www.ingramcontent.com/pod-product-compliance
Ingram Content Group UK Ltd.
Pitfield, Milton Keynes, MK11 3LW, UK
UKHW031424300625
460082UK00017B/212

* 9 7 8 1 0 0 9 6 4 3 0 3 0 *